THE
GLASS
CANDLESTICK
BOOK

VOLUME 1
AKRO AGATE TO FENTON

Identification and
Value Guide

Tom Felt and
Elaine & Rich Stoer

cb

COLLECTOR BOOKS
A Division of Schroeder Publishing Co., Inc.

Front cover: Fenton three-light Butterfly candleholder in ruby carnival, Atterbury crucifix in blue, Fenton No. 232 candlestick in cameo opalescent, Boston and Sandwich hexagonal candlestick in clambroth with blue top, Central No. T345 Chippendale candlestick in canary, Cambridge No. 3 Centennial lustre candlestick in carmen with locking bobeche, Duncan and Miller No. 2 Canterbury two-light candlestick in milk glass, and Cambridge No. 1338 three-light candlestick in forest green.

Back cover: Blenko No. 7634 handled candlestick in ruby, Fenton No. 5172 Swan candlestick in green opalescent, Central No. 691 cherub candlestick in crystal, Cambridge No. 500 Pristine candlestick in crystal, Anchor Hocking No. M902 colonial candlestick in milk glass, Fenton No. 3998 Hobnail hurricane candle lamp in ebony with pink pastel shade, and Cambridge No. 3 Everglade candelabrum in amber.

Cover design by Beth Summers
Book design by Terri Hunter

COLLECTOR BOOKS
P.O. Box 3009
Paducah, Kentucky 42002-3009
www.collectorbooks.com

Copyright © 2003 Tom Felt and Elaine & Rich Stoer

Searching For A Publisher?

We are always looking for people knowledgeable within their fields. If you feel that there is a real need for a book on your collectible subject and have a large comprehensive collection, contact Collector Books.

The current values in this book should be used only as a guide. They are not intended to set prices, which vary from one section of the country to another. Auction prices as well as dealer prices vary greatly and are affected by condition as well as demand. Neither the authors nor the publisher assumes responsibility for any losses that might be incurred as a result of consulting this guide.

CONTENTS

INTRODUCTION

Almost every manufacturer of glassware included at least one candlestick among their offerings to the public — and for most companies, candlesticks were a staple, offered in a bewildering variety of shapes and sizes. This volume is the first in a series that will attempt to present a comprehensive sampling of these candlesticks. It is, of course, impossible to include every candlestick ever made — in some instances because there just hasn't been enough research done on some of these companies, while in other cases we were not able to photograph or find original catalog representations suitable for publication. We also made a decision to omit most candelabra (using as a rough definition those items that have removable arms, bobeches, and candle cups), only including such items when it seemed to us that they had particular importance or interest to collectors of candlesticks. Similarly, we have omitted votive candleholders, tea lights, and most other holders requiring non-standard candles.

Our focus has primarily been on American-made candlesticks, though we plan in a later volume to include a section featuring a selection of imports. We will also include information on foreign reproductions whenever this information is available to us.

The arrangement of the book follows a standard format. Companies are listed alphabetically and are prefaced with a brief history. When possible, we show you examples of trademarks or labels used by the company. The listings for the candlesticks are presented chronologically, though sometimes this involves guesswork on our part. When possible, we show a photograph of each candlestick. If a photograph is not available, we provide a picture from an advertisement or company catalog. The accompanying text includes as much information as is available, including pattern numbers, names, dimensions, and dates of production, when known. Listings of colors and decorations, such as etchings and cuttings, have either been verified through research or the authors' personal knowledge, but necessarily are incomplete and should not be assumed to be comprehensive.

Many companies made candlesticks that closely resemble those made by other manufacturers. Whenever possible we have included additional pictures of the "lookalikes," but have set them apart in green shaded boxes.

We have also tried to avoid making identifications that cannot be supported by current research. On a few occasions, however, we have found the temptation to do so irresistible. When this happens, our conclusions will also be set apart in a green shaded box, not to be taken as gospel, but just as a reasonably informed guess.

In addition to a standard index, a visual index will also be found at the rear of this volume. It presents all of the candlesticks in the book in such a way that you can quickly browse through them to tentatively identify a candlestick, when you do not know its manufacturer.

The authors welcome comments from readers. You can write us in care of the publisher or e-mail us directly at tomfelt@bigfoot.com or rstoer@worldnet.att.net.

Pricing

Our approach to pricing is to assign a range for each listing. Rarer items will generally have a broader range than the less volatile commonplace ones. Prices shown are always for each piece. Since pairs are often more desirable than singles, you may be able to lean toward the high end of the range for each candleholder that is part of a pair.

We've spent several years compiling sales data from eBay and other auctions as well as from antique dealers and private collectors in an attempt to provide realistic values for each piece shown. Despite this effort we've not been able to gather any direct pricing information for several of the thousands of items shown in these volumes. Some of these we've attempted to price based on information from items of similar age, quality, and design. Others we don't feel that we can price with any degree of accuracy and have omitted their pricing information altogether.

In some cases our research has led us to figures that differ greatly from those published by other authors. When we vary from the "norm" in this manner it is based on good data or we wouldn't take such a stand. Like most authors, we are not attempting to set prices, but only to reflect what our own research has shown. As always, the final price is an issue to be settled between the buyer and seller.

All prices listed in this book are for items in excellent or mint condition. Chips, cracks, stains, scratches, worn paint, etc. all affect an item's value, often greatly (some scratches to the bottom of a piece are to be expected and will have no bearing on the value). The value of very old (nineteenth century) and very rare pieces is less affected by minor imperfections, but items that are more commonplace may be virtually un-saleable if damaged. We do not mean to discourage the purchase of an item just because it is flawed. Several of the pieces in our collection are less-than-perfect and we still enjoy them immensely. Simply remember to adjust its value accordingly when buying (or selling) a damaged piece.

An item's desirability (and thereby its value) is based on scarcity, design, quality, and condition. The following are some additional guidelines as to what's desirable in today's market. Keep in mind that these are generalities and will not apply in all cases:

1) If an item is available in color, the colored version will generally sell for more than the crystal.
   a) The most desirable colors are ruby and cobalt, sometimes bringing a price ten times that of the same piece in crystal. Dark amber is the least desirable, and often brings about the same price as crystal. Other colors fall somewhere in between.
   b) Items made from fusing two pieces of different colored glass together, such as those made by Boston & Sandwich, Fenton, and Heisey, are often worth far more than single color items of the same type.
2) Items with etched patterns (usually on the base) are worth more than plain ones.
3) Nice or elaborate wheel cuttings add value. Very simple ones add little or nothing.
4) Nice hand-painted designs add value (note the word "nice").
5) Items with heavy bands of gold trim are often worth less than the same item without.
6) Items with (factory) bobeches and prisms are worth more than the same piece without.
   a) Colored or etched bobeches can greatly add to the value of the item.
   b) Large, colored, or otherwise unusual prisms will generally add value.

SIZES

Sizes listed are taken from actual examples when available, otherwise they are taken from manufacturers' catalogs. Catalog sizes are often inaccurate and change for the same item from one catalog to another. Therefore our sizes will often not match the manufacturer's catalog's size. The items themselves also vary from one to another; i.e., bases are often formed by hand while the piece is still warm. The more the base is "flared" the shorter the candleholder will be and the wider the base will be, causing both dimensions to be different from the same piece with a slightly different shaped base. Size differences of ± ¼" or more from those listed are not unusual.

ACKNOWLEDGMENTS

This book could not have been written without the assistance of many people. Among them, we would like to express our special gratitude to John Boyd, Bill Burke, Frank Chiarenza, George Fogg, Esther E. Hall, Roger and Claudia Hardy, Rick Hirt, Jimee Hurst, Bob and Helen Jones, Beverly Kappenman, Woody Moore, Bruce Mueller and Gary Wickland, Nezka Pfeifer (Sandwich Glass Museum), Dean Six, Marty Smith, Roger Trudeau, Charles Upton, William P. Walker, John Weishar, and Jack D. Wilson.

AKRO AGATE COMPANY, Akron, Ohio (1911 – 1914), Clarksburg, West Virginia (1914 – 1951).

The company was initially founded to manufacture glass marbles. By the 1930s, Akro Agate was responsible for nearly 75% of all marbles sold in the United States. Eventually, increased competition forced them to seek additional lines and they began producing children's glassware. In 1936, they acquired the molds of the Westite Company of Weston, West Virginia, for items such as flower pots and planters and these were their strongest lines prior to World War II. They also did private mold work. However, it was the decrease in Japanese imports during the war that allowed them to expand their children's glassware production and it is these items for which Akro Agate is best known today. The factory eventually succumbed to the competition of the plastics industry and was bought in 1951 by the Clarksburg Glass Company of Clarksburg, West Virginia. Under this name, the new company, operated by a group of former Akro Agate employees, made glass for only about six months.

AKRO TRADEMARK,
THE CROW™

COLORS

Much of Akro Agate's production was in color, though some crystal was also made. Other transparent colors include amber, azure blue, brown, cobalt, green (sometimes called jade green), red, and topaz (1935 – 1936). The opaque colors include apple green, black, canary yellow, ivory, mottled green, onyx (ivory striped with maroon), orange (often referred to as pumpkin by collectors), royal blue, and white. Various marbleized combinations are known with white or ivory backgrounds, including blue, green, orange, or oxblood; other combinations include green/blue and lemonade/oxblood (yellow and red). Some children's pieces are also known in crystal with fired-on colors of yellow, green, blue, and red, but to date no candlesticks have been reported with this treatment.

AK-1.
INKWELL STYLE
CANDLEBLOCK,
TYPE I, IN BLUE

Inkwell style candleblock, type I. 2" tall and approximately 2¼" square. Production dates unknown. Made in transparent colors only, including crystal, amber, blue, green, and red. Other colors possible. The base is smaller than the type II candlestick (below) and the top is flat. Crystal: $6.00 – 8.00. Colors: $20.00 – 30.00.

AK-2. INKWELL STYLE CANDLEBLOCKS,
TYPE II (2 VERSIONS)

Inkwell style candleblock, type II. 2" tall and approximately 3" square. Production dates unknown, but probably 1940s. Common in crystal and made in amber, cobalt, red, and marbleized colors. Other colors likely. This style differs from type I by the addition of the raised rim around the candleholder and the wider base. There seem to be multiple versions of the type II candleblock, some with rounded panels, others with flattened panels. Also known with an opening for a ¾" candle, 1" deep, or with a ½" opening, 1½" deep. Crystal: $7.00 – 9.00. Marbleized colors: $30.00 – 35.00. Transparent red (and other unusual colors): $75.00 – 85.00.

In the late 1950s, Imperial made an almost identical candlestick, but smaller (1¾" high and approximately 2¼" square) as part of their Elysian pattern.

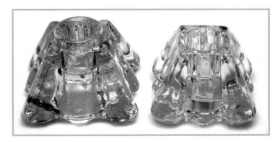

AK-2A. COMPARISON OF INKWELL STYLE CANDLEBLOCK, TYPE II (ON LEFT) AND IMPERIAL ELYSIAN CANDLEBLOCK (ON RIGHT)

Vertical rib candleblock, scalloped base. 1⅞" tall with a five-sided base, approximately 3¾" from point to point. Production dates unknown. Has not been documented in color. $40.00 – 50.00.

AK-3.
VERTICAL RIB
CANDLEBLOCK

Vertical rib candleblock, round base. 2⅛" tall. Production dates unknown. Has not been documented in color. $40.00 – 50.00.

(Photograph courtesy of Roger & Claudia Hardy.)

AK-4.
VERTICAL RIB
CANDLEBLOCK,
ROUND BASE

Ribbed candleholder. 3¼" tall with a 3½" diameter round base. Probably 1930s – 1940s. Made in apple green, black, canary yellow, ivory, mottled green, onyx, orange, royal blue, white, and various marbleized combinations. Other colors possible. $150.00 – 200.00.

AK-5. RIBBED
CANDLEHOLDER
IN APPLE GREEN

Low ribbed candleblock. 1¾" high. Production dates unknown, but probably 1930s – 1940s. Made in apple green and probably other opaque colors. Marked with the Crow™, MADE IN THE U.S.A. and the number 10-L. $125.00 – 150.00. *(Photograph courtesy of Roger & Claudia Hardy.)*

AK-6.
LOW RIBBED
CANDLEBLOCK IN
APPLE GREEN

Low plain candleblock. 1¾" high. Production dates unknown, but probably 1930s – 1940s. Made in canary yellow and other opaque colors. Very similar candleblocks were made by both the L. J. Houze Convex Glass Company and the Westite Company. Although the Akro Agate candleblock appears to be completely round, looking straight down at the base reveals that it actually has 16 panels. $300.00+. See page 8 for additional information on how to differentiate between the Akro Agate, Houze, and Westite candleblocks. *(Photograph courtesy of Roger & Claudia Hardy.)*

AK-7. LOW PLAIN CANDLE-
BLOCK IN YELLOW

LOOKALIKES

AK-7A. HOUZE NO. 851 CANDLEBLOCK IN MARBLEX, WESTITE CANDLEBLOCKS
IN CREAM AND GREEN TRANSPARENT

There were two other companies that produced a short candleblock similar to Akro Agate's, the L. J. Houze Glass Company of Point Marion, Pennsylvania, and the Westite Company of Weston, West Virginia. The differences between the candleblocks are minute.

The Houze candleblocks are marked very faintly on the bottom with the number 851. It may be necessary to use a magnifying glass or to turn the candleholder so that the light hits it properly to see the number. The underside of the base is recessed by 7/16". The bottom rim itself is completely round. The height of the candleblock is the same as Akro's (1¾"). These blocks were made in MarbleX, Houze's marbleized color, as well as jadite, transparent amber, green, and amethyst.

The candleblocks made by Westite are recessed on the underside of the base 9/16" and are not marked. They are 1 9/16" high, slightly shorter than either the Akro Agate or Houze candleblock. They also have a round bottom rim.

The green candleblock shown has a flat top rim. It is recessed on the underside ½" and is not marked. It is 1½" high, shorter than any of the other candleblocks, but is believed to also be a Westite product. However, there is a possibility it was made by a third unknown company.

The Akro Agate candleblocks are not marked and the underside of the base is recessed 9/16" (like the Westite candleblock). They are 1¾" tall, like the Houze candleblock. They have only been seen in solid, opaque colors. The most distinctive difference, however, is found on the bottom edge. Even though it appears at first glance to be round, it actually has 16 panels, whereas the bottom edge on the other three candleholders is completely round. *(Information provided by Roger & Claudia Hardy.)*

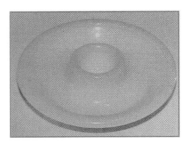

AK-8.
BRIDGE
CANDLE-
STICK IN
IVORY

Round saucer candleholder, known to researchers as a bridge candlestick because of its similarity to a set of four ashtrays made by Akro Agate, each with a different card suit in its center. 4" diameter. Production dates unknown. Made in ivory, possibly other opaque colors. Marked with the Crow™. Considered rare. $250.00+. *(Photograph courtesy of Roger & Claudia Hardy.)*

AK-9.
TWISTED STEM
CANDLESTICK IN
ORANGE

Twisted stem candlestick. 8⅛" high. Production dates unknown. The example shown is in orange and is from the only pair that has been reported to date. According to Roger and Claudia Hardy, it was a special order item that they acquired from a former Akro Agate employee. Unable to price. *(Photograph courtesy of Roger & Claudia Hardy.)*

Miniature candleholder. Called Banded Swirl by collectors. 1⅞" high, base: 2¾" diameter. Made in the 1940s. Available in crystal and white opaque. Also known in crystal with overall gold paint. Generally found with the plain handle seen in the accompanying photograph, but also made with a notched handle and additional waves circling the top part of the base. At least some of these candlesticks were made especially for the Lander Company of New York, a cosmetic retailer. They were intended to hold small perfume bottles in the shape of candles. Most have candle cups that are relatively shallow and flat on the bottom, sometimes with a number impressed inside; others are deeper and come to a point inside. Attribution of this candlestick to Akro Agate is based on examples found at the factory site by Roger and Claudia Hardy. Crystal: $6.00 – 10.00. White opaque: $10.00 – 15.00. (Candle insert doubles value.)

AK-10. MINIATURE CANDLEHOLDERS, PLAIN HANDLE, IN CRYSTAL, WHITE OPAQUE (WITH PERFUME BOTTLE), AND CRYSTAL WITH GOLD DECORATION

ANCHOR HOCKING GLASS CORPORATION, Lancaster, Ohio (1905 –

present). Founded as the Hocking Glass Company, they initially manufactured opal decorated goods and novelties. Almost from the beginning they seem to have been successful at introducing time-saving processes, leading to their becoming one of the first companies to produce an entirely machine-made tableware pattern in 1928. They went on to become one of the top producers of the glassware commonly referred to as "Depression glass" today. They readily survived the Depression years by perfecting machinery that could make up to 90 pieces of glassware per minute, giving them a highly competitive edge. (They were able to advertise tumblers at "two for a nickel," for instance — less than half their former price.)

They also had a history of active expansion. In the 1920s they took control of a number of other glass companies, including the Turner Glass Company, the Lancaster Glass Company, and, later, the Monongah Glass Company. By 1937, they had gone into the manufacture of bottles and jars. This led to a merger with the Anchor Cap Corporation, manufacturers of bottle closures. Ultimately, following the absorption of half a dozen additional companies with factories in as many cities, the new conglomerate became the Anchor Hocking Glass Corporation. In 1969, the name was changed once again to the Anchor Hocking Corporation. This reflected expansion into new areas of manufacture, most notably plastics. By 1978, they controlled 28 factories around the world and employed 14,000. They advertised themselves as "The most famous name in glass" and "The world's largest manufacturer of glass tableware." In the years since, they have continued to expand and diversify. The Anchor Hocking family now encompasses housewares, home furnishings, office products, hardware, and tools — and they still advertise themselves as "the company that brings more glassware into the home than anyone else."

Among Hocking's better known patterns from the Depression glass era are Block Optic, Bubble, Cameo, Manhattan, Mayfair, Miss America, Moonstone, Old Colony, Oyster and Pearl, Princess, and Queen Mary. Hocking is also the manufacturer of the Fire-King dinnerware and oven ware line, which was introduced in 1942 and remains very popular with collectors today.

ORIGINAL ANCHOR HOCKING TRADEMARK, USED 1937 – 1977, AND CURRENT TRADEMARK

COLORS

Opal	First color produced in 1905; continued to be made throughout the early years	Topaz	Introduced 1928 – 1930s
		Mayfair blue	Introduced about 1930 (a medium shade)
Amber	Mid 1920s – 1930s	Vitrock	Introduced 1932 (opaque white)
Blue	Mid 1920s – 1930s	Royal ruby	1938 – 1967, 1973 – 1977
Canary	Mid 1920s – 1930s	Blue	Introduced 1940, for use on Fire-King ovenware
Green	Mid 1920s – 1930s		
Rose (pink)	1926 – 1942 (later called flamingo and cerise)	Ivory	Introduced 1940, for use on Fire-King ovenware

Sapphire blue	Introduced 1941	Avocado	Introduced 1966
Moonstone	1942 – 1946 (opalescent crystal)	Honey gold	1966 – 1970s
Jade-ite	1948 – early 1960s (opaque green, used for Fire-King)	Aurora	Introduced 1968 (mother of pearl finish)
		Harvest amber	Introduced 1976 (for use on ovenware)
Forest green	1950 – 1965		
Shell pink	Introduced 1955 (called Pink Anchor-glass)		

FIRED-ON COLORS:

Turquoise blue	1956 – 1958 (for use on ovenware)
Milk glass	Introduced 1958
Anchorwhite	Introduced 1958 (for use on Fire-King; sometimes called Azur-ite)
Desert gold	Introduced 1961
Aquamarine	Introduced 1966

Peach lustre	1952 – 1963 (reintroduced as Royal lustre, 1976 – 1977)
Grey Laurel	Introduced 1953

Many other fired-on colors and decorations were offered over the years.

AH-1. BLOCK
OPTIC LOW
CANDLESTICK
IN GREEN

Block Optic low candlestick. 1¾" high with a 3¾" diameter round base. Made by Hocking, 1929 – 1933. Made in green and rose (pink); limited production in amber. Other pieces in the pattern were made in crystal and topaz, but the candlestick has not been seen in these colors. Amber: $20.00 – 25.00. Rose: $35.00 – 40.00. Green: $45.00 – 50.00.

Cameo candlestick. 3⅝" high with a 5" base. Made by Hocking, 1930 – 1934. Also known as Ballerina and Dancing Girl. Made in green; other pieces in the pattern were made in crystal (with a platinum rim), rose (pink), and topaz, but the candlesticks have not been reported in these colors. The pattern is reported to have been based on an etching originally made by the Monongah Glass Company, a company that had been absorbed by Hocking. $50.00 – 55.00.

The same blank without the machine-etched Cameo pattern was made by the Lancaster Glass Company and the Standard Glass Manufacturing Company, both divisions of the Hocking Glass Company (see volume 3 of this series).

Beginning in 1985, the Mosser Glass Company (see volume 3) began production of a half-size children's version of the Cameo candlestick, which they market as part of their Jennifer pattern. These are from new molds. No Cameo children's pieces were made by Hocking.

AH-2. CAMEO CANDLESTICK
IN GREEN

AH-3. RUFFLED
CANDLEHOLDER IN
ROSE

Ruffled candleholder. 2⅜" high, 6¼" across the top. Pattern and production dates unknown, but probably 1930s. Made in rose (pink). Other colors possible. $15.00 – 20.00.

Old Colony candleholder. Also known to collectors as Lace Edge and Open Lace. 3⅛" high with a 5" diameter base. 1935 – 1938. An earlier version of this line was introduced in 1928 by the Lancaster Glass Company (see volume 3 of this series) and advertised that same year by the Hocking Glass Sales Corporation, since at this time Hocking owned the controlling share of Lancaster's stock. The original version of the candleholder had a flat base and was offered cut by the Standard Glass Company, another Hocking division. It is 2" high with a 5¼" diameter base. The Hocking advertisement in figure AH-4b indicates that it was made in pink only; however a later Lancaster ad stated that it would be featured in pink, crystal, and green in 1929. The redesigned version, with ribs added to the turned down base and three little knobbed feet, is known in pink, usually found with a satin finish, and in fired-on red. Flat base: $40.00 – 60.00. Raised base, satin pink: $40.00 – 50.00; plain pink: $120.00 – 150.00; fired-on red: $20.00 – 25.00.

AH-4. Old Colony candle-holder (Hocking) in rose satin

AH-4A. Original Lancaster Glass Company version with flat base in green

AH-4B. Old Colony candleholder with flat base. From *The Pottery, Glass & Brass Salesman*, September 27, 1928

Some Snappy Cuttings at a Snappy Price

We recommend to the trade as a particularly good buy our No. 906 line, Cutting No. 30, illustrated herewith. This line consists of a full array of tableware, twenty-seven pieces in all, of a nice quality of glassware done in the now so popular open work border. The cutting, from the Standard Glass Manufacturing Company, is snappy and pleasing. Pink glass only. Ask us for particulars—especially about our popular priced assortments.

THE HOCKING GLASS SALES CORPORATION
129-131 Fifth Avenue, New York

Representing: Hocking—Lancaster—Standard Glass Companies

J. J. Collins, *President*

George E. Nicholson, *Sec.-Treas. and Gen. Mgr.*

Queen Mary. Two-light candlestick. 4" high, base 4" by 2¼", arm spread 4". Pattern also known as Prismatic Line and Vertical Ribbed by collectors. Ca. 1936 – 1949. Made in crystal (both plain and with a satin finish) and royal ruby, but scarce in that color; other pieces in the pattern were also made in pink, but the candlestick has not been reported in this color. First made about a year after Heisey's Ridgeleigh was introduced. Queen Mary was an inexpensive near-copy and the quality of the glass is very poor compared to Heisey. Crystal: $6.00 – 9.00. Ruby: $100.00 – market.

AH-5. Queen Mary candlesticks in crystal and royal ruby

A variant of this candlestick has been seen with a star-like or flower-like figure on the candle cups instead of the usual ridges (AH-5a.) It was offered on eBay by a seller in Auckland, New Zealand, and may have been made by an overseas subsidiary. Another unknown candlestick is shown here (AH-5b) because of its similarity to the Queen Mary candlestick, but it can easily be told apart because of the very different shape of its base and the way the ribbing appears on the candle cups.

AH-5A. Variant of Queen Mary pattern by unknown maker

AH-5B. Candleholder similar to Queen Mary by unknown maker

AH-6. No. 184 MANHATTAN
CANDLEHOLDER

No. 184 Manhattan. Called a "drip catch" candleholder. Also known to collectors as Horizontal Ribbed. 4⅜" square, 1⅜" high. The pattern was made ca. 1938 – 1943, with the candleholder remaining in production as late as 1957 – 1958. Crystal only; has been seen with an overall silver finish, giving it a mirror-like appearance. Some pieces in the pattern were made in pink, but the candleholder has not been seen in color. This was another art deco pattern reminiscent of Heisey's Ridgeleigh, but made primarily for the dime store trade. L. E. Smith's No. 38 two-light candlestick is often erroneously identified as Manhattan. (See volume 3 of this series.) The square candleholder is the only one in the pattern. $5.00 – 8.00.

AH-7. No. A881 OYSTER & PEARL CANLDEHOLDERS IN
ROYAL RUBY AND VITROCK WITH FIRED-ON DUSTY ROSE

No. A881 Oyster and Pearl candleholder. 3¼" high with a 4½" base. Ca. 1938 – 1940. Made in crystal, royal ruby, pink, and vitrock (white). The white candlesticks usually have fired-on green (Hocking's Springtime Green) or pink (Dusty Rose). Fired-on blue is possible, but has not been confirmed. The crystal candlesticks can be found etched. Crystal, vitrock, fired-on colors: $10.00 – 12.00. Pink: $15.00 – 20.00. Ruby: $20.00 – 25.00.

AH-8. BUBBLE
CANDLEHOLDER

Bubble candleholder. Also advertised as Bullseye and Provincial. 2" high with a 3½" base. Ca. 1940 – 1968 in crystal, 1950 – 1965 in forest green. Also known in black. The pattern was made in many other colors, including pink, royal ruby, and sapphire blue, so other colors are possible. Crystal: $2.00 – 4.00. Black: $10.00 – 15.00. Forest green: $135.00 – market.

AH-9.
No. M2781
MOONSTONE
CANDLEHOLDER

No. M2781 Moonstone candleholder. 2" high, 4" base. Ca. 1942 – 1946. Made only in opalescent crystal. Available as part of a four-piece buffet set, with a 9½" bowl and 10¾" underplate. Many other companies made hobnail patterns, some of them in opalescent crystal, such as Fenton's handmade French opalescent pieces. As with most of Anchor Hocking's machine-made patterns, Moonstone would have primarily been sold in dime stores as an inexpensive competitor to these other patterns. The candlesticks originally sold for 5¢ each. $6.00 – 9.00.

Hurricane lamp base. 7" high with shade. Base is 1¾" high, 4" wide at the bottom and 2⅝" wide at its top. Made in the 1940s and possibly later. Made in crystal, and fired-on white and green; has been reported in milk glass and jade-ite, but these may be the fired-on colors. $5.00 – 7.00.

AH-10.
HURRICANE
LAMP BASE

No. 984 candleholder. In early years called Berwick by Anchor Hocking and later sold as Hobnail, but often referred to by collectors today as Boop-ie or Ball Edge. 2½" high, 4¾" base. In production from the 1950s to the 1980s. Crystal and milk glass only; occasionally found in crystal with ruby or yellow stain. The candle cup usually has six deep ridges that hold the candle in place; a variant version of the mold has multiple fine ridges instead. This must have been a tremendously popular candlestick through-out its entire production period with the result that it is one of the most commonly found candlesticks today. It is also one of the most frequently misidentified, due to its resemblance to Imperial's Candlewick pattern. $2.00 – 4.00.

AH-11. No. 984 BERWICK CANDLE-
HOLDER, ALSO KNOWN
TO COLLECTORS AS BOOPIE

No. 981 candleholder. Referred to as Prescut in a 1950 hardware catalog. Called Stars and Bars by collectors. 1½" high with a diameter of 4". Made in the 1940s and 1950s. Originally sold for 5¢ each. $3.00 – 5.00.

AH-12.
No. 981 STARS
& BARS
CANDLEHOLDER

Candlestick, attributed to Anchor Hocking based on a family history that a pair had been brought home from the factory by a father who had worked there for 44 years. The intricate pattern on the base is also very similar to that of the No. 981 Stars & Bars can-dleholder above. 3¼" with a base diameter of 4¼". Made in the 1950s. In 1955, A. H. Dorman of New York advertised a console set with fired on colors of pink with black trim or turquoise with smoked trim. Note the variances between the two candleholders in the accompanying photograph. $4.00 – 6.00.

AH-13. CANDLESTICK (ATTRIBUTED TO
ANCHOR HOCKING), TWO STYLES

No. 581 candleholder. 2⅛" high, 3¾" wide at the top, 1⅝" base. Made in the 1950s, possibly earlier or later. Known in crystal, amethyst, forest green, blue, and ruby stain. Two styles of this candleholder are known. When used as a saucer candleholder, both have a ribbed candle cup that will hold a 1" candle. When reversed, one style has a second ribbed candle cup that will take a ½" taper, whereas the other style simply has an open well that measures 1½" and is without ribs to hold a candle in place. (See AH-14a.) Crystal: $2.00 – 4.00. Colors: $4.00 – 6.00.

AH-14. No. 581 CANDLEHOLDER IN FOREST GREEN, CRYSTAL, AND RUBY STAIN

AH-14A. No. 581, TWO STYLES, REVERSED, CRYSTAL AND RUBY STAIN

AH-15. No. 989 SKIRTED CANDLESTICK IN MILK WHITE

No. 989 skirted candlestick, 4½" high, 3½" octagonal base. Late 1950s to early 1970s. Made in milk glass as No. W989; probably also produced in crystal and desert gold. The inside of the candle cup is ribbed and marked in the center with the number "21." A handled version was also made, marked inside the candle cup with the number "12." It is pictured below. Milk glass: $3.00 – 5.00.

AH-16. No. M982 COLONIAL CANDLESTICK IN MILK WHITE, HAND PAINTED

No. M982 colonial candlestick. 4⅝" high, 3⅝" octagonal base. Late 1950s to early 1970s. Made in crystal, desert gold, and milk glass. Pairs in milk glass were offered in a gift box as No. W900/47, retailing for approximately 80¢ for the set in 1958 – 1959. The milk glass candlesticks were available with painted floral decorations. Identical to the No. 989 skirted candlestick seen above, with the addition of a handle containing two distinctive notches where it is meant to be gripped. The inside of the candle cup is ribbed and marked in the center with the number "12" (in comparison with the No. 989 candlestick, which is marked with the number "21"). Several other companies made handled colonial-style candlesticks, including Heisey, Westmoreland, Paden City, New Martinsville, Kemple, and Smith. The Anchor Hocking candlestick is easily recognized because of the notches on the handle and the fact that its base has a wider flare than the others. $4.00 – 6.00.

No. 784 Early American Prescut twin candelabra. Often referred to as EAPC. 5⅝" high, 7" x 4" at the base. Introduced in 1960 and still in production as late as 1998. Made in crystal only (plain or satin finish), but also known with ruby stain overall. Other pieces in the pattern were offered with amber, avocado, and blue stain, so these are also a possibility for the candelabra. There appear to have been three versions of this candelabra made. The earliest is the one on the left, without the center knob, as pictured in the 1960 – 1961 catalog. In place of the knob is a pressed star in a circle. Early advertisements, such as the one from the August 1961 *Chain Store Age* seen in the center, show that the knob must have been added within just a few months after the candelabra's initial appearance. The knob rises from a circular rim that fills the area between the two arms. At some point, the candelabra was simplified even further and the circular rim was omitted, with the knob emerging directly from the base of the candelabra. Because of its long production span, this third version seems to be the most common. $15.00 – 30.00.

AH-17. No. 784 EAPC TWIN CANDELABRA, 1960 – 1961 CATALOG

AH-17A. No. 784 EAPC TWIN CANDELABRA, *CHAIN STORE AGE*, AUGUST 1961

AH-17B. No. 784 EAPC TWIN CANDELABRA, CENTER KNOB AS COMMONLY SEEN

No. 4567 Wexford® candleholder/bud vase. 6" high. Introduced in 1967 and still in production in the 1980s. Some pieces of Wexford® are still being made today. The candleholder is known only in crystal, though a few pieces in the pattern were made in recent years in green and various fired-on colors or stains are possible (including green, blue, cranberry, and amber). Sold for dual use as both a candleholder and a bud vase. The extensive Wexford® pattern also includes a 2½" votive candleholder and a saucer-style candleholder. $3.00 – 5.00.

AH-18. No. 4567 WEXFORD CANDLE-HOLDER/BUD VASE

No. 120 Avocado candleholder. 2¼" high with a diameter of approximately 5" at the top and a 2¼" diameter base. Known in avocado only. Made in the late 1960s, early 1970s. Offered as part of a three-piece Accent Modern console set with a matching bowl. $5.00 – 8.00.

AH-19. AVOCADO CANDLE-HOLDER

No. 992 Candle-Stax®. 2¾" high, 3" diameter of small candleholder, 4" diameter of large candleholder. Introduced in 1974 and still in production in the 1980s. Marked on the inside of the candle cup with the Anchor™ and the letters "USA." Designed to be reversible and stackable. With the wide portion of the candleholder used as a base, it holds a 1" candle in a ribbed candle cup. Reversed, it holds either a 1½" or 2" wide candle. Sold with a decorator booklet offering hints on the various ways these candleholders could be arranged. Crystal or marigold iridescent. $4.00 – 6.00.

AH-20. No. 992 CANDLE-STAX®

AH-20A & B. No. 992 CANDLE-STAX®

No. 986 Star Design candleholder. 4½" wide, 1¼" high. Production dates unknown, but began in the early 1970s and they were still being made in the late 1980s – early 1990s. Crystal only, but also available with ruby stain. The Anchor Hocking candleholder has six rounded points and a ribbed candle cup, with small beads at the base of each point of the star and spikes between each point. An almost identical candleholder without the beads or spikes is made by the Indiana Glass Company (see IN-112+ in Volume 2 of this series). Paden City, Hazel Atlas, and Libbey also made similar star candleholders, but with only five points that are much sharper than the Anchor Hocking candleholder. $2.00 – 3.00.

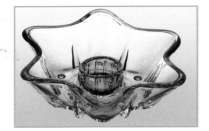

AH-21. No. 986 STAR DESIGN
CANDLEHOLDER

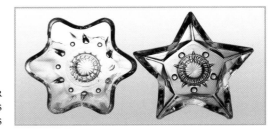

AH-21A. COMPARISON OF ANCHOR
HOCKING AND HAZEL ATLAS
STAR CANDLEHOLDERS

AH-22.
UNKNOWN
PATTERN
NUMBER

Unknown pattern number. 8¼" high with a 3" diameter base. Probably made in the 1980s or early 1990s. Known in milk glass only. Marked with the Anchor™ trademark. $5.00 – 8.00.

AH-23.
No. 280
BEDFORD
CANDLE-
STICK

No. 280 Bedford™ candlestick. (When sold as a pair, the pattern number is given as No. 200/174 in the catalogs.) 5½" high. Production dates unknown, but still being made in the late 1980s, probably longer. Known in crystal only. The Anchor™ appears inside the candle cup. $5.00 – 8.00.

ATTERBURY & COMPANY, Pittsburgh (1859 – 1899). The company was initially found-

ed as Hale, Atterbury & Company and known as the White House Factory. The founder and president of the company until his death in 1895 was Thomas Bakewell Atterbury, of the same family as Benjamin F. Bakewell, who founded Bakewell, Pears & Company. The Atterbury firm went through various changes of partnership. By 1863, the company was advertised as Atterbury, Reddick & Company and by 1864 as J. S. & T. B. Atterbury, when Thomas's brother James became a co-owner. The name was changed again to Atterbury & Company in 1865. The final name change occurred in 1865, when the firm became the Atterbury Glass Company. After both Atterbury brothers died the factory continued to be operated for a few more years. As late as 1901 there were reports that one of the Atterbury heirs was involved in estab-lishing a glass factory in Los Angeles.

Atterbury produced tableware, lamps, and novelties. They are especially well known for their many covered animal dishes. The company also offered many innovations in glassware, including glass shingles, which they hoped would prove more durable than slate. In the 1880s they received much publicity for developing a method for spinning glass into cloth, producing garments for men, women, and children in a variety of colors. Their production was large and varied and it is likely that they made other candlesticks, but the only one that can be attributed to them based on existing catalogs is the crucifix below. In the 1950s, the Imperial Glass Company (see volume 2 of this series) produced a candlestick that they called "Atterbury," advertising that it was reproduced from the "famous Belknap collection of early American antique milk glass."

COLORS

Atterbury was renowned for their opal glassware. They also produced flint (crystal) and opaque blue through most of their existence. Other colors made included opaque lavender, a light opaque green, mosaic glass (slag or marble glass in various color combinations), amber, transparent blue, and some ruby.

Crucifix. 8¼" high with a 4½" diameter base. Produced in the 1880s. Made in opal, opaque lavender, amber, and transparent blue, possibly also in crystal, blue opaque, and other colors. Opal: $50.00 – 80.00. Amber: $75.00 – 100.00. Transparent blue: $140.00 – 200.00. Opaque lavender: $250 to market.

AT-1A. CATALOG, CA. 1880, ORIGINAL BASE

AT-1. ATTERBURY CRUCIFIXES, MODIFIED BASE, IN OPAQUE LAVENDER AND TRANSPARENT BLUE

An early Atterbury catalog from about 1880 illus-trates this candlestick (AT-1a) with vines curling around the dome of the base. However, all the exam-ples we have seen have vines on the back of the cross and the upper part of the base, but not on the domed portion. This suggests that Atterbury modified the mold soon after it was put into production.

Complicating the situation, the mold for this can-dlestick was modified again, this time so radically that the third version appears to be an entirely new candle-stick with a changed candle cup and a hexagonal base. The cross and the Christ figure remained identical to the earlier version, and most examples still have the vines on the back although this detail is sometimes very faint. This last modification makes the candleholder appear very similar to a slightly taller model, known to have been made by the Cambridge Glass Co. While Atterbury may have made these modifications, we believe that Cambridge probably acquired the mold after Atterbury's demise and modified it to use as a second mold for their Crucifix candleholder (see CB-1a and CB-1b on p. 49 in the Cambridge chap-ter for more information).

In their *Glass Candlesticks, Book 2*, Margaret and Douglas Archer state that they have the earlier domed-based Atterbury candlestick in amber, which they believed to be a reproduction. However, it is likely that Atterbury also produced the amber version since this was one of their production colors.

BAKEWELL, PEARS & COMPANY, Pittsburgh (1808 – 1880). This was one of the

earliest glass companies established in the Pittsburgh area and one of the most successful. Founded by Benjamin F. Bakewell, Sr., the firm was originally known as Bakewell & Ensell. They went through a number of name changes, as various partners joined or withdrew from the company. Members of the Pears family were involved as early as 1816, with John Palmer Pears becoming president in 1842. The name was changed at that time to Bakewell & Pears. In 1844, following the death of Benjamin Bakewell, Sr., the firm was reorganized once again as Bakewell, Pears & Company.

Their earliest production was cut and engraved glassware, but they also made window glass, bottles, and flasks. In later years, they offered many pressed wares and are considered the first American factory to have successfully produced flint glass. Bakewell received many patents and among the patterns popularized by this company are Argus, Ashburton, and Princess Feather.

COLORS

In addition to crystal, Bakewell is known to have made amber, blue, green, opal, and opaque turquoise. Any of the other colors popular throughout the 1800s are possible.

Bakewell undoubtedly made many candlesticks. These include one depicting the figure of Rebecca at the Well, with the same figure appearing as the base of an accompanying comport in the Ribbon pattern. A corresponding male figure was reported by William Heacock in the June/July 1987 issue of the *Glass Collector's Digest*. Both figures are frosted, with the candle cups and bases of the candlesticks sometimes left clear. The Rebecca candlestick was reproduced by Fostoria (see volume 2 of this series) in the 1960s for the Henry Ford Museum. The Fostoria reproductions have a satin finish overall and are marked HFM on the left side, in the folds of the skirt just above the base, where the mark is easy to overlook.

BP-1. SMALL THISTLE
CANDLESTICK

Thistle candlestick. Made in two sizes. The one shown in the accompanying photograph, which is the smaller size, is 8¼" high with a 3⅞" diameter hexagonal base. The taller candlestick differs slightly in shape, as can be seen in the accompanying catalog reprint, and may be found with pewter inserts in the candle cups. The taller candlestick also has a scalloped candle cup. Known in crystal, opal, and opaque turquoise; other colors are possible. These candlesticks appear in an 1875 catalog, but probably were made for a number of years before and after that date. Similar candlesticks were made by other nineteenth century glasshouses, including McKee, who offered similar shapes as their "French" and "Boston" candlesticks. The Bakewell candlestick is manufactured in two parts, connected by a very thin wafer, almost imperceptible, with what looks like a more typical wafer above it actually being molded. Small: $35.00 – 50.00. Large, crystal: $45.00 – 65.00; opaque turquoise: $300.00 – 400.00.

BP-1A.
THISTLE
CANDLESTICKS,
CATALOG
CA. 1875

BARTLETT-COLLINS COMPANY, Sapulpa, Oklahoma (1914 to the present). For

many years, this company was the only independent manufacturer of glass tableware west of the Mississippi River. It was originally founded to make hand-pressed utilitarian glassware and lampshades. By the 1920s and 1930s, production had expanded to include blown ware, etching, and light cuttings. Around 1941, the company turned to machine-made glassware and discontinued all hand operations. In the years since, they have continued to turn out tableware in machine-made reproductions of earlier patterns, decorated tumblers, and kitchenware.

COLORS

Early production was in crystal and opal. By 1927, rose lustre, amber lustre, and crystal iridescent were being offered. During the Depression years, the company offered Nu-Rose and Nu-Green. By the 1950s, they were advertising such fired-on colors as Chinese Red, Snow White, and Lemon Yellow, often with gold trim and hand-painted or silkscreened decorations. In 1960, new "jewelled" colors were introduced as part of their Aurora line, including iridescent ruby, blue, amber, and smoke. The later sixties saw new "ceramic" (fired-on colors) such as Turquoise, Mandarin Orange, Green, Orchid, and White Matt. Popular colors late in the decade included Avocado and Sunset Gold (amber).

No. 87 candlestick. Made in the late 1920s, early 1930s. The accompanying catalog picture shows this candlestick as part of a console set with decoration 26, probably an etching. It was offered in Nu-Rose and was probably also available in Nu-Green. Many companies made similar spool-type candlesticks. This one seems to vary in the way that the candle cup tapers in toward the base. In color: $6.00 – 8.00. Decorated: $12.00 – 15.00.

BC-1. No. 87 CANDLESTICK
WITH DECORATION 26

BEACON GLASS COMPANY, Vineland, New Jersey (ca. 1946). Very little is known

about this company. They may have been new when they advertised in the July 1946 issue of *Giftwares* magazine, offering a 60-piece trial assortment. A second advertisement appeared the following month. Both advertisements listed showrooms around the country and in Canada where the Beacon line could be seen. Pieces shown in the initial advertisement were in wide optic, but other patterns described were "the sparkling thumbprint and the rich crackled." The ad went on to state that "Beacon has the 'eye-appeal' that excites admiration and stimulates buying… plus a popular price range… that makes it one of America's fastest selling glass lines."

COLORS

Colors mentioned in the advertisements were crystal, royal ruby, aquamarine blue, emerald, and amethyst.

The only known candleholder made by Beacon is the candleblock seen in the August 1946 advertisement from *Giftwares* magazine. It was offered as part of the No. 134X console set. 1¾" tall and 3⅜" wide. The candleblocks were listed in crystal only, while the accompanying bowl was available in crystal, emerald, blue, and ruby. $8.00 – 12.00.

This candleblock is very similar to Heisey's No. 1503 Crystolite rosette candleblock (1937 – 1955). (See HE-112 in Volume 2 of this series.) The Heisey candleblock was protected by a patent that was still in effect in 1946. Beacon modified their candleblock in several significant ways (as pointed out on the next page) that presumably protected them from patent infringement.

BE-1. BEACON NO. 134X CANDLEBLOCK

COMPARISON OF BEACON AND HEISEY CANDLEBLOCKS

BE-1A. SIDE VIEW   BE-1B. TOP VIEW   BE-1C. BOTTOM VIEW

BEACON NO. 134X CANDLEBLOCK ON THE LEFT, HEISEY NO. 1503 CRYSTOLITE ROSETTE CANDLEBLOCK ON THE RIGHT

The biggest difference between the two candleblocks is the number of "petals" around the top and the number of ribs on the base. The Beacon candleblock has six petals, while the older Heisey candleblock has eight. In between each petal on the Beacon candleblock appear six smaller petals. This results in the base of the Beacon candleblock having twelve ribs of alternating size, where the Heisey candleblock has only eight ribs, all the same size. The Beacon candleblock is 3⅜" wide, while the Heisey candleblock is 3¼". There is also a distinct difference in the quality of the crystal. The Heisey candleblock is good crystal, with the bottom cut and polished. The Beacon candleblock is unfinished on the bottom and appears not to have been fire polished, so that the glass is wavy.

BEAUMONT COMPANY, Morgantown, West Virginia (1918 – early 1990s). This company
was originally founded in 1905 as the Union Stopper Company (see volume 3 of this series), manufacturers of stoppers for non-refillable bottles, and pressed glass tableware and barware. The general manager was Percy Beaumont. He had previously been associated with a glass decorating firm originally located in Martin's Ferry, Ohio, that later moved to Grafton, West Virginia, which was known as the Beaumont Glass Company. (Upon Percy Beaumont's departure, this company changed its name to the Tygart Valley Glass Company.) When the Union Stopper Company was reorganized in 1918, it was renamed the Beaumont Company.

During the 1920s, Beaumont continued to make tableware and novelties, specializing in unusual colors and decorations. By later in the 1930s, however, they seem to have turned increasingly to lighting and stationers' glassware, lenses and signal glasses, chemical glassware, and the like. As late as the 1950s they still advertised themselves as manufacturers of novelties, including decorated vases. A 1954 catalog also offered a full line of Georgian pattern tumblers.

COLORS

During the 1920s and 1930s, Beaumont made crystal (sometimes with red edges or satin finish), ruby, cobalt blue, transparent pink and green (often with a satin finish), opaque jade green, and black. Their most unusual color is an opaque white called Ferlux. Originally developed for the manufacture of lighting goods, this semi-translucent white adapted well to tableware. It continued in production until 1936. In later years, opal, amber, dark green, and light blue were also offered (plain, satin, or with a crackled finish). Other colors are likely.

DECORATIONS

As might be expected, considering Percy Beaumont's background, many interesting decorations can be attributed to this company. These included etchings on crystal very similar to Fenton's Ming, San Toy, and other satin decorations. Hand-painted decorations on Ferlux include flowers, polka-dots, and plaids in bright colors. Metallic and solid-color bands were also popular.

Candlestick. 2½" high, 4½" diameter base with scalloped edge. Made in the 1920s or early 1930s. Known in Ferlux (opaque white), amber, and jade; other colors are likely. The Sears catalog for fall 1934 offered these candlesticks as part of a console set in amber or "milk white." Ferlux, plain: $10.00 – 12.00; decorated: $12.00 – 15.00.

BU-1. CANDLESTICK, FERLUX, HAND-PAINTED PLAID DECORATION

BU-1A. CANDLESTICK, FERLUX, HAND-PAINTED FLORAL DECORATION

One-light candlestick. 5" high, 4½" diameter scalloped base. Made in the 1920s or early 1930s. Known in crystal, cobalt, Ferlux (opaque white), and ruby. Other colors are possible. This candlestick can be confused with Paden City's No. 412 Crows' Foot candlestick, but has a more intricate "keyhole" design and a scalloped base. Crystal: $12.00 – 15.00. Ferlux: $16.00 – 18.00. Cobalt, ruby: $20.00 – 30.00.

BU-2. 1-LIGHT CANDLESTICK, COBALT

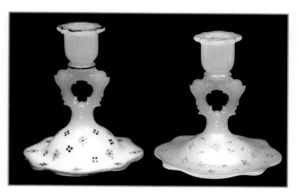

BU-2. 1-LIGHT CANDLESTICKS, FERLUX, HAND-PAINTED DECORATIONS

Two-light candlestick. 5" high, 4¾" diameter scalloped base. Made in the 1920s or early 1930s. Known in ruby and Ferlux (opaque white); probably also made in cobalt. Other colors are possible. This candlestick appears in crystal as No. 1480 in a Seneca Glass Company catalog with cutting 881. It isn't known if Seneca used blanks from Beaumont for cutting or if they borrowed the mold and produced the glassware themselves. Ferlux: $25.00 – 35.00. Ruby: $35.00 – 45.00.

BU-3. TWO-LIGHT CANDLESTICK, RUBY

Three-light candlestick. 6⅜" high, 7¾" arm spread, 4½" diameter round base. Made in the 1920s or early 1930s. Known in Ferlux (opaque white); probably also made in ruby and cobalt. Other colors are possible. This candlestick appears in crystal as No. 1480 in a Seneca Glass Company catalog with cutting 791. It isn't known if Seneca used blanks from Beaumont for cutting or if they borrowed the mold and produced the glassware themselves. Crystal: $35.00 – 45.00. Ferlux: $50.00 – 75.00.

BU-4. THREE-LIGHT CANDLESTICK, FERLUX

BU-5.
CORNUCOPIA
CANDLEHOLDER,
FERLUX

Cornucopia candleholder. 4½" high with a base measuring 3½" at its longest point. Made in the 1920s or early 1930s. Known in Ferlux (opaque white), ruby, and cobalt. Ferlux: $16.00 – 18.00. Cobalt, ruby: $20.00 – 30.00.

BU-6.
CRUCIFIX,
MADE FOR
WEISHAR BY
BEAUMONT

Crucifix. 10" high. According to John Weishar, of Island Mould in Wheeling, the original mold for this crucifix was carved by his grandfather, J. D. Weishar, in the late 1940s in response to a request by his wife for a crucifix more realistic than the ones commonly seen. It was sent to Beaumont who made 500 pieces in milk glass. They requested another mold with some alterations. However, before a second order could be placed, Mrs. Weishar passed away. After her death, her husband had the body of the milk glass crucifixes painted in gold leaf or in color and gave them away to friends. The original mold is still owned by Island Mould, and was leased briefly by Dalzell Viking (see DV-20 on p. 130) who made some candlesticks in crystal. The second mold was sold to the John E. Kemple Glass Works (see volume 3 of this series) in 1950. Opal, plain: $60.00 – 80.00; decorated with gold: $75.00 – 100.00. *(Photograph courtesy of John Weishar.)*

BISCHOFF SONS AND COMPANY, Huntington, West Virginia (1921 – 1935),
Culloden, West Virginia (1935 – 1959). This company manufactured stemware, barware, vases, and novelties, as well as lamp chimneys, lantern globes, lenses, and signal glass.

COLORS
There is very little information available on this company. Colors made seem to duplicate most of those typical of other West Virginia glass manufacturers, such as Blenko, including blue, brown, green, peach, red, and yellow.

BI-1.
No. 236
CANDLESTICKS,
TEAL BLUE AND
CHARCOAL

No. 236 candlestick. 5¾" high, according to the catalog, but actually 6⅜", with a 5" diameter base. Made in the 1950s. Known in teal blue, emerald green, ruby with a crystal base, and charcoal; other colors are likely. Available as part of a console set with a No. 230 handled bowl. $16.00 – 25.00.

No. 415 candlestick. 5¾" high. Made in the 1950s. Available colors unknown, but probably made in various colors. Offered as part of a console set with a No. 417 bowl. $15.00 – 20.00.

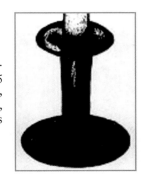

BI-2.
No. 415
CANDLESTICK,
FROM CATALOG,
CA. 1950S

BLENKO GLASS COMPANY, Milton, West Virginia (1921 to the present). This company was founded by William Blenko to manufacture stained glass. One of his earlier factories, established in Kokomo, Indiana, in 1893 had failed after little more than ten years, due to a reluctance on the part of buyers to purchase American stained glass, which was believed to be inferior to the English or European product. Subsequent factories in Point Marion, Pennsylvania, and Clarksburg, West Virginia, were even less successful, though Blenko received plaudits for the quality of his glass. At 67, in 1921, after working for several other glass companies, he decided to try once again to make glass on his own. Although orders were initially slow to come in, eventually the new factory, called Eureka Art Glass, was able to establish itself as one of the finest manufacturers of stained glass in the world, a reputation they still enjoy today.

The fortunes of Blenko remained precarious throughout the 1920s, however, and they were seriously threatened by the stock market crash of 1929, when new construction – and, therefore, orders for stained glass – ground to an almost complete halt. It was at this time that the company expanded production to include decorative glassware, mostly blown pieces in the brilliant colors developed for the company's stained glass production. The company became known as the Blenko Glass Company in 1930. In 1936, they were authorized by the Colonial Williamsburg Foundation to make exclusive reproductions of glassware found at Williamsburg, a partnership that continued for many years. Throughout the 1940s they adapted many traditional glassmaking techniques, such as the use of prunts and applied threads of glass, to modern shapes.

EARLY LABEL, USED
THROUGH THE 1970S

In 1946, Blenko hired Winslow Anderson, who designed all of the company's new patterns until his departure in 1952. From 1952 to 1963, Wayne Husted was the designer, followed by Joel Myers, from 1963 to 1972. John Nickerson (1970 – 1974) and Donald Shepherd (1975 – 1988) were the next designers to be associated with the firm, followed by Hank Adams (1988 – 1994), Chris Gibbons (1994 – 1995), and Matt Carter, who currently fills that position. Blenko is still active today, one of the few surviving handmade glass factories in the United States. Four generations of the Blenko family have been actively involved in the business to date.

COLORS

Considering Blenko's original goal to create antique art glass (stained glass), the company has specialized in the creation of a spectrum of colors that were often imitated by other West Virginia companies. Many of these colors were also offered with a crackled finish.

LATER LABEL

Color	Date	Color	Date
Alpine (blue)	1993	Desert green	1996 – 1997
Amber		Ebony	1999 – 2000
Amethyst	1991 to the present	Emerald green	1972 – 1973, 1991 to the present
Antique green	1980s – 1999	Gold	
Azure	1990 to the present	Grass green	1977 – 1978
Black		Honey	1965 – 1968
Blue, light		Jonquil	Early 1960s
Charcoal	Late 1950s, again in 1971	Juniper	
Chartreuse	Late 1940s, early 1950s	Kiwi	1998 to the present
Chestnut	1965 only	Lemon	1968 – 1969
Citron		Midnight blue	1986
Cobalt blue	1990 to the present	Olive green	1964 to 1976, 1993 to 1994

Opaline yellow	1986	Slate	1989
Orchid	1991 to the present	Surf green	1970 only
Peacock	1965 – 1966	Tangerine	1960s to 1981
Pine green	1974 only	Teal	1950s; 1997 – 1998
Plum	1967; 1988	Topaz	1991 to the present
Rose	1964 only	Turquoise	1960s to 1979, 2001 (limited edition)
Ruby		Violet	1994 to the present
Sapphire blue	1979 – 1985	Wheat	1969 – 1985
Sea green		Wisteria	Amethyst shading to blue
Seafoam	2000 to the present	Yellow	Early 1950s
Sky blue			

BL-1.
**No. 20, EARLY
1930S CATALOG**

No. 20. Made in the early 1930s. Any of the early colors are possible. $20.00 – 25.00. *(Catalog reproduction courtesy of Blenko Glass Company.)*

BL-2.
**No. 20H,
EARLY 1930S
CATALOG**

No. 20H. Made in the early 1930s. Any of the early colors are possible. $20.00 – 25.00. *(Catalog reproduction courtesy of Blenko Glass Company.)*

**BL-3. No 3612,
1930S CATALOG**

No. 3612. Made in the 1930s. Any of the early colors are possible. Offered with various bowls as part of a console set. $20.00 – 25.00. *(Catalog reproduction courtesy of Blenko Glass Company.)*

BL-4.
**No. 3747, 1930S
CATALOG**

No. 3747. Made in the 1930s. Any of the early colors are possible. Offered with a matching No. 3744 crimped bowl as part of a console set. $25.00 – 30.00. *(Catalog reproduction courtesy of Blenko Glass Company.)*

No. CW-11. Colonial Williamsburg glassware reproduction. 8¼" high, 5¼" diameter foot. Blenko was exclusively authorized to make glassware for the Colonial Williamsburg Foundation from 1937 to 1966. Made in crystal only. All pieces made for Williamsburg were copies of items excavated there and were produced using authentic eighteenth century methods. $60.00 – 75.00.

BL-5. TABLE SETTING FEATURING OLD WILLIAMSBURG GLASSWARE REPRODUCTIONS, INCLUDING THE No. CW-11 CANDLESTICK, *House and Garden*, SEPTEMBER 1942

No. 444CS spiral stem candlestick. 7" high, 3¼" diameter foot. Made ca. 1946 – 1951. Available in amethyst, marine crystal, ruby, sea green, sky blue, and turquoise. Offered with the No. 444B spiral stem compote as part of a console set. "A pleasing departure from the conventional is this skillful double twist," according to the 1946 catalog. $30.00 – 40.00.

BL-6. No. 444CS SPIRAL STEM CANDLE-STICK, TURQUOISE

No. 445CS candlestick with rosettes. 3½" high. Produced ca. 1946. Made in amethyst, chartreuse, marine crystal, ruby, sea green, sky blue, and turquoise. Called "rosette" because of the applied prunts appearing just below the candle cup, an example of a traditional manufacturing technique applied to contemporary glass. The candlestick was also made without the prunts. Offered in the 1946 catalog with the No. 444LB rosette bowl as part of a console set. Plain: $20.00 – 25.00. With rosettes: $30.00 – 35.00.

BL-7. No. 445CS CANDLESTICK WITH ROSETTES, SKY BLUE

No. 476CS. 7" high, 4⅛" diameter foot. Produced ca. 1946. Made in crystal with blue, green, or ruby rings and foot. Another example of traditional glassmaking techniques, with the heavy threads, or rings, applied by hand. Note in the accompanying photograph that, because these candlesticks were completely handmade, the shape can vary, as well as the size of the rings. Offered with the No. 476B footed bowl with matching rings as part of a console set. $50.00 – 70.00.

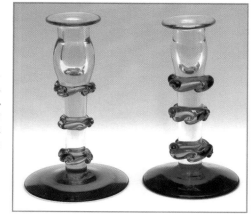

BL-8. No. 476CS, CRYSTAL AND GREEN AND BLUE RINGS

No. 902 candleholder. 1½" high, 5¼" in diameter. Introduced 1950. Made in amethyst, chartreuse, emerald, marine crystal, ruby, sea green, sky blue, and turquoise. Designed by Winslow Anderson. This was one of the pieces chosen by the selection committee of the Museum of Modern Art as "examples of some of the best in modern design for home furnishings in 1950" (from an advertisement appearing in *House Beautiful,* August 1950). $20.00 – 25.00.

BL-9. No. 902 CANDLEHOLDERS, RUBY AND EMERALD

BL-9A. No. 902 CANDLEHOLDER AND OTHER PIECES, FROM *House Beautiful,* AUGUST 1950

BL-10. No. 954 CANDLEHOLDER DISH, FROM 1950S CATALOG

No. 954 candleholder dish. 7" in diameter. Made in the 1950s in amethyst, chartreuse, emerald, marine crystal, ruby, sea green, sky blue, and turquoise. Offered with the No. 953 epergne as part of a console set. $30.00 – 35.00. *(Catalog reproduction courtesy of Blenko Glass Company.)*

BL-11. No. 990A CANDLEBLOCK

No. 990A candleblock. 2" high, 3⅛" in diameter. One of Blenko's classic designs, made from the 1950s to the present. Colors include crystal, ruby, sea green, sapphire, tangerine, turquoise, jonquil, rose, olive green, honey, plum, lemon, wheat, surf green, emerald, juniper, amethyst, gold, and teal. Other colors are possible. The sides and the bottom of the candleblock are mottled, while the top is smooth. Also offered with an accompanying 13¾" cylinder-style hurricane shade that surrounds the candleblock. The shades were available in all of the same colors and either plain or with a crackled finish. Also offered with the No. 7817 Bamboo hurricane shades in 1978. $10.00 – 15.00.

BL-12. No. 990B CANDLEBLOCK, TURQUOISE

No. 990B candleblock. 2" high, 3⅛" in diameter. Made 1974 – 1975 in crystal, wheat, pine, turquoise, and olive green. Almost identical to the No. 990A candleblock, except that it sits on three tapered feet. The sides are mottled and the top is smooth. Also available with the No. 675 15" hurricane shade. $10.00 – 15.00.

No. 6128 teardrop shaped candleblock. 1¼"
high and 3½" long. Made from 1961 to 1965.
Production colors include crystal, jonquil, olive
green, rose, sea green, turquoise, tangerine,
honey, cobalt, and black; other colors are possible. Reissued 2001 in crystal, topaz, emerald,
and amethyst as No. 2101. Colors in current
2002 catalog: $8.00. Other colors: $12.00 –
17.00.

BL-13.
No. 6128
TEARDROP
SHAPED
CANDLEBLOCKS,
COBALT AND
JONQUIL

No. 6326 candleblock. 1¾" high, 4" across. Made in crystal
(1963 – 1965); rose (1963 – 1964); olive green and turquoise
(1964 – 1965); honey, jonquil, sea green, and tangerine (1964
only). Reissued 1995 and still in the current (2001) catalog in
crystal, topaz, emerald, and amethyst as No. 2102. Colors in
current 2002 catalog: $9.00. Other colors: $13.00 – 18.00.

BL-14.
No. 6326
CANDLEBLOCK,
HONEY

No. 6411 candleholder. 3½" in diameter. Made in 1964 in crystal, jonquil, olive green, rose, sea green, tangerine, and turquoise. $15.00 –
20.00. *(Catalog reproduction courtesy of Blenko Glass Company.)*

BL-15.
No. 6411
CANDLEHOLDER,
ROSE, FROM
1964 CATALOG

No. 6424 vase/candlestick. 5" high. Introduced as a vase in
1964; it wasn't until 1969 that it was also shown as a candlestick. It remained in production until at least the early 1980s.
It was made both plain and with a crackled finish. Production
colors include crystal, jonquil, olive green, rose, sea green,
tangerine, turquoise, chestnut, honey, peacock, plum, lemon,
wheat, surf green, charcoal, and emerald; other colors are possible. In 1970, a stopper was added to convert the vase into
the No. 708 bottle. $25.00 – 35.00.

BL-16. No.
6424
VASE/CANDLE-
STICK,
EMERALD

No. 683 candleholder. 6⅝" diameter. Made in 1968 only. Offered
in crystal, honey, lemon, olive green, and turquoise. Designed to
hold a large candle. $10.00 – 15.00. *(Catalog reproduction courtesy of Blenko Glass
Company.)*

BL-17.
No. 683
CANDLEHOLDER,
TURQUOISE,
FROM 1968
CATALOG

BL-18.
No. 6824
CANDLE-
BLOCK, CRYS-
TAL CASED
OVER OLIVE
GREEN

No. 6824 candleblock. 6¼" high, 2½" diameter at the base, tapering up to 1⅜" diameter at the top. Made in 1968 only. Offered in crystal cased over honey, olive green, or turquoise. The candleblock is solid with spirals appearing in the center at the bottom. $40.00 – 60.00.

BL-19.
No. 6825
CANDLEHOLDER,
CRYSTAL CASED
OVER OLIVE
GREEN, FROM
1968 CATALOG

No. 6825 candleholder. Approximately 6½" in diameter. Made in 1968 only. Offered in crystal cased over honey, olive green, or turquoise. Matches the pattern appearing in the No. 6824 candleblock above. $40.00 – 50.00. *(Catalog reproduction courtesy of Blenko Glass Company.)*

BL-20.
No. 692
CANDLEBLOCK,
TURQUOISE,
FROM 1969
CATALOG

No. 692 candleblock, eight-pointed star. 4⅜" in diameter. Made in 1969 in crystal, lemon, olive green, turquoise, and wheat. $10.00 – 15.00. *(Catalog reproduction courtesy of Blenko Glass Company.)*

BL-21.
No. 7047
CANDLESTICK,
FROM 1970
CATALOG

No. 7047 candlestick. 11" high. Offered in 1970 only in crystal with colored trim (olive green, surf green, tangerine, turquoise, or wheat). A delightful example of the use of traditional glassmaking techniques to produce a piece that is thoroughly modern, whimsical, and sassy. $125.00 – 150.00. *(Catalog reproduction courtesy of Blenko Glass Company.)*

No. 712 vase/candleholder. Available in three sizes: 712S (6½" high), 712M (8" high), and 712L (9½" high). Introduced in 1971 in crystal, charcoal, olive green, tangerine, turquoise, and wheat. Small: $20.00 – 25.00. Medium: $25.00 – 30.00. Large: $30.00 – 35.00. *(Catalog reproduction courtesy of Blenko Glass Company.)*

BL-22. No. 712L, 712S, AND 712M VASE/CANDLEHOLDERS, TANGERINE, OLIVE GREEN, AND WHEAT, FROM 1971 CATALOG

No. 722 candleholder. Available in three sizes: 722S (6½" high), 722M (8" high), and 722L (9½" high). Made 1972 – 1974 in crystal, olive, turquoise, emerald, tangerine, wheat, and pine, both plain finish and crackled. Small: $15.00 – 20.00. Medium: $20.00 – 25.00. Large: $30.00 – 35.00. *(Catalog reproduction courtesy of Blenko Glass Company.)*

BL-23. No. 722 CANDLEHOLDERS, OLIVE, TURQUOISE, AND CRYSTAL, FROM 1972 CATALOG

No. 748 candlestick. Available in two sizes: 748S (5" high) and 748L (7" high). Made 1974 – 1975 in crystal, olive, turquoise, tangerine, wheat, and pine, both plain finish and crackled. Small: $10.00 – 15.00. Large: $15.00 – 25.00. *(Catalog reproduction courtesy of Blenko Glass Company.)*

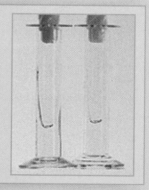

BL-24. No. 748L CANDLESTICKS, FROM 1974 CATALOG

No. 763 three-light candleblock, footed. 3¼" high and 6½" wide. Has a 1976 pattern number, but only appears in the 1981 catalog. Known only in crystal. The top is smooth, with all other surfaces textured, including the feet. A very similar candleblock, probably Swedish, appears on the next page. $20.00 – 30.00.

BL-25. No. 763 THREE-LIGHT CANDLEBLOCK

LOOKALIKE

BL-26. THREE-LIGHT CANDLE-BLOCK MADE BY KOSTA, SWEDEN

Three-light candleblock, footed. 3½" high and approximately 5¼" across at the widest point. Note the stylistic resemblance to the No. 763 candleblock (BL-25 on page 29). We have seen a slightly small version of this candleholder (2¾" high and 3¾" at its widest point) with a label indicating that it was made by Kosta of Sweden.

BL-27. No. 765 CANDLE-BLOCK, WHEAT

No. 765 candleblock. Part of the Bounty Collection. 2⅞" high, with a top diameter between 4¼" and 4½". The bottom is 2" in diameter. Made 1976 in crystal, green, olive, turquoise, and wheat. Smooth on top with roughly textured sides pressed with petals like a flower. The bottom has crosshatching on it. $10.00 – 15.00.

BL-28. No. 7634 HANDLED CANDLESTICKS, SAPPHIRE AND RUBY

No. 7634 handled candlestick. Part of the Americana Collection. 3½" high, 5¼" in diameter. Introduced in 1976 and remained in production until the 1990s. Colors include crystal, emerald, antique green, sapphire, cobalt, tangerine, turquoise, ruby, plum, wheat, olive, antique green, and teal; other colors are likely. In 1981, a version of this candlestick was introduced without a handle as No. 811 (see BL-38 on page 32). $20.00 – 25.00.

BL-29 & BL-30. No. 7635 AND No. 7636 CANDLESTICKS, FROM 1976 CATALOG

No. 7635 candlestick (left), 7" high, and No. 7636 candlestick (right), 5½" high. Part of the Americana Collection. Made 1976 – 1977 in crystal only. $20.00 – 25.00 each.

(Catalog reproduction courtesy of Blenko Glass Company.)

BL-31. SET OF THREE CANDLEBLOCKS, No. 77S, 77L, AND 77M

No. 77S, 77M, and 77L candleblocks, graduated. 3", 4", and 5" high, with a top diameter between 4½" and 4¾". The columns are 2¼" in diameter. Produced in 1977 and again in 1981 in crystal only. Smooth on top, but textured on all other surfaces. A similar set of candleblocks, without the figured pattern on top, is in current production. (See No. BL-42 on p. 33.) All sizes: $10.00 – 15.00 each.

No. 774 candleholder. Part of the Chinese Classics line. The height varies from 3½" to 4", depending on the amount of flare. Star-shaped base with six petals, opening to a diameter of approximately 7". Introduced in 1977 and reissued in 1981 and 1985. Known colors include crystal, turquoise, wheat, grass, antique green, and sapphire. Designed to hold either a standard taper or a wide candle. $10.00 – 15.00.

BL-32. No. 774 CANDLE-HOLDER, WHEAT

No. 7710 three-light candleblock. 10" wide. Made 1977 in crystal only. $20.00 – 30.00. *(Catalog reproduction courtesy of Blenko Glass Company.)*

BL-33. No. 7710 THREE-LIGHT CANDLEBLOCK, FROM 1977 CATALOG

No. 802 Diamonds candleblocks. Made in three sizes: 802S (2½" square), 802M (2½" by 5" high), and 802L (2½" by 7½" high). Made 1980 – 1981 in crystal only. Small: $8.00 – 10.00. Medium: $10.00 – 15.00. Large: $15.00 – 20.00. *(Catalog reproduction courtesy of Blenko Glass Company.)*

BL-34. No. 802S, 802L, AND 802M DIAMONDS CANDLE-BLOCKS, FROM 1980 CATALOG

No. 805 Diamonds candleblock. 2" square. Made 1980 in crystal only. $5.00 – 10.00. *(Catalog reproduction courtesy of Blenko Glass Company.)*

BL-35. No. 805 DIAMONDS CAN-DLEBLOCKS, FROM 1980 CATALOG

No. 808 Diamonds hurricane lamp. 5" square. Made 1980 in crystal only. $15.00 – 20.00. *(Catalog reproduction courtesy of Blenko Glass Company.)*

BL-36. No. 808 DIAMONDS HURRICANE LAMP, FROM 1980 CATALOG

BL-37.
No. 810
CANDLEHOLDER,
FROM 1981 CATALOG

No. 810 candleholder. 3¾" diameter. Introduced 1981 and reissued in 1985 in crystal only. $10.00 – 15.00. *(Catalog reproduction courtesy of Blenko Glass Company.)*

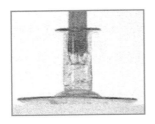

BL-38.
No. 811
CANDLESTICK,
FROM 1981
CATALOG

No. 811 candlestick. 3¾" high. Introduced in 1981 in crystal, wheat, antique green, tangerine, and sapphire. Appears to be identical to the No. 7634 candlestick, but without a handle. (See BL-28 on page 30.) $15.00 – 25.00. *(Catalog reproduction courtesy of Blenko Glass Company.)*

BL-39.
CANDLESTICK,
UNKNOWN
PATTERN
NUMBER,
COBALT

Candlestick. 9½" high, with a top diameter of 3½" and a base diameter of 3¼". Production dates unknown, but probably made in the 1980s. Known in cobalt blue and teal, with other colors likely. $25.00 – 30.00.

BL-40.
ROUND
CANDLEBLOCK,
UNKNOWN
PATTERN
NUMBER

Round candleblock. 2" high and 3¾" in diameter. Production dates unknown, but probably 1980s or 1990s. Known in crystal, but colors are also possible. Has a lightly textured finish. $15.00 – 20.00.

BL-41.
No. 84M, 84S,
AND 84L
CANDLEBLOCKS

No. 84 candleblocks. Available in three sizes: 84S (2" high), 84M (4" high), and 84L (6" high). Listed in the current catalog in crystal only, but known also in cobalt, dark green, and yellow. Current 2002 catalog: $27.00 for the set of three.

No. 877 candleblocks. Available in three sizes: 877S (2" high), 877M (3" high), and 877L (4" high). Made from 1987 to the present. Known in cobalt, green, and light blue, and probably made in other colors as well, but listed in the current catalog in crystal only. Similar in shape to the candleblocks shown in illustration BL-31 on page 30, but without the figured pattern on the tops. Current 2002 catalog: $24.00 for the set of three. *(Catalog reproduction courtesy of Blenko Glass Company.)*

BL-42. No. 877, THREE SIZES, FROM 2000 CATALOG

No. 85 candleblocks. Available in three sizes: 85S (2" high), 85M (4" high), and 85L (6" high). Known in yellow, but listed in the 2000 catalog in crystal only at $8.00, $9.00, and $10.00 respectively. *(Catalog reproduction courtesy of Blenko Glass Company.)*

BL-43. No. 85 CANDLEBLOCKS, THREE SIZES, FROM 2000 CATALOG

No. 990 candleholder (1¾" high and 4⅞" in diameter). No. 881 candleholder (2" high and 7" in diameter). The No. 881 candleholder was introduced in 1988, with the No. 990 being a later version of the candleholder in a smaller size. Both known in plum and possibly also made in antique green and other colors. The No. 881 was offered in the 2000 catalog in crystal only, while the No. 990 was available in both crystal and ruby. Used as the base for a tall hurricane shade, 12" and 13⅛" high respectively, in various colors. 2000 catalog price, small, in crystal, base only: $12.00; with hurricane shade: $46.00; ruby, with hurricane shade: $57.50. Large, in crystal, base only: $16.00; with hurricane shade: $70.00.

BL-44B. No. 881 CANDLEHOLDER IN PLUM WITH WHEAT HURRICANE SHADE

BL-44. No. 990 CANDLEHOLDER, PLUM

BL-44A. No. 881 CANDLEHOLDER, PLUM

No. 901 candleblock. Heart-shaped. 1⅛" high and 3½" wide. Made from 1990 to 2000. Known in tangerine, with other colors possible, but listed in the 2000 catalog in crystal only at $8.00.

BL-45. No. 901 CANDLEBLOCKS IN TANGERINE

BL-46. No. 9512 CANDLE-HOLDER, FROM 2000 CATALOG

No. 9512 candleholder. 2" high, 8" in diameter. Made from 1995 to 2000. Listed in the 2000 catalog in crystal only at $20.00. *(Catalog reproduction courtesy of Blenko Glass Company.)*

BL-47. No. 9515 CANDLEBLOCK, FROM 2000 CATALOG

No. 9515 candleblock. 4" high. Made from 1995 to 2000. Listed in the 2000 catalog in crystal only at $12.00. *(Catalog reproduction courtesy of Blenko Glass Company.)*

BL-48. No. 9517 CANDLEHOLDER AND No. 9516 CANDLE-HOLDER, FROM 2000 CATALOG

No. 9516 and 9517 candleholders. 2" and 4¾" high, respectively. Made from 1995 to 2000. Known in topaz and cobalt blue, and probably made in other colors as well, but only listed in crystal in the 2000 catalog at $9.00 and $15.00 respectively. *(Catalog reproduction courtesy of Blenko Glass Company.)*

BL-49. No. 9701 CANDLE-BLOCK, No. 9703 CANDLE-BLOCK, AND No. 9702 CANDLEBLOCK, FROM 2000 CATALOG

No. 9701 candleblock (4" high), No. 9702 candle-block (4" high), No. 9703 candleblock (2½" high). Made from 1997 to 2000. Listed in the 2000 catalog in crystal only at $12.00. *(Catalog reproduction courtesy of Blenko Glass Company.)*

BL-50. No. 9802 CANDLEBLOCKS (SET OF 3) FROM 2000 CATALOG

No. 9802 candleblocks. 3½" high. Sold as a set of three. Made from 1998 to the present. Listed in the 2000 catalog in crystal only, but also known in yellow. Current 2002 catalog: $30.00 for the set of three. *(Catalog reproduction courtesy of Blenko Glass Company.)*

BL-51. No. 9803 CANDLEBLOCKS FROM 2000 CATALOG

No. 9803 candleblock. 5" high. Made from 1998 to the present. Listed in the 2000 catalog in crystal only at $16.00. *(Catalog reproduction courtesy of Blenko Glass Company.)*

BOSTON AND SANDWICH GLASS COMPANY, Sandwich, Massachu-

setts (1825 – 1887). This company was initially operated from July 4, 1825 to April 3, 1826, as the Sandwich Manufacturing Company. It was then incorporated as the Boston and Sandwich Glass Company. In 1827 they began making pressed glass, only the third American company to do so. Deming Jarves, the founder, had previously also been one of the founders of the New England Glass Company (see volume 3 of this series). He is justly famous for the many improvements made in the manufacturing process under his leadership at Sandwich. Much of this is attributable to his talent for attracting highly talented men, such as Hiram Dillaway, the master mechanic and mold maker who was responsible for ten patents.

The output at Sandwich was immense, with an average of 100,000 pounds of glass produced every week. The glassware made was equally varied, including both pressed and blown. In addition, their decorating department did cutting, engraving, etching, and hand-painted designs. Their lacy pressed patterns are particularly popular with collectors today.

In 1858, Jarves resigned and founded a competing factory, the Cape Cod Glass Company (see p. 100), which was also located in Sandwich. It is often difficult to distinguish between the products of the New England Glass Company, Boston and Sandwich, and the Cape Cod Glass Company. It should be noted that all Sandwich candlesticks were made in two parts with a wafer, with the exception of the Madonna, which sometimes had a metal fitting. This means that any pressed base may be found with any pressed top or with a blown top. One or more blown knops were also sometimes inserted between the pieces to give additional height. The possible combinations are nearly limitless. The candlesticks shown below are just a sampling.

Boston and Sandwich remained in operation for nearly 30 years after Jarves's departure, eventually closing because of increased competition from the Pittsburgh area factories and labor problems. Between 1888 and 1907 three short-lived attempts were made to reopen the factory, but none of them were successful.

COLORS

All of the popular nineteenth century colors were made at Sandwich, including amber, amethyst, various shades of blue, canary, various shades of green, clambroth (alabaster), opal, opaque blue, and opaque green (in shades ranging from pale green to jade), among others.

Lacy candlestick. 9¼" high, with a base that is 3¼" across. Made ca. 1828 to 1835. Known in crystal. The candle cup and base are pressed, connected to a stem consisting of dual blown melon knops that provide additional height. This candlestick demonstrates one of the three styles of candle cup that will be found on Sandwich lacy candlesticks. This one has a Peacock Eye pattern. Crystal: $1,200.00 – 1,400.00.

BS-1. LACY CANDLESTICK (WITH CLOSE-UP OF THE SOCKET)

Lacy candlestick. Made ca. 1828 to 1835. Known in crystal. Made in two pieces, connected by a wafer. This candlestick demonstrates the second of three styles of candle cup that will be found on Sandwich lacy candlesticks. Crystal: $350.00 – 450.00. *(Photograph courtesy of the Sandwich Glass Museum.)*

BS-2. LACY CANDLESTICK

BS-3. GROUP OF LACY CANDLESTICKS

Group of lacy candlesticks, ranging from 5¼" to 9½". Made from ca. 1828 to 1845. Known in crystal. All made in two pieces attached by wafers; the two taller candlesticks also have blown melon knops that provide additional height. The two shorter candlesticks demonstrate the third style of candle cup, with a lily motif, that will be found on Sandwich lacy candlesticks. The three styles of candle cup shown in this grouping have been authenticated as Sandwich. According to Raymond E. Barlow and Joan E. Kaiser's *The Glass Industry in Sandwich*, any of these three candle cups attached to a pressed base by a wafer can be accepted as Sandwich.

The handled candlestick, which is very rare, was reproduced by Imperial in crystal and sapphire blue from 1976 to 1982 and again, in the early 1990s, by Dalzell Viking for the Smithsonian Institution, including in crystal with a ruby top. (See DV-4 on p. 126.) The reproductions are marked SI and are molded in two pieces like the originals, but do not have a true wafer (i.e., the mold seams are clearly visible on the wafer.). *(Photograph courtesy of the Sandwich Glass Museum.)*

BS-4. TWO CANDLESTICKS, PRESSED BASES, SCALLOPED CANDLE CUPS

Candlesticks, pressed bases, scalloped candle cups. Made from ca. 1830 to 1845. Known in crystal. Both candlesticks are made in two pieces, attached by wafers; the taller candlestick also has blown melon knops that give it additional height. Tall, crystal: $500.00 – 700.00. Short, crystal: $100.00 – 150.00. *(Photograph courtesy of the Sandwich Glass Museum.)*

BS-5. CANDLESTICKS, BLOWN AND PRESSED CANDLE CUPS

Candlesticks, one with a blown candle cup, the other with a pressed candle cup. Made from ca. 1835 to 1860. Both candlesticks are made in two pieces, attached by wafers. As can be seen, the taller candlestick has a blown candle cup with a blown knop center. Pittsburgh area manufacturers made similar combinations. Tall, crystal: $400.00 – 450.00. Short, crystal: $150.00 – 200.00. *(Photograph courtesy of the Sandwich Glass Museum.)*

BS-6. PETAL SOCKET CANDLESTICK, CANARY

Petal socket candlestick, wafer joined to a faceted stem. 7¼" high with a 4" diameter round base. Produced circa 1830 – 1845. This candlestick was an early example of what would become a gradual shift away from lacy patterns to a cleaner style that would typify later Boston & Sandwich candleholders. According to Barlow & Kaiser's *A Guide to Sandwich Glass*, the thin lipped petals indicate that this stick dates to the early- or mid-1830s. This may also have come in a larger "master" size. This same base was also offered with a hexagonal socket (BS-6a). Known in crystal, canary, and transparent blue. Other colors are likely. Crystal: $65.00 – 85.00. Canary: $125.00 – 150.00. Blue: $475.00 – 550.00.

BS-6A. HEXAGONAL SOCKET CANDLESTICK

Hexagonal candlestick with shallow socket. Made in three sizes: 7¼" high, with a 3⅜" base; 8¼" high, with a 3⁹⁄₁₆" base; and 9¾" high, with a 4⅜" base. The tall candlestick is referred to as the "master size" and is considered rare. Produced circa 1840 – 1860. Known in crystal, amber, canary, and clambroth; also the clambroth base can be found with opaque blue or green tops. Manufactured in two pieces, with the candle cup attached to the column by a wafer. The New England Glass Company made this same style base, but their version was manufactured in one piece. Small: Crystal: $60.00 – 85.00. Clambroth: $85.00 – 110.00. Amber, canary: $100.00 – 125.00. Clambroth/blue: $400.00 – 450.00. Clambroth/green: $1,200.00 – 1,500.00.
Medium: Crystal: $85.00 – 110.00. Clambroth: $100.00 – 120.00. Amber, canary: $125.00 – 150.00. Clambroth/blue: $500.00 – 600.00. Clambroth/green: $1,500.00 – 1,800.00.
Large: Crystal: $100.00 – 125.00. Clambroth: $120.00 – 150.00. Amber, canary: $150.00 – 200.00. Clambroth/blue: $600.00 – 800.00. Clambroth/green: $2,000.00 – 2,500.00.

BS-7. CLAMBROTH HEXAGONAL CANDLESTICKS, THREE SIZES

Petal and Loop candlestick. 7" high with a 4½" diameter round base. Produced circa 1840 – 1860. Known in crystal, amber, amethyst, apple green, blue, canary, clambroth, opal, and opaque light blue. Made in two parts and connected by a wafer. The base has seven loops on it. This candlestick has been reproduced, but the copy is made in one piece and has only six loops. The base to this candlestick was also used as the cover to a sugar bowl. Crystal: $80.00 – 100.00. Clambroth, opal, canary: $200.00 – 275.00. Amber: $250.00 – 400.00. Apple green: $500.00 – 800.00. Blue, amethyst: $800.00 – 1,100.00. Opaque light blue and other unusual colors: $1,200.00 to market.

BS-8A. PETAL AND LOOP CANDLESTICK, CANARY

BS-8. PETAL AND LOOP CANDLESTICK, APPLE GREEN

Hexagonal candlestick. 7½" high with a 3¾" base. Produced circa 1840 – 1860. Known in crystal, amethyst, and canary. Made in two parts and connected by a wafer. This candlestick was also made with a wider, 4½" diameter base. Raymond E. Barlow and Joan E. Kaiser, in their definitive *The Glass Industry in Sandwich*, refute the claim that the candlesticks with the wide base were made by workers for their own use, suggesting instead that they were intended for banks or counting rooms, where special stability was essential to prevent fires. Crystal: $60.00 – 80.00. Clambroth, opal, canary: $100.00 – 150.00. Amethyst: $600.00 – 800.00. (Add 50% to these prices for the wide base version.)

BS-9. HEXAGONAL CANDLESTICKS, CRYSTAL AND CANARY

Hexagonal candlestick. 7¼" high with a 3¾" base. Produced circa 1840 – 1860. Known in crystal, blue, amber, canary, amethyst, and green. Made in two parts and connected by a wafer. What is unusual about the example shown in the accompanying photograph is that the wafer is so thin as to be almost imperceptible. A very small bubble can just be made out, which is almost the only evidence that the wafer exists. Most candlesticks in this style will have a more typical, protruding wafer. Crystal: $75.00 – 90.00. Canary: $125.00 – 150.00. Amber, blue: $225.00- $250.00. Amethyst: $250.00 – 275.00. Green: $300.00 – 325.00.

BS-10. HEXAGONAL CANDLESTICK

BS-11. CRUCIFIX, OPAL

Crucifix. 11½" high. Produced circa 1840 – 1880. Known in crystal, amber, amethyst, blue, canary, transparent green, jade green, clambroth, opal, and opaque light blue. Made in two parts connected by a wafer. One of three styles of crucifix known to have been made by Sandwich. Crystal: $80.00 – 100.00. Clambroth, opal: $100.00 – 125.00. Canary, amber: $300.00 – 400.00. Blue, amethyst: $450.00 – 700.00. Opaque light blue, opaque jade green: $800.00 – 1,200.00.

BS-12. CRUCIFIXES WITH HEXAGONAL BASES, OPAL

Crucifix with hexagonal base. 9¾" high. Produced circa 1840 – 1880. Known in crystal, amethyst, cobalt blue, and opal. Made in two parts connected by a wafer. This crucifix appears to have two wafers, one immediately above the other, but in fact, only one wafer is a true one. An 11½" version of this candlestick was also made without the second pseudo-wafer. Crystal: $65.00 – 80.00. Clambroth, opal: $80.00 – 100.00. Canary, amber: $250.00 – 350.00. Blue, amethyst: $400.00 – 600.00.

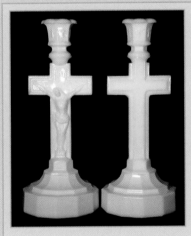

BS-13. CRUCIFIXES IN OPAL, FRONT AND BACK

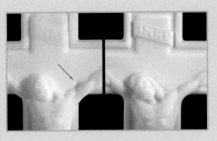

BS-13A. CLOSE-UP COMPARISON OF SANDWICH AND CAPE COD GLASS COMPANY CRUCIFIXES

Crucifix with twelve-sided base and crosses on the hexagonal candle cup. 12¾" high with a 4⅞" diameter base. Produced circa 1860 – 1887. This is almost identical to crucifixes made by the Cape Cod Glass Company and Hobbs, Brockunier and Company (both before and after the latter joined the United States Glass Company). All three Crucifixes were made in two parts, with the candle cup attached to the base by a wafer. The Hobbs/U.S. Glass Crucifix has many subtle details that make it comparatively easy to spot, such as a reinforcing ring around the candle opening. The Cape Cod version (CC-1 on p. 100) is much closer to the Boston and Sandwich, making it more difficult to distinguish between the two. In their book, *A Guide to Sandwich Glass*, Barlow and Kaiser reference differences in the way the wafer is applied as a determining factor but we have seen exceptions to this. The Cape Cod mold also appears to have been slightly modified at some point, making it even more similar to the Boston and Sandwich. The best way we have found to differentiate between the two is to look above Christ's left arm for a continuation of the groove that outlines the cross. The Boston and Sandwich Crucifix shows a corner of this detail, the Cape Cod does not. Other differences are pointed out in the appendix on Crucifix and religious candleholders, appearing in volume three of this series. In the late 1800s, Fostoria showed a candelabra using an almost identical base, raising the possibility that they may have made this style of candlestick as well. Barlow and Kaiser list several colors but we know them only in crystal and opal. Any other color should be considered rare. Crystal: $80.00 – 100.00. Opal: $100.00 – 125.00.

Dolphin candlestick with single step base and petal candle cup. 10¼" high. Produced circa 1845 – 1870. Known in crystal, blue, canary, green, lavender, opal, pink opaque, clambroth, and clambroth base with opaque green or blue candle cup. The latter was also sometimes decorated with gold. Made in two pieces, connected by a wafer. Sandwich made a number of other dolphin candlesticks, but the style with the single step base shown here seems to have been the most popular. Crystal: $150.00 – 200.00. Clambroth, opal: $225.00 – 300.00. Canary: $400.00 – 600.00. Light green: $1,000.00 – 1,200.00. Blue, amethyst, teal green, clambroth/blue: $1,800.00 – 2,250.00. Clambroth/green: $2,000.00 – 2,400.00.

This candlestick has been widely reproduced, most of them highly collectible in their own right. From 1925 to 1935, Heisey made their No. 110 Sandwich Dolphin in crystal and various colors. The Metropolitan Museum of Art sold reproductions, manufactured by Imperial in the early 1980s. They are marked MMA on the bottom of the base. General Housewares Corporation also sold a reproduction in the 1980s, imported from Taiwan and marked GHC on the base. Other differences between the reproductions and the original Sandwich dolphins are pointed out in the appendix on Dolphins at the end of this volume.

BS-14. DOLPHIN CANDLESTICK, SINGLE STEP BASE

Dolphin candlestick with double step base and petal candle cup. 10¼" high. Produced circa 1845 – 1870. Known in crystal, amethyst, blue, canary, green, opal, clambroth, and clambroth base with opaque green or blue candle cup. The head of this dolphin is smaller than the one appearing on the single step base seen above. Made in two parts, with the candle cup connected to the base by a wafer. A reproduction was made in 1924 in Bohemia (now Czechoslovakia). It also was produced in two parts, but features a larger dolphin, closer in size to the one on the single step base. Crystal: $200.00 – 250.00. Clambroth, opal: $300.00 – 400.00. Canary: $400.00 – 600.00. Light green: $1,000.00 – 1,200.00. Blue, amethyst, clambroth/blue: $1,800.00 – 2,250.00. Clambroth/green: $2,000.00 – 2,400.00.

BS-15. DOLPHIN CANDLESTICK, DOUBLE STEP BASE

Dolphin candlestick with a half step base. Known in two sizes: 9½" high with a 3½" base and 10¾" high with a 4" base. Circa 1845 – 1870. The base of this candlestick is known as the half step or short step base. It has a very small second step compared with the double-step base seen above. The 9½" size is only known to us in combination with the very rare dolphin and shell socket. This socket is wafer joined to the stem and features a dolphin on each of the six panels around the socket, with six scallop shells around the rim and six more on the knob beneath the candle cup. The 10¾" size can be found with the traditional petal socket and might also be found the dolphin and shell socket. Prices with petal socket: Crystal: $300.00 – 450.00. Canary, clambroth, opal: $600.00 – 800.00. Clambroth/blue: $2,000.00 to market. Clambroth/green: $2,500.00 to market. Prices with dolphin and shell socket: Crystal: $1,300.00 – 1,500.00. Clambroth, opal: $1,500.00 – 2,000.00. Canary: $2,000.00 – 2,400.00. Clambroth/blue: $4,000.00 to market. Clambroth/green: $5,000.00 to market.

BS-16. DOLPHIN CANDLESTICKS, HALF-STEP BASE (SOCKET BROKEN OFF LARGER EXAMPLE)

Imperial Glass Corporation reproduced this candlestick in the 10¾" size with a dolphin and shell socket from 1972 to 1983 in emerald, crystal, canary, moonstone blue, azure blue, and sky blue. Viking Glass Company also made this candlestick in crystal. In 1973 Dalzell Viking again made them in crystal and blue. (See DV-8 on p. 127.) Most of these reproductions were sold by the Metropolitan Museum of Art and all of them are marked MMA on the base. In addition, the head of the dolphin is solid glass on the reproductions, compared to the originals which are partly hollow. A later reproduction, with a copyright date of 1992, produced for the Metropolitan Museum by an unknown company, has a blown candle cup, a combination that to our knowledge has never been seen on an original Sandwich dolphin candlestick.

Dolphin candlestick with hexagonal base. 9" – 9½" high. Produced somewhere between 1845 and 1870. Rare in canary and crystal. No other colors have been reported. Made in two parts, with the candle cup attached to the body by a wafer. The base has three distinctive rings molded into the underneath. Although the originals are rare, this is probably the most reproduced of all dolphin candleholders. A Czechoslovakian copy dating to the late 1920s was made in two parts, but the candle cup is not attached by a wafer and the base does not have the concentric rings. The most frequently found reproductions are those made by Westmoreland from 1924 – 1984 in many different colors. There were slight changes made to the Westmoreland candlestick over the years but they're all one piece and do not have the rings. The later ones will be marked WG. The mold for the final Westmoreland version was also used by Viking in the mid-1980s and by Dalzell Viking from 1990 to 1998. (See DV-3 on p. 126.) Reproductions in cranberry were also made for the Smithsonian Institution. Finally a very similar stick that we believe to be a contemporary of the Boston & Sandwich is known in clambroth with a blue socket. The socket is wafer joined and this could easily be taken for a Boston and Sandwich if not for the lack of the rings beneath the base. Barlow & Kaiser's research indicates that all Boston & Sandwich hex-based dolphin candleholders have these rings. For now this stick remains a mystery but we believe it was made at about the same time as the Boston & Sandwich version. More information on how to differentiate between the original Sandwich dolphin candlesticks and the various reproductions will be found in the appendix on dolphin candleholders at the end of this volume. Crystal: $300.00 – 400.00. Canary: $800.00 – 1,200.00.

BS-17. DOLPHIN CANDLESTICK, HEXAGONAL BASE, 9" HIGH IN CANARY

BS-18. DOLPHIN CANDLESTICK, HEXAGONAL BASE, 6¾" HIGH

Dolphin candlestick with hexagonal base. Height varies from 6¾" to 7" with a 4" diameter base. Produced circa 1855 – 1870. Known in crystal, amethyst, blue, canary, green, jade, clambroth, and opal. Like the 9" version described above, this candlestick was made in two parts, with the candle cup attached to the base by a wafer. A series of concentric rings appear in the base. Crystal: $75.00 – 100.00. Clambroth, opal: $125.00 – 175.00. Canary: $200.00 – 300.00. Blue, amethyst, green: $800.00 – 1,200.00.

This piece was reproduced for the Sandwich Glass Museum, initially by Pairpoint from the late 1980s until 1990 in two parts (both in solid colors and in various color combinations) and then from 1990 to 1995 pressed as a single piece. Fenton also used the one piece mold from 1995 to 1998. (See FN-105 on p. 206.) The reproductions are marked SGM or SM under the base (sometimes very faintly). Current reproductions from this mold are once again being made by Pairpoint.

BS-19. CANDLESTICKS WITH PETAL CANDLE CUPS, CLAMBROTH WITH TRANSPARENT BLUE TOP, OPAL, AND CANARY

Column candlestick with petal candle cup. 9" high. Produced circa 1850 – 1865. Known in crystal, canary, opal, clambroth, and combinations of opal or clambroth with green or blue candle cups. Sometimes found with a sand finish, caused by deterioration of the glass. Made in two parts, with the candle cup attached to the base by a wafer. The base was also used by Sandwich as a shelf support. The candlestick has been reproduced in Taiwan for General Housewares Corporation and others and may be marked GHC. Unmarked reproductions are still in current production. The column on the original is hollow inside; the column on the reproductions is solid. Also the reproductions are made in one piece, without a wafer. Crystal: $125.00 – 150.00. Clambroth, opal: $250.00 – 300.00. Canary: $250.00 – 400.00. Blue: $600.00 – 800.00. Clambroth/blue combination: $800.00 – 1,000.00. Clambroth/green combination: $1,500.00 – 1,800.00.

Madonna candlestick. 12" high with a 6" diameter base. Also referred to as a caryatid. Produced circa 1870 – 1887. Made in crystal with satin finish. Can be found with the candle cup permanently affixed using a wafer or attached using a threaded connector concealed by a collar. The fixed socket version is 11" high with a 5¼" base. An addendum to the catalog, ca. 1880, shows two sizes of this candlestick with a ribbed candle cup. The smaller version is 9¾" high with a 4¾" diameter base. This figure was used as the base for a number of other items, including various styles of comport, fish bowls, etc. A very similar candlestick with a hexagonal base was patented in 1870 by Henry Whitney, of East Cambridge. It has been attributed to the New England Glass Company. Baccarat also made a similar candlestick, but with the figure reversed. Crystal: $600.00. Amber: $1,400.00 to market.

BS-20. MADONNA CANDLESTICK

BS-21. ASSORTMENT OF CANDLESTICKS FROM THE SANDWICH MUSEUM OF GLASS

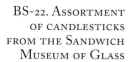

BS-22. ASSORTMENT OF CANDLESTICKS FROM THE SANDWICH MUSEUM OF GLASS

BOYD'S CRYSTAL ART GLASS, INC., Cambridge, Ohio (1978 to the present).

This company began making glass on October 18, 1978, operated by Bernard C. Boyd and his son, Bernard F. The senior Boyd had assisted Elizabeth Degenhart in running the Degenhart Glass Company. When she died, her will stipulated that he be given the first opportunity to buy the factory and its stock of 50 molds. As Boyd's Crystal Art Glass, the new company made a specialty of collectible items, such as covered animal dishes, salts, figurines, toothpick holders, etc. The senior Boyd died in 1988, but the company continues to be a family business, with Bernard F. now assisted by his son, John Bernard. They advertise that they still manufacture collectibles "the old-fashioned way, to the delight of visitors and collectors, with a man and a mould and not with an automated machine" — but do so with a modern flair, having inaugurated exclusive Internet sales in the year 2000.

COLORS

From the beginning, the creation of unusual colors was Boyd's hallmark. They now have 300 different colors formulated. Many of these are unique opaque shades and slag combinations. They also offer carnival and lustre finishes. In a brief history written by Bernard Boyd in 1980, he set forth the company's policy of offering items guaranteed to be collectible: "Each item made by Boyd's Crystal Art Glass is done in a run of one color — no color is ever repeated in the same mold… They stay in a run for approximately one month."

Our trademark is a Diamond B; every five years we add a line to it, so you can determine when the item was produced.		
First five years (1978-1983)	Second five years (1983-1988)	Third Five Years (1988-1993)
◇B	◇B	◇B
Fourth Five Years (1993-1998)	Fifth Five Years (1998-)	
◇B	◇B	

MARKS

Production items are marked with a B in a diamond. Every five years, the mark is modified, as set forth in the accompanying chart.

BO-1. WILDFLOWER CANDLEHOLDER IN CRANBERRY (DEGENHART MOLD)

Wildflower candleholder. 2¾" high with a 2¼" base and 3⅞" across the top. Produced November 1979 in purple variant, May 1980 in persimmon, and in cranberry in 2001. Other colors are likely. This was one of the early pieces made by Boyd and was made from a Degenhart mold. Persimmon, pink: $10.00 – 15.00.

BO-2. SLEIGH CANDLEHOLDER (IMPERIAL MOLD)

Sleigh candleholder. 3½" high, 6" long. Made from a mold that was originally owned by the Imperial Glass Company. Boyd manufactured this both with and without a candleholder element, but we don't believe that Imperial ever produced the candleholder version. Made in Old Lyme (August 12, 1985), carmel (October 4, 1985), milk white (October 23, 1985), Indian orange (November 11, 1985), rubina (December 9, 1985), azure blue (April 9, 1986), kumquat (December 5, 1986), white opal (November 23, 1987), and cobalt (January 26, 1989). Milk glass: $15.00 – 20.00. Other colors: $18.00 – 22.00.

(Photograph from original catalog, used by permission.)

BO-3. ALADDIN LAMP CANDLEHOLDER IN SEAFOAM GREEN (IMPERIAL MOLD)

Aladdin lamp candleholder. 3" to top of handle (2⅛" to top of bowl). This candleholder is from a mold that was originally owned by the Imperial Glass Company. Although the mark on the one shown here indicates that it was manufactured by Boyd somewhere between 1978 and 1983, Boyd's turn-records indicate that it was made in 1986. According to John Boyd, few of these were made because it was a difficult mold to work with. Because of this, the mold may have been overlooked when the mark was updated for the 1983 – 1988 period. He is confident that the following production dates are accurate: A test run was made in lemonade on May 29, 1985. Other colors include Indian orange (November 22, 1985), azure blue (April 10, 1986), seafoam (August 1, 1986), and misty vale (September 24, 1986). All colors: $28.00 – 35.00.

Candlewick candle bowl. 4⅜" diameter, 1¼" high. Introduced by Boyd in 1985 using a mold obtained when Imperial went out of business. Imperial did not use this mold for a candleholder; the candle cup was added by Boyd to the mold for the No. 400/33 4" jelly dish. The example shown is in mulberry mist and was made on March 12, 1985, as a test run of the new mold. Only 39 were made. Because these initial pieces were not considered production items, they are not marked with the usual molded Diamond-B. Instead, the name "Boyd" and the diamond-B are lightly engraved on the bottom. The inside of the bowl is signed in gold, "Good luck, Bernard F. Boyd." Following this successful trial run, the Candlewick candle bowl was also made in lilac (June 19, 1985), milk white (October 24, 1985), azure blue (April 2, 1986), seafoam (August 11, 1986), ruby (May 11, 1987), cobalt (June 19, 1987), and vaseline (September 24, 1992). Milk glass: $6.00 – 8.00. Other colors: $10.00 – 15.00.

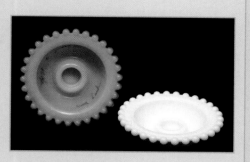

BO-4. CANDLEWICK CANDLE BOWLS IN MULBERRY MIST AND MILK WHITE (CAMBRIDGE MOLD)

Candlewick low candleholder. 3¾" high with a base diameter of 4½". This piece is made from Imperial's No. 400/170 mold, obtained after Imperial went out of business. Initially made in lemonade in a trial run of 18 pieces on May 23, 1985. The only other colors produced to date are lilac (June 14, 1985), milk white (October 24, 1985), and rubina (December 23, 1985). Milk glass: $6.00 – 8.00. Other colors: $10.00 – 15.00.

BO-5. CANDLEWICK LOW CANDLEHOLDERS IN MILK WHITE AND RUBINA (IMPERIAL MOLD)

Swan candleholder. Listed as a 4" swan, but actually approximately 2⅞" high and 4½" to 5" long. Made from Cambridge's No. 1050 swan candleholder mold. (See No. CB-69 on p. 69.) Produced by Boyd in royal plum carnival (May 9, 1995), vaseline (May 22, 1995), mint julep carnival (September 26, 1995), Capri blue (May 23, 1996), rosie pink (June 4, 1999), millennium surprise (March 15, 2000), spring beauty (May 2, 2001), and purple valor (December 5, 2001). $20.00 – 25.00.

BO-6A. SWAN CANDLEHOLDER IN SPRING BEAUTY (CAMBRIDGE MOLD)

BO-6. SWAN CANDLEHOLDER IN MINT JULEP CARNIVAL (CAMBRIDGE MOLD)

BRILLIANT GLASS PRODUCTS, Weston, West Virginia (ca. 1927 – 1929). This company reportedly relocated from Brilliant, Ohio, to Weston, West Virginia, around 1927. They produced opal ware, novelties, and other miscellaneous items. After going bankrupt in 1929, some of their molds (and possibly personnel, as well) were acquired by the Balmer-Westite Company. In 1930, that company became the Westite Company. When Westite burned in 1936, some of their molds were sold to the Akro Agate Glass Company.

COLORS

Very little is known about Brilliant Glass Products during their brief existence. They made opal ware and, as can be seen from the candlestick shown below, they also produced some slag glass.

BR-1. BRILLIANT
CANDLEBLOCK,
CARAMEL SLAG

Candleblock, hexagonal. Dimensions unknown. Produced between 1927 and 1929. Known in caramel slag, but could have been made in milk glass also. Alternating images are impressed on each panel of either a handled basket filled with flowers or a vase with palm fronds. The candleblock is impressed on the inside, "Brilliants [sic], Weston." Caramel slag: $22.00 – 28.00.

BROOKE GLASS COMPANY, Wellsburg, West Virginia (1983 – 2001). This company advertised that its location "has been the site of a glass manufacturing plant since 1879." The original Brooke Glass Company was founded in 1891 to manufacture bottles and prescription ware. It failed in 1897 and after sitting idle for two years, was leased by the North Wheeling Glass Company in 1899. It was then taken over by the Crescent Glass Company (see p. 125), which was founded in 1908. In 1983 Crescent became the Brooke Glass Company, located at 6th and Yankee Streets. According to a brochure put out by the company around 1992, "Colored glass is another specialty of Brooke Glass. Approximately twenty colors are currently available and new ones are constantly being developed." In March 2001, the company discontinued the manufacture of glass. They are still operating as a decorating company, using blanks and some pieces made for them from their own molds by the Mosser Glass Company.

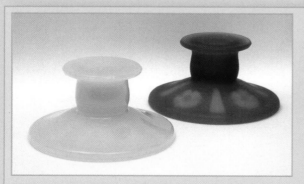

Candlestick. 2" high with a 3¾" base. Made in the 1990s. Known in custard, pink satin, and yellow satin, but probably also made in other colors. This candlestick is also known with a pressed flower design on the underside of the base, as seen in the accompanying photograph, in amber, opaline translucent delphite blue, and red with yellow highlights and satin finish (probably crystal with applied colors). Custard, amber: $4.00 – 6.00. All other colors, decorations: $6.00 – 10.00.

BK-1. BROOKE CANDLESTICKS, OPALINE BLUE AND
RED SATIN WITH YELLOW HIGHLIGHTS

BRYCE BROTHERS COMPANY, Hammondville, Pennsylvania (1893 – 1896), Mount

Pleasant, Pennsylvania (1896 – 1967). The involvement of the Bryce family in glass manufacture extends back to the early 1840s. The original Bryce brothers, James, Robert, and John, founded Bryce, McKee and Company in Pittsburgh around 1850. After various changes of name, the company was reorganized as Bryce Brothers in 1882 — two of the original brothers, Robert and James, being joined by five of the latter's sons, as well as one son of Robert's. In 1891, Bryce Brothers became factory "B" of the United States Glass Company.

Most of the Bryce clan took positions with U.S. Glass. However, in 1893, two of the younger generation, Andrew H. and J. McDonald Bryce, withdrew to found the new Bryce Brothers Company. They purchased the bankrupt Smith-Brudewold Company's plant at Hammondville, which they operated until 1896, when they moved to a brand new factory in Mount Pleasant. Their specialty was blown stemware and tumblers, with a full variety of offerings for the hotel and bar trade. From the beginning they also offered many forms of decoration, including etching, cutting, sand blasting, iridescent finishes, enameling, gold bands, etc. Bryce Brothers remained a major producer of blown stemware and tableware through most of the twentieth century. In 1948, they began using a logo that advertised "Bryce, hand blown, since 1841," apparently referring to the year when the original John Bryce got his first job in the glass industry, working for Bakewells and Company. In 1965, Bryce Brothers Company was purchased by Lenox, Inc., the Trenton, New Jersey, china manufacturer, who continues to operate the factory today under their own name.

COLORS

Color was an important part of Bryce's production, with many of their stemware lines offered in crystal and color combinations. By the early 1920s, colors mentioned in catalogs included amber, amberosa, amethyst, blue, canary, green, and ruby. Dark blue, light blue, and pink had been added by the late 1920s. In the 1930s, aurene (a gold tint) and black were made. Greenbrier was advertised in the early 1950s and, by 1955, Aztec gold, dusk, and milk glass had been added. In 1961, Morocco was advertised. Many of these colors were either made over a long span of time or were reintroduced throughout the years. Other colors are likely, as well.

Aquarius candlestick. 4½" high with a 4⅜" diameter base. Introduced 1950 to accompany the new Aquarius stemware line. The stemware line was advertised in 1961 with the statement that "No Bryce design has ever enjoyed more favor among discriminating hostesses than magnificent Aquarius." (*Living for Young Home-makers*, November 1961.) There was no mention of a candlestick still being part of the line at this time. The candlestick was made in crystal or in combinations of crystal with cobalt blue, amethyst, greenbrier, or aurene (gold tint) bowls and feet. Other colors are possible. This candlestick is unique in that it was also offered with a bowl that rests on the candle cup to transform the candlestick into a comport. It is unlikely that this combination was marketed for very long, since the result isn't very sturdy. With the bowl added, the comport stands 5" high. $15.00 – 20.00. With comport: $25.00 – 30.00.

BB-1. AQUARIUS CANDLESTICKS, WITH REMOVABLE BOWLS. NOTE CENTER CANDLESTICK TRANSFORMED INTO A COMPORT

CAMBRIDGE GLASS COMPANY, Cambridge, Ohio (1902 – 1958). The Cambridge

Glass Company was founded in 1900, when the National Glass Company signed a contract with the citizens of Cambridge, who offered a free site and a $30,000 bonus. The National Glass Company (see volume 3 of this series), which had been formed in 1893, but not finalized until 1899, claimed in 1901 to control the output of 21 factories, representing 70% of the producing capacity of table glassware, blown and pressed tumblers, and bar goods in this country. In fact, they had closed all but twelve of these factories, in an attempt to consolidate and make their operations more efficient. Rather than upgrading older plants, they embarked on building two large new factories, the Rochester Tumbler Company and the Cambridge Glass Company.

As a result, when Cambridge began producing glass in May 1902, they were one of the most modern and well-designed plants in the world. Arthur J. Bennett was hired to manage the factory and was named president. They immediately issued a 140-page catalog, which included "about everything that is made in table glass" (*Crockery and Glass Journal,* April 24, 1902), thus early establishing a reputation for a widely varied output. They also offered decorated ware right from the beginning, including gold decorations intended to compete with Bohemian imports.

Their most popular early patterns were their Nearcut lines of imitation pressed glass, though they also produced many of the colonial patterns that were so popular in the first decades of the twentieth century, as well as blown ware. They continued to expand their output, operating the Canton Glass Works of the National Glass Company for a brief period (and eventually acquiring their molds), which added druggist's ware and other utilitarian glassware to their line.

In 1907, a severe economic depression forced the already troubled National Glass Company into bankruptcy. Arthur Bennett was able to purchase the Cambridge plant and, through the rest of its existence it was operated as an independent factory. From 1911 – 1917, they added lamps to their product line, after purchasing the Byesville Glass and Lamp Company in Byesville, Ohio.

In 1916, Cambridge introduced the first of their famous colors. In 1937, they inaugurated a national advertising campaign, ultimately establishing themselves as one of the best known glass companies in the world, rivaled only by Fostoria and Heisey for name recognition among consumers. During these years, their output was vast, including blown and pressed stemware and tableware, with etchings and cuttings among their most sought after offerings. Among their many patterns, some of the most popular included Cambridge Square, Caprice, Cascade, Everglade, Gadroon, Georgian, Heirloom, Martha Washington, Mount Vernon, Pristine, Statuesque, and Tally Ho.

In 1939, Arthur Bennett sold his controlling interest in the factory to W. L. Orme, his son-in-law, who continued to operate the factory until 1954. At that time, as happened with so many other American glass companies, the company was forced to close in the face of increasing foreign competition and growing costs for fuel and labor. Later that year, it reopened as a worker-owned stock company, but only managed to stay in business for another four years, closing for good in 1958. In 1960, the Imperial Glass Company (see volume 2 of this series) purchased the Cambridge name, etching plates, and molds, putting many of them back in production in Imperial's colors. Cambridge remains one of the most popular collectibles in glassware today.

One of the discoveries that we made in researching this book is that Cambridge was not a company to let well enough alone. They seem to have constantly tinkered with their designs, making changes to the molds — sometimes slight and sometimes major. We have attempted to identify as many of these variations as possible in the pages that follow, but be aware that there are probably many more that we haven't identified.

COLORS

Initial production of Cambridge seems to have been limited to crystal. The 1903 catalog also offered opal, turquoise (opaque blue), amber, blue, and green, but use of these colors was not extensive. It wasn't until 1916 that color became a significant factor.

Ebony	Introduced initially in January 1916; reintroduced in 1922 and continued in production until at least the late 1940s and probably until the factory closed
Emerald	Introduced January 1916 (this early version of emerald is a darker shade than the later emerald)
Royal blue	Introduced January 1916 (this early version of royal blue was sometimes called cobalt and is a medium dark shade of blue)
Mulberry	Introduced June 1916 (this early shade of mulberry is a medium dark shade of amethyst, often found with a carnival finish)
Azurite	Introduced in 1922 (a light opaque blue)

Carrara — Introduced in 1923 and in production only briefly; the least common of the opaque colors (a white with rich opalescence)

Emerald — Introduced in 1923 and produced extensively until the early 1940s (a transparent shade of green, often referred to as "light emerald" to distinguish it from the earlier dark emerald of 1916 and the later dark emerald of 1949)

Helio — Introduced in 1923 and produced for no more than two years (an opaque lavender, sometimes called heliotrope)

Mulberry — Introduced in 1923 (very similar to the early version of mulberry; not as sparkling as the later color of amethyst)

Primrose — Introduced in 1923 and discontinued within a year or two (an opaque yellow, darker than ivory)

Topaz — Introduced in 1923 and produced until the early 1930s (a transparent yellow-green, sometimes called canary or vaseline)

Amber — First advertised in January 1924 and still in production in the 1950s; later advertisements called this color amber-glo

Cobalt blue 1 — Probably made around 1924 and only briefly in production (despite the name, a medium blue, lighter than the later cobalt blue)

Ivory — Introduced in 1924 (a light opaque cream color in the shade commonly called custard)

Jade — Introduced in 1924 (a medium opaque green, shading toward the blue side)

Cobalt blue 2 — Introduced in January 1925, continuing in production until 1926 (similar to the earlier cobalt blue, but a little darker in shade; not quite as dark as the later Ritz blue)

Rubina — First advertised in January 1925 and only produced briefly (red shading to green and then blue; because this effect was created by reheating the glass, some pieces will show considerable variation in colors)

Peach-blo — First advertised in August 1925; in 1934 the name was changed to Dianthus Pink

Bluebell — First made around 1926 and only in production for a short period, though it may have been briefly reintroduced in the 1940s as Tahoe blue (a rich, medium blue very similar to the Antique blue made by Imperial and other companies)

Avocado — Probably made around 1927 – 1928; the company's original name for this color is unknown (a rich green opaque on the yellow side)

Ritz blue — Probably first made around 1928 and continued until the early 1930s (darker than the earlier versions of cobalt blue, but still not as dark as most other companies' cobalt)

Willow blue — Introduced in August 1928; the name was changed to Eleanor blue in 1933 (a light, transparent blue, very similar to Moonlight blue)

Madeira — Introduced in June 1929 and only made for about a year (a light golden color, midway between canary yellow and amber)

Gold Krystol — Introduced in August 1929 (a light yellow with no hint of amber; replaced in 1949 by Mandarin gold, a darker yellow)

Amethyst — Introduced in February 1931 and remained in production until the factory closed in 1958 (a deep amethyst, darker and more rich than the earlier shades of mulberry)

Carmen — Introduced in February 1931 and discontinued in 1943, then reintroduced from 1950 – 1953 and again from 1955 – 1958 (a rich red, sometimes shading to amberina)

Royal blue — Introduced in June 1931 and continued in production until World War II when the required materials became scarce (a dark, cobalt blue)

Forest green — Introduced in September 1931 and still in production in 1940 (a dark shade of green tending toward the yellow side, often confused with the later Emerald)

Heatherbloom — Introduced in November 1931 and last advertised in 1935 (a transparent lavender; dichromatic, it changes shade from orchid to light blue depending on the light source)

Crown Tuscan — Introduced in September 1932 and in production until the factory closed in 1958 (an opaque pink that ranges from almost white to a dark tan; sometimes nearly translucent with opalescence on the edges)

Coral — Introduced in February 1935 for use in the Sea Shell line; probably identical to Crown Tuscan

Moonlight — Introduced by June 1936 and in production until 1951; reintroduced 1955 – 1956 (a light transparent blue, slightly deeper than the earlier Willow blue)

Windsor blue — Introduced in July 1937 (a light opaque blue, not as dark as the earlier Azurite). Total production span unknown.

LaRosa	Made from around 1938 to 1943, when it was discontinued because of wartime shortages of the raw materials needed (a medium-to-light transparent pink)
Pistachio	Made from 1938 to 1943 when this color, too, was discontinued due to wartime shortages (a very pale shade of transparent green, not to be confused with the less sparkling Pistachio produced after 1955)
Mocha	Made from 1938 to 1943 when this color was discontinued due to wartime shortages (a soft shade of amber, lighter than the earlier amber)
Mandarin gold	Introduced in August 1949 and in production until the company closed in 1958 (a medium shade of yellow, darker than the earlier Gold Krystol)
Emerald	Introduced in August 1949 and continued in production until the factory closed in 1958 (a rich, dark green, often confused with the earlier Forest green; darker than the earlier shades of emerald)
Ebon	Introduced in early 1954 and only made until July of that year (black with a velvety matte finish)
Milk glass	Introduced in early 1954 and only made until July of that year (opaque white with no opalescence)
Amber	Introduced after the factory reopened in 1955 (darker than the earlier shades of amber; often referred to as "late amber")
Pink	Introduced after the factory reopened in 1955 (only distinguishable from earlier shades of pink by the blanks on which it is found)
Pistachio	Introduced after the factory reopened in 1955 (a light transparent green, less sparkling than the earlier Pistachio)
Smoke	Introduced after the factory reopened in 1955 (a medium shade of transparent gray)
Sunset	Introduced after the factory reopened in 1955 (red shading through yellow or green to a light blue, topped by a thin line of yellow and red, also available with a crackle finish; similar to the earlier Rubina)
Violet	Introduced after the factory reopened in 1955 (a medium shade of opaque purple, lighter than the earlier Helio)
Mardi Gras	Introduced December 1957 (crystal with flecks of color)

Carnival colors were first made in 1908 and again, extensively, around 1916 – 1917 and possibly in the late 1920s for a third time:

Blue	On early royal blue glass	Marigold	On crystal glass
Green	On early emerald glass	Purple	On early mulberry glass

Other special finishes:

Cinnamon	Introduced in February 1930 (satin highlights on amber)
Jade	Introduced in February 1930 (satin highlights on light Emerald)
Krystol	Introduced in February 1930 (satin highlights on crystal)
Mystic	Introduced in February 1930 (satin highlights on Willow blue)
Rose du Barry	Introduced in February 1930 (satin highlights on Peach-blo)
Almond	Made in the mid-1930s (amber with a satin finish applied to one side of the piece with the other left clear)
Grape	Made around 1935 (amethyst with a satin finish applied to one side of the piece with the other left clear)
Jade green	Introduced in April 1935 (Forest green with a satin finish applied to one side of the piece with the other left clear)

Other, experimental colors are known. The definitive reference work on this subject is the Cambridge Glass Collectors' *Colors in Cambridge Glass*.

DECORATIONS

From the very beginning, Cambridge had a large decorating department, initially offering gold decorations in competition with Bohemian imports. Needle etchings, sand blast engravings, and copper wheel engravings were also among the earliest offerings. Cambridge also produced many rock crystal cuttings from the 1930s to the 1950s.

Wheel cuttings or engravings add value depending on their attractiveness and complexity. This is typically between 5% and 50%.

Third parties would sometimes buy Cambridge blanks and apply their own decorations. Some of the best known examples of this are the "Charleton" decorations done on Crown Tuscan by Abels, Wasserberg & Co., Inc. of New York. These decorations, in good condition, will add 50% – 200% to the value of a piece.

Cambridge's etchings are often collected in their own right and will add considerably to the value of a piece. Candle-light (1936 – early 1950s): add 180 – 220% to the values given below; Rose Point (1934 – 1958, with limited production by Imperial in the 1960s): add 120 – 160%; No. 746 Gloria (ca. 1930s): add 80 – 120%; Chantilly (ca. 1939 – 1956), No. 752 Diane (1931 – 1954), No. 762 Elaine (1933 – ca. 1954), No. 754 Portia (1932 – 1952), No. 773 Wildflower (1937 – 1958): add 40 – 60%; No. 744 Apple Blossom (1930 – late 1930s): add 35 – 40%; Cleo (ca. 1922 – mid-to-late 1930s), No. 748 Lorna (ca. 1930s), other lesser known etchings: add 20 – 40%. Some etchings were also available gold filled, which increases their desirability (add another 20 – 30% to the etched price if slight or no wear).

MARKS

Cambridge registered Nearcut as a trademark in 1904 and it will be found impressed on some pieces as late as 1920 (sometimes written as two words, Near Cut, one above the other). According to Harold and Judy Bennett's *The Cambridge Glass Book,* the C in a triangle was used between 1925 and 1954, though not all pieces were marked. A "Genuine Hand Made Cambridge" label was trademarked in 1927. The earliest versions of this label incorporate the C in a triangle. From March 1938 to 1958, the same label was used without the C in a triangle.

1904 – 1920

1927 – 1938   1938 – 1958

No. 1 crucifix candlestick. 9⅝" with a 3¾" hexagonal base. The candle cup is octagonal with a hexagonal lip around the opening. Produced circa 1903 to some-time after 1910. Known in crystal, opal, and turquoise. Early versions have the initials INRI (a rough translation of which is "Jesus, King of the Jews") on a plaque above Christ's head. This was removed at some point during its production. Crystal: $20.00 – 30.00. Opal: $35.00 – 45.00. Turquoise: $120.00 – 180.00.

There is considerable mystery surrounding a very similar, but shorter crucifix candleholder that comes from a mold originally owned by Atterbury & Co. (See AT-1 on p. 17.) This candleholder has been attributed to Cambridge by many authors and is often referred to as "the short version of the No. 1 crucifix." While we also suspect that it was manufactured by Cambridge at some point, as of yet, we've found no hard evidence to support this.

Here's what we know:

The mold used to manufacture this candleholder originated with the Atterbury crucifix mold. We know this due to numerous identical features that stand out upon a close comparison of the two. The most obvious is a vine pattern molded on the back side of both crosses (see CB-1b). This unusual and intricate detail is identical on both versions. In addition, the Christ figures are the same, right down to the small medallion at Christ's feet (a unique feature). It should be mentioned that the vine and medallion details were always subtle and are faint (or missing) on some of the hex based examples, while easily seen on others. (We've also noticed that the opal or milk glass examples are more prone to lose the fine details than the crystal and colored glass. This is true of other milk glass items as well and we assume that it has something to do with the formula.)

In its original form the Atterbury crucifix had few similarities to the No. 1 Cambridge but after heavy modifications to the mold the resulting candleholder bares a striking resemblance to the aforementioned No. 1. The simple round candle cup and base of the Atterbury were changed to shapes that are practically indistinguishable from the No. 1's. Given the unique shape of the candle cup on the No. 1 this had to be intentional. In fact, beside the height difference (8¾" vs. 9⅝") the only notable variation between the two is that the bottom of the cross on the shorter stick does not flair out to blend with the base.

CB-1. NO. 1 CRUCIFIX CANDLESTICK. THE CROSS ON THE LEFT IS MARKED INRI, THE ONE ON THE RIGHT IS NOT. ALTHOUGH BOTH ARE OPAL, NOTE THE DIFFERENCE IN THE COLORING.

CB-1A. GROUP OF CRUCIFIXES MADE FROM THE HEAVILY RE-WORKED ATTERBURY MOLD, POSSIBLY BY CAMBRIDGE

CB-1B. CLOSE-UP OF THE BACKS OF ATTERBURY AND UNCONFIRMED CAMBRIDGE CRUCIFIXES SHOWING IDENTICAL VINE PATTERNS ON BOTH. THE REWORKED VERSION IS ON THE RIGHT AND HAS ONLY FAINT TRACES OF THE VINES REMAINING.

Here's what we suspect:

While it's possible that Atterbury made these changes, there seems to be little reason for them to have done so. Other details such as color and glass formulas also point away from the modified versions having come from Atterbury. It's more likely that Cambridge, or another factory associated with the National Glass Company, acquired the mold after Atterbury's demise (Atterbury ceased operations in 1899) and modified it to serve as a second mold for producing the No. 1 crucifix.

Things that suggest this crucifix was made by Cambridge are its obvious similarity to their No. 1 along with a comparable milk glass formula. Things that suggest someone other than Cambridge manufactured this candleholder are that it's known in at least two colors not associated with the No. 1 crucifix (amber and blue). Keep in mind that the last statement doesn't imply that Cambridge never made the item, only that someone else may have made it in its modified form. If that's the case it would most likely have come from another factory associated with the National Glass Company who would have made it between 1899 and 1903.

We may never know the complete history of this mold but we suspect that one way or another it wound up in the hands of the Cambridge Glass Company. This smaller crucifix is known in opal, amber, and blue. Opal: $30.00 – 40.00. Amber: $65.00 – 90.00. Blue: $120.00 – 180.00.

CB-2. NO. 3 CRUCIFIX CANDLE-STICK, FROM THE 1903 CATALOG

No. 3 crucifix candlestick. Dimensions unknown, but the catalog picture makes it appear to be one or two inches taller than the No. 1 crucifix which would make it approximately 11½" high. Shown in a 1903 catalog in opal; crystal or other colors are possible. Discontinued before 1910. Very similar to crucifixes made by a number of other companies. The ironic thing is although we are showing the catalog illustration, we may actually have this in our collection and not know it (we have over 130 glass crucifix candleholders). Catalog drawings from this era are often just "suggestions" of what the item looks like and you sometimes can't take them too literally. However, Cambridge's other catalog depictions have been more accurate than most. If this one is as accurate as their others, the socket shape is dissimilar to anything we have. We hope to have this mystery solved by the time we publish the appendix on crucifix and religious candleholders in volume three of this series. Unable to price.

CB-3. NO. 200/34 CRUCI-FIX CANDLE-STICK, OPAL

No. 200/34 crucifix candlestick. 9½" high with 3⅞" diameter base. This was a later crucifix, made from around 1910 to the early 1920s. It shares an octagon base with similar candleholders from two other makers, Canton (CN-1 on p. 97) and Imperial. Of the three, the Cambridge has more detail in the Christ figure. Side-by-side comparisons of all three will appear in the section on crucifixes and religious candleholders in volume three of this series. Known in crystal and opal. Crystal: $15.00 – 20.00. Opal: $25.00 – 35.00.

CB-4. NO. 40 CANDLE-STICK, FROM 1903 CATALOG

No. 40 candlestick. Shown in the 1903 catalog on a page of opal novelties. Made in the shape of a miniature stove. Westmoreland's No. 236 handled candlestick is very similar. Although there are a number of differences between the two, the easiest details to identify are that the Cambridge candlestick has a plain top and a round finger grip. The Westmoreland candlestick has an ornate pattern on the top and the finger grip has a small point on the outside rim to make it easier to grasp. L. G. Wright also made a miniature stove candlestick in the Daisy & Button pattern. $30.00 – 40.00.

No. 41 candlestick. Shown in the 1903 catalog on a page of opal novelties. This candlestick may have only been in production for a couple of years. Some early molds used by Cambridge were transferred by the National Glass Company from other member companies, notably McKee, so it is possible that this one also originated elsewhere. $30.00 – 40.00.

CB-5. No. 41 CANDLESTICK, FROM 1903 CATALOG

No. 2630 Martha Washington candlestick. Our catalog lists this as 6" but it's actually 5" high. Made from around 1906 to sometime before 1920. Crystal only. According to a notation in a catalog from ca. 1920, the mold was apparently modified to become the No. 200/10 & 200/11 candlestick which appears to be lacking the panels (this version was listed as 5" high). (See CB-37 on p. 59.) $15.00 – 20.00.

CB-6. No. 2630 MARTHA WASHINGTON CANDLESTICK

No. 2630 candlestick. Made in two sizes, 7" (with a 4⅛" hexagonal base) and 9" (with a 5½" hexagonal base). In production by 1910 to sometime before 1920. Crystal only. According to a notation in a catalog from ca. 1920, the molds were apparently modified to become the No. 200/30, 200/31, 200/32, 200/33 candlesticks, which were listed as 6" and 8" high. The modified versions were skirted, with the only element remaining unchanged seemingly being the candle cup. (See CB-42 on p. 60.) Small: $20.00 – 25.00. Tall: $25.00 – 30.00.

CB-7. No. 3630 CANDLESTICKS, TWO SIZES

No. 2657 Colonial candlestick. 7" high, 4" diameter hexagonal base. In production by 1910 to sometime before 1920. Crystal only. According to a notation in a catalog from ca. 1920, the mold was apparently modified to become the No. 200/12, 200/13 candlestick. The modified version was skirted and appears to be round and without panels. (See CB-38 on p. 59.) $25.00 – 30.00.

CB-8. No. 2657 CANDLESTICK

No. 2672 bottle candlestick. 8¼" high with a 5⅜" base. The bottle had a capacity of five ounces. Introduced in 1908 and made until sometime after 1918. Probably crystal only. One of Cambridge's Nearcut novelties, with a pressed pattern in imitation of cut glass. $70.00 – 90.00.

CB-9A. No. 2672 BOTTLE CANDLESTICK, FROM 1910 CATALOG, ILLUSTRATING HOW CANDLE CUP/STOPPER LOOKS WHEN REMOVED

CB-9. No. 2672 BOTTLE CANDLESTICK

CB-10. No. 2750 CANDLESTICK, FROM 1910 CATALOG

No. 2750 Colonial candlestick. 7" high. In production by 1910, but only made for a few years before being replaced by the No. 2859 candlestick below. Crystal only. This seems to be the first of Cambridge's candlesticks to be part of a complete pattern. In the 1910 catalog this candlestick was one of more than three dozen items shown in Nearcut Colonial design 2750. The pattern continued to be expanded over the next few years with at least one additional candlestick added. (See No. CB-14 on page 53.) $15.00 – 20.00.

CB-11. No. 2859 CANDLESTICK, FROM CATALOG DATING BEFORE 1915

No. 2859 candlestick. 7" high. A redesigned version of the No. 2750 Colonial candlestick, in production before 1915 and, in turn, replaced by the No. 72 candlestick below around 1920. Crystal only. Plain crystal: $15.00 – 20.00. Cut crystal: $20.00 – 25.00.

CB-11A. No. 2859 CANDLESTICKS. NOTE RAYED PATTERN ON BOTTOM OF ONE

CB-12. No. 72 CANDLESTICK, AZURITE

No. 72 candlestick, also listed as No. 200/20 and 200/21. 7" high with a 3¾" base. This final version of the candlestick was made in the early 1920s. It was produced in crystal, ebony, and azurite; other colors are possible. Catalogs show this candlestick with the No. 894 and 5010 cuttings.

The differences between these three candlesticks are apparent from the pictures. The No. 2750 candlestick has a distinct rim both above and below the bulge on the candle cup and its base is stepped. The No. 2859 candlestick has a simpler base. The No. 72 candlestick has no ridge on either side of the bulge, which flows from the top of the candle cup all the way to the base in an unbroken line, with only a single, shallow step on the base. It is impressed with a rayed pattern on the bottom. Crystal: $15.00 – 20.00. Colors: $20.00 – 30.00.

A very similar candlestick, with a round base, was made by an unknown company (see below).

WHAT IS IT?

CB-13. UNKNOWN CANDLESTICKS, CANARY, AMETHYST, AND BLUE

Unknown candlestick. 7" high with a 3⅝" base. Known in crystal, amethyst, blue, ebony (with gold decoration), green, and vaseline. Is it Cambridge? Despite Cambridge's predilection for continually reworking their molds, apparently not, since none of the colors it has been seen in match known Cambridge colors. Nevertheless, it bears a marked similarity to the Cambridge No. 72. The diameter of the bulge on the candle cup is identical to that on the No. 72 candlestick; the diameter of the base, although round, also matches (if measured from one flat side to the other, rather than from point to point). The width of the panels on the column are also the same, though the diameter of the column is smaller than that of the No. 72 candlestick. Pending further research, this candlestick remains unknown. $20.00 – 30.00.

No. 2750 Colonial two-handle candlestick, also listed as No. 200/28. 6½" high with a 3" square base. (Listed in the catalogs as 7".) This was the second candlestick added to the No. 2750 Colonial pattern, probably around 1911; it remained in production until the early 1920s. It is known in crystal only. However, this may be another mold that was later modified by Cambridge, since the same shape is known in azurite, but without the handles. $15.00 – 20.00.

CB-14. No. 2750 TWO-HANDLE CANDLESTICK

No. 2759 three-prong candlestick. 5" high. This size would commonly be considered a toy or child's candlestick. Probably made only briefly, sometime between 1910 and 1915, in crystal only. This is an almost exact copy of Westmoreland's No. 1013 mini candelabra (q.v.), patented in 1910 and made for many years in crystal and colors. We believe, but have not been able to prove that the primary difference between them is barely perceptible in the catalog picture: the Westmoreland candlestick has a hexagon base, while the Cambridge toy has a square base, but oriented so that the point of the square faces forward. Such a candlestick is known, but the authors are not in agreement that it is the one depicted in the catalog picture. The bulge at the juncture of the arms also differs, being more ball-shaped on the Westmoreland candlestick. The square-based version is rarely seen. $50.00 – 75.00.

CB-15. No. 2759 THREE-PRONG CANDLESTICK, FROM CATALOG, CA. 1910 – 1915

No. 2760 Daisy Design candlestick. Pattern also known as Red Sunflower. 9" high. Made from 1910 to around 1920, probably in crystal only. Available clear or with the daisy in satin. Some pieces in the pattern are known with ruby stain and with the pattern partially filled with gold. This was part of one of Cambridge's early Nearcut patterns, described in the catalog as "medium pressed," with a "patented arch foot." This is another mold that was drastically reworked to become the No. 200/3 candlestick (see CB-32 on p. 58). $55.00 – 65.00.

CB-16. No. 2760 DAISY DESIGN CANDLE-STICK

No. 2777 Mission candlestick. 7" high. Production from sometime after 1910 to about 1920. This mold was then redesigned to become the No. 200/29 6" candlestick. (See CB-41 on p. 60.) At that time, the two bottom "steps" on the candlestick seem to have been removed. $15.00 – 20.00.

CB-17. No. 2777 MISSION CANDLESTICK

CB-18. No. 2780 STRAWBERRY CANDLESTICK IN GREEN CARNIVAL

No. 2780 Strawberry candlestick. 7" high with a 4⅝" base. Also known as Inverted Strawberry and Late Strawberry Variant. This is usually seen as a round candlestick, but it has been found with the skirt "blocked" to form a square base. The pattern was made from around 1911 to 1918. It is known in crystal, clear, and with ruby stain. The candlestick was also made in marigold and green carnival (the latter on early emerald). Purple and blue carnival are also possible (on mulberry and royal blue, respectively), since other pieces in this pattern have been reported with those finishes. This was a Nearcut pattern, described in the catalog as a "rock crystal design, light pressed." This mold may have been redesigned to become the No. 200/15 (No. 72) candlestick. (See CB-40 on p. 59.) Crystal: $80.00 – 100.00. Carnival: $250.00 – market.

No. 2798 birthday candlestick, also listed as No. 200/9. 3" high with a 2" base. Made from around 1912 to sometime in the 1920s. Known in crystal and pink (probably peach-blo, but see below for information on reissues in color). This candlestick has been reissued/reproduced in transparent slag colors of blue and peach, possibly using the original mold, though the panels and depth of the candle cup are a fraction larger than the original. More recent reproductions from Taiwan, made for Biedermann in the late 1980s, appear to be from the original mold. Also seen are two miniature versions of the candlestick, 1½" high with a base diameter of 1¼" and 1¼" high with a base diameter of 1", respectively. These are probably from Taiwan, as well. (See CB-19a.) Crystal: $12.00 – 15.00. Colors: $15.00 – 25.00.

CB-19. No. 2798 BIRTHDAY CANDLESTICK

CB-19A. BLUE SLAG TOY CANDLESTICK, UNKNOWN MANUFACTURER, AND REPRODUCTION FROM TAIWAN IN BACKGROUND, WITH MINIATURE SIZES IN FRONT

CB-20. No. 2818 CANDLESTICK, FROM EARLY CATALOG

No. 2818 candlestick. 6" high. Production dates unknown, but probably sometime between 1910 and 1915 in crystal only. $45.00 – 65.00.

CB-21. No. 2825 OLD ROSE CANDLESTICK, FROM EARLY CATALOG

No. 2825 Old Rose candlestick. 5" high. Production dates unknown, but probably sometime between 1910 and 1915 in crystal only. $60.00 – 75.00.

No. 2862 candlestick. Originally offered in a 6½" size (later also offered as No. 200/16 and 200/17, with the height listed as 6"). A 7½" size was also made, with a 4⅜" diameter base (later offered as No. 200/18 and 200/19, with the height listed as 7"). Introduced sometime before 1915 and in production through the mid-1920s. Reported colors include crystal, ebony, azurite, helio, mulberry, light emerald, primrose, amber, and jade; other colors are possible. Available with at least three copper wheel engravings (No. 5016, 5017, and 5018) and one plate etching (No. 510). Other companies made almost identical candlesticks. Duncan and Miller's No. 66 candlestick (made in 4", 6", and 7½" sizes) has the bulge higher up on the stem and has three mold seams. (See DM-13 on p. 147.) The New Martinsville Glass Company's No. 19 candlestick (7½" high) and Paden City's No. 114 candlestick (6¼" and 7½" high) also have the bulge higher up on the stem, but only have two mold seams. Crystal, amber: $25.00 – 30.00. Helio, primrose: $40.00 – 50.00. Other colors: $30.00 – 45.00.

CB-22. No. 2862 CANDLESTICKS, HELIO AND AZURITE

No. 2889 candlestick. Also listed in the 6" height as No. 66 (in opaque colors), No. 200/22, and No. 200/23. Made in a 7" height as No. 101, No. 200/24, and No. 200/25. Originally offered in 1916 and continued in production until the early 1920s. Known in crystal, ebony, and azurite; other colors are possible. An advertisement for Geo. Borgfeldt and Co. of New York in the *Pottery, Glass, and Brass Salesman*, March 23, 1916, showed this candlestick as No. 3010 in their "new jet black decorative glass ware," which they called Ravenware, "sold exclusively by us." Coin gold decorated and encrusted edges were also advertised. Available with at least two copper wheel engravings (No. 2195 and 4077) and two plate etchings (No. 529 Dresden and 530). Some of the catalog pictures do not clearly show the rim beneath the candle cup and this has led to some confusion with New Martinsville's No. 14 candlestick and Paden City's No. 112 candlesticks, both of which taper down from the candle cup to the base with no demarcation. The Cambridge candlestick has a column that is almost straight, with a barely perceptible taper, and rims that separate it from the candle cup and base. The underside of the base may have rays or be plain (when found in one of the opaque colors). Crystal: $20.00 – 30.00. Colors: $30.00 – 40.00.

CB-23. No. 2889 (No. 66) CANDLESTICK IN EBONY

No. 916 candlestick. Also listed as No. 73 and No. 200/26. 6½" high. Made from sometime after 1910 to around 1924. Listed in crystal, azurite, and ebony. Available with at least one plate etching (No. 529) and three copper wheel engravings (No. 896, 4099, and 5011). This same style of candlestick was also made by a number of other companies. The Jefferson Glass Company and, later the Central Glass Works, offered an 8" size as part of the Chippendale pattern. (See CE-9 on p. 104.) It can be differentiated from the Cambridge candlestick both by the size and because it does not have a pressed star in the base. The New Martinsville Glass Manufacturing Company and the Paden City Glass Company also made this candlestick with a pressed star base in a series of heights ranging from 3½", 5½", 7", and 8½". Again, size can help determine the difference. Although listed as 6½", the Cambridge candlestick can vary in actual height from 6⅜" to 6½", but still falls in between the sizes offered by the other two companies. Crystal: $20.00 – 25.00. Colors: $25.00 – 30.00.

CB-24. No. 916 CANDLESTICK IN EBONY

No. 2800/107 Community Crystal Design candlestick. 7½" high with a 3¾" diameter hexagonal base. Made from around 1915 to 1920 in crystal only. The example pictured has a gravic cutting, giving it serrated edges. Around 1921, the mold was reworked to become the No. 2800/235 candlestick, which is identical except for having the center band removed. (See CB-30 on p. 57.) This candlestick bears a striking similarity to Heisey's No. 5 candlestick (which had been patented in 1904 and remained popular for many years) but with the addition of the bands at the top, middle, and bottom of the column. $30.00 – 35.00.

CB-25. No. 2800/107 CANDLE-STICK, WITH UNKNOWN CUTTING

CB-25A. No. 2800/107 CANDLESTICK, FROM 1915 CATALOG

CB-26. No. 2800/108 CANDLESTICK

No. 2800/108 Community Crystal Design candlestick. 9" high with 4⅛" diameter base. Made from around 1915 to 1920 in crystal only. Around 1921, the mold was reworked to become the No. 200/7 candlestick. (See CB-35 on p. 58.) The main change in the reworked version is that the bottom of the column flares out rather than having a slight bulge. $25.00 – 30.00.

CB-27. No. 2800/109 CANDLE-STICKS, WITH UNKNOWN CUTTING

No. 2800/109 Community Crystal Design candlestick. 8" high with a 4" square base. Made from around 1915 to 1920 in crystal only. The example shown has an unknown cutting on two sides of the column. Around 1921, this mold was reworked to become the No. 200/5 candlestick. (See CB-34 on p. 58.) The main difference between the two candlesticks is that where the neck meets the column, it does so in a straight line, compared to the No. 200/5, which curves upward at that juncture. Also, the No. 2800/109 has a beveled edge on the candle cup, whereas on the No. 200/5, the edge is rounded. $25.00 – 30.00.

CB-28. No. 2800/110 CAN-DLESTICK, FROM CATA-LOG, CA. 1915

No. 2800/110 Community Crystal Line candlestick. 7" high. Made from around 1915 to 1920 in crystal only. Around 1921, the mold was reworked to become the No. 200/8 candlestick. (See CB-36 on p. 59.) At that time, the trophy-like handles which attach just below the candle cup on the No. 2800/110 candlestick were moved up to attach to the candle cup itself. $50.00 – 65.00.

No. 2800/111 Community Crystal Line candlestick. Made in heights 7" and 10". Produced from around 1915 to 1920 in crystal and ebony. Around 1921, the molds were reworked to become the No. 200/1 and 200/2 candlesticks. (See CB-31 below.) The most notable differences between the two candlesticks are that the foot was completely reworked, becoming square instead of petal-shaped, and the shape of the candle cup was modified. Crystal: $45.00 – 60.00. Ebony: $60.00 – 75.00.

CB-29. No. 2800/111 CANDLE-STICK, FROM CATALOG, CA. 1915

No. 2800/235 Community Crystal Design candlestick. Also listed as No. 200/6 and No. 72. In England, this candlestick was marketed as part of the No. 2800 Tudor line. Sometimes referred to by collectors as Hexagon. 7½" high with a 3⅞" hexagonal base. This was a redesigned version of the No. 2800/107 candlestick. (See CB-25 on p. 56.) It probably was first made around 1921 or a little earlier and then continued in production until around 1930. Known in crystal, ebony, azurite, carrara, helio, primrose, and jade; other colors are possible. British advertisements, which show this candlestick as part of a trinket set, mention its availability with rainbow lustre effects. It was offered with at least four copper wheel engravings (No. 4077, 4084, 4085, and 5009) and one etching (No. 510). Known in two shapes, one thicker around the middle than the other, both of which seem to have been in production at the same time.

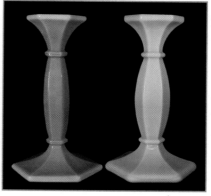

CB-30. No. 2800/253 (No. 72) CAN-DLESTICKS, HELIO AND AZURITE. NOTE VARIANCE IN THICKNESS OF THE CENTER COLUMN.

Around 1940, a taller 8½" version was made as the No. 1440 candelabrum with locking bobeche and prisms. (The height of the assembled candelabrum was 9".) This version was probably in production until the factory closed in 1958, since it was still being sold as part of the liquidation proceedings in 1962 by Ebeling & Reuss of Pittsburgh. In *The Cambridge Glass Book*, Harold and Judy Bennett show this candlestick without a bobeche in ebony. It seems likely that this mold was among those purchased by Imperial and that it became their No. 1440 candlestick, which was made from 1969 to 1979. If so, this mold is now owned by Lancaster Colony and was reissued by their Indiana Glass Company Division in the 1980s.

As mentioned in the discussion of the No. 2800/107 candlestick, this version also bears a striking resemblance to Heisey's popular No. 5 candlestick, but with the addition of the bands at the top and bottom of the column. A 1919 catalog from the United States Glass Company also shows an almost identical candlestick, called No. 52 and cut top and bottom.

Crystal: $20.00 – 25.00. Ebony, jade, azurite: $25.00 – 30.00. Helio, primrose: $50.00 – 60.00. Carrara: $60.00 – 70.00.

No. 200/1 candlestick, also listed as No. 68. 10" high, with a 4" square base. Also made in a 7½" height as No. 200/2 and No. 69. Modified around 1921 from the earlier molds used for the No. 2800/111 candlesticks, with the feet completely reworked to become square, rather than petal-shaped, and the candle cups also redesigned. (See CB-29 above.) Production probably continued until around 1930. Known colors include crystal, ebony, azurite, carrara, helio, and primrose; other colors are possible. Known with at least two copper wheel engravings (No. 4077 and 5014) and one etching (No. 510); also with a black enamel line decoration. Crystal: $25.00 – 30.00. Ebony, jade, azurite: $35.00 – 40.00. Helio, primrose, carrara: $60.00 – 75.00.

CB-31. No. 200/1 (No. 68) CANDLE-STICKS, TWO SIZES, PRIMROSE AND EBONY

CB-32.
No. 200/3
CANDLESTICK,
FROM CATALOG,
CA. 1920 – 1921

No. 200/3 candlestick. 8" high. Made in the early 1920s. An annotation in a catalog from around 1920 – 1921 indicates that this candlestick was reworked from the mold originally used for the No. 2760 Daisy Design candlestick, but with the Prescut daisy pattern removed and the foot completely changed. (See CB-16 on p. 53.) $25.00 – 30.00.

CB-33. No. 200/4
CANDLESTICK,
FROM CATALOG

No. 200/4 candlestick, later listed as No. 653. 8" high. Initially made in the early 1920s. Known in crystal only, though colors are possible. Offered in the early years with at least four engravings (No. 4084, 4085, 5009, and 5016). A modified version of this candlestick was also offered as No. 35, as part of the Mount Vernon pattern, with a diamond point motif added to the shaft. (See CB-86 on p. 74.) If this was from the same mold, it must have been changed back to its original form, because it was reissued in 1951 with plain panels as No. 653 for use as a base for the Cambridge Arms accessories. A version of the candlestick is also known with an extension added above the candle cup. This mold is currently owned by the Mosser Glass Company, who have reproduced it in cobalt, vaseline, ruby, jadite, and ebony (sometimes marked with an underlined M at the bottom of the candle cup). $30.00 – 35.00.

CB-34. No. 200/5 (No. 70) CANDLE-
STICKS, EBONY AND AZURITE

No. 200/5 candlestick. Also listed as No. 70 and No. 102. 8" high with a 4" square base. Made in the early 1920s. Modified around 1921 from the earlier No. 2800/109 candlestick. (See CB-27 on p. 56.) Known in crystal, ebony, and azurite; other colors are possible. Available with at least one copper wheel engraving (No. 5012) and two etchings (No. 529 Dresden and Adams). The main difference between this and the earlier candlestick seems to be that where the neck meets the column it does so with a slight upward curve. Also, the edge of the candle cup is rounded, unlike the No. 2800/109, which is beveled. Crystal: $25.00 – 30.00. Colors: $35.00 – 40.00.

CB-35.
No. 200/7
CANDLESTICK,
FROM CATALOG,
CA. 1920 – 1921

No. 200/7 candlestick. 9" high. Modified around 1921 from the earlier No. 2800/108 candlestick. (See CB-26 on p. 56.) Production dates unknown, but probably made in crystal only. Offered with at least five copper wheel engravings (No. 4084, 4085, 5009, 5013, and 5015). Plain: $25.00 – 30.00. Cut: $30.00 – 45.00.

No. 200/8 candlestick. 7½" high. Modified around 1921 from the earlier No. 2800/110 candlestick. (See CB-28 on p. 56.) Production dates unknown, but probably made in crystal only. The main difference from the earlier candlestick is that the trophy-like handles on the modified version attach directly to the candle cup, whereas on the earlier version, they attached underneath it. $50.00 – 65.00.

CB-36. No. 200/8 CANDLE-STICK, FROM CATALOG, CA. 1920 – 1921

No. 200/10, 200/11 candlestick. The difference in numbering appears to be due to the candlestick being offered either unfinished or cut top and bottom. 5" high. Made in the early 1920s. An annotation in a catalog from ca. 1920 indicates that this candlestick was apparently a modification of the earlier No. 2630 Martha Washington candlestick, with its panels removed. (See CB-6 on p. 51.) $15.00 – 20.00.

CB-37. No. 200/10 CANDLESTICK, FROM CATALOG, CA. 1920 – 1921

No. 200/12, 200/13 candlestick. The difference in numbering appears to be due to the candlestick being offered either unfinished or cut top and bottom. 7" high. Made in the early 1920s. An annotation in a catalog from ca. 1920 – 1921 indicates that this candlestick was apparently a modification of the earlier No. 2657 Colonial candlestick, but so completely changed that the two candlestick bear little resemblance to one another. (See CB-8 on p. 51.) $25.00 – 30.00.

CB-38. No. 200/12 CANDLESTICK, FROM CATALOG, CA. 1920 – 1921

No. 200/14 candlestick. 6" high. Made in the early 1920s. An annotation in a catalog from ca. 1920 – 1921 indicates that this candlestick was modified from the mold for an earlier No. 991 (or possibly No. 2991) candlestick. The earlier candlestick is unknown and, considering how drastically some of the other early molds were reworked, it may have born little resemblance to the No. 200/14 candlestick. $20.00 – 25.00.

CB-39. No. 200/14 CANDLESTICK, FROM CATALOG, CA. 1920 – 1921

No. 200/15 candlestick, also listed as No. 74. 7" high. Made in the early 1920s. Produced in crystal, azurite, and ebony. Probably redesigned from the mold made for the earlier No. 2780 Strawberry candlestick, with the Prescut strawberry pattern removed and the plain oval base replacing the original scalloped base. (See CB-18 on p. 54.) Crystal: $30.00 – 40.00. Colors: $50.00 – 65.00.

CB-40. No. 200/15 CANDLE-STICK IN EBONY WITH GOLD TRIM

CB-41. No. 200/29 CANDLESTICK, FROM CATALOG, CA. 1920 – 1921

No. 200/29 candlestick. 6" high. Made in the early 1920s. Probably crystal only. An annotation in a catalog from ca. 1920 – 1921 indicates that the mold for this candlestick was reworked from the earlier No. 2777 mission candlestick. (See CB-17 on p. 53.) $15.00 – 20.00.

CB-42. No. 200/30, 200/32 CANDLESTICKS, FROM CATALOG, CA. 1920 – 1921

No. 200/30, 200/31 (8" high), 200/32, 200/33 (6" high). The dual sets of numbering for each height appears to be due to the candlesticks being offered either unfinished or cut top and bottom. Made in the early 1920s. An annotation in a catalog from ca. 1920 indicates that these candlesticks were apparently a modification of the earlier No. 2630 candlesticks, with the skirted base added and only the candle cup remaining seemingly the same. (See CB-7 on p. 51.) They may have been modified yet again in 1942 to become the No. 1596 and 1598 candlesticks. (See CB-157 on p. 93.) Small: $20.00 – 25.00. Tall: $25.00 – 30.00.

CB-43. No. 65 DORIC COLUMN CANDLESTICKS, ORIGINAL VERSION IN EBONY (ON LEFT), PRIMROSE, AND HELIO

No. 65 Doric Column candlestick. 9½" high with a 4⅜" square base. Made from 1922 until sometime around 1925. Known colors include crystal, ebony, azurite, carrara, emerald, helio, primrose, amber, ivory, jade, and rubina; other colors are possible. Sometimes decorated with coin gold encrustation. *China, Glass, and Lamps,* in the January 14, 1924, issue indicated that Cambridge was selling these candlesticks as part of a console set with the Ram's Head bowl.

Like so many of Cambridge's other candlesticks, this one went through at least two design iterations. The top of the columns on the earliest candlesticks made from 1922 to 1923 have an indentation 2" from the top, apparently intended to give them the appearance of a traditional candle cup. (See the ebony example in the accompanying photograph.) The design was then modified to make the candlestick look more like a true Doric column. The rim above the base was also changed from a button and line pattern to a laurel design. Crystal, amber, emerald: $80.00 – 90.00. Ebony, jade, azurite: $90.00 – 110.00. Ivory, primrose, helio, carrara: $100.00 – 125.00. Rubina: $225.00 – market.

CB-44. No. 1271 CANDLESTICKS, COMMONLY SEEN VERSION IN TOPAZ AND VARIANT IN AMBER

No. 1271 candlestick. 6¼" high with a 3¾" diameter base. Production dates unknown, but probably ca. 1922 or 1923 until around 1930. Known colors include crystal, ebony, emerald, helio, primrose, topaz, amber, peach-blo, and gold krystol; other colors are possible. Around 1930, this candlestick appears to have been redesigned, with a rim added to the candle cup, the length of the column shortened from 3⅛" to 2¾", and the base turned down to form a rim, 3⅜" in diameter. The variant is 6½" high and was offered with at least one etching, No. 732. The mold for this candlestick was probably further reworked to become the 1402/80 Tally Ho candlestick by adding horizontal grooves to the candle cup and stem. (See CB-93 on p. 76.) Crystal, amber: $15.00 – 20.00. Helio, primrose: $40.00 – 50.00. Other colors: $22.00 – 30.00.

No. 1273 candlestick. 9" high with a 4⅛" diameter base. Probably also made from ca. 1922 or 1923 to the early 1930s. Known colors include crystal, ebony, azurite, emerald, primrose, amber, ivory, peach-blo, gold krystol, and carmen; other colors are possible. Also known with the base turned down to form a rim and the candle cup modified, as described on the previous page. Crystal, amber: $25.00 – 30.00. Gold krystol, ebony, peach-blo, ivory, topaz: $40.00 – 55.00. Helio, primrose, topaz: $65.00 – 85.00.

In late 1930, both sizes of candlestick were offered with Cambridge's patented lock bobeche as "lustre cut prism candlesticks." This required the addition of a flange above the rim on which to "lock" the bobeche. This flange may be marked "Pat. Applied For."

CB-44A. No. 1273 CANDLESTICK, PRIMROSE

LOOKALIKES

A number of companies made candlesticks that all bear a basic resemblance to one another. In most cases, the easiest way to tell them apart is the shape of the candle cup. The McKee candlestick, which has a candle cup very similar to that on the Heisey candlestick, can be differentiated because it has two bands at the top and bottom of the column, unlike all of the others which only have single bands. The Fostoria candlestick is the most completely different from the others, since the "bands" are larger and more accurately described as knobs. Color may also be a reliable differentiating

CB-44B. HEISEY NO. 100, MCKEE NO. 151 IN AMETHYST, CAMBRIDGE NO. 1273 IN EMERALD, TIFFIN NO. 75 IN SKY BLUE, FOSTORIA NO. 2324 IN AMBER

factor, as in the case of some of Cambridge's very distinct opaque colors, for instance. (Ebony is the exception to that rule, since Tiffin also made their candlestick in black.)

The Heisey candlestick was probably the earliest (1921 – 1929) and was covered by a design patent. The McKee and Cambridge candlesticks came out a year later. The Tiffin and Fostoria candlesticks date to about 1924, with the latter also receiving a design patent.

Twist Stem candlestick. Made in two sizes: 6⅞" with a 3¾" base and 8⅜" with a 4½" base. Made ca. 1922 – 1926. The smaller size is known in mulberry, bluebell, and amber; the larger size in azurite, light emerald, mulberry, primrose, topaz, jade, and rubina. Other colors are possible.

A number of other companies made twist stem candlesticks, but the only one that is easily confused with the Cambridge candlestick is the U.S. Glass Company's No. 66, produced at their Tiffin plant and advertised in 1922. It was made in two versions. The earliest version has a base almost identical to that of the Cambridge candlestick and also has the "ribbon" between the twists. In the later version, the Tiffin candlestick has a less defined rim to the base and does not always have the ribbons. The shape of the candle cup on the Tiffin versions is different than that of the Cambridge candlestick.

However, thanks to research done by Douglas Archer, Bill and Phyllis Smith, and Fred Bickenheuser (reported in *Glass Review,* October 1983 and

CB-45. TWIST STEM CANDLESTICKS, TWO SIZES, MULBERRY AND EMERALD

CB-45A.
COMPARISON OF
TIFFIN NO. 66
IN AMBERINA
AND CAM-
BRIDGE TWIST
STEM IN RUBINA

also in the Archers' *The Collector's Encyclopedia of Glass Candlesticks*) it is actually quite easy to differentiate between the candlesticks of the two companies. The Cambridge candlestick was made in a two part mold and, therefore, will only have two mold seams. The Tiffin candlestick was made in a three part mold and has three seams.

Amber: $25.00 – 30.00. Jade, bluebell, light emerald, azurite, topaz, mulberry: $30.00 – 35.00. Primrose: $35.00 – 40.00. Rubina: $85.00 – 90.00.

CB-46.
BALL STEM
CANDLESTICKS
IN PRIMROSE
AND EMERALD

Ball stem candlestick, unknown pattern number. 9⅜" high with a 4⅝" diameter base. We have been unable to find any documentation for this candlestick, but it is known in colors that can be distinctively identified as Cambridge. Probable production dates are ca. 1922 – 1924. Known colors include azurite, helio, primrose, ivory, and royal blue. Azurite, ivory, emerald: $70.00 – 80.00. Primrose, royal blue, helio: $80.00 – 100.00.

CB-46A, CB-46B, CB-46C. CAMBRIDGE CANDLESTICK IN AZURITE, NEW MARTINSVILLE NO. 10 CANDLESTICK IN BLUE, HEISEY NO. 102 CANDLESTICK, PAIRPOINT CANDLESTICK (FROM *THE JEWELERS' CIRCULAR*, MAY 10, 1922)

The New Martinsville Glass Mfg. Co.'s No. 10 candlestick, advertised in 1925, is almost identical. However, it is a little taller (10" in height), with other slight variances. The New Martinsville candlestick has a ring around the base about ⅞" from the rim. It also has a "gather" of glass at the base of the stem that extends down into the cupped base approximately ½", compared to the Cambridge candlestick which is hollow all the way up to the bottom of the stem. In Cambridge's opaque colors, there may also be a "lozenge" in the center of the underside of the base. (This irregularity in the glass does not appear in examples of the Cambridge candlestick in transparent colors.) The rim just above the ball on the New Martinsville candlestick is slightly thicker, 3⅞" in diameter, compared to only 3½" in diameter for the Cambridge candlestick. Also, the rim below the candle cup on the New Martinsville candlestick has less of a defined edge and tapers down toward the stem, whereas the rim on the Cambridge candlestick has almost no taper. And, finally, the New Martinsville candlesticks are not fire polished and have a slightly pebbly finish, with much rougher mold seams that sometimes show a 40 degree twist.

The Cambridge candlestick is ordinarily seen with a domed base, as in the accompanying photographs. However, it has also been seen with the base turned down to form a rim.

Heisey also made a ball stem candlestick at about the same time as the Cambridge and New Martinsville candlesticks. However, the Heisey No. 102, produced 1922 – 1929, is not likely to be confused with either of the other two candlesticks. It was made in crystal only, has a completely different shape candle cup, and its base is almost flat.

Pairpoint also made a ball stem candlestick, advertised in 1922 as being available in blue, amethyst, canary, alabaster, and turquois [sic], but again probably would not be confused with the Cambridge candlestick, both because of the higher quality of the glass and the likelihood of its being found cut or engraved, and the fact that the ball is hollow.

Vase candlestick. Original pattern number unknown. Available 9½" high with a 3" diameter base and 13" high with a 3⅝" base. Known in ebony, azurite, primrose, helio, royal blue, and ivory; other colors are possible. Based on color, these would have had a production period between 1922 and 1931. $30.00 – 45.00 (9½" size). $50.00 – 80.00 (13" size). *(From the collection of Charles Upton)*

CB-47. VASE CANDLESTICKS, 9½" IN HELIO AND 13" IN ROYAL BLUE

No. 109 Dolphin candlestick. 9½" with a 5" diameter base. In production from around 1923 to 1927. Known in crystal, mulberry, ivory (plain and with caramel stain), Ritz blue, rubina, peach-blo, amber, emerald, and bluebell. Also known in crystal with a stained socket and base. Some colors have been seen with satin finishes. Many other companies made dolphin candlesticks. One of the most distinctive features of Cambridge's dolphin is the domed base with its impressed diamond pattern, which matches the Mount Vernon pattern. However, a variant of this candlestick with a plain, flat base in crystal, emerald, peach-blo, and amber will also occasionally be found. This was an interim design brought out in 1928. It stands 8¾" high. The mold was once again completely reworked around 1936. At that time, the base became a square slab with indented corners. The section between the candle cup and the dolphin's tail was also removed. (See CB-113 on p. 82.) Crystal, amber: $70.00 – 85.00. Peach-blo, emerald: $100.00 – 130.00. Bluebell, Ritz blue, mulberry: $135.00 – 185.00. Ivory, rubina: $400.00 to market. Ivory with caramel stain: Cannot price. *(From the collections of the authors and Charles Upton)*

CB-48. No. 109 DOLPHIN CANDLESTICKS IN BLUEBELL AND IVORY WITH CARAMEL STAIN

CB-48A. No. 109 DOLPHIN CANDLESTICKS, EMERALD, PEACH-BLO, AND COBALT BLUE. (NOTE REDESIGNED BASE IN CENTER.)

No. 437 candlestick, 9½" high with a 4⅜" diameter base; No. 438 candlestick, 8½" high with a 3⅞" diameter base; and No. 439 candlestick, 7½" high. In production from around 1922 to 1928. Known colors include crystal, ebony, azurite, emerald, helio, primrose, topaz, amber, cobalt blue, ivory, rubina, peach-blo, avocado, and Ritz blue; other colors are likely. A similar candlestick, found with fired-on colors, has been attributed to the Indiana Glass Company. The main differences can be seen in the accompanying photograph (CB-49a): the rings on the Indiana candlestick are not as rounded and prominent; also, the foot is proportionately taller. The Indiana candlestick also has very rough mold seams. The Cambridge version was a popular blank for decorations, including Cambridge's own Cleo etching and various designs from the Lotus Glass Company. Crystal, amber: $35.00 – 40.00. Peach-blo, emerald, topaz, Ritz blue, ebony, azurite: $45.00 – 50.00. Primrose, helio, avocado, cobalt, blue, ivory: $50.00 – 60.00. Rubina: $90.00 – 100.00.

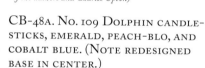

CB-49. No. 437 AND 438 CANDLESTICKS IN RITZ BLUE, PRIMROSE, DARK AMBER, AND AZURITE

CB-49A. No. 437 IN LIGHT AMBER, No. 438 IN CRYSTAL WITH APPLIED DECORATION, AND CANDLESTICK ATTRIBUTED TO THE INDIANA GLASS COMPANY WITH FIRED-ON GREEN

CB-50. No. 1595
CANDLESTICKS,
AMBER, MULBERRY,
AND COBALT BLUE I

No. 1595 candlestick. 9" high with a 4⅛" diameter base. Production dates unknown, but probably ca. 1923 – 1926. Known in crystal, ebony, emerald, mulberry, amber, cobalt blue 1, and bluebell; other colors are possible. The original pattern number for this candlestick is not known. In 1940, it was reissued as the base for the No. 1595 candelabra in crystal only. Crystal, amber: $25.00 – 30.00. Other colors: $30.00 – 35.00.

CB-51. No. 624
CANDLESTICK, EMERALD

No. 624 candlestick, 3⅛" high with a 3½" square base, ca. 1927 – 1930; and No. 635 candlestick, 5" high with a 3" square base, ca. 1927. These two candlesticks are very similar to each other, differing primarily in height and diameter of the base. Known in emerald and amber, but could have been made in any of the colors being made in the late 1920s. The No. 635 candlestick is not shown in the 1930 catalog reprint, so may have been made for only a short period. However, it was probably redesigned in 1932 to become the No. 1402/76 Tally Ho candlestick. (See CB-92 on p. 76.) $20.00 – 25.00.

CB-52. No. 635
CANDLESTICK, AMBER

CB-53. No. 625
CANDLESTICK,
FROM CATA-
LOG, CA. 1930

No. 625 candlestick. Dimensions unknown. Made from around 1927 to 1930. Production colors are not known, but could include any of the colors being made in the late 1920s. Offered with at least one etching (No. 703) as part of a console set, with a No. 1004 8" bowl. This candlestick may have been reworked to become the No. 3500/108 Gadroon candlestick. (See CB-98 on p. 78.) $15.00 – 20.00.

CB-54.
CANDLESTICK,
UNKNOWN
PATTERN
NUMBER, IN
EMERALD
WITH No. 703
ETCHING

Unknown pattern candlestick. 4¼" high with a 5" diameter base. Made ca. 1927 – 1929. Known in amber, emerald, and peach-blo; other colors are possible. Offered with at least three etchings, No. 703, No. 732, and Rosalie. $30.00 – 35.00.

CB-55. No. 626
CANDLESTICK IN
CARMEN

No. 626 candlestick. 3½" high. Ca. 1927 – 1934. Known in crystal, carmen, and crown Tuscan; other colors are likely. Crystal: $10.00 – 15.00. Colors: $25.00 – 30.00.

No. 627 candlestick; also listed as No. 3400/627 and as No. 2 when part of the Centennial Line (later renamed Victorian Line and, eventually, Martha Washington). 4" high with a 4⅝" diameter base. Ca. 1927 – 1936. Made in crystal, ebony, emerald, amber, peach-blo (or Dianthus pink), gold krystol, amethyst, carmen, royal blue, forest green, heatherbloom, and moonlight; other colors are possible. Extensively used as a blank for etchings (including No. 731, 738, 739, 744 Apple Blossom, 746 Gloria, 748 Lorna, and Cleo) and cuttings (including No. 515, 530, 534, 541, 542, and 644). Crystal, amber, ebony: $15.00 – 20.00. Peach-blo, emerald, gold krystol, amethyst: $25.00 – 30.00. Moonlight, forest green: $35.00 – 40.00. Carmen, royal blue, heatherbloom: $40.00 – 45.00.

CB-56. No. 627 (No. 2) CANDLESTICK IN GOLD KRYSTOL

No. 3 Centennial Line candlestick (later known as Victorian Line). This candlestick was made in three versions. Version 1 was first listed as 9½" in height and then as 10". Made ca. 1927 – 1931. Listed in crystal, emerald, amber, peach-blo, gold krystol, and carmen; other colors are possible. Available as a candlestick or with a patented lock bobeche and prisms.

Version 2 replaced the earlier candlestick in 1932 when the pattern was renamed Martha Washington. It was 9" high. This version has an extension added to the candle cup around which a bobeche could rest, but was also offered as a candlestick. Production dates are unknown, but probably continued through the 1930s. Known in crystal, carmen, and royal blue with a crystal foot; other colors are possible.

Version 3 was in production ca. 1939 to sometime before 1949. In 1953 it became part of the Heirloom pattern as No. 5000/70. Also listed as 9" in height. May have been made in crystal only. It was also available as a candelabrum, listed as 9½", with various pattern numbers, depending on the style of bobeche and prisms used. (For other candlesticks in the Heirloom pattern, see p. 95.)

Crystal: $50.00 – 60.00. Amber, peach-blo, emerald, gold krystol: $65.00 – 75.00. Carmen, royal blue with crystal foot: $75.00 – 100.00. Add $40.00 – 50.00 for four-tab locking bobeche and prisms.

CB-57. No. 3 CENTENNIAL CANDLESTICK, VERSION 1, FROM CATALOG CA. 1931

CB-57A. No. 3 CANDLESTICKS, VERSION 2, IN CARMEN, SHOWN BOTH WITH AND WITHOUT BOBECHE AND PRISMS

CB-57B. No. 3 (No. 5000/70) CANDLESTICK, VERSION 3, FROM CATALOG CA. 1953

No. 628 low candlestick. Listed as 3½", though actual heights vary from 3⅛" to 3⅞". Base diameter of 4¾". In production from ca. 1927 until the factory closed. As so often happened with Cambridge candlesticks there were various modifications made over the years. Although subtle, the changes can be seen in the roundness of the center knob, its distance from the candle cup and the base, and the way in which it connects with the base. Also known with a domed base, making it 4" high. Since other companies made similar candlesticks (see page 66), this is a particularly confusing candlestick to pin down.

CB-58. No. 628 LOW CANDLESTICK, TWO EARLY VERSIONS, IN DIANTHUS PINK AND AMBER

Reported production colors include crystal, emerald, amber, amethyst, royal blue, forest green, dianthus pink, ebon, and milk glass. Considering its long production period, other colors are likely.

This blank was used for many decorations. Cuttings include No. 500 Windsor, 538, 539, 540, 600 Celestial, 821 King Edward, 942 Belfast, 951 Broadmoor, 979 Vesta, 1003 Manor, 1004 Montrose, 1070 Lynbrook, 1081 Rondo, and Laurel Wreath. Etchings include No. 520, 704, 732, 758, 766 Chintz, Candlelight, Daffodil, Elaine, Magnolia, Portia, Rose Point, and Wildflower.

In 1951, this was one of the candlesticks used as a base for the Cambridge Arms accessories. (See p. 96.) In 1961, when the Imperial Glass Company reissued Cambridge Arms, they included this candlestick in crystal as part of the line.

Crystal, amber: $10.00 – 15.00. Dianthus pink, emerald, forest green, amethyst: $15.00 – 20.00. Ebon, milk glass, royal blue: $30.00 – 35.00.

CB-58A. No. 628 LOW CANDLE-STICK, LATER VERSION, IN EBON

LOOKALIKES

Paden City's No. 119 candlestick, patented in 1926, is particularly problematic, since it is quite possible that Cambridge also made a version of the No. 628 candlestick with the knob at the base of the stem, immediately above the base. This might, in fact, be the earliest version of the No. 628 candlestick, perhaps initially modified to avoid infringement of Paden City's patent. The Welkers, in their *Cambridge, Ohio Glass*

CB-58B. L. E. SMITH No. 805 3¼" CANDLE-STICK IN GREEN AND PADEN CITY no. 119 3" CANDLESTICK IN BLUE

CB-58C. McKEE No. 100 3½" CANDLESTICK (FROM UNIDENTIFIED CATALOG)

in Color, Book II, show such a candlestick in avocado (a color that was probably only made briefly around 1927). In Book I, they also show a pair in what might be bluebell; Sherry Riggs and Paula Pendergrass, in *20th Century Glass Candle Holders,* also show this same color with Cambridge's No. 704 etching (again dating to around 1927). Complicating matters, however, the Welkers' "bluebell" candlesticks have what appears to be the Wildflower etching, gold encrusted, which is much harder to explain since Wildflower was not offered until the late 1930s — long after bluebell was discontinued and the No. 628 candlestick can be documented in its familiar form.

The Smith candlestick is less confusing, except that late Cambridge catalogs show a drawing of the No. 628 with what appears to be a rim on the base. However, that seems to be due to the nature of the artist's quick sketch, since all of the late candlesticks that we have seen have a flat base without a rim.

McKee's No. 100 candlestick is listed as 5" in the catalog, but that is actually the diameter of the base, its true height being 3½". It was made in green, rose, and possibly other colors. It differs from the others primarily in the shape of the candle cup.

CB-59. No. 630 CANDLESTICK, FROM CATALOG, CA. 1930

No. 630 candlestick. 4" high. Produced ca. 1927 – 1930. Any of the colors made during this period are possible. Very similar to the No. 878 candlestick on the following page, but with a completely round rim on the candle cup and base. $15.00 – 25.00.

No. 878 candlestick. 4" high with a 4¾" diameter base. Produced ca. 1928 – 1930. Known in crystal and emerald; any of the other colors from this period are possible. Used as a blank for at least three etchings (No. 731, 738, and 739). Very similar to the No. 630 candlestick on page 66, except that the rim of the candle cup and base are ten-sided. Both candlesticks appear in the 1930 catalog, indicating that neither is a redesigned version of the other. Crystal: $10.00 – 15.00. Colors: $15.00 – 20.00.

CB-60. No. 878 CANDLESTICK IN EMERALD

CB-61. No. 631 CANDLESTICK, FROM CATALOG, CA. 1927

No. 631 candlestick. 9" high. Ca. 1927. Any of the colors made around this time are possible. $40.00 – 60.00.

No. 632 candlestick. 2" high. Ca. 1927. Any of the colors made around this time are possible. Other companies made similar rolled-edge candlesticks; one distinguishing characteristic of this one is that it has no foot, but rests instead on the rolled-down edge (a trait it shares with Fostoria's No. 2372 candlestick). $12.00 – 15.00.

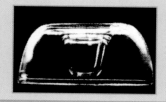

CB-62. No. 632 CANDLESTICK, FROM CATALOG, CA. 1927

No. 636 candlestick. 9½" high with a 5" diameter base. Ca. 1927 to the 1930s. In late 1930, a patented locking bobeche and prisms were added and it was sold as a 10½" No. 1272 candelabrum until the early 1940s. This has four locking "nubs" to hold the bobeche (instead of two as on some other Cambridge candelabra) and says "Pat applied for" on the extended part of the socket. Offered in crystal, ebony, emerald, amber, peach-blo, gold krystol, and carmen; other colors are possible. Known with at least one cutting (No. 629). Crystal, amber: $35.00 – 40.00. Peach-blo, emerald, gold krystol, ebony: $40.00 – 45.00. Carmen: $65.00 – 90.00. Add $40.00 – 50.00 for four-tab locking bobeche and prisms.

CB-63. No. 636 CANDLESTICK IN EMERALD AND No. 1272 CANDELABRUM IN CRYSTAL (WITH EXTENDED SOCKET TO HOLD LOCKING BOBECHE AND PRISMS)

No. 637 candlestick. Made in two versions. Also listed as No. 687, with a more rounded knob. 3½" high with a 3⅞"diameter base with a turned-down rim. Ca. 1927 to the early 1930s. Known in crystal, emerald, amber, peach-blo, and bluebell; other colors are likely. Known with at least one cutting (No. 1074 Cambridge Rose) and one etching (No. 731 Rosalie). Crystal, amber (without etching): $8.00 – 10.00. Peach-blo, emerald, bluebell (all with Rosalie etching): $25.00 – 35.00.

CB-64. No. 637 CANDLESTICK IN BLUEBELL

CB-65. No. 639 CANDLESTICKS, DARK AMBER AND PISTACHIO

No. 639 candlestick. Also listed as No. 745 and No. 4073/639, with the latter having impressed patterns on the underside of their bases (flowers and leaves on the No. 745 — not to be confused with the floral pattern on the similar No. 10 Everglade candlestick mentioned below — and a striated design on the No. 4073/639). 4⅛" high with a 3¾" diameter base. The No. 639 candlestick was made ca. 1927 to the 1940s; however, by the time of the 1940 catalog, it had been redesigned with the addition of a raised rim and panels on the candle cup and scallops on the disc beneath the candle cup. Known in crystal, emerald, topaz, amber, bluebell, avocado, and carmen; other colors are likely. Known with at least one engraving (No. 650). Crystal, amber: $8.00 – 10.00. Emerald, bluebell, avocado: $15.00 – 20.00. Carmen: $25.00 – 30.00.

Two other candlesticks were also in production in 1940, very similar to the redesigned version of the No. 639: the No. 10 Everglade candlestick (see CB-80 on p. 73) and the No. 72 Martha Washington candlestick (see CB-91 on p. 76).

CB-65A. No. 4073/639 CANDLESTICK AND No. 745 CANDLESTICK, BOTH IN EMERALD

CB-66. No. 227 CANDLESTICK IN EMERALD

No. 227 candlestick (cupped base). 1⅜" with a base diameter of 3⅞". No. 227½ (flat base) candlestick. 1½" high with a base diameter of 4⅛". Ca. 1927 – 1930. Known in crystal, emerald, jade, primrose, and topaz, but probably also made in other colors. Available with at least one etching, No. 704. The No. 227 candlestick, with its cupped base, is distinctive; however, the same style of low candlestick with a flat base was made by many other companies, making them very difficult to attribute with certainty, unless they are in a distinctive color or have a known decoration. The candle cup of the Cambridge No. 227½ is slightly tapered and the diameter of its top rim is 1⅞"; the "flat" base is slightly pushed up in the center — all characteristics shared by candlesticks from other manufacturers. Crystal: $6.00 – 8.00. Emerald, topaz, jade: $10.00 – 15.00. Primrose: $15.00 – 20.00. Please refer to p. 49 for pricing on etched Cambridge.

CB-66A. No. 227½ CANDLESTICK IN BLUEBELL, WITH No. 704 ETCHING

CB-67. No. 824 THREE-LIGHT LOW CANDLESTICK IN EMERALD

No. 824 three-light low candlestick. 4⅜" high. The base is 9⅛" long by 3¾" wide. Ca. 1928. Known in crystal, emerald, and peach-blo; other colors are possible. Probably not made very long before being redesigned, first as the No. 3500/154 Gadroon candlestick in 1935 and, ultimately, as the No. 74 Caprice candlestick. (See CB-101 on p. 79.) Crystal: $25.00 – 35.00. Colors: $30.00 – 40.00.

No. 747 candlestick. 3" high. Ca. 1928 – 1930. Known in crystal, peach-blo, and willow blue; any of the other colors made during this period are possible. Offered with at least two etchings, No. 741 and 747 Cleo. Crystal: $25.00 – 30.00. Colors: $30.00 – 35.00.

CB-68. No. 747 CANDLESTICK, FROM CATALOG, CA. 1928

No. 1050 (or No. 1041/1050) candleholder. Listed as No. W 98 swan candlestick in milk glass. 3" high and 4½" long. Ca. 1928 until sometime in the 1930s. Although the Swan line continued to be made for years, the candlestick does not appear in the 1940 catalog. It was reissued in milk glass in 1954. Other colors offered included crystal, ebony, emerald, and peach-blo; additional colors are likely, since other swans from the same line have been reported in amber, gold krystol, carmen, crown Tuscan, moonlight blue, Mandarin gold, and smoke. The Swan line included seven sizes of swan, ranging from the 3" individual nut up to a 16" punch bowl. The candleholder is identical to the No. 1041 candy dish, with a candle cup added. The mold is currently owned by Boyd's Crystal Art Glass, who have reissued it in various colors since 1995. (See BO-6 on p. 43.) Crystal: $35.00 – 45.00. Colors: $50.00 – 65.00.

CB-69. No. 1050 SWAN CANDLEHOLDER, FROM CATALOG, CA. 1930

No. 823 centerpiece, four-light. Introduced for the holiday trade in 1928; probably only in production for a brief period. Known in emerald, amber, and peach-blo; other colors are possible. Shown here with a No. 1108 figurine and decoration No. D845. Other figurines may be found. Complete with figurine as shown: $350.00 – market.

CB-70. No. 823 CENTERPIECE, FROM CATALOG, CA. 1929

No. 638 candelabra, three-light. Also listed as No. 3400/638. 6" high. Generally referred to as Keyhole or Ring Stem by collectors. Introduced in 1928 and in production until the 1940s. Known in crystal, ebony, emerald, amber, peach-blo (or dianthus pink), willow blue, gold krystol, forest green, and moonlight blue; some colors were offered both plain and satin finish. Other colors are possible.

Initially, the base was ten-sided or decagon, 4¼" in diameter. It was modified around 1939 to a 5⅜" round foot. Many etchings were offered on this candlestick, including No. 731, 739, 744 Apple Blossom, 748 Lorna, 752 Diane, Blossom Time, Candlelight, Chantilly, Elaine, Portia, Rose Point, and Wildflower. Silver decoration D/971-S was also available on ebony.

CB-71. No. 638 CANDELABRA IN AMBER, DECAGON BASE

Patented as D78,400, filed January 25, 1929, and approved April 30, 1929. The designer was given as Jess Clair Kelly. This was the first of Cambridge's popular Keyhole designs and was soon followed-up by the one- and two-light versions on the following pages.

Crystal, amber: $30.00 – 40.00. Other colors: $40.00 – 45.00.

CB-71A. No. 638 CANDELABRA IN EMERALD SATIN, DECAGON BASE

CB-72. No. 646 CANDLESTICKS IN CARMEN WITH PORTIA ETCH, FOREST GREEN, AND AMBER WITH PORTIA ETCH, ALL WITH DECAGON BASE

No. 646 candlestick. Also listed as No. 3400/646. 5" high with a 4⅝" diameter decagon base (early version) or a 5⅛" diameter round base (later version). Generally referred to as Keyhole or Ring Stem by collectors. In later catalogs, it was listed as part of the Caprice pattern as No. C-646. Introduced in 1930 and remained in production until the factory closed in 1954. Known in crystal, ebony, emerald, amber, gold krystol, amethyst, carmen, royal blue, forest green, heatherbloom, crown Tuscan, moonlight blue, Windsor blue, and ebon (black with a matte finish). Also offered with the "Springtime" finishes (satin highlights on amber, emerald, crystal, willow blue, and peach-blo).

Initially, the base was ten-sided or decagon. It was modified to be round around 1939. Many etchings were offered on this candlestick, some gold filled, including No. 731, 744 Apple Blossom, 752 Diane, Blossom Time, Candlelight, Chantilly, Elaine, Gloria, Portia, Rose Point, Roselyn, and Wildflower. Other known decorations include D970-S, D/971-S silver decorations and D/450 gold band decoration on ebony, D/1041, D/1047, D/1059, and D/1061.

Also offered as the No. 648/19 candelabra, with the addition of a bobeche and prisms. Versions of the candlestick will be found with either two nubs of glass on the rim to hold a locking bobeche or an extension around which the bobeche could rest.

Crystal, amber: $15.00 – 20.00. Emerald, ebony, gold krystol, amethyst, forest green, peach-blo, moonlight blue: $25.00 – 35.00. Carmen, crown Tuscan, heatherbloom, royal blue, ebon: $35.00 – 45.00. Windsor blue: $75.00 – 90.00. Add for bobeche and prisms: $25.00 – 30.00.

CB-72A. No. 646 CANDLESTICK, ROUND BASE, WITH CANDLELIGHT ETCHING

CB-73. No. 647 TWO-LIGHT CANDLESTICK, ORIGINAL VERSION, FROM CATALOG, CA. 1930

No. 647 two-light candlestick. Also listed as No. 3400/647. Generally referred to as Keyhole or Ring Stem by collectors. In 1935, it was listed as part of the Krystolshell line and, in later catalogs, it was included as part of the Caprice pattern as No. C-647. 5½" high with a 4¾" diameter base. Introduced in 1930 and remained in production until the factory closed in 1954. Known in crystal, ebony, emerald, amber, peach-blo (dianthus pink), gold krystol, amethyst, carmen, royal blue, forest green, heatherbloom, crown Tuscan, coral, moonlight blue, and Windsor blue; other colors are possible. Also offered with the "Springtime" finishes (satin highlights on amber, emerald, crystal, willow blue, and peach-blo).

Many etchings were offered on this candlestick, some gold filled, including No. 744 Apple Blossom, 752 Diane, Blossom Time, Candlelight, Chantilly, Elaine, Portia, Rose Point, Roselyn, and Wildflower. Other known decorations include D/450 gold band decoration on ebony, D/1041, D/1047, D/1059, and D/1061.

Cuttings include No. 500 Windsor, 542, 600 Celestial, 621, 629, 644, 821 King Edward, 942 Belfast, 979 Vesta, 1003 Manor, 1004 Montrose, 1021, 1053 Harvest, 1059 Ivy, 1068 Granada, 1072 Bexley, and Laurel Wreath.

This candlestick went through a number of design changes. The first version has no finial at the top of the arch above the keyhole; it was essentially identical to the three-light No. 638, with the middle candle cup removed. As with the other early keyhole candlesticks, it has a decagon base. This version was apparently only made for a few months in 1930.

The second version, also only briefly produced in the later months of 1930, has a pair of curlicues added to the top of the arch. It also has a decagon base.

The third version, introduced early in 1931, has the now familiar finial, which remained a part of its design for the remainder of its existence. It, too,

CB-73A. No. 647 TWO-LIGHT CANDLE-STICK IN AMBER, SECOND VERSION, DECAGON BASE

initially had a decagon base; around 1934, this was replaced with a round base, 5⅜" in diameter.

Also offered as the No. 1268 and 1269 candelabra, with the addition of bobeches and prisms. Versions of the candelabra will be found with either two nubs of glass on the rims of the candle cups to hold locking bobeches or extensions around which the bobeches could rest.

Crystal, amber: $20.00 – 25.00. Peach-blo, emerald, gold krystol, forest green, ebony, amethyst, crown Tuscan, coral, moonlight blue, heatherbloom: $40.00 – 55.00. Carmen, royal blue: $60.00 – 70.00. Windsor blue: $125.00 – market. Add for bobeches and prisms: $50.00 – 60.00. Please refer to p. 49 for pricing on etched Cambridge. *(Crown Tuscan from the collection of Charles Upton)*

CB-73B. No. 647 TWO-LIGHT CANDLESTICKS IN ROYAL BLUE, CROWN TUSCAN WITH CHARLETON DECORATION, AND AMETHYST

No. 1274 two-light lustre-cut prism candelabrum. 13½" high. The last of the Keyhole candlesticks. Introduced in 1931 and probably only in production for a year or less. May have been made in crystal only, though colors are possible. Advertised with the No. 560 rock crystal cutting as a piece "created to anticipate the prevailing trend toward Victorian accessories." The mold was probably redesigned in 1932 to become the No. 38 Mount Vernon candelabrum (see CB-87 on p. 75) and again around 1940 to become the No. 1441 candelabrum (see CB-156 on p. 92). $150.00 – 175.00.

CB-74. No. 1274 TWO-LIGHT CANDELABRUM, FROM CATALOG, CA. 1931

No. 640 three-light candlestick. Dimensions unknown. Appears on a catalog page dating to the spring of 1929. Any of the colors made around this time are possible. Crystal: $25.00 – 35.00.

CB-75. No. 640 THREE-LIGHT CANDLESTICK, FROM CATALOG, CA. 1929

No. 1155 three-footed candlestick. 2¼" high, 5" across. No. 1156 three-footed candlestick. Dimensions unknown. Both of these candlesticks were made from the same mold and then shaped differently during the finishing process, so variations are likely. The No. 1155 eventually became part of the Everglade pattern and was made from 1929 to 1940. The No. 1156 seems to have only been made briefly around 1929. Known in emerald, cinnamon, jade, krystol, mystic, and rose du Barry (the latter being satin highlights on amber, emerald, crystal, willow blue, and peach-blo, respectively; the same colors are possible without the satin finish). Sometimes marked on the bottom with the C in a triangle. This candlestick was reissued by Imperial in the 1970s in aurora jewels and white carnival, but with the sides turned up, doubling its height to 4½". Crystal: $15.00 – 22.50. Colors: $20.00 – 30.00.

CB-76. No. 1155 THREE-FOOTED CANDLESTICK IN CINNAMON

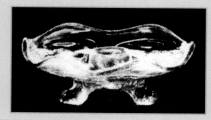

CB-77. No. 1156 THREE-FOOTED CANDLESTICK, FROM CATALOG, CA. 1929

CB-78. No. 1209 (No. 2 EVER-GLADE) CANDLESTICK, SATIN FINISH

CB-78B. No. 33 EVERGLADE CANDLESTICK, FROM CATA-LOG, CA. 1933

No. 1209 candlestick. Originally known as Leaf Line. Later listed as No. 2, 32 and 33 in the Everglade pattern, with the different pattern numbers denoting variations in the way the three leaves that form the candlestick were shaped during the final finishing of the candlestick. The pattern was then renamed Arcadia and this candlestick was listed as No. 74. The height varies considerably depending on how the leaves were shaped; the irregularly shaped base is a little more than 5" in diameter. Produced from 1931 to the mid-1940s.

Known colors include crystal, amber, carmen, forest green, and moonlight blue, with all colors available clear, satin finish, or with satin highlights. One catalog lists the pattern under the heading "Pearl Mist," which presumably refers to this method of decoration. Other colors are possible. This candlestick has also been reported in opalescent blue, probably an experimental color. The candlestick was also used as the base for the No. 1210 10" vase and the No. 1214 12" vase (with removable insert vases).

This was one of Cambridge's most unusual patterns, with all the pieces employing motifs from nature. Although it had been identified as Everglade as early as 1933, in 1941 some new pieces were added and the pattern was renamed Arcadia, with a series of patents taken out at that time. Four years later, in 1944, it was still being advertised with the claim that "Arcadia combines freshness and originality of form with an entirely new decorative treatment of finely engraved leaf patterns which give matchless sheen and brilliance to the crystal" — on "new and lovely shapes," even though some of the shapes were more than a decade old at that time.

The mold was owned by Imperial and is currently in the possession of the Summit Art Glass Company. It has been reissued in cobalt carnival.

Crystal: $30.00 – 35.00. Amber, forest green, moonlight blue: $50.00 – 65.00. Carmen: $85.00 – 100.00.

CB-78A. No. 32 EVER-GLADE CANDLESTICK, FROM CATALOG, CA. 1933

CB-79. No. 1211 (No. 3 EVERGLADE) CANDELABRUM IN AMBER

No. 1211 candelabrum. Originally known as Leaf Line. Later listed as No. 3 in the Everglade pattern. The pattern was then renamed Arcadia and this candlestick was listed as No. 75. 6" high. Produced from 1931 to the mid-1940s. Known colors include crystal, amber, carmen, forest green, Eleanor blue, and moonlight blue, with all colors available clear, satin finish, or with satin highlights. One catalog lists the pattern under the heading "Pearl Mist," which presumably refers to this method of decoration. Also known in ebony; other colors are possible. Also offered as the No. 1216 flower holder, with two vase inserts. Crystal: $65.00 – 80.00. Amber: $80.00 – 90.00. Forest green, moonlight blue, Eleanor blue: $90.00 – 120.00. Ebony: $200.00 – market. Carmen: $250.00 – market.

The mold is currently owned by the Summit Art Glass Company.

No. 10 Everglade candlestick. 4" high with a base diameter of 3⅞". Made from 1933 to 1940. Known in crystal, emerald, amber, and willow blue; other colors are possible. It has been seen in an opalescent blue, probably an experimental color. In 1940, the height given in the catalogs was changed from 4" to 3½", indicating that the mold had been reworked. A top rim was removed and a ring was added to the stem. Crystal, amber: $15.00 – 20.00. Emerald, willow blue: $25.00 – 30.00.

Very similar to the earlier No. 639 candlestick (see CB-65 on p. 68) and the No. 72 Martha Washington candlestick (see CB-91 on p. 76), both of which were in production at roughly the same time as the No. 10 Everglade candlestick. The primary difference is the addition of the pressed flower and leaf pattern on the underside of the base. (Note that a variant version of the No. 639 candlestick, listed as No. 745, also has a pressed pattern of flowers and leaves, but is different from the Everglade pattern.)

CB-80. No. 10 EVERGLADE CANDLESTICKS IN WILLOW BLUE (REDESIGNED VERSION) AND AMBER (ORIGINAL VERSION)

No. 62 Everglade candlestick. 3½" high. Made from ca. 1936 to 1940. Known in crystal and moonlight blue (plain, satin finish, or with satin highlights); other colors are possible. The mold was owned by Imperial and is currently in the possession of the Summit Art Glass Company. It has been reissued in cobalt carnival. Crystal: $20.00 – 25.00. Moonlight blue: $25.00 – 30.00.

When the Everglade pattern was renamed Arcadia in 1940, a number of new pieces were added that were not a part of the original Everglade line, including two candlesticks. See No. 3800/72 (CB-148 on p. 91) and No. 3800/73 (CB-149 on p. 91).

CB-81. No. 62 EVERGLADE CANDLESTICK, FROM CATALOG, CA. 1940

No. 1192 candlestick. Also listed as No. 3400/1192. 6" high. In production from 1930 to the 1940s. Known in crystal, ebony, emerald, amber, peach-blo (dianthus pink), gold krystol, amethyst, carmen, royal blue, forest green, and moonlight blue; other colors are possible. Offered with at least one engraving (No. 642) and four etchings (No. 746 Gloria, Diane, Elaine, and Portia). Also available as the No. 1270 lustre cut prism candlestick, with a patented lock bobeche. Very similar to the No. 3120 line of stemware. Crystal: $25.00 – 35.00. Amber, peach-blo, gold krystol, emerald: $35.00 – 40.00. Amethyst, forest green, moonlight blue, ebony: $40.00 – 45.00. Royal blue, carmen: $50.00 – 70.00. Add for bobeche and prisms: $25.00 – 30.00.

CB-82. No. 1192 CANDLE-STICK IN CARMEN

No. 1191 candlestick. 6" high with a 4⅛" diameter round base. Rarely found on a square base with notched corners and a raised lip. (See CB-083a, courtesy of the Cambridge Glass Museum.) Introduced in 1931 and probably only made for a brief period. Known in crystal, ebony, and emerald; other colors are possible. Also offered as a No. 1193 12" vase with an insert vase. Crystal: $175.00 – 200.00. Colors: $350.00 – market.

CB-83A. No. 1191 CANDLESTICK IN EMERALD, VARIANT BASE

CB-83. No. 1191 CANDLESTICKS

CB-84. No. 1223
CANDLESTICK IN
AMBER

No. 1223 candlestick. 5⅜" high with a 4¼" base. Shown on a 1931 catalog page as part of a console set with a No. 1224 11" oval bowl. Probably only made for a brief period. Known only in amber but any colors from this period are possible. $25.00 – 30.00.

No. 3011 candlestick; also listed as No. 60. Part of a pattern originally named the Figured Stem Line (later Figure Stem Line), then renamed Sea Shell (or Seashell). Also offered as part of the Venus Table Set. The pattern is also known as Statuesque and commonly referred to as the Cambridge Nude line. 9" high. Produced from 1931 to ca. 1949. Known in crystal, amber, amethyst, carmen, royal blue, forest green (or emerald), crown Tuscan (or coral), Windsor blue, and moonstone (crystal with satin finish); other colors are possible. May be found with solid color or with the nude stem in crystal and the candle cup in color.

The pattern was patented on August 25, 1931, as D85,618, with Will Cameron McCartney, the corporate secretary and sales manager, named as designer.

Offered with at least one engraving (No. 639), gold encrusted Rose Point etching, and decoration D/1007-8 on crown Tuscan. Available as a candlestick or with a bobeche and prisms.

Crystal, moonstone: $125.00 – 150.00. Amber, amethyst, forest green, crown Tuscan: $200.00 – 225.00. Royal blue, carmen: $300.00 – 350.00. Windsor blue: $450.00 – market. Add for bobech and prisms: $50.00 – 80.00.

This mold is currently owned by the Summit *(Windsor blue from the collection of Charles Upton)*

CB-85. No. 3011 CANDLESTICKS IN
CROWN TUSCAN AND WINDSOR BLUE.

No. 35 Mount Vernon candlestick. 8" high. Ca. 1932 to the 1940s. Reported in crystal, amber, carmen, royal blue, forest green, heatherbloom, crown Tuscan, pistachio, Mandarin gold, and milk glass. The latter color indicates that this candlestick must have been reissued in 1954. The same shape was also used for the No. 36 lustre cut prism candlestick (or candelabra) with bobeche and prisms and as the No. 1613/1614 and No. 1613/1614 hurricane lamps. (See CB-86a.) The candelabra will either have nubs to hold a locking bobeche in place or an extension around which the bobeche can rest. This candlestick may have been modified from the earlier No. 200/4 candlestick. (See CB-33 on p. 58.) Crystal: $40.00 – 50.00. Colors: $50.00 – 100.00. Hurricane Lamp, complete with extended socket, bobeches, prisms, and hurricane globe (any etching): $275.00 to market.

CB-86. No. 35
MOUNT VERNON
CANDLESTICK,
FROM CATALOG,
CA. 1932

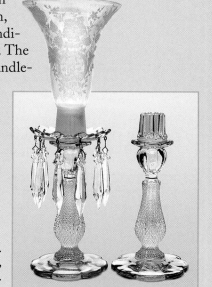

CB-86A. No. 35 CANDLESTICKS, WITH EXTENSION.
EXAMPLE ON LEFT IS FITTED WITH A BOBECHE,
PRISMS, AND HURRICANE SHADE.

No. 38 Mount Vernon candelabrum. 13½" high. Introduced in 1932 and probably only produced for a short time. Known in crystal, gold krystol, carmen, and heatherbloom; other colors are possible. This candelabrum seems to have been redesigned from the earlier No. 1274 two-light candelabrum, with the Mount Vernon diamond point motif added to the finial and portions of the base. (See CB-74 on p. 71.) The mold may have been modified yet again to become the No. 1441 candelabrum around 1940. (See CB-152 on p. 92.) Crystal: $125.00 – 175.00. Colors: $350.00 – market.

CB-87. No. 38 MOUNT VERNON CANDELABRUM, FROM CATALOG, CA. 1933

No. 130 Mount Vernon candlestick. 4" high with a 4½" diameter scalloped base. Introduced in 1932 and made until the 1940s. Known in crystal and amber; reintroduced in milk glass in 1954 as No. W 76. Also offered as the No. 131 4½" candelabrum with bobeche and prisms, and as the No. 1607 9" hurricane lamp. $15.00 – 22.00.

CB-88. No. 130 MOUNT VERNON CANDLESTICK IN AMBER

No. 110 Mount Vernon two-light candlestick. 5" high. This was a late addition to the pattern, introduced in 1940 and probably only made for a brief period, then reintroduced very briefly, ca. 1954, in milk glass. Also offered as a candelabrum with No. 19 bobeches and prisms. Crystal: $45.00 – 60.00. Milk glass: $90.00 – 120.00. Add for bobeches and prisms: $50.00 – 60.00.

CB-89. No. 110 MOUNT VERNON TWO-LIGHT CANDLESTICK

No. 1307 three-light candlestick. Also listed as No. 68 three-holder candlestick and No. 1545 three-light candelabrum. Made in various heights, ranging from 5" to 6½", depending on the size of the base and the shape of the foot. Diameter of the foot varies from 4⅝" to 5".

The tall version was introduced in 1932. By ca. 1937, the shorter version was also being made, with both sizes appearing in the 1940 catalog. An intermediate version is also known, which may be the one shown in later catalogs from the 1950s. The shorter version was also made with an extender added to the center candle cup to hold a locking bobeche.

Known in crystal, emerald, amber, amethyst, carmen, royal blue, forest green, crown Tuscan (or coral), dianthus pink, and moonstone (crystal with satin finish); other colors are possible.

Used as a blank for various etchings, including No. 758, 764, Diane, Elaine, Portia, Rose Point, Wildflower, D/995 Chintz, D/997, and D-1001.

CB-90. No. 1307 THREE-LIGHT CANDLESTICK IN DIANTHUS PINK, TALL BASE

Crystal, moonstone, amber: $25.00 – 35.00. Dianthus pink, forest green, amethyst, emerald: $35.00 – 45.00. Carmen, royal blue, crown Tuscan: $45.00 – 65.00. Please refer to p. 49 for pricing on etched Cambridge.

CB-90A. No. 1307 THREE-LIGHT CANDLESTICK IN AMBER, SHORT BASE

CB-91. No. 72
MARTHA WASHINGTON
CANDLESTICK, FROM
CATALOG, CA. 1940

No. 72 Martha Washington candlestick. 4½" high. Ca. 1932 to the 1940s. Offered in crystal, amber, gold krystol, carmen, royal blue, forest green, and heatherbloom; other colors are possible. The Martha Washington pattern (earlier known as Centennial and Victorian Line) was reintroduced in 1953 as Heirloom, but this candlestick does not seem to have been included. Crystal, amber: $15.00 – 20.00. Gold krystol, forest green: $25.00 – 30.00. Royal blue, carmen, heatherbloom: $30.00 – 40.00.

It is very similar in style to the earlier No. 639 candlestick (see CB-65 on p. 68) and the No. 10 Everglade candlestick (see CB-80 on p. 73), both of which were in production at roughly the same time as the No. 72 candlestick. See also the later No. 5000/68 Heirloom candlestick (CB-167 on p. 95).

CB-92. No. 1402/76 TALLY HO
CANDLESTICK IN AMBER
AND CANDELABRUM

No. 1402/76 Tally Ho candlestick. 5" high with a 3" square base. This was part of an extensive pattern line introduced in 1932 and was still in production in the early 1940s. Known in crystal, amber, carmen, and royal blue. Other pieces in the pattern were made in amethyst and Windsor blue, so additional colors are possible. Also offered as a candelabrum with a lock-on bobeche. This candlestick was probably a redesigned version of the earlier No. 635 candlestick. (See CB-51 on p. 64.) Crystal, amber: $20.00 – 25.00. Carmen, royal blue: $40.00 – 60.00. Add for bobeche and four prisms: $20.00 – 30.00.

This mold is currently owned by the Summit Art Glass Company.

CB-93. No. 1402/80
TALLY HO
CANDLESTICK
(EARLY VERSION),
FROM 1933 CATALOG

No. 1402/80 Tally Ho candlestick. 6½" high. This was the second candlestick added to the Tally Ho line in 1933, but seems to have been in production for less than a year, since the same pattern number was reassigned to another candlestick in 1934. (See below.) Known in crystal, amber, carmen, and royal blue; other colors known for pieces in the Tally Ho pattern are also possible. Also offered as the No. 1402/81 candelabrum, with bobeche and prisms. This was probably a reworked version of the earlier No. 1271 candlestick. (See CB-44 on p. 60.) Crystal, amber: $35.00 – 40.00. Carmen, royal blue: $50.00 – 75.00. Add for bobeche and prisms: $25.00 – 30.00.

CB-94.
No. 1402/80
TALLY HO
CANDLESTICK
(LATER VERSION),
FROM 1934
CATALOG

No. 1402/80 Tally Ho candlestick. 6" high. Produced from 1934 to the 1940s. Known in crystal, amber, carmen, royal blue, and forest green; other colors are possible. Available with at least one etching, Elaine. Also offered as the No. 1402/81 candelabrum, with bobeche and prisms. This was the second candlestick with the same pattern number (see above), either superseding the earlier version or possibly a modification of that mold. Crystal, amber: $35.00 – 40.00. Carmen, royal blue: $50.00 – 75.00. Add for bobeche and prisms: $25.00 – 30.00.

No. 3500/31 Gadroon candlestick. 6" high with a base diameter of 4½". Made from 1933 to the 1940s. Reported in crystal, ebony, amber, gold krystol, dianthus pink, amethyst, carmen, royal blue, forest green, crown Tuscan, moonlight blue, and milk glass. (The latter color would suggest this candlestick was reissued in 1954.) Also offered as the No. 3500/32 candelabrum with bobeche and prisms.

Made in two different versions. The earlier version (seen in the accompanying photograph) had ridges on the base. By 1940, small rams' heads had been added on either side of the candle cup and the ridges were removed from the base, replaced by four equidistant ribs. This made the candlestick suitable as a blank for decorating. Known etchings include Chantilly, Elaine, Rose Point, and Valencia.

The later version of the candlestick, with the rams' heads, was reissued by Imperial in cobalt with the Aurora jewels carnival finish from June 1, 1970 to April 1, 1972.

Crystal, amber: $20.00 – 25.00. Gold krystol, dianthus pink, milk glass, ebony, moonlight blue, amethyst, forest green: $25.00 – 45.00. Carmen, royal blue, crown Tuscan: $45.00 – 60.00.

CB-95. No. 3500/31 GADROON CANDLESTICKS IN AMETHYST AND CARMEN, 6", ORIGINAL VERSIONS WITH RIDGED FEET

No. 3500/74 Gadroon candlestick. 4" high with a base diameter of 4⅝". Made from 1934 to the 1940s. Known in crystal, amber, carmen, royal blue, and crown Tuscan; other colors are likely. The example pictured is a puzzle: it is opaque white with rich opalescence, appearing to be in Cambridge's carrara — however that color was only in production for a brief period more than a decade before the first appearance of this candlestick in a catalog. Either the candlestick was first made much earlier than we believe, the color was reintroduced at a later date, or one of the companies that owned the mold after Cambridge's closing reissued it in this color.

The No. 3500/74 candlestick is a shorter version of the No. 3500/31 candlestick discussed in the preceding entry. It has the rams' heads on either side of the candle cup and the base has only the four equidistant ribs. There is no evidence available to indicate that this candlestick was ever made with a ridged foot, as the taller No. 3500/31 was. Known etchings include Elaine and Rose Point. This candlestick may have been reissued by Imperial and has more recently been reissued by Fenton, but marked with the Fenton logo. (See FN-92 on p. 203.)

Crystal, amber: $20.00 – 25.00. Crown Tuscan: $25.00 – 30.00. Royal blue, carmen, carrara: $30.00 – 45.00.

CB-96. No. 3500/74 GADROON CANDLESTICK, 4", IN CARRARA

No. 3500/94 Gadroon two-light candlestick. Commonly called Ram's Head. Also available as the No. 3500/95 candelabrum with bobeches and prisms. 6" high. Introduced in 1934 and probably only made for a few years. Known in crystal only. This mold was redesigned to become the No. 657 two-light candlestick, with the ram's head between the arms replaced by a cornucopia, while retaining the rams' heads on either sides of the candle cups. (See CB-147 on p. 91.) Crystal: $30.00 – 35.00. Add $50.00 – 60.00 for bobeches and prisms.

CB-97. No. 3500/94 GADROON TWO-LIGHT CANDLESTICK, FROM 1934 CATALOG

CB-98. No. 3500/108
GADROON CANDLESTICK
IN AMBER

No. 3500/108 Gadroon candlestick. 2½" high with a 3⅞" diameter base. A somewhat late addition to the pattern, in production by 1940. Known in crystal, ebony, amber, amethyst, carmen, royal blue, forest green, and moonlight blue; other colors are possible. Used as a blank for various etchings, including Diane, Elaine, Portia, Rose Point, and Wildflower; also D/450 gold band decoration on ebony. This candlestick was probably reworked from the mold for the No. 625 candlestick. (See CB-53 on p. 64.) The candle cup is very similar to that of the No. 67 Caprice candlestick, which was in production during the same time period as the Gadroon candlestick. (See CB-106 on p. 80.) Crystal, amber: $8.00 – 10.00. Ebony, amethyst, forest green, moonlight blue: $12.00 – 15.00. Carmen, royal blue: $18.00 – 25.00.

CB-99. No. 1338 THREE-LIGHT
CANDLESTICK IN AMBER,
ORIGINAL VERSION

No. 1338 three-light candlestick. Originally introduced as part of the Gadroon pattern (sometimes listed as No. 3500/1338) and also sold as part of the No. 3400 pattern. Later incorporated into the Caprice line. Listed as No. W 91 in milk glass. 6" high with a 5¼" x 4¾" base. In production from 1933 to 1956. Known in crystal, amber, carmen, royal blue, forest green, dianthus pink, moonlight blue (plain and with the Alpine satin finish), LaRosa (plain and Alpine finish), Mandarin gold, emerald, and milk glass; other colors are possible. Also a popular blank for decorations, including at least nine etchings (Apple Blossom, Chantilly, Diane, Elaine, Portia, Rose Point, Roselyn, Valencia, and Wildflower) and the D/1018 gold stippled edge decoration.

Made in two versions. The earliest form had crosshatching on the balls beneath the candle cups. By 1940, a version without the crosshatching was in production, with both styles shown in the catalog. Crystal: $30.00 – 40.00. Amber, crystal alpine: $40.00 – 50.00. Carmen, Ritz blue: $125.00 – 175.00. All other colors: $70.00 – 100.00. Please refer to p. 49 for pricing on etched Cambridge.

This mold is owned by the Summit Art Glass Company, who reissued the candlestick in light blue in 1985.

CB-99A. No. 1338 THREE-LIGHT CANDLE-
STICK IN FOREST GREEN, LATER VERSION

CB-100. No. 1577 FIVE-LIGHT
CANDLESTICK, FROM 1940 CATALOG

No. 1577 five-light candlestick. 6" high, 11" in length. Ca. 1940. Crystal only. Very similar to the No. 1338 three-light candlestick above, though not listed as Caprice in the catalog. There are two versions known, one with a rim on the center candle cup to hold a bobeche and prisms. This mold is owned by the Summit Art Glass Company. $145.00 – 165.00. Add $30.00 – 40.00 for bobeche and prisms.

No. 3500/154 Gadroon three-light low candlestick. This seems to have been the precursor to the No. 74 Caprice three-light candlestick. (See below.) It was illustrated in the October 1935 issue of the *Crockery and Glass Journal* as "being offered plain, etched, or cut." The only difference between the two is that the No. 3500/154 does not have the familiar Caprice pattern pressed on the underside of its base, and therefore was suitable as a blank for decorating. The example pictured was shown with Rose Point etching. Plain: $35.00 – 40.00. Etched: $120.00 – 135.00.

CB-101. No. 3500/154 GADROON THREE-LIGHT CANDLESTICK, FROM *CROCKERY AND GLASS JOURNAL*, OCTOBER 1935

No. 74 Caprice three-light candlestick. Listed as 4" high, with actual heights ranging from 3⅞" to 4¼". The base is 9½" long by approximately 4¼" wide. Introduced in 1936 as part of the Caprice line and probably modified from the No. 3500/154 above. Continued in production until the 1940s. Known in crystal and moonlight blue, both clear and with the Alpine finish. Crystal: $35.00 – 40.00. Moonlight blue: $115.00 – 135.00.

The difference in base height noted above is because the base seems to have been modified yet again at some point. The shorter base was made first. It can be seen clearly that the difference in height is in the mold rather than in the way the piece was shaped during the manufacturing process. On the short base, the two loops that radiate out from the center candleholder extend all the way to the edge of the base, while the pointed ray that bisects the loops ends just below the first loop. On the taller base, there is ⅜" between the loops and the edge of the base, and the pointed ray bisects both loops. Other similar variations can be seen as well.

It is likely that all three of the candlesticks discussed here (the No. 3500/154 and both versions of the No. 74)

CB-102. No. 74 CAPRICE THREE-LIGHT CANDLESTICK, SHORT BASE

were originally derived from the earlier No. 824 three-light candlestick. (See CB-67 on p. 68.)

The mold (for the taller base version) is currently owned by the Summit Art Glass Company, who made some pieces in vaseline, cobalt, and cobalt carnival in 2001 – 2002. They also produced this candlestick in various two-tone combinations of cobalt and vaseline.

CB-102A. No. 74 CAPRICE THREE-LIGHT CANDLESTICK, TALLER BASE

No. 1355 two-holder candlestick. Although originally not part of a pattern line, this candlestick was later listed as Caprice. 6⅞" with a 6" base. Made from 1934 until 1956. Known in crystal and moonlight blue (plain or Alpine finish, with satin highlights). Also offered as the No. 1356 two-holder candelabra with bobeches and prisms added. Crystal: $40.00 – 50.00. Moonlight blue: $140.00 – 175.00. With bobeches and prisms (No. 1356), crystal: $100.00 – 130.00; moonlight blue: $300.00 – 350.00.

CB-103. No. 1356 TWO-HOLDER CANDELABRA IN MOONLIGHT BLUE

CB-104. No. 1358 THREE-HOLDER CANDELABRA WITH REMOVABLE INSERT HOLDING TWO EPERGNE VASES

No. 1357 three-holder candlestick. Although originally not part of a pattern line, this candlestick was later listed as Krystolshell and then as Caprice. 6" high with a 6" base. Made from 1934 until 1956. Known in crystal and moonlight blue (plain or Alpine finish, with satin highlights). Also offered as the No. 1358 three-holder candelabra with bobeches and prisms added. This is a three-light version of the No. 1355 two-holder candlestick, with its center finial replaced by an additional candle cup. Like most of the candlesticks from this period, it was also available with a removable insert that holds two epergne vases. The mold is currently owned by the Summit Art Glass Company. Crystal: $60.00 – 75.00. Moonlight blue: $135.00 – 155.00. With bobeches and prisms (No. 1358), crystal: $125.00 – 140.00; moonlight blue: $345.00 – 375.00.

CB-105. No. 1457 THREE-LIGHT CANDLESTICK

No. 1457 three-light candlestick. 7" tall with a 6" base. In production by 1940 and made until 1956. Known in crystal only. Also offered as the No. 1458 three-light candelabra with bobeches and prisms added. This candlestick was never listed as part of a pattern, even though it is clearly based on the No. 1357 three-holder candlestick above, which was in later years considered to be part of the Caprice line. A taller, three-light candelabra was also made, with different shaped candle cups and with the center arm extended upward by the addition of a faceted ball between the foliage and the candle cup; it stands 9¾" high. $65.00 – 80.00. With bobeches and prisms (No. 1458): $130.00 – 160.00.

CB-106. No. 67 CAPRICE CANDLESTICK IN MOONLIGHT BLUE

No. 67 Caprice candlestick. Also listed as No. C-67. 2½" high with a 4" diameter scalloped base. Introduced in 1936 with the rest of the pattern and in production until the factory closed in the 1950s. Known in crystal, moonlight blue, and LaRosa (both plain and with the Alpine satin finish); considering its unusually long production period, other colors are possible. The candle cup bears a strong resemblance to that on the No. 3500/108 Gadroon candlestick, which was introduced at about the same time. (See CB-98 on p. 78.) Crystal: $12.00 – 16.00. Colors: $25.00 – 30.00.

CB-107. No. 68 CAPRICE TRIANGLE CANDLEHOLDER, FROM CATALOG, LATE 1930S

No. 68 Caprice triangle candleholder. 2" by 2¼". Introduced in 1936 and discontinued before 1940. Offered in crystal and moonlight blue, both plain and with the Alpine satin finish. This was made from the same mold as the No. 204 triangle cigarette holder, with a candle well added to the inside bottom. Unable to price.

No. 69 Caprice two-holder candlestick. 7½" high. In production by 1938 until the early 1940s. Known in crystal and moonlight blue; probably also made in LaRosa. Available with single prisms hanging from each candle cup or as a candelabrum, with bobeches and additional prisms. This is another candlestick whose design seems to have evolved. In addition to the style shown, it was also made in two other very different versions. The first had candle cups in the shape of shells, possibly as part of the Sea Shell or Krystolshell lines, and was discontinued before 1939. A third version, production dates unknown, does not have the fans in between where the arms join the body and the center finial. The mold for the style shown is currently owned by the Summit Art Glass Company. Crystal: $125.00 – 150.00+. Moonlight blue: $800.00 – market.

CB-108. No. 69 CAPRICE TWO-HOLDER CANDLESTICK, FROM 1940 CATALOG

No. 70 Caprice candlestick with prism. Also listed as No. C-70. Also considered part of the Sea Shell and Krystolshell lines. 7" high with a 4½" base. Made from 1936 to 1954. Offered in crystal, moonlight blue, and LaRosa (both plain and with the Alpine satin finish); other colors are possible. Patented as D99,448, filed March 10, 1936, and approved April 28, 1936. The designer was given as Wilbur L. Orme, vice president of the company. (A similar shape was later used for the No. 499 Virginian candlestick and the No. 497 Martha candelabrum. See CB-120 on p. 84 and CB-146 on p. 90.) The mold is currently owned by the National Cambridge Collectors, Inc. The Mosser Glass Company makes a 3½" miniature version of the No. 70 candlestick in moonlight blue and cobalt as part of their Lindsey pattern. Crystal: $30.00 – 35.00. Moonlight blue (plain or Alpine): $60.00 – 75.00.

CB-109. No. 70 CAPRICE CANDLESTICK IN MOONLIGHT BLUE WITH ALPINE SATIN FINISH

No. 72 Caprice two-light candlestick. Also offered as part of the Sea Shell line and later included in the Corinth pattern as No. 3900/72. 5⅛" high with a 5⅜" diameter base. Made from 1941 to 1954. Known in crystal, moonlight blue, LaRosa (both plain and with the Alpine satin finish), and smoke; other colors are possible. There were two versions of this candlestick. The original version, made from 1940 to 1942, has round candle cups. The revised version has the ribbed candle cups seen in the accompanying photograph. A popular blank for decorations. Cuttings include No. 568 Achilles, 720 Adonis, 732 Carnation, 824 Lucia, 985 Maryland, 1003 Manor, 1020, 1022 Plymouth, 1064, 1065, 1066 Thistle, 1067 Silver Maple, Laurel Wreath, Roxbury, and Tempo. Etchings include Candlelight, Chantilly, Daffodil, Diane, Elaine, Magnolia, Portia, Rose Point, and Wildflower. Also offered as the No. 78 and 79 candelabra, with the addition of bobeches and prisms. For other candlesticks in the Corinth pattern, see No. 3900/67 (CB-158 on p. 93) and 3900/74 (CB-160 on p. 94). Crystal: $30.00 – 35.00. Moonlight blue, LaRosa: $100.00 – 125.00. Smoke: unable to price. Please refer to p. 49 for pricing on etched Cambridge.

CB-110. No. 72 CAPRICE TWO-LIGHT CANDLESTICK WITH WILDFLOWER ETCHING

No. 73 Caprice reflector candlestick. Also sold as part of the Sea Shell line. Dimensions unknown. Introduced in 1941 to ca. 1945. Made in crystal and briefly reissued in milk glass in 1954. According to Sherry Riggs and Paul Pendergrass, in their *Glass Candleholders of the Depression Era and Beyond*, also made in moonlight blue. The mold, which is not complete, is currently owned by the Cambridge Collectors of America, Inc. $350.00 – market.

CB-111. No. 73 CAPRICE REFLECTOR, FROM 1941 CATALOG PAGE

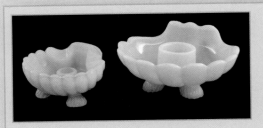

CB-112. SEA SHELL CANDLEHOLDERS (TWO SIZES) IN WINDSOR BLUE

Sea Shell candleholder. Pattern number unknown. Available in two sizes. The larger measuring 2" high and 4" across, the smaller being 1⅝" high and 2¾" across. The smaller size holds a miniature candle or could be used as a cigarette holder/ashtray. Known in ebony and Windsor blue; other colors are possible, especially coral and moonstone (crystal with satin finish). Has been reproduced in vaseline, probably by the Summit Art Glass Company. Both sizes: Ebony: $30.00 – 40.00. Windsor blue: $50.00 – 70.00. *(From the collection of Charles Upton)*

CB-113. No. 50 DOLPHIN IN MILK GLASS (No. W 109) WITH FLARED PETALS ON THE CANDLE CUP AND ORIGINAL VERSION IN CORAL.

No. 50 Dolphin candlestick. Variously listed as part of the Krystolshell, Sea Shell, and Mount Vernon patterns. 7¾" with a 4⅜" square base. In production from around 1936 to the early 1940s; reissued again in 1954. Production colors from the 1930s include crystal, amber, amethyst, carmen, royal blue, forest green, crown Tuscan (called moonstone in one catalog), and coral. The crown Tuscan or coral candlesticks are sometimes seen with ornate gold and enamel decoration, done by Charleton.

In 1954, the candlestick was made in milk glass only, as No. W 109, with the petals at the top of the candle cup flared. This harks back to the pattern number of the earlier Dolphin candlestick, No. 109, which had been modified to become the No. 50 candlestick. (See CB-48 on p. 63.)

This version of the Dolphin was also offered as a No. 51 candelabrum with the addition of a short extender above the candle cup around which rested a bobeche and prisms (CB-113a). In later catalogs, it was listed as the No. 1612 candelabrum and by that time had been redesigned with the addition of a much longer extender. The same version was also used as the base for the No. 1612/1614 and 1612/1615 hurricane lamps (16" and 18", respectively, depending on the size of globe used) (CB-113b). In 1940, it was this version that appeared in the catalog as the No. 50 candlestick (with the extender but without a bobeche). This was probably an economy during the wartime years, allowing production of both the candlestick and candelabrum from a single mold. In 1954, a candelabrum was made in milk glass as No. W 110, with the short extender.

This mold is currently owned by the Summit Art Glass Company (q.v.) who have reissued the Dolphin in iridized (a mother of pearl or rainbow effect sprayed on the heated glass), cobalt blue, red, and rubina. The latter color was only made in a single batch, due to difficulties in controlling the color.

CB-113A. No. 50 DOLPHIN WITH SHORT EXTENDER

Crystal: $80.00 – 90.00. Amber, forest green, amethyst: $160.00 – 185.00. Carmen, royal blue: $200.00 – market. Milk glass: $125.00 – 145.00. Crown Tuscan: $140.00 – 165.00. Add for short extended socket, bobeche, and prisms: $40.00 – 50.00. Hurricane Lamp, complete with ribbed extended socket, bobeches, prisms, and hurricane globe: Small globe (any etching): $350.00 to market. Large Globe (any etching): $400.00 to market.

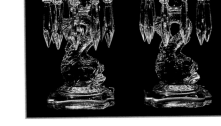

CB-113B. No. 1612/1614 HURRICANE LAMP WITH WILDFLOWER ETCHING AND No. 1612/1615 HURRICANE LAMP WITH GOLD ENCRUSTED ROSE POINT ETCHING

No. 66 footed candleholder. Also listed as No. SS66. Part of the Sea Shell and Krystolshell patterns. 4" high with a 3¼" base. Produced ca. 1935 to the 1940s; reissued in coral in 1950. Offered in crystal (clear and moonstone or satin finish), amber, amethyst, royal blue, forest green, crown Tuscan, and coral. The coral candleholders are sometimes seen with ornate gold and enamel decoration by Charleton. The mold is currently owned by the Summit Art Glass Company who have reissued the candleholder in transparent blue and vaseline. Crystal, amber: $45.00 – 55.00. Amethyst, forest green, crown Tuscan, coral: $65.00 – 75.00. Royal blue, coral decorated: $75.00 – 85.00. (Summit reissues: $30.00 – 35.00.)

CB-114. No. 66 FOOTED CANDLEHOLDER IN CORAL

CB-114A. No. 66 FOOTED CANDLEHOLDER IN MOONSTONE

No. 67 two-holder candlestick. Part of the Sea Shell and Krystolshell patterns, but generally called Dolphin by collectors. 5" high with a 4" base. Introduced ca. 1935 and only made for a few years. Offered in crystal (clear and moonstone or satin finish), amber, amethyst, royal blue, forest green, crown Tuscan, and coral. Crystal, amber: $55.00 – 65.00. Amethyst, forest green, crown Tuscan (coral): $80.00 – 100.00. Royal blue: $100.00 – 125.00.

CB-115. No. 67 TWO-HOLDER CANDLESTICK IN CORAL

Lyre candelabrum. Pattern number and dimensions unknown. Made 1936 – 1939, probably in crystal only. Advertised both with the standard scalloped bobeches and with bobeches in the shape of shells, suggesting a possible relationship with the Sea Shell and Krystolshell lines. This candelabrum was redesigned in June 1939 to become the much more ornate No. 1474 Regency two-light candelabrum. Among other changes, a center finial was added and the rectangular molded base was replaced with a round applied foot. (See CB-155 on p. 93.) $225.00 – 300.00.

CB-116. LYRE CANDELABRUM

No. 1580 epergnette. 5⅜" high with a 5" diameter base. Ca. 1937 – 1938. Crystal only. Shown in the catalog with a No. 1579 ball shaped vase. Also available as No. 1583 (with crimped top vase), No. 1588 (with bobeches, prisms, and No. 78 vase), No. 1589 (with bobeches, prisms, and No. 93 vase), No. 1590 (twin hurricane lamp), and No. 1591 (with No. 93 footed, crimped top vase). Patented as No. D105,954, filed July 30, 1937, approved September 7, 1937. The designer was given as Jess Clair Kelly. $25.00 – 30.00.

CB-117. No. 1580 EPERGNETTE

CB-118. No. 493 VIRGINIAN CANDLESTICK

No. 493 Virginian candlestick. 2¾" high with a 3¾" base. Ca. 1937 to the 1940s. Crystal only. $20.00 – 25.00.

CB-119. No. 507 VIRGINIAN CANDELABRUM

No. 493 Virginian candlestick. 6½" high. Ca. 1937 to the 1940s. Crystal only. Offered with the D/1054 gold decoration. Also available as the No. 507 7" candelabrum, 7½" high with the addition of a bobeche and prisms, with a 4½" base. $55.00 – 75.00.

CB-120. No. 499 VIRGINIAN CANDLESTICK

No. 499 Virginian candlestick with prism. 7½" high with a 4¼" diameter base. Ca. 1937 to the 1940s. Crystal only. The unusual shape allowing a single prism to be suspended beneath the candle cup is similar to that of the patented No. 70 Caprice candlestick with prism. (See CB-109 on p. 81.) $50.00 – 60.00.

CB-121. No. 501 TWO-LIGHT VIRGINIAN CANDLESTICK

No. 501 two-light Virginian candlestick. 6" high with a 4½" by 5¾" diamond-shaped base. Although the pattern was introduced in 1937, this candlestick was probably only made in the early 1940s. Crystal only. Also offered as the No. 509 and 511 candelabra with bobeches and prisms added. There are three other versions of this candlestick, at least one of which was shown as part of the Pristine pattern and also designated as No. 501. (See CB-136 on p. 88.) It seems likely that the Pristine candlestick was issued first and that the mold was then redesigned to become part of the Virginian line, though it is also possible that both were in production at the same time. The Pristine candlestick does not have the center medallion or the serration on the edges of the arms; also, its base is rectangular (though a version of the candlestick without the serration but with a diamond-shaped base is also known). $50.00 – 60.00.

No. 502 Virginian two-holder candlestick. 5½" high with a 5⅜" diameter base. Made ca. 1937 to the 1940s. Crystal only. Offered with at least one cutting, No. 951 Broadmoor, the D/1050 and D/1054 gold decorations, and one etching, Diane. Also available as the No. 512 two-light candelabrum, with the addition of bobeches and prisms, and the No. 669 epergne. $40.00 – 45.00. Add for bobeches and prisms: $40.00 – 60.00. Please refer to p. 49 for pricing on etched Cambridge.

CB-122. No. 502 VIRGINIAN TWO-HOLDER CANDLESTICK, WITH DIANE ETCHING

No. 488 Pristine candlestick. 4" high. Made from ca. 1937 to the early 1940s. Crystal only. Early examples of the candlestick are cut top and bottom; this practice was discontinued around 1939 to allow the company to reduce prices. $20.00 – 25.00.

CB-123. No. 488 PRISTINE CANDLESTICK, FROM 1940 CATALOG

Pristine round candlesticks. No. 489, 1¾" high; No. 490, 2¾" high; No. 491, 3¾" high. Made from ca. 1937 to the early 1940s. Crystal only. Early examples of these candlesticks are cut top and bottom; this practice was discontinued around 1939 to allow the company to reduce prices. $15.00 – 20.00.

CB-124, CB-125, AND CB-126. No. 489 PRISTINE ROUND CANDLESTICKS, SMALL, MIDDLE, AND TALL SIZES, FROM 1940 CATALOG

No. 492 square candlestick, also listed as No. P.492 and No. 3797/492, 1¾" high, 2" by 2" square; No. 493 square candlestick, also listed as No. P.493 and No. 3797/493, 2⅜" high, 2⅛" by 2⅛" square; No. 495 square candlestick, also listed as No. P.495 and No. 3797/495, 3⅛" high, 2¼" by 2¼" square. These three candleblocks were originally issued as part of the Pristine pattern and later incorporated into the Cambridge Square line. They were made from ca. 1937 until the factory closed in 1958. They were offered in crystal, ebony, and ebon (black with a matte finish). In ebon, they were available with two gold decorations, D/1 Birds and D/2 Stars. The square candleblocks match the round candlesticks above, with the same beveled insets on each of the flat sides. Early versions were cut top and bottom. The molds are currently owned by the Summit Art Glass Company. For other candleholders in the Cambridge Square line, see No. 3797/67 (CB-163) and No. 3797/69 (CB-164) on p. 95. Crystal: $15.00 – 20.00. Ebony: $18.00 – 22.50.

CB-127, CB-128, AND CB-129. No. 492, 493, AND 495 SQUARE CANDLESTICK IN EBONY

No. 494 Pristine candlestick. 3½" high with a 3⅜" diameter round base. Made from 1937 to 1958. Crystal only. Available with the D/1050 gold decoration. Also offered as the No. 506 candelabrum, with a bobeche and prisms added, and as the No. 54 hurricane lamp.

There were two versions of this candlestick. The original design only has two steps on the base. By 1940, it had been reworked to add a third step. Early examples of the candlestick are cut top and bottom; this practice was discontinued around 1939 to allow the company to reduce prices. $15.00 – 20.00.

CB-130. No. 494 PRISTINE CANDLE- STICK, FIRST VERSION

CB-130A. No. 494 PRISTINE CANDLESTICK, REDESIGNED VERSION, FROM 1940 CATALOG

No. 496 Pristine Table Architecture™ interchangeable candlestick and flower trough. 5" high. Made from 1937 to the early 1940s. Crystal only. Early versions of these candleholders were offered cut top and bottom or full-cut; this practice was discontinued around 1939 to allow the company to reduce prices. $35.00 – 45.00.

CB-131. No. 496 PRISTINE TABLE ARCHI-TECTURE™ INTERCHANGEABLE CANDLE-STICK AND FLOWER TROUGH, FROM 1940 CATALOG

This unique addition to the Pristine line was patented as No. 2,115,962, filed April 23, 1937, and approved May 3, 1938. The inventor was given as Wilbur L. Orme, the vice president of the company. It was described as a "table decorating unit" and the patent application stated that "One of the objects of this invention is to provide a modest shaped candlestick unit ... which may be utilized in groups in decorative schemes in numerous positions and in various combinations wherein the hostess or interior decorator may secure a variety of tasteful settings." When laid flat, the recessed areas formed a flower trough.

By themselves or in combination with various available bowls, the possible combinations were virtually unlimited, as can be seen from the Table Architecture™ brochure reproduced here.

In May 2000, an exhibition entitled "American Modern, 1925 – 1940, Design for a New Age" opened at the Metropolitan Museum of Art, including the Table Architecture™ candlesticks. At that time, it was reported that the Metropolitan Museum had commissioned a mold to reproduce this candlestick (clearly marked, as all MMA reproductions are). As of this writing, these reproductions are currently being offered in sets of two for $89.95, or as a grouping of three with a centerpiece bowl for $150.00.

CB-131A. TABLE ARCHITECTURE™ BROCHURE, UNDATED

No. 503 Pristine three-light candlestick. 6" high. Made from 1937 to the early 1940s. Crystal only. Early versions of this candlestick are cut top and bottom; this practice was discontinued around 1939 to allow the company to reduce prices. Similar in shape to the patented No. 496 interchangeable candlestick and flower trough shown on the previous page. $35.00 – 45.00.

CB-132. No. 503 PRISTINE THREE-LIGHT CANDLESTICK, FROM 1937 BROCHURE

No. 497 Pristine one-light candlestick. 5½" high. Made from 1937 to the early 1940s. Crystal only. Available with a single prism or as the No. 505 candelabrum, with a bobeche and nine prisms. The latter has three steps on the base, rather than two as on the candlestick. Early versions of this candlestick are cut top and bottom; this practice was discontinued around 1939 to allow the company to reduce prices. Offered with at least one cutting, No. 951 Broadmoor. This candlestick is based on the design of the patented No. 502 two-light candlestick, following, with one arm removed. $45.00 – 55.00.

CB-133. No. 497 PRISTINE ONE-LIGHT CANDLESTICK, FROM 1937 BROCHURE

No. 502 Pristine two-light candlestick. Also listed as No. 1616, and available as the No. 520 and 521 candelabra, with bobeches and prisms. 6¼" high with a 5¼" diameter base. Made from 1937 to the early 1940s. Known in crystal and crown Tuscan. The 1940 catalog shows two versions of the base, one a thicker slab than the other. Early versions of this candlestick are cut top and bottom; this practice was discontinued around 1939 to allow the company to reduce prices. Offered with at least one cutting, No. 951 Broadmoor, and with No. D/1050 gold decoration. This design was patented as D103,538, filed January 21, 1937, and approved March 9, 1937. The designer was Will Cameron McCartney. Crystal: $50.00 – 55.00. Crown Tuscan: market. With bobeches and prisms (No. 520 and No. 521), crystal: $100.00 – 125.00. Crown Tuscan: market.

CB-134. No. 520 PRISTINE TWO-LIGHT CANDELABRA

No. 498 Pristine candlestick. 7" high. Made from 1937 to the early 1940s. Crystal only. Early versions of this candlestick are cut top and bottom; this practice was discontinued around 1939 to allow the company to reduce prices. Offered with the No. D/1050 gold decoration. Also available as the No. 507 candelabrum, with the addition of a bobeche and prisms. $50.00 – 55.00. With bobeches and prisms (No. 507): $75.00 – 80.00.

CB-135. No. 498 PRISTINE CANDLESTICK, FROM 1937 BROCHURE

Two-way candelabrum. 5½" high (6" with the bobeches added) with a 2⅞" x 5" base. Advertised in the winter 1936 – 1937 issue of *Creative Design* as a "two-way candelabrum." Crystal only. Also No. 501 Pristine two-light candlestick. 5" high. Probably made ca. 1937 in crystal for no more than a year or two.

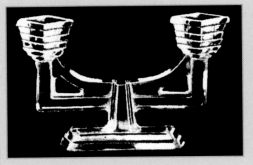

CB-136. TWO-WAY CANDELABRUM

The evolution of this candlestick is unusually complicated. The initial version, with the finial between the arms, was probably not part of a pattern. When Pristine was issued in 1937, the finial was removed. The next phase in its design history was when the base was redesigned, changing from rectangular with steps to a diamond-shape. All three of these candlesticks were apparently only made very briefly, since they do not appear as part of the Pristine line in the 1940 catalog. Instead, the mold seems to have been reworked one final time to become the No. 501 Virginian two-light candlestick (retaining the same pattern number that it had while part of Pristine). At that time, serration was added to the arms, a ridged design to the underside of the base, and an ornate medallion was placed between the arms, coming full circle from the original finial. (See CB-121 on p. 84.) $45.00 – 50.00. Add for bobeches and prisms: $40.00 – 60.00.

CB-136B. NO. 501 PRISTINE TWO-LIGHT CANDLESTICK, DIAMOND-SHAPED BASE. *(From the collection of Helen and Bob Jones)*

CB-136A. NO. 501 PRISTINE TWO-LIGHT CANDLESTICK, RECTANGULAR BASE, FROM 1937 BROCHURE

No. 500 Pristine one-light candlestick. Also listed as No. P.500 Leaf candlestick. 6½" high. Made from 1941 to around 1949. Listed in crystal only. Sherry Riggs and Paula Pendergrass, in their *20th Century Glass Candle Holders*, indicate that it is also available in moonlight blue. Known with at least two etchings, Rose Point and Wildflower. This candlestick was advertised as one of Cambridge's "innovations in the best modern spirit," a claim that was underscored by their almost surrealist 1947 ad campaign featuring illustrations resembling paintings by Salvador Dali. Plain: $40.00 – 50.00.

CB-137. NO. 500 PRISTINE ONE-LIGHT CANDLESTICK

CB-137A. NO. 500 PRISTINE ONE-LIGHT CANDLESTICK AND OTHER PIECES, FROM *HOUSE BEAUTIFUL*, MAY 1947

No. 499 Pristine Calla Lily candlestick. Also listed as No. P.499. 6½" with a 4¾" diameter base. Made from 1942 to 1958. Offered in crystal, ebony, Mandarin gold, and late emerald; other colors are possible. Used as a blank for at least three etchings, Chantilly, Paisley, and Rose Point, and three cuttings, No. 1053 Harvest, No. 1066 Thistle, and No. 1067 Silver Maple. Reissued by Imperial as No. 1936-499 in crystal, amber, heather, and verde, beginning January 1, 1962. Crystal: $22.00 – 26.00. Colors: $32.00 – 36.00.

CB-138. No. 499 Pristine Calla Lily candlesticks, ebony and Mandarin gold

No. 504 Pristine two-light candlestick. 7" high. Introduced in August 1942 and probably only in production briefly. Crystal only. $45.00 – 50.00.

CB-139. No. 504 Pristine two-light candlestick, from 1942 catalog

No. 510 Pristine ball candlestick. Also listed as No. P.510. 2⅜" high and 2¾" in diameter. Made from 1942 to 1958. Crystal only. Also offered in various combinations with peg nappies, vases, globes, etc. Used as part of the Cambridge Arms set in later years. Other, unidentified companies made round candleblocks. Note the bulbous shape and relative depth of the candleholder (visible in the picture); also, the Cambridge ball candlestick will have a ⅝" indentation on the underside of the base. Imperial's No. E-18 Elysian candleblock is slightly smaller (2¼" high), but otherwise identical, except that both the tops and bottoms are flat without the indentations found on the Pristine candleblock. Orrefors also made a similar spherical candleblock, 2¾" in diameter and 2½" tall, ground flat on the bottom. $18.00 – 22.00.

CB-140. No. 510 Pristine ball candlestick

No. 511 Pristine two-ball candlestick. 2¼" high, 8½" long. Introduced in August 1942 and only in production for a brief period. Crystal only. $50.00 – 60.00.

CB-141. No. 511 Pristine two-ball candlestick

No. 512 Pristine three-ball candlestick. 2¼" high, 8½" by 8½" by 8½". Introduced in August 1942 and only in production for a brief period. Crystal only. $80.00 – 100.00.

CB-142. No. 512 Pristine three-ball candlestick

CB-143. No. 1604
HURRICANE LAMP,
PATENT DRAWING

No. 1604 hurricane lamp. 10" high with globe. Introduced in 1940; production dates unknown, but probably only made for a few years in the 1940s. Crystal only. Offered with Rose Point etching. Patented as D121,759, filed February 6, 1940, approved August 6, 1940. Designer given as Arthur J. Bennett, president of the company. $45.00 – 55.00.

CB-144. No. 494
MARTHA
CANDLESTICK,
WITH CHANTILLY
ETCHING

No. 494 Martha candlestick. 4" high (5" with the extender added, as seen in the photograph) with a 5" diameter base. Made from late 1939 to 1958. Crystal only. Offered with at least two etchings, Blossom Time and Chantilly. Also available as the No. 1617 hurricane lamp. $20.00 – 25.00.

No. 495 Martha 2-light candlestick. 5½" high with a 5¼" diameter base. Made from late 1939 to 1958. Listed in crystal only. Sherry Riggs and Paula Pendergrass, in their *20th Century Glass Candle Holders,* indicate that it is also available in moonlight blue. Known with at least one cutting, No. 1070 Lynbrook, and several etchings, including Blossom Time, Chantilly, Diane, Elaine, Portia, Rose Point, and Wildflower. Also offered as the No. M. 496 two-light candelabrum, with the addition of bobeches and prisms. $45.00 – 55.00. With bobeches and prisms: $75.00 – 90.00.

CB-145. No. 495 MARTHA
TWO-LIGHT CANDLESTICK, WITH
WILDFLOWER ETCHING

CB-146. No. 497
MARTHA
CANDELABRUM,
WITH CHANTILLY
ETCHING

No. 497 Martha candelabrum. 7¼" with a 5" base. Made ca. 1940, probably in crystal only. Known with at least two etchings, Chantilly and Rose Point. The unusual shape allowing a single prism to be suspended beneath the candle cup is similar to that of the patented No. 70 Caprice candlestick with prism. (See CB-109 on p. 81.) $30.00 – 35.00. Please refer to p. 49 for pricing on etched Cambridge.

No. 657 two-light candlestick. 5¼" high with a 5½" diameter base. Also available as the No. 658/1 and 658/2 candelabra with bobeches and prisms. Appears in the 1940 catalog; probably only in production for a few years in the 1940s. Known in crystal only and used as a blank for at least three etchings (Elaine, Rose Point, and Wildflower). Redesigned from the earlier No. 3500/94 Gadroon two-light candlestick, with a cornucopia replacing the ram's head that appeared between the arms of the earlier candlestick, but with the rams' heads on either sides of the candle cups retained. (See CB-97 on p. 77.) To complicate matter further, there are at least two versions of the redesigned No. 657 known: one with plain arms and one with a series of vertical lines incised midway on each arm (as seen in the accompanying photograph). $40.00 – 50.00.

CB-147. No. 657 TWO-LIGHT CANDLE-STICK, WITH ELAINE ETCHING

No. 3800/72 Arcadia candlestick. 3½" high with a 4" diameter base. Produced from 1940 to around 1944. Known only in crystal and pearl mist (crystal with satin highlights). Arcadia was a "new" pattern brought out in 1941; in fact, some of the pieces in the line were originally part of the Everglade pattern, made in the 1930s. (For Everglade candlesticks that became part of Arcadia, see No. 1209 and No. 1211 on p. 72.) The No. 3800/72 candlestick was one of two new candlesticks added to Arcadia. (A mold was ordered for a third one, the No. 3800/71 2¼" candlestick, but canceled before it was made.) The No. 3800/72 candlestick was later reissued by Imperial in various carnival colors. $15.00 – 20.00. (Imperial reissues: $15.00 – 20.00.)

CB-148. No. 3800/72 ARCADIA CANDLESTICK

No. 3800/73 Arcadia two-light candlestick. 6" high with a 5" diameter base. Produced from 1940 to around 1944. Known only in crystal and pearl mist (crystal with satin highlights). The mold for this candlestick is currently owned by the Summit Art Glass Company. $35.00 – 40.00.

CB-149. No. 3800/73 ARCADIA TWO-LIGHT CANDLESTICK

No. 1 Star candlestick. 2½" across. Made from late 1939 to 1958. Known in crystal, amethyst, and moonlight blue; other colors are possible. No. 2 Star candlestick. 4" across. Made from late 1939 to 1958. Known in crystal, forest green, and moonlight blue; other colors are possible. No. 3 Star candlestick. 5" across. Made from late 1939 to sometime in the 1940s. Known in crystal, amethyst, royal blue, and moonlight blue; other colors are possible. No. 4 Star candlestick. 11" across. Introduced in 1942 and only made for a brief period. Probably crystal only, though moonlight blue is also possible.

This set of candleblocks ranges from the tiny No. 1 (advertised in 1940 as "made to hold the new small diameter taper candle" or ½" size) to the massive No. 4, which takes a 1½" thick candle. The latter weighs a hefty 5½ pounds. The different sizes were designed to be sold "mix or match," with the catalog suggesting that "Many interesting and novel arrangements may be made by using all of one or a combination of the various sizes." All sizes will be found with cut bottoms, sometimes polished, sometimes not. Crystal: No. 1 or No. 2: $8.00 – 12.00. No. 3: $12.00 – 15.00. No. 4: $40.00 – 50.00. Colors: No. 1 or No. 2: $12.00 – 18.00. No. 3: $20.00 – 30.00.

CB-150. No. 3 STAR candleblock in amethyst, No. 4 STAR candleblock in crystal, No. 2 STAR candleblock in moonlight blue, with No. 1 STAR candleblock in crystal in foreground.

CB-151. No. 3121
CANDELABRUM

No. 3121 candlestick. 7" high. Made from ca. 1940 to 1958. In later years, this candlestick seems to have been offered only with a bobeche and prisms as a 7½" candelabrum. Crystal only. Offered with various etchings, including Diane, Elaine, Portia, Rose Point, and Wildflower. Designed to accompany the No. 3121 stemware line. A version of this candlestick with a ball at the bottom of the stem has been seen mounted in a base made by the Sheffield Silver Company. $35.00 – 45.00.

CB-152. No. 1441 TWO-LIGHT
CANDELABRUM

No. 1441 two-light candelabrum. 10⅛" high with a 5⅞" diameter base. Made ca. 1940 in crystal only. Also available with bobeches and prisms. This very ornate candelabrum bears a resemblance to two earlier ones and was probably reworked from the mold for the No. 38 Mount Vernon candelabrum (see CB-87 on p. 75), which in turn was modified from the earlier No. 1274 two-light candelabrum (see CB-74 on p. 71). To complicate matters even further, the "final" candelabrum was also made in at least three versions: the one shown in the accompanying photograph, a version with a ball at the top of the knob in the center of the keyhole, and a version with a crosshatch pattern in the fan-shaped finial. A three-light version was also made as No. 1443, with an additional candle cup in place of the center fan. Two-light: $125.00 – 150.00. Three-light: $160.00 – 190.00.

No. 1504 flower circle in two sizes, 5½" and 7½" long; and No. 1505 flower bar, 6" long. Appear in the 1940 catalog. Probably only in production for a brief period. Crystal, amber, and light emerald. The catalog shows several examples of ways in which these pieces could be combined to form elaborate floral table decorations. Crystal: $18.00 – 22.50 each piece. Amber, emerald: $22.00 – 30.00 each piece.

CB-153. No. 1504 FLOWER CIRCLES
AND No. 1505 FLOWER BARS

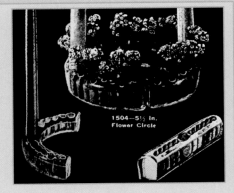

1504—5½ in.
Flower Circle

CB-153A. Nos. 1504 & 1505 SHOWING
SUGGESTED USAGE, FROM 1940 CATALOG

CB-154. No.
1602 CRUCIFIX

No. 1602 crucifix. 8⅝" high with a 4⅜" diameter round base. This was the last of the four crucifixes made by Cambridge. It appears in the 1940 catalog, so it was probably brought out sometime in the 1930s. Made in crystal and crystal with a satin finish only. $60.00 – 75.00.

No. 1474 Regency two-light candelabrum. 10½" high. Made from June 1939 to sometime in the 1940s. Crystal only. This was redesigned from the earlier Lyre candelabrum made in 1936, but with a number of changes including the addition of a center finial and the replacement of the original rectangular base with an applied round foot. (See CB-116 on p. 83.) Also offered as the No. 1442 candelabrum with bobeches and prisms added. $160.00 – 185.00. With bobeches: $225.00 – 250.00. *(Photograph courtesy of Esther E. Hall.)*

CB-155. No. 1474 REGENCY TWO-LIGHT CANDELABRUM

No. 1554 small cornucopia centerpiece, 6" high, 11½" long; and No. 1574 large cornucopia centerpiece, 7½" high, 13½" long. Introduced in 1941. Probably only in production for a brief period. Crystal only. Patented as D129,657, filed August 8, 1941, approved September 23, 1941. The designer was given as Wilbur L. Orme, who by that time had succeeded A. J. Bennett as president of the company. The large cornucopia centerpiece weighs six pounds and has a ground and puntied bottom. Small: $100.00 – 125.00. Large: $125.00 – 150.00. *(From the collection of Helen & Bob Jones.)*

CB-156. No. 1574 LARGE CORNUCOPIA CENTERPIECE

No. 1596 candlestick. 6½" high with a 4½" diameter hexagonal base. Made from 1942 until the factory closed in 1958. Crystal only. Also available as the No. 1597 7" candelabrum with the addition of a bobeche and prisms. In later years, this was one of the candlesticks used as a base for the Cambridge Arms. (See p. 96.)

No. 1598 candlestick. 8" high. A taller version of the No. 1596 candlestick, this one was also introduced in 1942 but had been discontinued by the end of the decade. Also available as the No. 1599 candelabrum with the addition of a bobeche and prisms.

These two candlesticks were probably reworked versions of the earlier No. 200/30 and 200/32 candlesticks, with the skirts flared out more. (See CB-42 on p. 60.) No. 1596 (6"): $15.00 – 20.00. No. 1598 (8"): $25.00 – 30.00.

CB-157. No. 1596 CANDLE-STICK

No. 3900/67 and No. 3900/68 Corinth candlestick. Approximately 5" high with a 5¼" diameter base. Height will vary because the No. 3900/67 has the rim of the candle cup turned down, while the No. 3900/68 has it turned up. Made from 1948 to 1958. Probably crystal only. Used as a blank for at least one cutting, No. 1068 Granada, and several etchings, including Candlelight, Chantilly, Diane, Elaine, Portia, Rose Point, and Wildflower. The No. 3900/68 candlestick can be turned upside down and used as a small comport. $25.00 – 30.00. Please refer to p. 49 for pricing on etched Cambridge.

CB-158. No. 3900/67 CORINTH CANDLESTICK, FROM 1949 CATALOG

CB-159. No. 3900/68 CORINTH CANDLESTICK

CB-160. No. 3900/74 CORINTH THREE-LIGHT CANDLESTICK

No. 3900/74 Corinth three-light candlestick. 6" high with a 5" diameter base. Made from 1948 to 1958. Probably crystal only. Used as a blank for various etchings, including Candlelight, Chantilly, Diane, Elaine, Portia, Rose Point, and Wildflower. Also offered as the No. 3900/75 epergne, with an insert holding a pair of vases. $20.00 – 25.00.

There was also a No. 3900/72 two-light candlestick in the Corinth pattern. It was originally issued as the No. 72 candlestick in the Caprice pattern. (See CB-110 on p. 81.)

CB-161. No. 4000/67 CASCADE CANDLESTICK IN LATE EMERALD

No. 4000/67 Cascade candlestick. Listed as No. W 88 in milk glass. 4½" high with a 5" diameter base. Made from 1948 to 1954. Offered in crystal, Mandarin gold, late emerald, and milk glass. In 1953 – 1954, this candlestick was briefly included as part of the Caprice pattern as No. 68. Crystal: $20.00 – 25.00. Mandarin gold, late emerald: $30.00 – 35.00. Milk glass: $28.00 – 32.00.

CB-162. No. 4000/72 CASCADE TWO-LIGHT CANDLESTICK

No. 4000/72 Cascade two-light candlestick. 5⅝" high with a 5¼" diameter base. Made from 1948 to the early 1950s. Offered in crystal only. $25.00 – 35.00.

CB-163. No. 3797/67 CAMBRIDGE SQUARE CUPPED CANDLESTICK

No. 3797/67 Cambridge Square cupped candlestick. 2⅛", 4½" wide, with a 2½" square base. Made from 1952 to 1958. Offered in crystal and ebon (black with a matte finish). Available in ebon with two gold decorations, D/1 Birds and D/2 Stars, and in crystal with Triumph (a platinum band applied around the upper rim). Also offered as the No. 3797/68 two-piece hurricane lamp. Reissued by Imperial in regal ruby from July 1, 1962 to January 1, 1964. In current production in light green slag with a matte finish, made by the Summit Art Glass Company. Crystal: $8.00 – 10.00. Ebon: $15.00 – 22.00. (Imperial reissue: $15.00 – 22.00. Summit reissue: $12.00 – 15.00.)

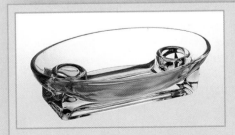

CB-164. No. 3797/69 CAMBRIDGE SQUARE TWO-LIGHT CANDLESTICK

No. 3797/69 Cambridge Square two-light candlestick. 2" high by 7½" long. Made from ca. 1954 to 1958. Offered in crystal and ebon (black with a matte finish). Available in ebon with the D/1 Stars gold decoration, so the D/2 Birds decoration is also possible. Crystal: $30.00 – 35.00. Ebon: $40.00 – 50.00.

Note: There were three square candleblocks that were also considered a part of the Cambridge Square line, Nos. 3797/492, 3797/493, and 3797/495. They were originally introduced as part of the Pristine pattern. (See CB-127 et al. on p. 85.)

No. 1715 candleholder. 1½" with a top diameter of 1¾" and a bottom diameter of 3⅜". Made from 1953 to 1954. Offered in crystal, Mandarin gold, and late emerald. The candleholder could also be reversed and used as an ashtray, available in Stackaway sets of four. $8.00 – 12.00.

CB-165. No. 1715 CANDLEHOLDER IN LATE EMERALD, WITH REVERSED ASHTRAY AND STACKED SET IN BACKGROUND

No. 5000/67 Heirloom candlestick. 3½" high. The diameter of the bowl is 4¼" and the diameter of the base is 3". Made from 1953 to 1954 in crystal only. Although this candlestick was new in 1953, it was part of a pattern that was originally made in the late 1920s and 1930s as, variously, the Centennial Line, Victorian Line and, ultimately, Martha Washington. This pattern is also very similar to Fostoria's No. 2574 Raleigh (originally introduced in 1939, but still in production in the 1950s). $20.00 – 25.00.

CB-166. No. 5000/67 HEIRLOOM CANDLE-STICK

No. 5000/68 Heirloom candlestick. 4½" high. Made from 1953 to 1954 in crystal only. Very similar to the earlier No. 72 Martha Washington candlestick, made in the 1930s. (See CB-91 on p. 76.) $20.00 – 25.00.

One other candlestick in the Heirloom pattern, the No. 5000/70 9" candlestick (also offered as the No. 5000/71 candelabrum base and the 5000/72 candelabrum) was a carryover from the earlier Martha Washington pattern. (See CB-57b on p. 65.)

CB-167. No. 5000/68 HEIRLOOM CANDLE-STICK, FROM 1953 CATALOG

No. 1957/120 Sonata two-light candlestick. Dimensions unknown. Made ca. 1956 to 1958. Made in crystal and, possibly, carmen. This and the candlestick below were the only new ones added to the line after the factory reopened in 1956 as a worker-owned stock company. Unable to price.

CB-168. No. 1957/120 SONATA TWO-LIGHT CANDLESTICK, FROM 1956 CATALOG

No. 1957/121 Sonata candlestick. 5⅜" high with a 3¼" diameter base. Made ca. 1956 to 1958 in crystal and carmen. Crystal: $35.00 – 40.00. Carmen: $45.00 – 55.00.

CB-169. No. 1957/121 SONATA CANDLESTICK IN CARMEN

CAMBRIDGE ARMS

Crystal witchery ... with Cambridge Arms

You can create endless decorative arrangements with these exciting new *switchabouts* in Cambridge Crystal

The units shown below go together in many, many exquisite combinations—from simplest flower holder to elaborate candlestick arrangements—a challenge to your ingenuity and a compliment to your good taste. Featured and demonstrated at leading stores. Items range from about $1 to $4. No finer gift for the home or bride!

Cambridge Arms Basic Units

Cambridge Arm becomes a candleholder . . .

now a flower centerpiece . . .

now a lazy susan

Send for these booklets
A book of Cambridge Arms settings plus "The Art of Making Fine Glassware" are yours for 10c. Send for them.

50th year GENUINE HAND MADE Cambridge MADE IN U.S.A.

The Cambridge Glass Company, Cambridge, Ohio

CB-170. FROM *Living for Young Homemakers*, DECEMBER 1951

The Cambridge Arms have been referred to several times in the previous pages. This group of accessories were intended to be used by themselves or with any candlestick. The candlesticks that Cambridge specifically used as part of the set included the No. 510 Pristine ball candlestick (see CB-140 on p. 89), the No. 628 low candlestick (see CB-58 on p. 65), the No. 653 8" candlestick (originally No. 200/4 – see CB-33 on p. 58), and the No. 1596 6½" candlestick (see CB-157 on p. 93).

The Cambridge Arms were introduced in 1949 and made until 1958 when the factory closed. They will generally be found in crystal only, though the peg nappy and bird figure are known in late emerald and the small peg vase in ebon (black with a matte finish). They were offered with at least one cutting, No. 1053 Harvest.

The pieces available to be mixed and matched included the No. 1563 Cambridge arm itself (a central candle cup with three arms radiating from it, each containing an additional candle cup), the No. 1562 vase arm (with open loops at the end of the three arms to hold tapered vases), the No. 2355 epergne vases used with the foregoing, the No. 1633 small peg vase, the No. 1634 large peg vase, the No. 1363 peg nappy, the No. 19 bobeche with prisms, and the No. P431 13" bowl. In addition, there was a No. 1636 bird figure, the No. 1138 figural bird flower block, and the No. 1606 hurricane shade. Not surprisingly, the advertisement seen here offers these units as "a challenge to your ingenuity"! The pieces could be bought individually, as desired, or an 11 piece set was offered that could be arranged 29 different ways — for candles, flowers, or even as a lazy Susan. There were sets as large as 24 pieces. Catalogs offered at least 58 different sets. Some of the arrangements shown have the various accessories put together almost like tinker toys.

There were three patents for the arms. The first, D151,067, filed September 19, 1947, and approved September 21, 1948, was apparently never put into production. It consisted of three arms, but instead of a center candle cup had a finial. D154,701, filed April 7, 1949, and approved August 2, 1949, was for the vase arm (called an "epergne spider or similar article"). D154,796, filed April 25, 1949, and approved August 9, 1949, was for the version of the Cambridge arm that was actually manufactured. Wilbur L. Orme, president of the company, was given as designer for all three items.

Farber Brothers offered the arms with three chrome-encased nappies inserted in a chrome candlestick as part of their Krome-Kraft line in 1950.

Heisey made an almost identical peg nappy for use with their No. 1619 Block Five candlestick in 1951. It is slightly smaller (4¾" in diameter compared to 5" for the Cambridge one); also the Cambridge peg has ridges on it, while the Heisey one is smooth and marked with the Diamond H at the bottom of the peg. Jeannette and Colony Glassware (see CL-8 on p. 111) both also made peg nappies for use in some of their candlesticks.

Imperial reissued the Cambridge arm, small peg vase, peg nappy, and bobeche with the No. 628 candlestick from the 1960s to 1970.

CANTON GLASS COMPANY, Marion, Indiana (1903 – 1958), Hartford City, Indiana

(1958 – 1999). The original Canton Glass Company was founded in 1883 in Canton, Ohio, and moved to Marion, Indiana, after being destroyed by fire. In 1899, they became part of the National Glass Company. In 1902, National closed the factory, dismantling the plant and removing all equipment and molds to the Cambridge Glass Company. It was at this time that a new company was incorporated, retaining the Canton name, but erecting a brand new factory. The founder was Leon Nussbaum, who remained active in the management of the firm until his death in 1929. His son then became president until his death in 1945. In 1952, after the Paden City Glass Manufacturing Company went out of business, most of their molds were acquired by Canton. In 1958, the company was moved to Hartford City, Indiana. A company office was still in existence in 1999, but no longer manufacturing glassware; however, as of this writing, it no longer appears in current directories.

The company produced pressed and blown glassware, including tableware, tumblers, stemware, bar and soda fountain goods, photographic supplies, druggist, hospital, and laboratory glassware, automotive devices, sidewalk and skylight glass, and extensive private mold work. Their letterhead in 1938 stated that they were manufacturers of "best quality pot glass in all colors." Much further research is needed on this company, who undoubtedly made many candlesticks in addition to the ones noted below.

LABEL FROM THE 1950S

COLORS

In the 1920s, in addition to crystal, blue and opal were also offered. In 1932, ruby, cobalt, rose, green, crystal, and gold amber were advertised. By 1935, it was reported that eighteen colors were being made, including deep purple. Colors in the 1950s included amber, blue, gold, green, and jet black. The 1962 catalog offered light blue, light green, dark green, royal blue, amber, and smoke.

Crucifix candlestick. 9½" high. Appears in a catalog ca. 1919 – 1924. Offered in crystal, opal, and blue. Crystal: $20.00 – 25.00. Opal: $30.00 – 50.00. Blue: $130.00 – 175.00.

CN-1. CRUCIFIX CANDLESTICK IN OPAL

No. 2027 Colonial candlestick. 7" high. Appears in a catalog dated ca. 1919 – 1924. Offered in crystal and opal. Almost identical to Gillinder and Sons' earlier No. 14 candlestick, except that the Gillinder piece does not have the pattern on the base. Crystal: $20.00 – 25.00. Opal: $25.00 – 30.00.

CN-2. No. 2027 COLONIAL CANDLESTICK, FROM CATALOG, CA. 1919 – 1924

Florence candlestick. 9" high. Appears in a catalog dated ca. 1919 – 1924. Offered in crystal with ground and polished top and bottom. $30.00 – 35.00.

CN-3. FLORENCE CANDLESTICK, FROM CATALOG, CA. 1919 – 1924

CN-4. FLORENCE JUNIOR CANDLESTICK, FROM CATALOG, CA. 1919 – 1924

Florence junior candlestick. 3½" high. Appears in a catalog dated ca. 1919 – 1924. Offered in crystal. This would be considered a toy size by collectors. $35.00 – 40.00.

CN-5. No. 2038½ TOY CANDLESTICK, FROM CATALOG, CA. 1919 – 1924

No. 2038½ imitation cut candlestick. 3½" high. Appears in a catalog dated ca. 1919 – 1924. Offered in crystal. This would be considered a toy size by collectors. The New Martinsville Glass Manufacturing Company also made a very similar toy. (See CN-6 below for further information.) $35.00 – 40.00.

CN-6. No. 2938 IMITATION CUT GLASS CANDLESTICK, FROM CATALOG, CA. 1919 – 1924

No. 2038 imitation cut candlestick. 7½" high. Appears in a catalog dated ca. 1919 – 1924. Offered in crystal. A larger version of the toy candlestick above. Other companies made very similar candlesticks with imitation cut edges. The Canton candlestick differs from these in having the imitation cut motif only on the body of the candlestick itself, with a clearly demarcated candle cup that is plain, without the "cutting." The Tarentum Glass Company's "Electric" candlesticks (5" and 8" heights) and the New Martinsville Glass Manufacturing Company's No. 15 candlesticks (available in 3½", 5½", 7", and 8½" sizes) both have the "cutting" extending all the way up to the top rim of the candlestick. A third, unknown candlestick (7" high) is shaped like the Tarentum/New Martinsville examples, but with the "cutting" only extending to the constriction, or "neck," and not all the way to the top. The pattern of the serration on all of these candlesticks also appears to differ from that used on the Canton. $25.00 – 30.00.

CN-7. CASUAL CANDLEHOLDER, GREEN SWIRLED BASE WITH CRYSTAL TOP

Casual candleholder. 2¼" high, with a diameter of 4¼" at the top and 1½" at the bottom of the base. Advertised in 1951 in crystal with green, blue, or gold base, and amber with a black base. A crystal and black combination is also possible, since *Giftwares and Home Fashions* for August 1951 mentions "four color tones combined with crystal." The bottom of the candleholder is ground. The Casual pattern was available in a complete line of decorative and useful accessories, including a cigarette set, vases, relish dishes, flared bowls, nut dishes, a covered candy dish, and handled bonbon. The trade journal above described the pattern as "handmade glass of sparkling color tones that radiate in flowing swirls from the thick base to the crystal contours of each piece." $25.00 – 30.00.

In 1952, after the Paden City Glass Manufacturing Company went out of business, most of their molds were acquired by Canton. According to William P. Walker, author of a book on Paden City glass (forthcoming as of this writing), it appears that Canton did not make any use of these molds. They also acquired Paden City's unsold inventory, which consisted of several freight car loads of glass, which they sold through their 1954 catalog, including the following:

CN-8. No. 192 CANDLESTICK, FROM 1954 CATALOG (PADEN CITY MOLD)

No. 192 candlestick. Included as part of the "191 line" by Canton, called Party line by Hazel Marie Weatherman. 3½" high with a 4⅞" diameter round base. Offered by Canton in crystal in their 1954 catalog; originally made by Paden City in the 1920s in crystal, amber, black, blue, green, and possibly other colors. $12.00 – 15.00.

No. 215 candlestick. Called Hotcha by Hazel Marie Weatherman. 4⅞" high with a 4³⁄₁₆" diameter round base. Offered by Canton in crystal in their 1954 catalog; originally made by Paden City in the 1930s in crystal, black, ruby, and probably other colors. $25.00 – 30.00.

CN-9. No. 215 CANDLESTICK, FROM 1954 CATALOG (PADEN CITY MOLD)

No. 330 single candlestick. Called Luli by Hazel Marie Weatherman. 6½" high with a 5" diameter round base. Offered by Canton in crystal in their 1954 catalog; originally made by Paden City in the 1930s. This mold is currently owned by the Summit Art Glass Company, who reissued this candlestick in ruby in 2001. The Summit version has a domed base, making it 6¾" high with a 4⅜" diameter base. $30.00 – 35.00.

CN-10. No. 330 SINGLE CANDLESTICK, FROM 1954 CATALOG (PADEN CITY MOLD)

No. 444 single candlestick. Called Vale by Hazel Marie Weatherman. 6¼" high with a 4⅞" diameter round base. Offered by Canton in crystal in their 1954 catalog; originally made by Paden City in the 1930s in crystal and probably light blue. Sometimes confused with Imperial's Candlewick, which includes a similar candlestick, but with only three beads forming the stem, rather than four. $20.00 – 25.00.

CN-11. No. 444 SINGLE CANDLESTICK (PADEN CITY MOLD)

No. 444 two-way candlestick. Called Vale by Hazel Marie Weatherman and sometimes also referred to as Nine Ball. 5" high with a 5¼" diameter round base and an arm spread of 6". Offered by Canton in crystal in their 1954 catalog; originally made by Paden City in the 1930s in crystal and light blue. Sometimes confused with Imperial's Candlewick; however this candlestick is very different from any that appear in that line. $30.00 – 35.00.

CN-12. No. 444 TWO-WAY CANDLESTICK (PADEN CITY MOLD)

No. 900 single candlestick. Called Nadja by Hazel Marie Weatherman. 4¾" high with a 5" diameter round base. Offered by Canton in crystal in their 1954 catalog; originally made by Paden City in the 1930s in crystal, forest green, and possibly other colors. $25.00 – 30.00.

CN-13. No. 900 SINGLE CANDLESTICK (PADEN CITY MOLD)

CN-14. No. 900 TWO-WAY CANDLE-STICK, FROM 1954 CATALOG (PADEN CITY MOLD)

No. 900 two-way candlestick. Called Nadja by Hazel Marie Weatherman. 6" high. Offered by Canton in crystal in their 1954 catalog; originally made by Paden City in the 1930s in crystal and possibly forest green. $30.00 – 35.00.

CN-15. No. 1503 SINGLE CANDLE-STICK (PADEN CITY MOLD)

No. 1503 single candlestick. Called Trance by Hazel Marie Weatherman. 3" high with a 4⅞" diameter round base. A version of this candlestick has also been seen with a square base, but it isn't known if this was made by Canton or Paden City. The candlestick with the round base was offered by Canton in crystal in their 1954 catalog and originally made by Paden City in the 1940s. $12.00 – 15.00.

CAPE COD GLASS COMPANY, Sandwich, Massachusetts (1859 – 1869). Founded
by Deming Jarves, who had previously established the Boston and Sandwich Glass Company (see p. 35) only half a mile from his new company. However, a serious disagreement with the directors led to his resignation and the creation of a competing factory, initially as the Cape Cod Glass Works. Its output of tableware, lamp goods, and other standard ware was often nearly identical to that of the more well-established Sandwich firm, though Cape Cod's production was considerably smaller. Distinguishing between the products of Cape Cod, Sandwich, and the New England Glass Company can be very difficult.

John William Jarves had joined his father at the Cape Cod factory, but died young. The elder Jarves's dreams of a wholly family-owned business died when his son did. The firm was reorganized as the Cape Cod Glass Company in 1864, with the establishment of a board of directors consisting of outside investors. When Deming Jarves died in 1869, the decision to close the factory had already been made, with none of his surviving children interested in continuing the business and with various mounting problems discouraging the stockholders from a willingness to invest further.

In addition to the two candlesticks shown, Cape Cod is also known to have made a toy candlestick, but other candlesticks are also likely to have been offered by this firm.

COLORS
Cape Cod made all of the popular colors of the time, including crystal, canary, opal, sapphire blue, and probably many others. Various color formulas were also perfected at Cape Cod, including four pastel opaque colors, pearl gray opal, lilac opal, rose-colored opal, and turquoise.

CC-1. CALVARY CANDLE-STICK IN OPAL

Calvary candlestick. Crucifix with twelve-sided base and crosses on the hexagonal candle cup. 12¾" high with a 4⅞" diameter base. Produced circa 1859 – 1869. Very similar to Crucifix candleholders made by the Boston and Sandwich Glass Company and Hobbs, Brockunier and Company (both before and after the latter joined the United States Glass Company). All three Crucifixes are the same size and were made in two parts, with the candle cup attached to the base by a wafer. The Hobbs/U.S. Glass Crucifix has many subtle differences that make it comparatively easy to spot, like a reinforcing ring around the candle opening, a wider cross and much less detail in the Christ figure than either of the other companies renderings. However, the Boston and Sandwich version (BS-13 on p. 38) is almost identical to the Cape Cod making it much more difficult to distinguish between the two. Furthermore, the Cape Cod mold appears to have been modified at some point, removing three circles on Christ's right leg (see CC-1a) and making the area where the candle cup attaches smaller. This made it even more similar to the Boston and Sandwich version. In their book, *A Guide to Sandwich Glass*, Barlow and Kaiser reference differences in the way the wafer is applied as a determining factor in who manufactured the candlestick but we have seen exceptions to this method. The exception appears to occur when the original "hidden" wafer didn't adhere properly. Rather than waste the piece a more conventional wafer was inserted and the stick was saved, but the additional wafer now makes the Cape Cod Crucifix appear to be the Boston & Sandwich when using this method of distinguishing between the two. The before mentioned circles on

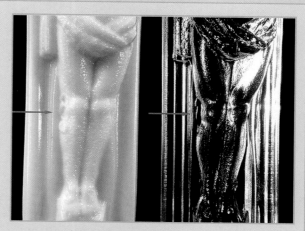

CC-1A. Close-up showing detail of Christ's leg

Christ's leg were never in the Boston & Sandwich mold, so if you have one with the circles it's a Cape Cod, but as you see in illustration CC-1a, the circles were removed at some point leaving only a trace of their existence behind. The best way we have found to differentiate between the two is to look above Christ's left arm for a continuation of the groove that outlines the cross. The Boston and Sandwich Crucifix shows a corner of this detail, the Cape Cod does not (see BS-13a on p. 38). Other differences are pointed out in the appendix on Crucifixes and religious candleholders in volume three of this series. Fostoria made a candelabra using an almost identical base, raising the possibility that they may have made this style of candlestick as well. Known in opal and crystal. Any other color should be considered rare. Crystal: $75.00 – 100.00. Opal: $100.00 – 125.00.

Dolphin candlestick. 6½" high with a 4" scalloped base. Called a "Dolphin French candlestick" in a list compiled by Deming Jarves in 1867. Circa 1855 – 1870. This base has 16 scallops around its circumference and is known with two different sockets, attached via a wafer. The shorter version, shown here, has a round socket with 12 petals around the rim. Belknap's *Milk Glass* shows the same base with a much taller, octagonal socket. Belknap lists the height of that version at 8¼".

There is some uncertainty about the manufacturer of this candlestick. We're attributing it to Cape Cod but with a disclaimer that it could be Boston & Sandwich. Belknap describes the taller version as "Sandwich," but both the Cape Cod Glass Company and the Boston and Sandwich Glass Company were located in the town of Sandwich so we aren't sure of his inference. Ray Barlow and Joan Kaiser clearly define how they use the term "Sandwich glass" in their introduction to *A Guide to Sandwich Glass*: "It is simple to describe Sandwich glass. It was all glass that was produced within Sandwich, Massachusetts, a town on Cape Cod that was founded in 1637." The same dolphin candlestick shown here is pictured in that book, but they only refer to it as Sandwich and don't specifically assign it to a company. The last sentence of their description seems to infer that they place it in the Cape Cod category but they never actually say so. That sentence reads: "A list of glassware manufactured by the Cape Cod Glass Company includes both short and tall dolphin candlesticks, in clear, opal, and blue." We think this descrip-

CC-2. Short dolphin candlestick

tion nicely fits the candlestick shown here, since this and the taller version are identical except for the height and the shape of the candle cup. (Usually companies made a small and large version and would describe them as such, as opposed to "short and tall.") Furthermore, most Boston & Sandwich sockets were used on more than one base, but we have never seen these sockets on any other candlestick. Regardless of who the manufacturer was, all of these candlesticks are rare. Blue would have to be considered very rare. Crystal: $250.00 – 300.00. Opal: $375.00 – 450.00. Blue: $700.00 to market.

CENTRAL GLASS WORKS, Wheeling, West Virginia (1863 – 1939). Sometimes referred

to as the East Wheeling Glass Works. Founded as a co-operative factory by a group of glassworkers, including John Oesterling, who became the first president. He was succeeded in 1883 by Nathan B. Scott, who had been sales manager and secretary of the company. In 1891, Central became factory O of the newly formed United States Glass Company. However, the plant was only operated for a short period by the combine and many of its molds were moved to other member factories. Nathan Scott resigned and was instrumental a few years later in engineering the purchase of the factory, which had lain idle since 1893, by a group of local investors. In 1896, the factory reopened with Scott once again established as its president. Although Scott had been a United States Senator since as early as 1887, he also remained president of the company until his death in 1924.

CA. 1909 – 1920S

Central's early output included tableware, novelties, and lighting goods. Among many patterns known to collectors today, the most famous was their Silver Age pattern, or Coin glass, as it is better known. The reopened plant specialized in pressed and blown stemware, both cut and etched, and hotel and barware of all kinds. Throughout its history, Central sold large quantities of glassware outside the United States, particularly in England.

In 1919, they purchased the molds for the famous Chippendale pattern, which had been originated by the Ohio Flint Glass Company in 1907 and then made by the Jefferson Glass Company from 1908 to 1918. Central also obtained the rights to the Krys-Tol trademark. Pieces marked Krys-Tol might be from any of the three companies. With Prohibition affecting the market for many of Central's major products, this proved to be a timely acquisition, becoming their major line during the 1920s. In 1933, the molds were sold once again to George Davidson & Company in England.

1919 – 1920S

In 1922, they began yet another new venture with the production of "off-hand table and fancy ware," produced without molds. These art glass pieces included candlesticks in heights ranging from 10" to 18". A spectacular example in cobalt blue and opal can be seen in the Oglebay Institute Glass Museum's collection and is included in their publication, *Wheeling Glass, 1829 – 1939*.

By the 1930s, the Depression was taking its toll. The company closed for a while in 1932 and only reopened when Prohibition was repealed. Even then, they were not able to fully recover and in 1939 they closed for good. At that time, the molds were sold to the Imperial Glass Corporation.

Considering how many years Central was in business, there is relatively little information available about their lines. It is likely that there are many additional candlesticks made by this company that are unknown at present.

1930S

COLORS

Central's production in the pre-U.S. Glass years was primarily crystal, but also included opal, blue opaque, amber, canary yellow, electric blue, and cobalt blue. The re-opened factory seems to have produced crystal only. In 1922, as mentioned above, the company began producing free-hand ware in amethyst, royal blue, canary, and Pomona green, with either white or black edging. These same colors were used for pressed pieces as well, both clear and with satin finish. By 1924, celeste blue, mirror black, and Chinese jade had been added. In 1925, amber shading to white opalescent was advertised as new. Later ads that same year also mention rose, light blue, emerald, amber, and purple. In 1927, orchid was introduced (known as lavender to collectors today). Ruby and topaz were also made in the 1920s. Golden sapphire was introduced in 1931. Other colors are possible.

CE-1. No. 730
CANDLESTICKS

No. 730 candlestick. 10" high with a 3½" square base. This pattern appears in a Central catalog dating to ca. 1885. Unlike most block patterns from the nineteenth century, the motif on this one is more like bricks, laid crossways and overlapping one another. The pattern has been named Picture Window by collectors. $100.00 – 150.00.

No. 691 candlestick. 10¼" high with a 5" diameter round base. Made by Central ca. 1885 – 1891. After Central became part of the U.S. Glass Company, the mold was removed to Factory C (the old Challinor, Taylor plant), and this candlestick remained in production until the mid-1890s. Offered by Central in crystal only (all clear, with a satin finish, or with just the cherub etched). U.S. Glass also offered this candlestick in opal. A very similar candlestick was also made by Baccarat in the nineteenth century and may have been copied by Central. $100.00 – 150.00.

CE-2. No. 691 CANDLESTICK

No. T305 Chippendale toy candlestick. 2¼" high with a 2½" hexagonal base. Made ca. 1919 to the mid-1920s. Crystal only. Sometimes marked Krys-Tol on the top of the base. Originally made from 1910 to 1918 by the Jefferson Glass Company. $25.00 – 30.00.

CE-3. No. T305 CHIPPENDALE TOY CANDLESTICK, MARKED KRYS-TOL

No. T310 Chippendale candlestick. 6½" high with a 3¾" diameter hexagonal base. Made ca. 1919 to the mid-1920s; previously made ca. 1910 – 1918 by the Jefferson Glass Company. Known in crystal only, though colors are possible. May be marked Krys-Tol. $20.00 – 25.00.

CE-4. No. T310 CHIPPENDALE CANDLESTICK

Is It Chippendale?

Toy candlestick. 4⅜" high with a 2½" diameter base. Very similar to the No. T310 candlestick above, but with a hollow base. Known in crystal only. $35.00 – 40.00.

CE-5. TOY CANDLESTICK, POSSIBLY CHIPPENDALE

No. T314 Chippendale candlestick, 4½" high with a 3" diameter hexagonal base; No. T317 Chippendale candlestick, 7½" high with a 4⅝" diameter hexagonal base; and tall Chippendale candlestick, pattern number unknown, 9½" high with a 5" diameter hexagonal base.

Made by Central from 1919 to the mid-1920s in the two smaller sizes; we have not found catalog evidence that the 9½" size was also reissued by Central, but it seems likely that it was. This was the earliest of the Chippendale pattern candlesticks, patented by Benjamin W. Jacobs for the Ohio Flint Glass Company in 1907 and then produced by Jefferson from 1908 to 1918. Known in crystal and canary. Sometimes marked Krys-Tol or "PAT JUNE 11 1907 Krys-Tol." The small size is popular with collectors of toy glassware. An almost identical candlestick, listed as 4" high, was advertised by Westmoreland in 1910 as No. 1015S and remained in production through the end of the 1920s. Toy: $35.00 – 40.00. Medium: $30.00 – 40.00. Large: $40.00 – 60.00.

CE-6. No. T317 CHIPPENDALE CANDLESTICKS, THREE SIZES

CE-7. No. T332
CHIPPENDALE
CANDLESTICK,
FROM EARLY
CATALOG

No. T332 Chippendale candlestick. Also listed as No. T333, with puntied bottom and cut top. 9" high. Made by Central from 1919 to the mid-1920s. Made prior to that by Jefferson from ca. 1910 to 1918. Known in crystal only. May be marked Krys-Tol. An almost identical candlestick was made by Josef Inwald, A.G., a Czechoslovakian manufacturer, in the 1920s – 1930s. $30.00 – 35.00.

CE-8. No. T335
CHIPPENDALE
CANDLESTICK

No. T335 Chippendale candlestick. Also listed as No. T336 with a cut top. 8½" high with a five-sided scalloped base, approximately 4⅜" wide, and a ribbed column. Made by Central from 1919 to the mid-1920s. Made prior to that by Jefferson from ca. 1910 to 1918. Known in crystal only. May be marked Krys-Tol. A close copy of this candlestick was also made by Josef Inwald, A.G., of Czechoslovakia, ca. 1925 – 1935. $35.00 – 40.00.

CE-9.
No. T340
CHIPPENDALE
CANDLESTICK

No. T340 Chippendale candlestick. 8" high with a 4" square base. Made by Central from 1919 to the mid-1920s. Previously made by Jefferson ca. 1910 – 1918 in crystal and Corona (a white opaque glass resembling marble). Offered by Central in crystal as No. T340 and in moonstone as No. T341. Puntied bottom and cut top. May be marked Krys-Tol. Used as a blank for at least two cuttings, No. 10 and 12. Very similar candlesticks were made by both the New Martinsville Glass Mfg. Company and the Paden City Glass Mfg. Company in a series of heights: 3½", 5½", 7" and 8½". Both the New Martinsville and Paden City candlesticks will have a pressed star in the base, whereas the Chippendale candlesticks have a puntied bottom or a plain unfinished bottom. Cambridge also made a somewhat similar candlestick as their No. 916. (See CB-24 on p. 55.) $25.00 – 30.00.

CE-10.
No. T345
CHIPPENDALE
CANDLESTICK
IN CANARY

No. T345 Chippendale candlestick. Also offered as No. T346 with puntied bottom and cut top. 9½" with a 4" square base. Made 1919 to the mid-1920s. Known in crystal, green, and canary. May be marked Krys-Tol. Although most of the Chippendale molds were obtained from the Jefferson Glass Company, it is unknown whether this one was among them or whether it originated at Central. Crystal: $35.00 – 40.00. Colors: $50.00 – 65.00.

No. T355 Chippendale candlestick. Also offered as No. T356 with a puntied bottom. 9½" high. Made by Central from 1919 to the mid-1920s, who apparently added the thick rim on the candle cup. Known in crystal only. Originally made by Jefferson from ca. 1910 to 1918 in crystal and canary with a much thinner rim on the candle cup. May be marked Krys-Tol. $25.00 – 30.00.

CE-11. No. T355 CHIPPENDALE CANDLESTICK, FROM *CROCKERY & GLASS JOURNAL*, MAY 6, 1920

No. T360 Chippendale candlestick. Also offered as No. T361 with cut top and puntied bottom and as No. T362 with cut top and with the PresCut floral design etched. 8½" high with a 4½" diameter hexagonal base. Made 1919 to the mid-1920s. Known in crystal only. May be marked Krys-Tol. Although most of the Chippendale molds were obtained from the Jefferson Glass Company, it is unknown whether this one was among them or whether it originated at Central. $45.00 – 60.00. *(From the collection of Helen & Bob Jones.)*

CE-12. No. T360 CHIPPENDALE CANDLESTICK

No. T370 Chippendale candlestick. Also offered as No. T371 with the PresCut floral design on the column etched and with a cut top and puntied bottom. 8½" high with a 4¼" diameter hexagonal base. Originally issued by Jefferson from ca. 1910 to 1918 and called Hepplewhite. Made by Central from 1919 to the mid-1920s. Known in crystal only. The bottom of the candle cup and the column feature a PresCut flower design. May be marked Krys-Tol. $35.00 – 40.00.

CE-13. No. T370 CHIPPENDALE (HEPPLEWHITE) CANDLESTICK

Candlestick. Called Memphis by Hazel Marie Weatherman. 6½" high. Made ca. 1923 in satin finish blue, black, canary, green, and amethyst, both plain and etched. Plain satin blue, green, black: $20.00 – 30.00. Amethyst, canary: $30.00 – 35.00. Etched: add 10 – 25%.

CE-14. MEMPHIS CONSOLE SET, FROM 1923 ADVERTISEMENT

LOOKALIKES

Various companies made very similar candlesticks. Paden City Glass Mfg. Company's No. 116 candlestick, made in 7" and 9½" heights, seems to differ only noticeably in that the ring at the top of the Central candlestick is immediately below the candle cup, whereas the ring on the Paden City candlestick is separated from it by approximately ⅛". The Westmoreland No. 1042, made in 6½" and 9" heights, has a differently shaped candle cup and the ring at the bottom of the column is separated from the base, rather than touching it as the Central one does. (Westmoreland also made the same candlestick as No. 1803, with the column crackled.) The Lancaster Glass Company's No. 85 candlestick (not pictured) is similar to the Westmoreland one, but without a ring at the bottom of the column.

CE-14A. PADEN CITY No. 116 CANDLESTICK, FROM CATALOG

CE-14B. WESTMORELAND No. 1042 CANDLESTICK, FROM CATALOG

CE-15. No. 2000 CANDLESTICKS IN COBALT BLUE, JADE GREEN, CANARY, TRANSPARENT GREEN STRETCH, AND WHITE OPALESCENT

No. 2000 candlestick, often referred to as trumpet shaped. Originally advertised as Chippendale Krys-Tol. Called Zaricor by Hazel Marie Weatherman. Made in two heights: 9" and 7". Produced from 1924 to sometime in the 1930s. Known in many colors, including amber shading to white opalescent, amethyst, blue, canary, celeste blue, Chinese jade, cobalt blue, green, mirror black, pink, sapphire, white opalescent, and crystal with fired on colors. Many of the colors were also offered with a satin finish or an iridescent stretch finish. Various etchings and other decorations are also possible. Short, crystal with fired on colors: $14.00 – 18.00; black, green, jade, sapphire, pink: $15.00 – 20.00; white opalescent, amber opalescent: $35.00 – 40.00; cobalt, canary: $35.00 – 40.00. Tall, crystal with fired on colors: $18.00 – 22.00; black, green, jade, sapphire, pink: $30.00 – 35.00; white opalescent, amber opalescent: $45.00 – 50.00; cobalt, canary: $45.00 – 50.00.

A number of other companies made this particular style candlestick, making it very difficult to identify with absolute certainty. John Madeley and Dave Shetlar, in their *American Iridescent Stretch Glass*, offer a number of useful hints. Part of what follows is indebted to their research.

The 9" height was only made by one other company, Diamond Glass-Ware Company (see DI-7 on p. 133), and it is fairly easy to differentiate between the candlesticks in this height. The Central candlestick has a rounded top rim with no mold seams; similarly the base is curved and the mold seams stop just above the place where the base curves down. The Diamond candlestick, on the other hand, has visible mold seams on the top rim and the base is a ⅜" high straight-sided rim. (For a comparison of the candle cups on these two candlesticks, see p. 134.)

The smaller size was made in six versions that we know of, only some of which can be associated to known companies. Once again, the Central version has a rounded top rim with no mold seams; similarly the base is curved and the mold seams stop just above where the base curves down. The Vineland Flint Glass Works' candlestick has three small rings beneath the candle cup, compared to all the others, which only have two. The Northwood Company's No. 719 candlestick is shorter (only 6¼" to 6½" high), has a less elongated candle cup, and the hollow portion only extends about a third of the way up the inside of its column. The Co-operative Flint Glass Company's No. 481 candlestick is the most similar to Central's, but comes from a three-part mold, a characteristic shared by other Co-operative candlesticks, unlike all of the other trumpet-style candlesticks that are from two-part molds. Another very similar candlestick is closer to 6⅞" and has a candle cup with a top rim that is ⅛" thick; the hollow part of its base extends halfway up its column and is only slightly rounded at the top when looked at through the side of the candlestick. Yet another unknown candlestick is 6¾" in height and has no measurable top rim; the hollow portion of its base also extends about halfway up the column, but comes to a slight point when seen from the side. We have found no documentation for this last style.

CE-15A. No. 2000 CANDLE-STICK IN CANARY STRETCH AND CELESTE BLUE

CE-16. LOW CANDLEHOLDER IN ROSE

Low candleholder. 2¾" high with 4¼" diameter base. Made in the early 1920s. Known in black and rose; other colors are likely. The octagonal top is very similar to the one used on Heisey's No. 114 candlestick in the mid-1920s. Known with at least one etching, No. 530 Harding (the etching used by President Warren G. Harding and his wife as their private dinner service). $14.00 – 18.00. With Harding etching: $25.00 – 30.00.

No. 1426 spiral candlestick. 4" high. Introduced in December 1925 as an addition to Central's spiral stemware line. Offered in crystal, amber, emerald, light blue, and rose. Plain, crystal, amber: $10.00 – 15.00; etched: $12.00 – 18.00. Plain, emerald, blue, rose: $15.00 – 20.00; etched: $18.00 – 22.00.

CE-17. No. 1426 SPIRAL CANDLE-STICK IN AMBER

No. 1426 spiral candlestick. 8" high. Introduced in December 1925 as an addition to Central's spiral stemware line. Offered in crystal, amber, emerald, light blue, and rose. The accompanying drawing is from an advertisement. The authors have never seen this size, so production seems to have been limited. Plain, crystal, amber: $20.00 – 25.00; etched: $25.00 – 30.00. Plain, emerald, blue, rose: $25.00 – 30.00; etched: $30.00 – 35.00.

CE-18. No. 1426 SPIRAL CANDLESTICK, FROM *CROCKERY & GLASS JOURNAL*, DECEMBER 17, 1925

No. 2010 candlestick. 3⅝" high, 3¾" base. Pattern is known as Frances to collectors today. Introduced in 1928. Known in amber, black, green, orchid, and rose. $25.00 – 30.00.

CE-19. No. 2010 FRANCES CANDLESTICK IN GREEN

Rolled edge candleholder, unknown pattern number. 2⅝" to 3" high, up to 5½" at its widest point, and with a 2½" diameter foot. It appears in a 1927 catalog. Known in amber, green, and rose; other colors are likely. On some candlesticks, the mushroom top is turned down more than on others, unlike the flared example in the accompanying photograph. $25.00 – 35.00.

CE-20. ROLLED EDGE CANDLEHOLD-ERS IN ROSE, WITH SILVER OVERLAY

No. 2000 candlestick. 3⅛" with a 4½" diameter base. Made in the early 1930s. Known in crystal, amber, black, blue, green, orchid, and rose, both clear and with satin finish. Sometimes seen with a ruffled base. Known with at least two etchings, Balda and No. 530 Harding (the etching used by President Warren G. Harding and his wife as their private dinner service). Plain, crystal, amber: $8.00 – 10.00; etched: $10.00 – 12.00. Plain, black, green, rose: $10.00 – 12.00; etched: $12.00 – 15.00. Plain, blue, orchid: $12.00 – 15.00; etched: $15.00 – 20.00.

CE-21. No. 2000 CANDLESTICK IN BLACK

CE-22. CANDLE-STICK, UNKNOWN PATTERN NUMBER WITH LORRAINE CUTTING

Candlestick, unknown pattern number. 5¼" high with a 4⅝" diameter base. These candlesticks appear in the spring and summer 1933 catalog for Larkin Premiums with the Lorraine cutting "in floral and bow-knot design." They are known in amber, black, green, and rose, with other colors possible. $45.00 – 60.00. Cut or etched: add 10 – 20%.

CE-23. No. 1470 10 OPTIC CANDLESTICK WITH GREEN TOP

No. 1470 candlestick. 7" high with a 4½" diameter base. The base of this candlestick matches the stemware line known as 10 Optic to collectors. Production dates unknown, but probably sometime in the late 1920s or 1930s. Known in green and rose with crystal stems; other color combinations are possible. The Imperial Glass Company reissued this pattern with Cambridge's Wildflower etching after Cambridge closed in 1958, but there is no indication that the candlestick was among the reissued items. $40.00 – 50.00.

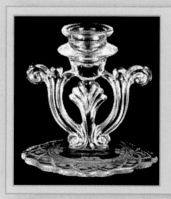

CE-24. CANDLE-STICK, UNKNOWN PATTERN NUMBER, FROM UNDATED CATALOG

Candlestick, unknown pattern number. 5" high. Production dates unknown. Probably made in crystal only, though colors are possible. This candlestick appears in an undated catalog from the Seneca Glass Company as No. 1480 with their No. 834 cutting. It isn't known if Seneca used blanks from Central for cutting or if they borrowed the mold and produced the glassware themselves. In 1940, this was one of the molds acquired by the Imperial Glass Corporation who reissued this candlestick as No. 148 from ca. 1944 to 1956. Plain: $25.00 – 30.00. With a Central etching: $35.00 – 40.00.

CHALLINOR, TAYLOR & COMPANY, Tarentum, Pennsylvania (1884 – 1891).

Also known as the Standard Glass Works. When this company opened its factory in 1884, it had the largest glass melting furnace in the United States. Although only in business for a relatively brief period of time, they produced a number of tableware patterns and novelties in crystal, amber, blue, and canary. They are most famous for their opaque colors: opal, black, olive, and turquoise — as well as mosaic glass (or slag glass, as it is commonly referred to today). Their covered animal dishes are especially sought after by collectors.

In 1891, they joined the United States Glass Company as Factory C. Advertisements from 1892 indicate that the newly formed combine moved a number of molds for candlesticks from other member companies to the Challinor plant, which then took over production of candlesticks previously made by the Central Glass Company; Hobbs, Brockunier; and others. Although only the one candlestick below has been documented as originating at Challinor, it is quite possible that some of the other candlesticks made by the United States Glass Company (see volume 3 of this series) were also initially made by Challinor.

In 1893, the Challinor factory was destroyed by fire and was not rebuilt by U.S. Glass.

Crucifix candlestick. 10¾" with a 4⅜" by 3⅜" rectangular base. Made by Challinor between 1884 and 1891 and by U.S. Glass, as their No. 11 candlestick, from 1891 to 1893. Made in crystal, opal, and turquoise (opaque blue) by Challinor, and in opal and crystal by U.S. Glass. Also known with gold trim. Although many companies made crucifix candlesticks in the late nineteenth – early twentieth centuries, this one is unique in showing Christ carrying the cross on the way to Calvary. The Cristalleries de St. Louis in France show an almost identical figurine on a bust (without the candleholder) in their 1905 catalog, but we have no way of knowing if it might be an earlier piece that served as inspiration for the Challinor candlestick, or the other way around. Crystal: $60.00 – 75.00. Opal: $125.00 – 150.00. Turquoise: $300.00 – 350.00.

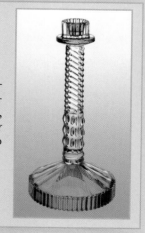

CH-1. CRUCIFIX CANDLESTICK IN TURQUOISE

COLONY GLASSWARE, a division of Pitman-Dreitzer & Company, Inc.; now operating as

Colony, a division of the Lancaster Colony Corporation. Pitman-Dreitzer was established in 1930 as a representative and manufacturer of china and glassware. The earliest reference to Colony Crystal dates to 1939. We have found no evidence that Colony had their own factory. It appears that Pitman-Dreitzer placed orders with different factories in West Virginia and Indiana, with advertisements frequently mentioning Dunkirk as point of origin. This leads us to believe that much of Colony's glass was made by the Indiana Glass Company. Some Colony glassware was also imported.

Not surprisingly, when Indiana Glass Company merged with the Lancaster Glass Company (previously the Lancaster Lens Company) to form the Lancaster Colony Corporation in 1962, Pitman-Dreitzer became a division. The Pitman-Dreitzer name disappears from advertising in the mid-1960s. Colony is still an active division of Lancaster Colony today.

Considering that the distinction between Colony Glassware and the Indiana Glass Company is often blurry at best, with some lines issued under both company's names, further information will be found in the section devoted to the Indiana Glass Company in volume 2 of this series.

LOGO, INTRODUCED CA. 1954 – 1953

CURRENT LOGO

Candlestick. 9" high, with a 4⅜" diameter base. Advertised as new from Pitman-Dreitzer in the July 1937 issue of the *Crockery and Glass Journal*, shown with a bobeche and six prisms. Known in crystal only. This probably predates the formation of Pitman-Dreitzer's Colony Glassware division. Actual manufacturer unknown, but possibly imported. $12.00 – 16.00.

CL-1. PITMAN-DREITZER CANDLESTICK, POSSIBLY IMPORTED

CL-2. TWO-LIGHT CANDLE-HOLDER (PATENT DRAWING)

CL-2. D140,747. Filed December 26, 1944; approved April 3, 1945.
CL-3. D140,974. Filed January 29, 1945; approved April 24, 1945.
CL-4. D141,721. Filed April 9, 1945; approved June 26, 1945.
CL-5. D142,474. Filed March 13, 1945; approved October 2, 1945.

This fascinating series of jeweled design candleholders were patented in 1945 by Charles L. Fordyce, who assigned the patents to Pitman-Dreitzer. Several other pieces in the pattern were also patented, indicating that a certain amount of effort went into developing the line, though only the three-light candleholder has been seen by the authors. This would have been at about the time that the Colony Glassware division was established.

CL-3. CANDLE-HOLDER (PATENT DRAWING)

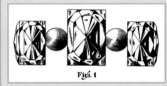

CL-4. THREE-LIGHT CANDLEHOLDER, SIDE VIEW (PATENT DRAWING)

CL-4A. THREE-LIGHT CANDLEHOLDER

CL-5. TWO-LIGHT CANDLE-HOLDER (PATENT DRAWING)

CL-6. DOG-WOOD CANDLE-BLOCKS WITH CRANBERRY STAIN

Dogwood candleblock. 1⅝" high, approximately 3" wide. This was one of the first patterns to be advertised by Colony Glassware in 1948. Offered in crystal with satin finish on the petals or with cornflower blue, cranberry, or ruby stain. (The actual colors vary considerably and were used in conjunction with a yellow stain on the rim of the candle cup.) Plain: $6.00 – 8.00. Stained: $10.00 – 12.00.

CL-7. DOGWOOD TWO-LIGHT CANDLE-BLOCK, WITH CORNFLOWER BLUE STAIN

Dogwood two-light candleblock. 1¾" high, approximately 7" long and 5" wide. This was one of the first patterns to be advertised by Colony Glassware in 1948. Offered in crystal with satin finish on the petals or with cornflower blue, cranberry, or ruby stain. (The actual colors vary considerably and were used in conjunction with a yellow stain on the rims of the candle cups and the centers of the other blossoms.) These candlesticks have also been seen with a Continental Crystal label. It is not known at present if this was a division of Colony or Pitman-Dreitzer. Plain: $10.00 – 12.00. Stained: $15.00 – 20.00.

Epergne hostess set. 9" high assembled. Consists of a 4½" base, a triangular arm with four holders, and three peg nappies. Advertised in *Giftwares*, January 1952, stating that "Cleverly designed removable sections permit its use as Candelabra, Buffet Server, Fruit Bowl, or striking centerpiece." Crystal only. It was shipped F.O.B. Indiana and was probably made for Colony by the Indiana Glass Company. Note similarity of the peg nappies to those used in the Cambridge Arms assortment. (See p. 96.) $40.00 – 50.00.

CL-8. EPERGNE HOSTESS SET

Lana hurricane lamp. 13" high overall, 7" high shade, 6½" high candleholder with a 3½" diameter base. Advertised in July 1962 as part of Colony's Optic Crystal Import Collection. Also known in amber and aquamarine. Actual manufacturer unknown. By this time, Pitman-Dreitzer had become a division of the Lancaster Colony Corporation. $20.00 – 25.00.

CL-9. LANA HURRICANE LAMP IN AMBER

Harvest footed candleholder. 4" high with a 3" diameter base and 4½" diameter bowl. Introduced ca. 1963 by Colony and made for a number of years in milk glass. Actual production was by the Indiana Glass Company who reissued this pattern in 1967 under their own name in carnival finishes, including blue, lime, and amber. The Harvest pattern, with its grape and leaf motif, included a number of serving and accessory pieces and was available in both 15-piece and 35-piece luncheon sets. Milk glass: $6.00 – 8.00. Amber iridescent: $9.00 – 12.00. Blue iridescent, green iridescent: $12.00 – 18.00.

CL-10. HARVEST FOOTED CANDLEHOLDER IN MILK GLASS

CL-11. CROWN THUMBPRINT
FOOTED CANDLEHOLDER IN
GOLD

Crown Thumbprint footed candleholder. Collectors also know this pattern as King's Crown or as Thumbprint. 3⅛" high with a 2⅞" diameter base and 3¾" diameter bowl. Originally made by Indiana Glass Company, ca. 1958 to the early 1960s in crystal (with ruby, cranberry, or blue stain on the rims) and milk glass. (See IN-81 in book 2 of this series.) Indiana then reissued this candleholder in 1966 for Colony Glassware in cobalt, gold (amber), and olive green. (By this time, both Indiana and Colony were divisions of Lancaster Colony.) In 1986, the pattern was reissued a final time by Indiana, this time for Tiara Exclusives, but the footed candleholder was not included. There is considerable confusion about this pattern and it has an unusually complicated history. It was originally introduced by Adams and Company of Pittsburgh in December 1890 as XLCR (or Excelsior), and continued to be made by the United States Glass Company after Adams joined that combine in 1891. U.S. Glass reissued the pattern as Dubonnet in 1943 and again from 1952 to 1962 as, variously, Thumbprint, Old Thumbprint, and King's Crown (the name by which it is best known by collectors today). It has often been reported that Indiana bought the molds from U.S. Glass, modifying some of them; however, as can be seen from the overlapping dates of production (with Indiana first advertising the pattern in 1958 and U.S. Glass including it in catalogs up to 1962), this clearly cannot have been the case. And, in fact, Ruth Hemminger, Ed Goshe, and Leslie Pina report in their *Tiffin Glass, 1940 – 1980,* that interoffice correspondence exists from 1959 in which officers of the U.S. Glass Company complain about Indiana's having "pirated" the pattern. Although "borrowing" one another's patterns was not unusual in the glass industry, in Indiana's defense it should be noted that many other companies made the same pattern, including the D. C. Jenkins Glass Company, the Imperial Glass Company, L. G. Wright, and the Rainbow Art Company (the latter using molds purchased from U.S. Glass) — and Indiana, itself, who claimed that two of the stemware pieces in the pattern could be traced back to a catalog of their own that predated 1910. All these complications aside, it does not appear that any of these other companies, including U.S. Glass, ever made a sherbet-style footed candleholder. Gold, olive: $6.00 – 8.00. Milk glass, crystal, ruby stained: $10.00 – 12.00. Cobalt: $12.00 – 15.00.

CL-12. SANDWICH GLASS CANDLESTICKS IN SUNSET,
BLUE, AND GREEN (DUNCAN MOLD)

Sandwich Glass candlestick. 4" high with a 4⅜" diameter base. Advertised in October 1967 as "Authentic Sandwich Glass, since 1825, a Colony exclusive." Also referred to as Star and Scroll pattern in the same advertisement. In fact, this was a reissue of Duncan & Miller's No. 41-121 Early American Sandwich candlestick, which had initially been made in crystal and milk glass from 1940 to 1953 (first by Duncan and later by Tiffin — see DM-68 on p. 161). The mold was obtained by the Indiana Glass Company in the 1960s who reissued the candlestick for Colony in crystal and possibly other colors. In 1972, Colony once again made this candlestick in blue, green, and sunset (amberina) exclusively for Montgomery Ward for one year only as part of their 100th anniversary. Many Early American Sandwich pieces were later reissued in various colors for Tiara Exclusives, but this candlestick was not among them. $20.00 – 25.00.

CONSOLIDATED LAMP & GLASS COMPANY, Fostoria, Ohio (1894 – 1896), Coraopolis, Pennsylvania (1896 – 1964). This concern originated in 1894 with the purchase of the Fostoria Shade and Lamp Company, which was the largest factory manufacturing lamps and lamp shades in the United States. The new company quickly established its own reputation for fine lamps and other goods, greatly aided by the talents of Nicholas Kopp, who had been general manager of the Fostoria Shade and Lamp Company and retained that position with Consolidated. He had a reputation for developing brilliant new colors and innovative designs.

In 1895, the company demonstrated its success by contracting for a second factory to be built in Coraopolis. The intention was to run both factories. However, when the Fostoria plant was badly damaged by fire, it was decided to move all of the workers to the new location.

Although Consolidated's output remained primarily lamps, shades, and globes, they also produced tableware and novelties from the beginning. As lighting needs changed, the Consolidated continued to meet them, remaining the largest manufacturer of lighting glassware through much of its existence.

In 1926, their art glass division introduced Martelé, the first of a series of sculpted glassware designs that vied with French art glass in elegance and artistic merit. Once again they were indebted to a brilliant designer, Reuben Haley, who was quick to respond to the development of art deco and the work of Rene Lalique in France. Other lines that followed included Catalonian and the very modernistic Ruba Rombic. Consolidated could truthfully claim in their advertisements that they were making glass "different from anything else made in this country."

In 1933, the company succumbed to financial difficulties and closed temporarily. Following the death of Reuben Haley in September of that year, his son Kenneth, who was a designer at the Phoenix Glass Company, obtained control of the molds created by his father and some of them were put into production by Phoenix. However, Phoenix was unable to produce the same fine finishes offered by Consolidated. After the Consolidated reopened under new ownership in 1936, the Haley molds were eventually returned.

Later production included blown, cased vases and, beginning in the early 1950s, hand-painted milk glass, including reissues of some of their earlier molds adapted to a new market. Ultimately, however, the company found itself facing increasing operating losses. When the glassworkers demanded higher wages in 1962, the owners decided they could no longer continue to subsidize a failing business. It was sold and about half the molds were removed to the Sinclair Glass Company in Hartford, Indiana. The remainder of the molds were scrapped. For a while, Sinclair shipped finished blanks to the Consolidated for decorating. However, in 1963, the workers at Coraopolis went on strike and a major fire damaged the plant. In 1964, it was closed for good.

Consolidated glassware from the 1920 – 1930s period (the Martelé era) has become highly sought after. As will be noted from the descriptions below, several of the candlesticks are considered by collectors to be among the most difficult items to find today.

COLORS

During the Consolidated's earliest years, the company was famed for pioneering bright, innovative colors developed by Nicholas Kopp. Most of them were available solid, cased, or satin finish. Although we don't know of any candlesticks made during this period, with the emphasis being on lamps, tableware, and novelties, it gives a good sense of the company's reputation for color to cite the various shades mentioned in ads. 1894: opal, ruby, green, half green (probably a paler color), royal blue, rose, yellow, canary; 1895: mauve; 1896: pearl, orange, terra cotta; 1897: marine, turquoise; 1899: magenta, Mandarin, emerald, cerise, Nile, Cyrano (red); 1902: azure, royal copper (deep red), gold dust (a "burnished gold"); 1903: roughed ruby, sage.

Later colors with their approximate dates of introduction are as follows:

1925	Black satin
1926	French crystal (crystal base with frosted highlighting)
	Martelé was also available with fired-on colors (which could include "a predominating color with one, two, or three complementary colors"); these included ruby, coral, amethyst, yellow, turquoise, brown, blue, and green
1927	Emerald green
	Spanish rose
	Honey (a colored wash on crystal)
	Amethyst (a colored wash on crystal)
	Jade (a colored wash on crystal)

Dec. 1927	Jungle green (a deep emerald green)
	Smoky topaz (a brownish color)
1928	Lilac (a lavender-pink finish on crystal)
	Sunshine (a yellow finish on crystal)
	Jade (an apple green finish on crystal)
	Silver (a silver gray finish on crystal, also known as Silver Gray and Silver Cloud)

Other colors from around this time include crystal with a touch of opalescence, powder blue, black, and red. The above colors probably remained in production until 1933, when the company temporarily closed. When the company reopened, French crystal continued to be made along with three new colors:

1937	Pink (with satin finish)
	Green (with satin finish)
	Daylight blue (with satin finish)
Mar. 1937	Coronation blue
1938	Custard with colored highlights (blue, brown, and red)
1939	Pink crystal (a solid pink, also available frosted)
	Green crystal (a solid green, on the blue side; also available frosted)
1940s	Cased aqua blue (sometimes iridized)
	Cased ash-rose pink (sometimes iridized)
1951	Milk glass

CS-1. No. 2560 MARTELÉ IRIS LOW CANDLE IN
CORONATION BLUE AND WITH PINK WASH

No. 2560 Martelé low candle. Known as Iris. 3⅞" high with a 5½" diameter base. Made 1926 – 1932 and again from 1936 to the early 1940s, then reissued in milk glass in the 1950s. Known in crystal, French crystal (with satin highlights), amethyst, blue, jade green, light green, orchid, pink, russet, sepia, coronation blue, and milk glass. The motif on this candlestick is floral. The milk glass candlesticks may be found decorated with gold or colored highlights. Crystal, blue, milk glass: $20.00 – 40.00. Other colors: $50.00 – 75.00.

CS-2. No. 2561
MARTELÉ IRIS
(FRUIT AND
FLOWERS) HIGH
CANDLE WITH
GREEN WASH

No. 2561 Martelé high candle. Known as Iris or Fruit and Flowers. 10" high with a 5½" diameter base. Made 1926 – 1932 and possibly again from 1936 to the early 1940s. Offered in crystal, French crystal (with satin highlights), amethyst, blue, jade green, light green, orchid, pink, russet, and sepia. All colors: $125.00 – market.

(From the collection of Bill Burke.)

No. 2643 Martelé candle. Listed in catalogs as 8", but actually closer to 6¾" high, with a base that is approximately 5⅜" x 3⅝". Known as Hummingbird, because of the central motif of the hummingbird and flowers. Made ca. 1926 to 1932. Known in amethyst and jade (washes on crystal), but probably also made in other Martelé colors, including French crystal. All colors: $150.00 – market. *(Photograph courtesy of Bruce Mueller and Gary Wickland, from their collection.)*

CS-3. No. 2643 MARTELÉ HUMMINGBIRD CANDLE WITH AMETHYST WASH

Martelé candlestick, pattern number unknown. 3⅛" high with a 5¼" diameter oval base. Known as Orchid. Probably made ca. 1928, since it is known in lilac, sunshine, and jade (colored washes on crystal), all shades that were new that year; other Martelé colors are possible, including French crystal. The pattern on the base has been variously described as orchids and as dogwood. $75.00 – 95.00.

CS-4. MARTELÉ ORCHID CANDLE WITH GREEN WASH

No. 2576 Santa Maria ship candlestick. 5¼" high with a 4⅜" diameter base. This pattern was introduced in 1926, with the ship candlestick appearing in the 1931 catalog. It is one of Consolidated's rarest pieces, indicating that production was very limited. The pattern is known in French crystal, as well as with amber, amethyst, yellow, sepia, jade, and aqua washes. At least one piece in the pattern has been found with a Martelé label. All colors: $750.00 – market.

CS-5. SANTA MARIA SHIP CANDLE-STICKS, GREEN AND SEPIA WASHES *(From the collection of Bill Burke.)*

No. 2562 Santa Maria dolphin candlestick. At least one piece in the pattern has been found with a Martelé label. 9" high with a 4" square base. This pattern was introduced in 1926, with the dolphin candlestick appearing in the 1931 catalog. It is one of Consolidated's rarer pieces, indicating that production was very limited. The pattern is known in French crystal, as well as with amber, amethyst, yellow, sepia, and aqua washes. It is possible that this candlestick was reissued in milk glass in the 1950s; however, in the absence of any documentation for production of the dolphin in this color, unmarked examples in milk glass are more likely reproductions made by Kenneth Haley in 1948. (See below.) All colors: $800.00 – market. *(From the collection of Bill Burke.)*

The dolphin candlestick was actually reproduced by two companies. The K. R. Haley Glassware Company, owned by Kenneth Haley, who previously worked for Consolidated and then Phoenix and was the son of Reuben Haley, designer of the Santa Maria line, produced this candlestick in 1948 in crystal and milk glass, both plain or decorated. The Imperial Glass Company also made this candlestick from 1969 to 1980 in various colors, including milk glass. The Imperial version is marked on the base with the IG trademark and is stippled on the underside of the base. The milk glass versions believed to be either Haley or Consolidated have ground bottoms.

CS-6. SANTA MARIA DOLPHIN CANDLESTICK, WITH SEPIA WASH

Reportedly, neither of these reproductions were made from the original Consolidated mold. According to Jack D. Wilson's *Phoenix & Consolidated Art Glass*, Kenneth Haley stated that he had a new mold made. The same source says that Imperial also used a new mold. After comparing the Consolidated original with both the Imperial reproductions and the milk glass reproductions, however, the authors were unable to detect any differences, indicating that if new molds were made, they were exceptionally close copies.

CS-7. NO. 1131 CATALONIAN CANDLES IN SPANISH ROSE, EMERALD, AND CRYSTAL WITH AMETHYST WASH

No. 1131 Catalonian Old Spanish candle. 2¾" high, 5⅜" across the top, with a 3⅞" base. Made from 1927 to 1932 and probably again from 1936 to the early 1940s. Offered in crystal, emerald, Spanish rose, and crystal with amethyst, honey, and jade washes. This pattern was advertised as "the glass of old Spain" and was designed to emulate seventeenth century handmade glassware. The shapes were irregular and the glass itself has a rough finish, full of bubbles and striations, giving it a deliberately crude appearance. This was another of Reuben Haley's designs, with at least two patents granted in 1929. $30.00 – 50.00. *(From the collection of Bill Burke.)*

CS-8. NO. 1124 CATALONIAN CANDLESTICKS IN EMERALD GREEN AND WITH TRANSLUCENT RED AND GREEN WASHES. NOTE VARIATIONS IN HEIGHT. *(From the collections of the authors and Bill Burke.)*

No. 1124 Catalonian Old Spanish candle. Height ranges from 2¾" to 3¼", depending on whether the base is flattened or not; base diameter ranges from 4½" to 4⅝". Made from 1927 to 1932 and probably again from 1936 to the early 1940s. Offered in crystal, emerald, Spanish rose, and crystal with many different washes, some opaque and some translucent, including rainbow blue shading to crystal. This pattern was advertised as "the glass of old Spain" and was designed to emulate seventeenth century handmade glassware. The shapes were irregular and the glass itself has a rough finish, full of bubbles and striations, giving it a deliberately crude appearance. This was another of Reuben Haley's designs, with at least two patents granted in 1929. $30.00 – 35.00+.

Reissued from 1956 to 1962 as part of the Regent pattern in milk glass, with hand-painted decorations: No. 1326 Violet, 1330 Green Leaf Ivy, 1384 Pine Cone, 1434 Assorted Flowers, 1449G Abstract, 1500G French Daisy, 1501G French Daisy, 1502G Lily, 1503G Dogwood, 1505G Magnolia, 1506G Poppy, 1507G Pussy Willow, 1509G Wheat, 1510G Roses, 1511G Bamboo, 1512G Palm Tree, 1528G Golden Wheat, 1529G Golden Lustre, 1530G Pearl Lustre, and 1543G Gold Lines. $25.00 – 30.00.

CS-8A. NO. 1124 CATALONIAN CANDLESTICKS IN VARIOUS COLORED WASHES. *(From the collection of Bill Burke.)*

CS-8B. NO. 1124 REGENT CANDLESTICKS IN MILK GLASS, WITH HAND-PAINTED DECORATIONS. *(From the collections of the authors and Bill Burke.)*

No. 805 Ruba Rombic candle. 2½" high. Introduced as "an epic in modern art" in February 1928 with a seven-page spread in *The Gift and Art Shop;* probably only in production until the factory temporarily closed in 1933. Offered in French crystal, jungle green, smoky topaz, and various delicately cased colors, including jade, lilac, sunshine (sometimes called honey), and silver gray. Pieces in the pattern are known in other colors, including opalescent, black, and red. This extraordinary pattern was designed by Reuben Haley and was covered by three patents issued in 1928. This is one

CS-9. RUBA ROMBIC CANDLES IN OPALESCENT AND FRENCH CRYSTAL

of the most sought-after patterns from the art deco era. According to advertising copy, the name is derived from "Rubaiy (meaning epic or poem), Rombic (meaning irregular in shape)," though it is more likely that "Ruba" is a derivative of Reuben, the designer. All colors: $250.00 – market. *(From the collection of Bill Burke.)*

CS-9A. RUBA ROMBIC CANDLES IN SMOKY TOPAZ AND JUNGLE GREEN

No. 708 Martelé candle. Sometimes also referred to as Fairy or Dance of the Nudes, though the only pattern appearing on the Line 700 pieces are vines and flowers, so neither name is really appropriate. The original pieces in the line were called Vine in early catalogs. 3¾" high, with a 3¾" base. Made from 1929 to 1932 and probably again 1936 to the early 1940s. Offered in crystal, French crystal (with satin highlights), jade, powder blue, and honey; also known with gray and sepia washes. Other colors are possible, including black satin, bright ruby, matte red, and custard (with color highlights), since other pieces in Line 700 pattern have been seen in these colors. The pattern is very similar to Lalique's Sauterelle, but without the grasshoppers found on the earlier French pattern. Crystal: $35.00 – 40.00. Other colors: $60.00 – 60.00.

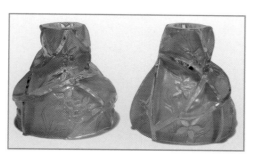

CS-10A. No. 708 MARTELÉ VINE CANDLES WITH SEPIA WASH

CS-10. No. 708 MARTELÉ VINE CANDLE IN FRENCH CRYSTAL *(From the collection of Helen and Bob Jones.)*

Martelé Tropical Fish candlestick. Between 4¼" and 4½" high, with an approximately 4½" to 5¼" diameter base. (Note difference in height and diameter of base in the pair shown in CS-11a.) Production dates are unknown, but probably late 1920s or early 1930s. Known in French crystal, crystal with green, amber, or brown washes, and blue, with other colors possible. This is considered one of Consolidated's rarest items. It was probably designed to go with their large fish bowl. It features a pair of fish in heavy relief on the underside of the base. Alll colors: $400.00 – market.

CS-11A. MARTELÉ TROPICAL FISH candlesticks WITH AMBER WASH *(Photograph courtesy of Bruce Mueller and Gary Wickland, from their collection.)*

CS-11. MARTELÉ TROPICAL FISH candlestick WITH BROWN WASH *(From the collection of Bill Burke.)*

There was also a Martelé Cockatoo candlestick produced (not pictured). It was 4" high with a 5½" diameter base. Production dates are unknown, but probably late 1920s or early 1930s. Known in amethyst, green, and honey washes; other colors are possible. It features an exotic bird molded on the underside of the base.

Martelé Love Birds candleholder. 3" high with an oblong base ranging from 6⅞" to 7⅜" by 4". Production dates unknown, but probably made in the late 1920s or early 1930s. Known in French crystal, amethyst opalescent, green opalescent, crystal with amethyst, and sepia washes, with other Martelé colors possible. This is considered one of Consolidated's rarest items. The design features a pair of love birds molded on the underside of the base. All colors: $450.00 – market. *(From the collection of Bill Burke.)*

CS-12. MARTELÉ LOVE BIRDS CANDLEHOLDER WITH AMETHYST WASH

CS-12A. MARTELÉ LOVE BIRDS CANDLEHOLDER, TOP VIEW

No. 2840 Dancing Nymph candleholder. Also referred to as Dance of the Nudes. Originally part of the Martelé line. 3" high with a base that is 5¾" long and 5¼" wide. Production was ca. 1928 – 1932, and possibly again after 1936; however, in 1939 when the line was expanded to a full luncheon set, the candleholders were no longer being made. Known in crystal, French crystal (with satin highlights), jade (green wash on crystal), and with ruby stain, with other colors or treatments possible. This is considered one of Consolidated's rarer items. The design consists of a pair of nude figures impressed on the underside of the base. Crystal: $175.00 – 200.00. Colors: $350.00 – market.

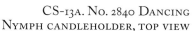
CS-13. No. 2840 DANCING NYMPH CANDLEHOLDER WITH GREEN WASH

CS-13A. No. 2840 DANCING NYMPH CANDLEHOLDER, TOP VIEW

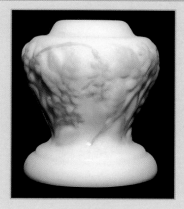

Unknown candleholder. 3¼" high with a 2¾" base. All of the characteristics of this candleholder — design, color, applied decoration — indicate that it was made by Consolidated, though to date no original catalog documentation has been found. When Consolidated introduced their custard color in August 1938, the *Crockery and Glass Journal* described the pieces as "carved designs in ivory against a background of either ivory or several soft-toned colors. These same items — vases, bowls, candlesticks — are made in reverse colors, with the figures in color against ivory. The most popular colors were blue, brown, and red." This appears to be a very close description of this candleholder. Pieces in custard are scarce, indicating that it was in production only briefly. The similarity of the design to Consolidated's earlier Martelé Vine pattern is also worth noting. Unable to price. *(From the collection of Helen & Bob Jones.)*

CS-14. UNKNOWN CANDLEHOLDER, POSSIBLY CONSOLIDATED

No. 5460 Con-Cora hobnail candlestick. 3¾" high with a 4" diameter base. Produced from 1957 to 1962. Made in milk glass; according to advertisements, the line was available in "pastel pink, turquoise, white, blue, and lemon yellow," probably referring to applied colors. Many Con-Cora pieces were hand-decorated; among the decorations offered were Ivy, Violet, Pussy Willow, and Rose. The Con-Cora line was a mix of old, reissued items and new, beaded-edge designs like the candlestick, which were probably copied from Imperial's very popular Candlewick pattern. $15.00 – 25.00. *(From the collections of the authors and Bill Burke.)*

CS-15. No. 5460 CON-CORA HOBNAIL CANDLESTICKS IN MILK GLASS, WITH VARIOUS HAND-PAINTED DECORATIONS

CO-OPERATIVE FLINT GLASS COMPANY, Beaver Falls, Pennsylvania

(1879 – 1937). This was the first successful glass cooperative to be established in the United States, the result of a general strike called in late November against the pressed glass factories in Pittsburgh. Rather than waiting out the lengthy strike, a number of workmen from McKee & Bros. chose to relocate to Beaver Falls, where the town gave them a tax free lease for ten years and a $25,000 cash bonus. They were in production by June 1879, advertising that they were "manufacturers of tableware, bar bottles, bird cups, shop furniture, candy jars, lantern globes, lamp chimneys, etc." This breadth and variety of product seems to have typified their output throughout most of their existence. The factory burned in 1889, but was immediately rebuilt, even larger than before. They offered a number of very successful full tableware lines and many novelties, such as a bell-shaped butter dish with a metal clapper, so that it could be used to summon the family to dinner.

By the 1920s, the Co-operative was a pioneer in the introduction of color to their glassware lines and had a considerable trade in hotel, soda fountain, and restaurant ware, while continuing to produce novelties, giftware, and specialties like furniture knobs and bird baths. Unfortunately, like so many other companies, the Co-operative Flint Glass Company was unable to withstand the economic ravages of the Depression, closing in 1937.

COLORS

There is small evidence of color in the early years. Opal is mentioned for the first time in 1892. Some early patterns were offered with amber, green, ruby, and blue stains. In 1898, green was advertised. By the 1920s, the Co-operative entered heavily into production of colored glassware, so that by 1929 they could advertise "all lines available in all popular colors." It can probably be assumed that many of the colors below remained in production until the factory closed in the 1930s:

By 1923	Amethyst		1924	Amber
	Blue			Cobalt
	Canary			Ruby
	Green		1925 – 1927	Sunset (red shading to yellow at the edges)
	Turquoise		1926	Rose
	Black (called Midnight Glass)			Aquamarine blue
			By 1932	Topaz

Small crucifix candlestick. 9½" high. Made ca. 1892 to sometime after 1911. Known in crystal, green, and opal. A number of other companies made crucifixes very similar to this one, especially Gillinder and McKee, with only subtle variances between them. Some details to look for on the small crucifix is the lack of a banner saying "INRI" at the top of the cross, the relatively small size of the Christ figure, and the area below the feet, which bulges out and then ends with a straight line (unlike the

CO-1. SMALL CRUCIFIX CANDLESTICK IN OPAL

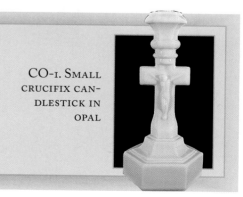

CO-1A. SMALL
CRUCIFIX CAN-
DLESTICK IN
GREEN

Gillinder crucifix, which is rounded at the bottom); also, the modeling of the figure of Christ is lacking in detail. Crystal: $25.00 – 30.00. Opal: $40.00 – 60.00. Green: $150.00 – 200.00.

Large crucifix candlestick. 11½" high. Made ca. 1892 to sometime after 1911. Offered in crystal and opal. A number of other companies made crucifixes very similar to this one, including New England Glass Company, Sandwich, Cambridge, McKee, and Hobbs, Brockunier. In order to identify the Co-operative crucifix, careful comparison must be made of the shape of the candle cup, the position of the pseudo-wafer (which is not a true wafer, since this candlestick was molded in a single piece), and the size and shape of the niche at the base of Christ's feet. Crystal: $50.00 – 60.00. Opal: $70.00 – 100.00.

CO-2. LARGE CRUCIFIX CANDLESTICKS
IN OPAL, FRONT AND REAR VIEWS

CO-3. No. 322 OR
RAY CANDLESTICKS
IN BLUE, CRYSTAL
(CUT), AND
AMETHYST, TWO
SIZES

No. 322 candlestick. Also offered as part of the Ray pattern, 7¼" with a 3⅜" diameter hexagonal base; Ray or Douglass (or Douglas) candlestick, 9⅛" with a 4⅛" diameter hexagonal base. Made ca. 1903 to the 1920s. Known in crystal, amber, amethyst, black, blue, and canary; other colors are possible. The Ray and Douglass patterns were both extensive colonial lines. Crystal, amber: $25.00 – 30.00. Other colors: $35.00 – 45.00.

CO-4. No. 344 CANDLESTICKS,
TWO VERSIONS

No. 344 candlestick. 5" high with a 3⅜" diameter hexagonal base and an impressed 24-point star on the bottom. Production dates unknown, but probably ca. 1903 until sometime after 1911. Known in crystal only. Made in two versions. The one shown on the right is the catalog version. The one on the left has a rim part way up its column, making it look as if it might have been part of the Ray or Douglass patterns. (See the No. 322 candlestick above.) Curiously, the candlesticks shown were purchased as a pair and may have come from the factory mismatched. The version on the right is very similar in shape to Heisey's No. 5 candlestick, also made in a 5" height from 1904 to 1931, but with a ground and polished pontil on the bottom. $15.00 – 20.00.

No. 279 candlestick. Called Sawtooth by collectors. 6¾" high with a 3¼" diameter base. According to Mrs. John Kemple, whose husband later purchased the mold, Co-operative first made this candlestick ca. 1902 – 1928, though it is possible it remained in production until the factory closed in 1937. (The interview with Mrs. Kemple appears in Jack D. Wilson's *Phoenix & Consolidated Art Glass*.) Known colors include crystal, blue, green, opal, and rose; other colors are possible. Crystal: $8.00 – 12.00. Opal: $10.00 – 15.00. Colors: $15.00 – 22.00.

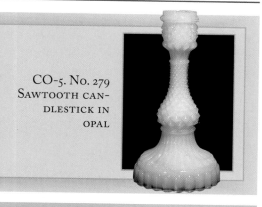

CO-5. No. 279 SAWTOOTH CANDLESTICK IN OPAL

LOOKALIKES AND THE HISTORY OF A MOLD

The origins of the Sawtooth candlestick are not clear. Some sources attribute the design to McKee; however, we have been unable to document this. McKee did make a candlestick with a similar shape, as seen here from an 1899 advertisement, but instead of the sawtooth motif, it featured a block pattern with alternating rows of imitation fine-cut crosshatching. In the interview with Mrs. Kemple, mentioned above, she attributed the mold to Sandwich in the 1840s, but there is no evidence to support this.

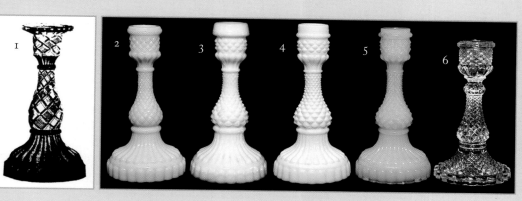

CO-5A. & CO-5B. 1. MCKEE PURITAN CANDLESTICK (*CHINA, GLASS AND LAMPS*, JUNE 15, 1899). 2. GILLINDER NO. 2 CANDLESTICK. 3. KEMPLE NO. 40 CANDLESTICK (REISSUE OF CO-OPERATIVE/PHOENIX CANDLESTICK WITH REDESIGNED TOP). 4. PHOENIX REISSUE OF THE CO-OPERATIVE CANDLESTICK. 5. CO-OPERATIVE CANDLESTICK. 6. U.S. GLASS NO. 3 CANDLESTICK.

A similar candlestick was also made by Gillinder & Sons from ca. 1896 to 1913. Although almost identical, it can be easily told apart from the Co-operative candlestick. Instead of the sawtooth pattern, with its sharp points, the Gillinder candlestick has flattened diamonds.

The Co-operative mold itself had an extensive history. When Co-operative went out of business in 1937, the Sawtooth candlestick was among a group of molds acquired by the Phoenix Glass Company, reportedly in settlement of a debt. Phoenix then produced the candlestick in milk glass with various finishes applied, including pink, antique blue (dark blue highlights), pearl lustre (lightly iridized), and caramel lustre (a highly iridized rich yellowish-beige). They marketed the candlestick as part of their Early American line until sometime around 1942.

Both the Co-operative and Phoenix catalogs show an identical candlestick, with a rim around the top of the candle cup and a small ⅛" lip above it. However actual candlesticks often have an additional flange extending above that to make a total of ⅜". This seems to be the case with the Phoenix reissues. It seems likely that these candlesticks with the extra lip are in the form that they would have come from the mold and that, initially, it was intended for the additional flange to be ground off during the final finishing of the candlestick. In practice, however, it probably turned out to be easier and less expensive to simply leave the additional rim in place.

In 1946, H. M. Tuska, a New York distributor, purchased the Co-operative molds from Phoenix, including the Sawtooth candlestick, and unsuccessfully attempted to have them made by Westmoreland. Later in the same year, he sold the molds to the John E. Kemple Glassworks (see volume 3 of this series), who modified the rim of the candle cup to give it a rounded appearance. After Kemple's death in 1970, the mold was acquired by Wheaton Industries and the candlestick was sold as part of their Wheatonware line up until 1979. The Kemple/Wheaton candlesticks were made in milk glass and a variety of colors. The mold for this candlestick is now in the custody of the Wheaton Historical Association.

The United States Glass Company also offered a version of this candlestick as their No. 3; it differs in having a scalloped base and the ring beneath the candle cup is beaded, rather than plain. It was made in two sizes, 6¼" and 7½".

CO-6. CAN-DLESTICKS, UNKNOWN PATTERN NUMBER, IN BLACK, CRYS-TAL, AND BLUE, THREE SIZES

Candlestick, unknown pattern number. Made in three sizes: 5⅝" with a 3⅜" hexagonal base; 7" high with a 3½" hexagonal base; 8⅜" high with a 4" hexagonal base. Production dates not known, but probably in the 1920s. Known in amethyst, aquamarine blue, canary, cobalt blue, crystal, and midnight black; other colors are possible. The attribution to Co-operative is made by James Measell and Berry Wiggins, in their *Great American Glass of the Roaring 20s & Depression Era*. Small, crystal: $10.00 – 12.00. Medium, crystal, amber: $25.00 – 30.00; other colors: $35.00 – 45.00. Large, crystal, amber: $35.00 – 40.00; other colors: $45.00 – 55.00.

Candlestick, unknown pattern number. This is the short version of the No. 448, 449, and 450 candlesticks below. Height varies from 3" to 3¼" with a 4⅛" to 4¾" diameter base. Production dates not known, but probably mid-1920s to the 1930s. This appears to be the candlestick, offered as part of a console set with gold decoration, that was shown in pink by Sears in their fall 1928 catalog. Made in crystal, amber, amethyst, blue, green, rose, ruby, and sunset; other colors are possible. Also found with fired-on colors and gold decorations. This mold was one of the ones acquired by the Phoenix Glass Company when Co-operative went out of business in 1937, reportedly in settlement of a debt. It appears in a Phoenix catalog, but with no indication of colors made. Crystal, amber: $8.00 – 12.00. Green, rose: $10.00 – 15.00. Black, amethyst, blue, canary, ruby: $20.00 – 30.00. Sunset: $50.00 – 60.00.

CO-7. CANDLESTICKS, UNKNOWN PATTERN NUMBER, IN ROSE AND SUNSET

CO-8. No. 448 CANDLESTICK IN SUNSET, No. 449 CANDLESTICK IN BLACK WITH SIL-VER OVERLAY, AND No. 450 CANDLESTICK IN CANARY

No. 448 candlestick, listed in the catalog as 7", but actual height varies to as much as 7⅝" with a 3⅝" diameter base; No. 449 candlestick, listed in the catalog as 9", but actual height ranges from 8¾" to 9" with a 4¼" diameter base; No. 450 candlestick, listed in the catalog as 10", but actual height ranges from 10¼" to 11" with a 4⅝" diameter base.

Production dates are unknown, but probably mid-1920s to the 1930s. Known in crystal, amethyst, blue, canary, midnight black, ruby, and sunset; other colors are possible. Co-operative's sunset is reminiscent of Wheeling peachblow, shading from yellow to red and then back to yellow. Cambridge experimented with a similar color that they called tomato, and prior to the correct identification through ongoing research of Co-operative's sunset, these candlesticks were erroneously attributed to Cambridge.

Small, crystal, amber: $10.00 – 12.00; black, amethyst, blue, canary, ruby: $20.00 – 30.00; sunset: $40.00 – 50.00. Medium, crystal, amber: $12.00 – 15.00; black, amethyst, blue, canary, ruby: $25.00 – 35.00; sunset: $50.00 – 60.00. Large, crystal, amber: $15.00 – 20.00; black, amethyst, blue, canary, ruby: $30.00 – 40.00; sunset: $60.00 – 80.00.

No. 456 candlestick. 8" high. Appears in an undated catalog, probably from the 1920s. Any of the colors from that period are possible. $20.00 – 35.00.

CO-9. No. 456 CANDLESTICK, FROM CATALOG, CA. 1920S

No. 473 candlestick. 7" high. Appears in an undated catalog, probably from the 1920s. Any of the colors from that period are possible. $25.00 – 35.00.

CO-10. No. 473 CANDLESTICK, FROM CATALOG, CA. 1920S

No. 481 candlestick. 7" high with a 3⅞" diameter base. Appears in an undated catalog, probably from the 1920s. Any of the colors from that period are possible. Several other companies made very similar candlesticks, but we believe the Co-operative Flint version can be differentiated from the others because it comes from a three-part mold, unlike all of the other trumpet-style candlesticks that are from two-part molds. See the discussion of Central's No. 2000 candlestick on p. 106 for further details. Blue, black: $20.00 – 30.00. Canary and all stretch colors: $25.00 – 35.00.

CO-11. No. 481 CANDLESTICKS IN CANARY STRETCH AND BLUE

No. 503 candlestick. 5½" with a 4⅞" diameter base. Appears in an undated catalog, probably from the 1920s. Known in blue and black, with any of the colors from the period possible. Designed for a 1½" diameter candle, one of only a few candlesticks from this period that take a larger than ordinary candle. Heisey's 5" No. 104 candlestick (1924 – 1929) is somewhat similar in shape, but has a solid, thicker stem, whereas the Co-operative candlestick is hollow halfway up. $25.00 – 30.00.

CO-12. No. 503 CANDLESTICK IN BLUE

No. 505 candlestick. 2½" with a 4¼" diameter saucer base. Appears in an undated catalog, probably from the 1920s. Known in amberina (possibly Co-operative's sunset, but without as much variation of color due to the

small size of the candlestick), but any of the colors from this period are possible. This mold was one of the ones acquired by the Phoenix Glass Company when Co-operative went out of business in 1937, reportedly in settlement of a debt. It appears in a Phoenix catalog, but with no indication of colors made. The United States Glass Company's Tiffin factory also made what appears to be an identical candlestick in the late 1920s as their No. 319-201 handled candlestick in various colors, most often seen with a satin finish. We believe the only differentiating factor between them may be the sharpness of the rim where the stem meets the candle cup on the Co-operative piece. Another, similar candlestick was made by Westmoreland as their No. 1062, but it differs in having an additional bulge at the top of the stem before joining the candle cup. Sunset: $50.00 – 60.00; other colors: $20.00 – 25.00.

CO-13. NO. 505 CANDLE-STICK, FROM CATALOG, CA. 1920S

CO-14. No. 507 CANDLESTICK IN AMBER

No. 507 candlestick. 2⅞" high with a base diameter of 3⅞". Appears in an undated catalog, probably from the 1920s. Known in amber, but any of the colors from that period are possible. $10.00 – 12.00.

No. 567 candlestick. Called Wig-Wam by collectors. 3" high with 3¾" diameter base. Made from 1929 until the 1930s. Known in crystal, aquamarine, cobalt blue, green, rose, ruby, and milk glass. This was part of a console set, advertised as a "modernistic design." Hazel Marie Weatherman, in her *Colored Glassware of the Depression Era 2*

shows the bowl from this set on a catalog page from the L. E. Smith Glass Company (see volume 3 of this series) and indicates her belief that Smith also made the candlesticks. If so, her attribution of a date of ca. 1930 to the catalog page must be incorrect, since Co-operative was still advertising the console set in 1930 and it would be unlikely that Smith would have acquired the molds until after Co-operative went out of business in 1937. Current employees of Smith have no recollection of this candlestick. Crystal: $10.00 – 12.00. Aqua, rose, green, black: $15.00 – 20.00. Cobalt, ruby, milk glass: $18.00 – 25.00.

CO-15. No. 567 WIG-WAM CANDLESTICKS IN AQUAMARINE, CRYSTAL, AND COBALT

CRESCENT GLASS COMPANY, Wellsburg, West Virginia (1908 – 1983). Founded by

Henry Rithner, Sr., formerly of the Consolidated Lamp and Glass Company and the Fostoria Glass Company. When the original Crescent plant was destroyed by fire in 1911, they purchased the abandoned Riverside Glass Works factory of the National Glass Company. They made a variety of products, ranging from blown tumblers and bar goods to lantern globes and headlight lenses. The company remained in operation until 1983, still under the control of the third generation of the Rithner family. In 1983, the name was changed to the Brooke Glass Company (see p. 44), which continued to manufacture glass until 2001, when the factory became a decorating firm only.

Liberty Bell candlestick. 4⅜" high with a 3¼" diameter base. Made for the Bicentennial in 1976. One side of the bell has the date 1776, the opposite side is inscribed 1976. Known in crystal, amber, blue, and red, both clear and with satin finish; other colors are likely. Attribution of this candlestick to Crescent was made by Paula Pendergrass and Sherry Riggs in their *Glass Candleholders.* $6.00 – 10.00.

CR-1. LIBERTY BELL CANDLE-STICKS IN RED AND AMBER, WITH SATIN FINISHES. CANDLESTICK ON LEFT IS REVERSED, SHOWING BICENTENNIAL DATE OF 1976; CANDLESTICK ON RIGHT READS 1776 AND HAS THE LIBERTY BELL CRACK

DALZELL VIKING, New Martinsville, West Virginia. In operation from April 1987 to July 1998.

Kenneth Dalzell, formerly of the Fostoria Glass Company, bought the old New Martinsville/Viking factory one year after its closing (see volume 3 of this series) and reopened it under the name Dalzell Viking. The company began remaking many items originally made by New Martinsville/Viking, Westmoreland, and other companies including many candlesticks. In addition they did private contract work for the Smithsonian, Sandwich, Oglebay, and Heisey Museums. Financial problems finally led to the closing of the company in July of 1998. The molds were sold to various other companies.

Colors

The Dalzell Viking colors that we're aware of are amethyst, azure blue (light), black, blue (medium), cobalt blue, crystal (plain or with hand-painted accents), cranberry mist, evergreen (sold only through outlet stores), golden (a sunny yellow), green mist (teal green), ice blue (light gray based blue), light evergreen (a deep emerald), pink, plum, peach, ruby, sage (pale lettuce green). Most were available with a satin finish.

Hexagonal candlestick. 7½" high with 3½" base. Made from 1988 to at least 1996 for the Metropolitan Museum of Art. Marked MMA on the bottom. Offered in crystal, cobalt, and amethyst, though not all of these colors seem to have been in production for that entire period. This was a reproduction of a candlestick from the Metropolitan's collection dated ca. 1850 – 1870, made by the New England Glass Company. Earlier, from 1979 to 1984, this same reproduction had been made for the Museum by the Imperial Glass Corporation in crystal, cobalt, amethyst, and canary yellow. Other reproductions are known, unmarked, that probably are imports from Asia or, possibly, Czechoslovakia. $20.00 – 25.00.

DV-1. HEXAGONAL CANDLESTICK IN AMETHYST. (REPRODUCTION OF NEW ENGLAND GLASS COMPANY CANDLE-STICK, MADE FOR METROPOLITAN MUSEUM OF ART)

No. 1937 dolphin candlestick. 4" high. Produced 1988 – 1998. Made in black, green, pink, crystal, cranberry mist, golden mist, cobalt, and ruby. This is a reissue of Westmoreland's No. 1049 small dolphin and was made from an original mold. It is not marked as Westmoreland dolphins had been since the 1950s. Unmarked Westmoreland dolphins are from before the fifties when they used an earlier version of the mold (see the comparison of the depression-era Westmoreland next to the later version in DV-2a). Dalzell's colors are also different from Westmoreland's. This candlestick has also been produced by the Viking Glass Company, probably during the mid-1980s. We believe the Viking colors were milk glass and black. The Viking version may be marked with a 'V' beneath the base. Crystal: $6.00 – 10.00. Golden mist, pink, black, green: $12.00 – 18.00. Ruby, cobalt, cranberry mist: $20.00 – 25.00.

DV-2. No. 1937 DOLPHIN CANDLESTICKS IN COBALT AND GREEN. (WESTMORELAND MOLD)

DV-2A. COMPARISON OF DALZELL VIKING NO. 1937 DOLPHIN CANDLESTICK AND EARLIER VERSION OF WESTMORELAND NO. 1049 DOLPHIN CANDLESTICK IN PINK

DV-3. No. 1938 DOLPHIN CANDLESTICKS IN RUBY, GOLDEN MIST, AND CRANBERRY MIST

No. 1938 dolphin candlestick. 9¼" high. Produced from 1990 to 1998. Colors were cobalt, cranberry mist, crystal, golden mist, and ruby. Black satin was made exclusively for sale through the Dalzell Viking outlet. This is a reissue of Westmoreland's No. 1049 large dolphin and is made from the original type 3 mold (see the appendix for further information).

While all of the large Westmoreland dolphins from the type 3 mold (solid head) are marked with the W over G, the Dalzell dolphins are not. Like the small dolphins, the colors are also different from Westmoreland's. This mold is currently being made in a color very similar to cranberry mist by the Mosser Glass Company. Crystal: $14.00 – 16.00. Yellow, pink, black, green: $20.00 – 25.00. Ruby, cobalt, cranberry mist: $25.00 – 35.00.

DV-4. No. 9000 HANDLED CANDLESTICK. (REPRODUCTION OF SANDWICH CANDLESTICK, MADE FOR SMITHSONIAN INSTITUTION)

No. 9000 handled candlestick. 5½" high with a 3¾" square base. Made beginning in 1990 in all crystal, crystal with a ruby top, and other colors. This was a reproduction of a rare Sandwich candlestick (see BS-3 on p. 36.) Produced for the Smithsonian Institution and marked SI on the underside of the base, adjacent to the handle. Made in two pieces, similar to the original candlestick, except that the pieces are not connected with a true wafer, but instead are probably joined together using an adhesive. The Imperial Glass Corporation produced this same candlestick earlier for the Smithsonian from 1976 to 1982 in crystal and sapphire blue. Crystal: $20.00 – 25.00. Colors: $25.00 – 30.00.

No. 9001 and No. 2210 Neo Classical candlestick, 9½" high; No. 9002 Neo Classical candlestick, 7½" high. Introduced about 1991, the 9½" size was still being sold in 1998 as No. 2210. Made in cobalt, crystal, evergreen, black, and ruby. Originally made for the Smithsonian Institution, early versions will be marked SI. Crystal: $10.00 – 12.00. Colors: $18.00 – 22.00.

DV-5A. FROM A 1991 CATALOG

DV-5. NO. 2210 NEO CLASSICAL CANDLESTICK, 9½"

No. 2171 candlestick. 7½" high. Produced from 1991 to 1998. Made in crystal, cobalt, cranberry mist, and ruby. This is a re-issue of Imperial's No. 41790 Collector's Crystal. The colors are different from Imperial's so only the crystal should be difficult to identify. This mold was apparently leased from the Indiana Glass Company, who had previously reissued this candlestick in crystal from 1986 to 1989. In 1992, it was made for Tiara Exclusives in dusty rose, by Fenton. (See FN-98 on p. 205.) Crystal: $8.00 – 10.00. Colors: $15.00 – 20.00.

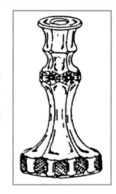

DV-6. NO. 2171 CANDLESTICK, FROM 1991 CATALOG

No. 606 Empress candlestick. 8½" high with a 4½" diameter round base. Made in 1992 for Tiara Exclusives in azure blue. This was a reissue of a candlestick probably originally made by the Indiana Glass Company in the 1920s or early 1930s. (See IN-4 in book 2 of this series.) The mold was modified by adding ribs to the base, whereas the original candlesticks have ribs on the column only. The other pieces in Tiara's Empress pattern are from molds originally belonging to McKee.

DV-7. NO. 606 EMPRESS PATTERN IN AZURE BLUE, FROM 1992 TIARA EXCLUSIVES CATALOG

Dolphin candlestick. 10⅞" with a 4" square base. This is a reproduction of Sandwich's dolphin candlestick with a half step base and dolphin candle cup (see BS-16 on p. 39). Made in 1993 in crystal and azure blue for the Metropolitan Museum of Art. Marked MMA on the bottom. Made in two parts, but held together by adhesive rather than a true wafer. (What appears to be a wafer can be easily differentiated from a true one because it has mold seams.) Imperial Glass Corporation produced this same candlestick earlier for the Metropolitan Museum in emerald, crystal, canary, moonstone blue, azure blue, and sky blue. The reproductions also differ from the originals in that the head of the dolphin is solid, whereas in the Sandwich version, the head is partially hollow. Crystal: $30.00 – 40.00. Azure blue: $45.00 – 50.00.

DV-8. DOLPHIN CANDLESTICK IN AZURE BLUE. (REPRODUCTION OF SANDWICH CANDLESTICK, MADE FOR THE METROPOLITAN MUSEUM OF ART)

No. 970 candlestick. 4" high with a 4⅛" base. Produced from 1993 to 1998. Made in cranberry mist, crystal, cobalt, forest green, and ruby. Made from New Martinsville/Viking's No. 970 mold and sold with the original stock number. Crystal: $6.00 – 8.00. Forest green: $12.00 – 18.00. Cobalt, ruby, cranberry mist: $20.00 – 25.00. Note the price sticker on the candlestick in DV-9a and several of the other items in this chapter. These must be supplied from the factory as we've seen Dalzell Viking glass in many different stores with this same style of label. Each shows the item number, a "Reg. Price" and "OUR PRICE" ("OUR PRICE" always appears to be half the Reg. Price).

DV-9. No. 970 CANDLE-STICK IN CRANBERRY MIST. (NEW MARTINSVILLE/VIKING MOLD)

DV-9A. No. 970 CANDLESTICK IN FOREST GREEN. (NEW MARTINSVILLE/VIKING MOLD)

DV-10. No. 8127 CANDLESTICK IN BLACK. (NEW MARTINSVILLE/VIKING MOLD)

No. 8127 candlestick. 5½" high with a 3½" base. Produced from 1993 to 1998 in black, ruby, and crystal. This is a reissue of New Martinsville/Viking's No. 11 Colonial candlestick. Crystal: $8.00 – 10.00. Black: $10.00 – 15.00. Ruby: $15.00 – 20.00.

DV-11. No. 4554 CANDLESTICK. (NEW MARTINSVILLE/VIKING MOLD)

No. 4554 candlestick. 5¼" high with a 5" base. Produced from 1993 to 1998. Made in cobalt, crystal, ruby, and light yellow. Other colors are possible. This is a reissue of New Martinsville/Viking's No. 4554 Janice candlestick. The Dalzell version tends to have a slightly higher base and poorer glass quality. Crystal: $8.00 – 10.00. Yellow: $12.00 – 18.00. Cobalt, ruby: $18.00 – 22.00.

DV-12. No. 8566 SQUIRREL TAIL CANDLESTICK IN COBALT. (NEW MARTINSVILLE/VIKING MOLD)

No. 8566 Squirrel Tail candlestick. 6½" high. Produced 1994 – ?. Made in cobalt and crystal. This is a reissue of New Martinsville/Viking's No. 415 one-light Flame candlestick. Although New Martinsville/Viking made cobalt glass, we don't believe this candlestick was produced in cobalt by them. That would make all cobalt examples Dalzell Viking's. Any found with a satin finish are also Dalzell's. Crystal: $8.00 – 10.00. Cobalt, black: $15.00 – 20.00.

Cornucopia candlestick. 3⅞" tall with a 4⅜" diameter round base. Production dates unknown. Made in black and possibly other colors. This is a reissue of New Martinsville/Viking's No. 653 candlestick. The Dalzell candlestick has a rough pontil mark on the base which is not present on the New Martinsville original. Crystal: $6.00 – 8.00. Black: $12.00 – 18.00.

DV-13. CORNUCOPIA CANDLESTICK IN BLACK. (NEW MARTINSVILLE/ VIKING MOLD)

No. 5213 candlestick. 4½" high with a square serrated base. Introduced in 1994. Known in crystal and black. This is a reissue of New Martinsville/Viking's No. 5213 Princess Plaza candleholder. Crystal: $8.00 – 10.00. Black: $12.00 – 15.00.

Note: The early New Martinsville/Viking versions of the No. 5213 and No. 5515 candleholders had a plain edge on the base. Later, New Martinsville/Viking changed both to a serrated edge. Therefore, either of these that are found with a plain edge came from New Martinsville/Viking. Those with a serrated edge may have been manufactured by either New Martinsville/Viking or Dalzell Viking.

DV-14. No. 5213 CANDLESTICK IN BLACK. (NEW MARTINSVILLE/ VIKING MOLD)

No. 5515 three-light candlestick. 6¾" high, rectangular serrated base. Produced 1994 – ? in crystal and black. This is a reissue of Viking's No. 5515 Princess Plaza. Crystal: $25.00 – 35.00. Black: $35.00 – 45.00.

DV-15. No. 5515 PRINCESS PLAZA THREE-LIGHT CANDLESTICK IN BLACK. (NEW MARTINSVILLE/ VIKING MOLD)

No. 2157 candlestick. 2⅜" high with a 4" base. Produced from 1994 to 1998. Known in crystal and crystal with a yellow stained candle cup and a red stained base. Available with a rayed, twisted optic, or diamond pattern on the base. Advertised as "Jewel Tones" these seem to be a reissue of Imperial's No. 134 candlestick, but with different patterns impressed on the underside of the base. $3.00 – 5.00.

DV-16. No. 2157 CANDLESTICKS IN CRYSTAL AND YELLOW/RED STAIN. (IMPERIAL MOLD)

DV-17. Jewel tones candlestick in green, hexagon base.

Candlestick, hexagon base. 3½" high with a 4⅛" base. Appeared in the 1995 catalog, advertised as "Jewel Tones." Known in green; probably also made in crystal and possibly other colors. The origin of this mold is not known, but it is very similar to a candlestick made by the Liberty Works in the late 1920s, except that the latter has a thicker stem and has ribs in the base. $10.00 – 12.00.

DV-17A. Comparison of Dalzell Viking hexagon base candlestick (on left) with candlestick believed to have been made by Liberty Works

DV-18. No. 1405 Ipswich candlestick in light evergreen. (Made from Heisey mold for Heisey Collectors of America)

No. 1405 Ipswich candlestick. 6" high with a 4¾" diameter round base. Made 1994 in light evergreen and ruby, exclusively for the Heisey Collectors of America. Marked on the column, "94 HCA" with a "D" underneath. This was a reissue using the original Heisey mold, now owned by the HCA, of a candlestick originally made from 1932 to 1936 in crystal, moongleam, flamingo, and sahara. The Heisey originals are not only in very different colors, but are also usually marked with the Diamond H at the bottom of the column, just above the base. (Light evergreen is a deeper emerald shade than moongleam.) $35.00 – 40.00.

DV-19. No. 1550 Dolphin (Fish) candlestick in ice blue. (Made from Heisey mold for Heisey Collectors of America)

No. 1550 Dolphin (Fish) candlestick. 5" high. Made 1995 in ice blue in a limited edition for the Heisey Collectors of America, as a souvenir for the Fourth Annual Percy Moore Memorial Dinner held in September of that year. Some sample pieces were also made in cobalt. Marked on one side, "HCA 95," and on the other side, "D." This was a reissue using the original Heisey mold, now owned by the HCA. The Heisey original, designed by Royal Hickman, was made in crystal only from 1942 to 1948. In 1982, Imperial reissued this candlestick for the HCA in sunshine yellow, both plain and frosted. The Imperial reissues are marked IG. Ice blue: 45.00 – 50.00. Cobalt: $55.00 – 65.00.

DV-20. Crucifix. (Weishar mold)

Crucifix. 10" high. Briefly leased from Island Mould and made about 1995 in crystal only. For the history of this mold, originally created in the late 1940s by J. D. Weishar and later used by Kemple, see BU-6 on p. 22. $35.00 – 40.00.

DELL GLASS COMPANY, Millville, New Jersey. Very little is known about this company.

According to Hazel Marie Weatherman, they were in operation during the 1930s; however, since the only trade journal reference we have found is from 1946 (uncovered through research done by Helen Jones) — and since Dell is not mentioned in the 1944 edition of the *Glass Factory Year Book and Directory* — it seems more likely that they were founded sometime in 1945. It isn't known how long they remained in production.

Tulip candleholder. 3¾" high. Made 1945 – 1946. Offered in amethyst, green, turquoise, and crystal; amber is also possible, since some pieces in the pattern have been found in that color. The Montgomery Ward fall-winter catalog for 1945 – 1946 offered these candleholders along with other pieces in the Tulip pattern in amethyst and turquoise, as "original designs made exclusively for Wards and to be found no other place." This seems to have been the only appearance of the pattern in a Montgomery Ward catalog.

DL-1. TULIP CANDLE-HOLDER IN AMETHYST

In the February 1946 issue of *China and Glass,* "Dell Tulip" was announced as new in blue, amethyst, and green, presumably indicating that the exclusive arrangement with Wards was at an end. (Note that some sources incorrectly date this pattern to the 1930s.) The candleholder shown in DL-1 was made from the same mold as the ivy vase, also offered by Montgomery Ward. The Tulip pattern can be found both with stippling (or beads) between the "tulips" and without. The stippling does not appear in the Montgomery Ward catalog, but is seen in the photograph in *China and Glass,* suggesting that it may have been added when the "new" pattern became generally available in 1946. There is also a second candlestick in the Tulip pattern, about 3" high with a base diameter of 5¼". (See DL-2.) Crystal, amber: $22.00 – 25.00. Green: $25.00 – 30.00. Amethyst, blue: $30.00 – 35.00.

DL-2. TULIP CANDLESTICK IN AMETHYST

DIAMOND GLASS-WARE COMPANY, Indiana, Pennsylvania (1913 – 1931).

This company was formed in 1913 when Thomas and Alfred Dugan resigned from what had been the Dugan Glass Company. The factory was originally built in 1892 as the home of the Indiana Glass Company; however that company was beset with financial woes and was forced to close its doors in 1894. The factory was then leased to Harry Northwood and was the site of the Northwood Company until they joined with the National Glass Company in 1899. In 1904 the plant was sold to a group of investors who formed the Dugan Glass Company, which it remained until 1913. While under the management of the Dugan brothers the company had introduced a line of iridescent glassware known today as carnival glass. The Diamond organization expanded this popular line and also specialized in fine handmade light cut and decorated tableware. After succumbing to a fire on June 27, 1931, the company was never reopened.

COLORS

Known colors include:

after glow (pink iridescent), 1927 – 1929
amber, 1920s
amethyst, late 1920s
amethyst iridescent stretch, 1921
antique ivory, 1926
black, 1926 – 1931
blue iridescent, 1920s
blue satin, 1925
cerulean blue, 1913 – 1920
cobalt blue, 1920s
Egyptian lustre (black glass with a bronze, blue, green, and ruby shading), 1921 – 1923

golden (iridescent marigold on crystal), 1921 – 1923
green, 1920s
green iridescent, 1921 – 1923
jade green, 1924
pearl lustre (iridescent crystal), 1921 – 1923
pink, 1920s
Ritz blue (cobalt), late 1920s
royal lustre (cobalt blue glass with a silver iridescence), 1921 – 1923
Vesuvius blue, 1924
ruby iridescent (opaque red-orange), 1924 ?
ruby iridescent stretch, 1924

DI-1. CANDLE BOWL IN GOLDEN LUSTRE

Candle bowl. two-light. 3¼" high with a length of 11¼". Produced circa 1924 – 1925. Made in black, golden lustre, green iridescent, iridescent blue (possibly Vesuvius), after glow, and pearl lustre. The bottom is marked "Pat. Applied For." It was designed by Harry Wallace Thomas and the patent was filed March 21, 1924, and approved May 12, 1925, as D67,330. Black: $35.00 – 50.00. Golden lustre: $85.00 – 90.00. Stretch colors: $50.00 – 75.00.

DI-2. No. 625 CANDLEHOLDER IN GREEN

No. 625 candleholder. 3¾" high with base sizes varying from 4⅝" to 5" in diameter. Circa 1920s. Made in amber, black, crystal, green, and pink. There is some uncertainty involving attribution of this candlestick. William Heacock, James Measell, and Berry Wiggins, in their *Dugan/Diamond*, attribute it to Diamond. Sandra McPhee Stout, in her *Depression Glass III*, reprints a catalog page from 1929 showing it with a hand-painted decoration to match Noritake's Azalea pattern, and says it was made by the Indiana Glass Company. Further support for this attribution is provided by the fact that all of the other items in the Azalea assortment match shapes found in Indiana's Moderne Classic line. Either both companies made identical candlesticks, a third company bought pieces from both and combined them to create the Azalea assortment — or this candlestick was, in fact, made only by Indiana. The authors tend toward the latter view, but present it here under rule of doubt. The pattern was dubbed Sherman by Hazel Marie Weatherman, who listed it as unknown. Black: $10.00 – 14.00.

DI-3. TALL BLOWN CANDLEHOLDER OR VASE IN BLACK

Tall blown candleholder or vase. There were several variations of these candle-vases made at Diamond. Heights varied from 7" to 10". Some had vertical ribs and some were plain. The one shown is 9¾" high with a 3½" base. Circa 1920s. Made in green iridescent, Harding blue stretch, golden lustre, cobalt, and black. Other colors are likely. Offered as part of a console set and also came decorated with hand-painted flowers. Offered in the 1925 Butler Bros. catalog in black with gold encrusted decoration. $35.00 – 50.00.

DI-4. MAE WEST CANDLEHOLDER IN EGYPTIAN LUSTRE

Tapered candleholder. 8" high with a 4¾" base. Circa 1923 – 1925. Made in black, blue satin, blue iridescent, blue with a crackle finish, cobalt blue, Egyptian lustre, green stretch, jade, marigold, royal lustre, and ruby iridescent. Dubbed Mae West by collectors, this was often sold as part of a console set. Two other companies made candlesticks similar to Diamond's. Duncan & Miller's No. 91 is taller (9¼") and was advertised in crystal only. (See DM-17 on p. 148 for a picture of Duncan's No. 91 candlestick.) The Fostoria Glass Company's No. 2275, which will be included in volume 2 of this series, was also made in different sizes than Diamond: 7"

and 9½". These have a thick rim that tapers inward at the base. Josef Inwald, A.G., a Czechoslovakian manufacturer, also made a candlestick very similar to the Duncan one in the 1920s – 1930s. Harding blue, black: $40.00 – 50.00. Cobalt, stretch colors: $55.00 – 65.00. Ruby luster, royal luster: $50.00 – 75.00. Egyptian luster: $120.00 to market.

DI-4A. MAE WEST CANDLE-HOLDER IN COBALT BLUE WITH WHITE ENAMEL DECORATION

DI-4B. MAE WEST CANDLEHOLDER IN BLUE WITH WHITE ENAMEL DECORATION AND CRACKLE FINISH

Candleholder, unknown pattern number. 8⅛" high with a 5" base. Made circa 1920s. Known in iridescent green, Harding blue stretch, and royal lustre. Other colors are likely. $35.00 – 55.00.

DI-5. CANDLE-HOLDER, UNKNOWN PATTERN, IN ROYAL LUSTRE

No. 713 candleholder. 2⅞" high with a 4½" base. Hexagonal candle cup. Produced around 1924. Made in amber, black, blue, green, pink, and crystal. Can be found with a "hammered gold" or "Jack and the Bean Stalk" decoration. This was also offered with a crimped base with a diamond optic. Many other companies made similar candlesticks. Diamond's can be identified by the ring around the outside center of the candle cup. $10.00 – 14.00.

DI-6A. NO. 713 CANDLE-HOLDER IN CRYSTAL WITH GOLD AND ENAMEL DECO-RATION

DI-6B. NO. 713 CANDLE-HOLDER IN PINK WITH CRIMPED BASE

DI-6. NO. 713 CANDLE-HOLDER IN AMBER WITH GOLD DECORATION

Trumpet shaped candleholder. 9" high with a 4⅜" base. Circa 1925. Made in black, Harding blue stretch, iridescent green, crystal, also crystal that has been painted with either red, green, or blue. Can be found with hand-painted decorations or silver overlay. Central Glass Company made a very similar candleholder in this size but the Central candlestick has a thicker rim and no mold seam at the rim's edge (see DI-7b on p. 134 and CE-15 on p.

DI-7. TRUMPET CANDLE-HOLDER IN AMETHYST WITH SILVER OVERLAY

DI-7A. TRUMPET CANDLE-HOLDER IN HARDING BLUE STRETCH WITH WHITE ENAMEL DECORATION

DI-7B. COMPARISON OF SOCKET SHAPES, CENTRAL ON THE LEFT, DIAMOND ON THE RIGHT

106). A ribbed version was also made as part of Diamond's 900 line (known to collectors as Adams Rib) in pink, blue, and other colors. Plain trumpets, black: $20.00 – 25.00; blue stretch: $35.00 – 40.00; amethyst with silver overlay: $40.00 – 45.00. Adams Rib, amber, pink: $18.00 – 25.00; blue: $25.00 – 30.00.

DI-8. ADAMS RIB CANDLESTICKS IN BLUE AND PINK, WITH GOLD DECORATION

DI-9. SPINDLE CANDLEHOLDER

Spindle candleholder. 8¾" high. Circa late 1920s. Known colors include after glow, blue iridescent, golden lustre, and green iridescent. Other colors are possible. Iridescent colors: $35.00 – 45.00. After glow: $60.00 to market. *(Artist's rendition.)*

DI-10. VICTORY CANDLESTICK IN GREEN

Victory candlestick. 3" high with a slightly scalloped round base, approximately 4½" in diameter. Produced 1928 – 1932. Made in Ritz blue, black, amber, green, and pink. Amethyst is also listed for this pattern but we have no evidence that the candlestick was ever produced in that color. Ritz blue and black command the highest prices. Amber, green, pink: $25.00 – 30.00. Blue, black: $100.00 – 115.00.

No. 716 candleholder. three-light. 3½" high with a 4¼" diameter base. Circa 1930 – 1931. Known in black and pink. Seen in a drawing by Charles E. Voitle, executive secretary of the National Association of Manufacturers of Pressed and Blown Glassware, dated 1930 and reproduced in William Heacock, James Measell, and Berry Wiggins' *Dugan/Diamond*. $15.00 – 25.00.

DI-11. NO. 716 CANDLEHOLDER IN BLACK

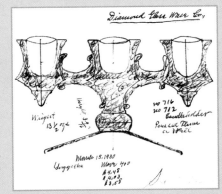

DI-11A. ORIGINAL SKETCH, 1930

No. 99 candleholder. 3" high with a 4" base. Circa 1930 – 1931. Known colors are blue, pink, yellow, and black. Can be found with Jack and the Bean Stalk or other silver decorations ("with the decoration placed on the left side as is now so modish"). Offered with four candleholders and a bowl as Diamond's No. 99 console set. $20.00 – 25.00.

DI-12. No. 99 CANDLEHOLDER IN BLACK WITH SILVER DECORATION

The Diamond Glass-ware Company also made a line of items with a swan motif, including a candlestick. Fenton acquired these molds after Diamond closed. See FN-26 on p. 187 for further information.

DITHRIDGE AND COMPANY, Pittsburgh (1827 – 1890), Jeannette, Pennsylvania

(1890 – 1902). This was one of the oldest and most respected companies in the Pittsburgh area, founded in 1827 as the Fort Pitt Glass Works, a name it continued to be popularly known by through many changes of ownership. Around 1839, Edward Dithridge became a glassblower at the factory (at that time known as Curling, Robertson, and Company). He eventually became a partner and then the sole owner. In 1867, his son George joined the firm, which became Dithridge and Son. Upon the senior Dithridge's death in 1873, the business was reorganized once again as Dithridge and Company. The only advertisements in the trade journals from 1879 to 1880 consistently refer to the Dithridge Chimney Company, Ltd., possibly a sister factory also under the proprietorship of E. D. Dithridge. At any rate, it isn't until around 1880 that the company is mentioned as having added bar goods and tumblers to their line of manufactures.

In 1890, the old Pittsburgh plant was abandoned and a new factory was built in Jeannette, Pennsylvania. Here, lamps and shades became their major output, soon supplemented by a large variety of salts and peppers, molasses cans, stamp plates, and other small goods in many colors. By 1899, they were able to advertise that they had "the largest, newest, and best line of opal decorated novelties ever shown." They continued to turn these novelties out in immense quantities over the next three years. However, at the end of 1901 it was reported that the Dithridge plant in Jeannette had been bought by the Pittsburgh Lamp and Brass Company, along with the Kopp Lamp and Glass Company's works. This merger, henceforth known as the Pittsburgh Lamp, Brass, and Glass Company, became the largest lamp manufacturer in the company. Although frequent reports on the new conglomerate in the trade journals and advertisements mention lamps only, assortments of Dithridge novelties appear in Butler Brothers catalogs up until at least 1906. We have not been able to determine if the new company continued to manufacture these lines, or if the molds were sold to another firm. Under the Pittsburgh Lamp, Brass, and Company, the Jeannette plant continued to operate until sometime around 1935.

COLORS

Because Dithridge's production was primarily lamps, they made all of the popular colors for that branch of manufacture, including canary, pink, blue, rosina (graduating from deep to light rose), and many others, including various opaque colors. At Jeannette, opal and turquoise (opaque blue) were specialties.

No. 42 candlestick. 5" high with a 4½" diameter base. Made from ca. 1900 to 1901 in opal and turquoise (blue opaque). May be found decorated. The mold work on this candlestick is quite detailed, with the rope handle ending in carefully delineated tassels. A Butler Bros. catalog from 1905 shows a very similar candlestick as part of their Our Victor assortment, in "new fancy shapes, richly embossed all over satin etched glass in asst. blue, lavender, and green tints with hand painted floral decorations, such as violets, forget-me-nots, etc., the embossed work and edges profusely decorated in gold bronze." The shape is identical to the Dithridge No. 42, but the design on its base, as drawn by the artist, is different, probably because it represents the hand-painted decoration, although it is also possible that the mold may have been reworked. Opal: $35.00 – 40.00. Turquoise: $45.00 – 50.00.

DT-1. No. 42 CANDLESTICKS IN OPAL AND TURQUOISE

No. 40 handled footed candlestick. 4¼" high with a 4½" six-pointed base. Made 1899 – 1900 and probably longer. Known in opal, plain, or satin finish. Turquoise is also a likely color. The number "40" is impressed on the underside of the base. Offered as part of Dithridge's Victoria assortment and initially advertised by them in 1899. Often found decorated with hand-painted floral sprays and gold bronze on the edges. A number of other companies made similar candlesticks. The most distinctive feature on the Dithridge No. 40 are the "fronds" that appear on the points on the base, a design found on a number of matching pieces made by Dithridge, known to collectors today as Ray End. $25.00 – 35.00.

DT-2. No. 40 RAY END HANDLED FOOTED CANDLESTICK IN OPAL

DT-3. HANDLED CANDLESTICKS IN OPAL AND TURQUOISE

Handled candlestick. 4⅛" high with a 4½" six-pointed base. Made ca. 1903 – 1906 in opal, turquoise, and satin crystal. Often found decorated with hand-painted floral sprays and gold bronze on the edges. The detail on this candlestick is relatively crude, with roses on the base that look like little more than lumps. At least three other companies made similar candlesticks, all with well-defined detail on the handle and rims of the candle cup and base. Gillinder's No. 4 candlestick, McKee's Cinderella candlestick, and the third one by an unknown maker, can be seen side by side in the Gillinder chapter in volume 2 of this series, but can be easily differentiated from the Dithridge candlestick because they do not have the lumpy flowers on the base. A better quality version of this candlestick with well-defined flowers was also made by Vallerysthal in France and may have been the original design copied by everyone else. The earliest reference we have found for the Dithridge candlestick is in Butler Brothers' March 1903 catalog, where it is included in two assortments that contain other known Dithridge pieces. One is in opal and the other is in "a clouded crystal, handsomely tinted and hand decorated with raised gold and silver tracing." The candlestick is shown as part of a similar turquoise assortment in Butler Brothers' August 1906 catalog. Opal, crystal: $25.00 – 30.00. Turquoise: $35.00 – 40.00.

Candlestick. 6½" high with a 3⅞" square base. Made ca. 1902 to possibly as late as 1911. Known in opal only, but turquoise is also a possibility. Offered as part of Butler Brothers' "Unexcelled" assortment of hand-decorated opal ware in their fall 1902 catalog, which includes a number of other known Dithridge pieces. It is described as a "6½ in. extra large candlestick — wide base, fancy shape" and is offered as part of the "popular embossed rose design," which probably links it to the candlestick above — though it must be noted that the roses on this candlestick are better detailed. This mold either became very worn or underwent modifications. Although the roses and leaves on the decorated example in the accompanying photograph are still sharp, the design on the candle cup has all but disappeared. $25.00 – 30.00.

DT-4. CANDLESTICKS IN OPAL

DT-5. No. 89 CANDLESTICK IN OPAL

No. 89 candlestick. 5¼" high with a three-sided base that is 4" from point to point. Known in opal only, but turquoise is also a possibility. This candlestick appears as part of an assortment of Dithridge pieces in Butler Brothers' 1905 catalog, offered with hand-painted floral decorations and gold bronze on the edges. The example in the accompanying photograph has a satin finish. $25.00 – 30.00.

DRITZ-TRAUM COMPANY, New York. This company was primarily an importer that

did not manufacture their own glass. However, they did apparently design at least some of the pieces they sold, such as the Chateau candlesticks seen here. It is quite possible that these may also have been made abroad for Dritz-Traum, most likely in England.

Chateau candlestick. 2⅝" high with a 4¼" square base. Made ca. 1937 – 1938 in crystal only. Advertised in the fall 1938 Sears catalog as an "early American design." $10.00 – 12.00.

DR-1. CHATEAU CANDLESTICK

No. 9648 Chateau candlestick. 3¼" high with a 3⅜" diameter round base. Advertised in 1937 as part of a console set, stating that "You and your customers will be surprised to learn that this new, expensive looking line of sparkling, imported polished crystal is really 'inexpensive.'" Made in crystal only. $12.00 – 15.00.

DR-2. CHATEAU CONSOLE SET, FROM *Crockery and Glass Journal,* APRIL 1937

Chateau candelabrum. 7" high with a 4" diameter octagonal base. Advertised in 1937 in crystal only. Available with or without prisms. This item was designed by David Traum, who received a patent, D105,445, filed March 12, 1937, and approved July 27, 1937. The ridges on the base are reminiscent of Heisey's Ridgeleigh, which had been introduced just a couple of years previously in 1935. $25.00 – 30.00.

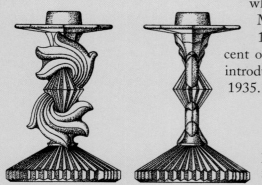

DR-3A. PATENT DRAWING

DR-3. CHATEAU CANDELABRUM (THE TWO FRONT PRISMS HAVE BEEN REMOVED TO BETTER SHOW THE CANDLESTICK)

DUNBAR GLASS CORPORATION, Dunbar, West Virginia (1912 – 1953). Origi-

nally founded as the Dunbar Flint Glass Company, this firm initially made flint glass lamp chimneys only. Other blown glass products were gradually added and the plant continued to expand, taking over the adjacent Bournique Art Glass Company in 1914. In 1921, a reorganization occurred and the name was changed to Dunbar Flint Glass Corporation. They acquired the idle Pennsylvania Glass Company in 1924, as they continued to grow, and in 1927 began the production of pressed glassware. In 1930, the name changed a final time to the Dunbar Glass Corporation. By this time, their production was considerably varied, but with their specialty being serving pieces, beverage sets, and vases offered with a wide range of decorations. In 1936, a table setting displayed at the Merchandise Mart's annual show was voted first choice in balloting by some 500 buyers, beating out Heisey, who came in second, and seventeen other exhibitors. In the 1940s, they went heavily into the manufacture of kitchenware, producing heat-resistant coffee makers, tea kettles, sauce pans, and double boilers. In 1943, it was stated that they were making more than 10,000 different shapes. These ranged from totally handmade to semi-automatic, with the company quick to utilize developments in technology. Their last advertisements in 1952 featured glass mounted in steel frames.

COLORS

During the 1920s and early 1930s, color was limited to rose pink and Bermuda green (also called Nile green, which was a pastel green, typical of the era). Amber was also made in the 1920s. Other colors reportedly produced in the 1930s include cobalt blue, ruby, and Stiegel green, but in much smaller quantities. Several luster finishes were offered, sometimes just covering portions of an article: blue, lavender, pearl, red, rose, and yellow (in 1924); amber, blue iridescent, peach, and wine (in 1926); amethyst, garden green, gunmetal blue, and light amber (in 1935); mother of pearl (in 1937). Opaque glass was offered as early as 1935 in refrigerator sets. "Mellow milk glass" was introduced in 1951; this was blown milk glass with various decorations and finishes.

DECORATIONS

Dunbar specialized in decorated glass of all types, ranging from the very simple to the highly ornate. A quick review of Dunbar advertising reveals gold encrustation and gold bands, light cuttings, etchings, hand painting, antique silver bands, overall brocade etchings, enamel designs, decals, and sand blast decorations — all at popular prices. As mentioned above, several colored lusters were offered. In 1935, Dunbar premiered their Carioca pattern — full of bubbles and roughly textured, very similar to Consolidated's Catalonian and Morgantown's El Mexicano.

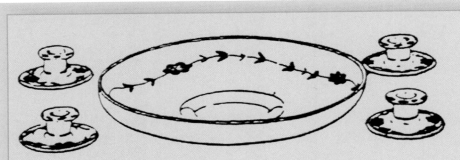

DB-1. CONSOLE SET, FROM *POTTERY, GLASS & BRASS SALESMAN*, AUGUST 4, 1927

Candlestick. Advertised in 1927 in amber, Bermuda green, and rose pink, plain or with luster finish. Available with light cutting or other decorations. This is the standard spool-shape candlestick that was made by at least ten other companies. $15.00 – 20.00.

Candlestick, sold under various pattern numbers as part of decorated console sets. 3¼" high with a 5" diameter base. Made from the 1920s to the 1930s in crystal, Bermuda green, and rose pink, either plain or with satin finish. Available with hand-painted decorations, cuttings, coin gold on black enamel, and other fired-on colors. There were at least two versions of this candlestick. Some drawings in the 1931 catalog have a scalloped base, while others are round. Another version of the candlestick, possibly Dunbar, has three small feet. The U.S. Glass Company's Tiffin factory made a very similar candlestick. It is slightly taller (3⅜") and the base, instead of being flat, has a ⅛" turned-down rim. The Tiffin candlestick will sometimes be found satin finished with a brocade etching on the base. $15.00 – 20.00.

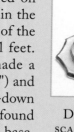

DB-2. CANDLESTICK, WITH SCALLOPED BASE, IN ROSE PINK

DB-2A. U.S. GLASS NO. 326 LOW CANDLESTICK

No. 1349 candlestick. Also listed as No. 6380-5 with a cutting. Offered in the 1931 catalog in Bermuda green and rose pink. Has a distinctive square, scalloped base. $18.00 – 23.00. *(Catalog reprint courtesy of the West Virginia Museum of American Glass.)*

DB-3. No. 1349 CANDLESTICK, FROM 1931 CATALOG

No. 4250-12 candlestick. 2½" high with a 5" diameter round base. Listed in the 1931 catalog in crystal, hand decorated with a deep etching, heavily encrusted with coin gold and a black border. Still in production in 1935. Other colors (especially Bermuda green and rose pink) are possible. A similar candlestick, which is 3¼" high, has been attributed to the Lancaster Glass Company. It has a knob just above the base that may be missing from the Dunbar candlestick. Unfortunately the picture shown here from the 1931 catalog, reproduced courtesy of the West Virginia Museum of American Glass, is not very clear. $12.00 – 15.00.

DB-4. No. 4250-12 CANDLESTICK, FROM 1931 CATALOG

Terrace or dining room set. Advertised as new in July 1935. This appears to be a pair of cylinder shades with candleholders inside, possibly made of plastic or wood, accompanying a No. 701 triplette rose bowl. $15.00 – 20.00.

DB-5. TERRACE SET, FROM *CROCKERY & GLASS JOURNAL,* JULY 1935

DB-6. HURRICANE
LAMP, FROM
AMERICAN HOME,
APRIL 1949

Hurricane lamp. Shown in *American Home*, April 1949, with a grape leaf cutting on the shade. Base only: $5.00 – 8.00. With globe: $18.00 – 25.00.

DB-7. No. 1330
BLOWN CANDLE-
STICK IN MEL-
LOW MILK
GLASS, FROM CA.
1951 CATALOG

No. 1330 blown candlestick. 4" high. Appears in catalog R-362. Available in crystal, cranberry (probably a stain), and "mellow milk glass" (Dunbar's name for blown milk glass). Offered with a variety of hand-painted and enamel decorations. Crystal: $8.00 – 12.00. Decorated milk glass: $12.00 – 18.00.

No. 104 Contrast hurricane. 14" high with a 3" diameter globe. One of 17 different designs combining glass with ebonized steel frames. Introduced in 1952 and made until the end of 1953, when the company discontinued production of glassware. Designed by Michael Lax, who later also designed for Duncan and Fenton. (See DM-97 on p. 170 and FN-59 on p. 195.) The line also included a larger hurricane (No. 101, 18" high with a 4" diameter globe) and two other lighting devices: the No. 103 candelabra (an ebonized stand holding three 3" diameter globes, with an overall height of 20") and the No. 112 wall hurricane (16" high, 10" long, and 5" wide, with a pair of 3" diameter globes).

DB-8. CONTRAST PATTERN, ADVERTISED
IN *HOUSE & GARDEN*, AUGUST 1952

DUNCAN (GEO.) AND SONS, Pittsburgh, Pennsylvania (1874 – 1891)
DUNCAN & MILLER GLASS COMPANY, Washington, Pennsylvania (1893

– 1955). The Duncan & Miller Glass Company of Jefferson Avenue, Washington, Pennsylvania, evolved from many prior names and associations. The story begins in 1865 when Daniel C. Ripley and five other investors formed Ripley & Company of Pittsburgh, Pennsylvania. George Duncan became a partner in the Ripley concern in 1867. Daniel C. Ripley died in 1871 and by 1873 the other investors had either died or been bought out by the Ripley heirs and George Duncan. In 1874 George purchased the remainder of the business from the Ripley family and two months later sold (for $1.00) half-interest in the firm to his son, James E., and his daughter, Susan. At that time the company name was changed to Geo. Duncan & Sons. George died in 1877 and the remaining half of the business was purchased by his son, James E., and A.H. Heisey (who was married to George's daughter, Susan). In 1891 Geo. Duncan & Sons joined the newly formed United States Glass Co. combine. They operated as Factory D of U.S. Glass until the factory was destroyed by fire in 1892. In 1893 James E. Duncan, his brother Harry B. Duncan, and John E. Miller (a talented glass designer and long-time employee of Geo. Duncan & Sons) built a new glass factory in Washington, Pennsylvania, under the name of Geo. Duncan's Sons and Co. In 1900 that name was changed to the Duncan & Miller Glass Company. Duncan & Miller remained in Washington, Pennsylvania, until 1955 when their trademark and other assets were sold to the U.S. Glass Company, which by that time had only one factory, the old Factory R in Tiffin, Ohio. Many of Duncan's skilled workers were relocated to Tiffin where they continued to operate as the Duncan & Miller Division of U.S. Glass until they also closed in 1980. Duncan's old Jefferson Avenue factory was sold to a company that recapped tires, but before the new owners were able to move in the plant was completely destroyed by a fire on June 29, 1956.

COLORS

Most of Duncan's early glassware was produced in crystal; however some colors were listed dating back to the Ripley years. The peak of the Geo. Duncan & Sons color period occurred around the mid 1880s with some colors remaining in production until fire destroyed the factory in 1892. Known colors from Duncan's early years (1867 – 1891) include amber, amethyst, blue (medium), canary (vaseline), cobalt, crystal, green, old gold (light amber), opal, pink, ruby, and rubina (ruby, shading to amber or other colors). Stained pieces, where the color is applied to the surface of crystal glass, are known in amber, blue, and ruby. Some items were available in gold-trimmed or with an etched (satin) finish.

Production of colored glassware at the Duncan & Miller Co. was limited until the mid-twenties when color was in vogue at all of the glass companies. The production of colored glassware continued into the next decade, but by the end of the thirties most of the Depression era colors were discontinued: green (ca. 1924 – 1937), amber (ca. 1925 – 1937), rose (ca. 1926 – 1931), ebony (ca. 1930 – 1933), cobalt blue (royal blue, ca. 1931 – 1937), ruby (ca. 1932 – 1936 and then, again, ca. 1948 – 1953), sapphire blue (a pale, ice blue, ca. 1936 – 1937). Sienna (pale amber on the pink side) was briefly made in 1940. In about 1941 – 1942 Duncan introduced a series of popular opalescent colors: Cape Cod blue, cranberry pink, and jasmine yellow; green opalescent was also made, but probably only experimentally. The post-war years saw the introduction (or reintroduction) of more colors, including chartreuse (ca. 1949 – 1952), milk glass (beginning in 1950), Biscayne green (a medium dark green, ca. 1952 – 1953), Key Largo blue (ca. 1952), smoky avocado (ca. 1953), teakwood brown (ca. 1953), aqua (turquoise, ca. 1955), and golden honey (ca. 1955). Amber, ruby, and possibly other stains were also offered during this period. Mercury (a silver, mirror-like finish) and frost (satin finished crystal, ca. 1934) were other decorations used.

After 1955, the colors produced by the Duncan & Miller Division of U.S. Glass (1955 – 1980) were primarily the Tiffin factory colors: dawn (Tiffin's twilight, a lavender similar to Heisey's alexandrite or Fostoria's wisteria, ca. 1951 – 1980, but advertised as dawn, beginning in 1957, when used with Duncan molds), pine (a dark green, ca. 1952 – 1956), milk glass (ca. 1957 – 1963), Copen blue (light blue, ca. 1958 – 1970), black (late 1950s and again in the late 1970s), smoke (a brown similar to Duncan's teakwood, late 1950s and again in the 1970s), persimmon (early 1960s), golden banana (bright yellow, ca. 1961 – 1962), plum (amethyst, ca. 1961 – 1962), empire green (a bright green, ca. 1961 – 1962), Tiffin rose pink, ca. 1962 – 1963), citron green (similar to Duncan's earlier chartreuse, but darker, ca. 1964), desert red (a mostly amber/orange amberina, ca. 1965 – 1978), flame (a mostly red amberina, production dates unknown), and greenbriar (a smoky green, late 1960s).

DM-1. ROMAN I CANDLEHOLDER IN BLUE

Roman I candleholder. 10½" high with a 5½" diameter base. Originated by Ripley & Co., probably in the 1860s. We surmise this from the base, which is mold-marked with "RIPLEY & Co" and "PAT PENDING." The patent referred to was issued in February of 1870 so the mold was logically produced before that time. This candlestick was shown in an 1877 Geo. Duncan & Sons catalog where it was listed in crystal, blue, and opal. These have a spool-shaped Britannia metal candle cup with two thin horizontal bands at the center. In 1877 they sold for $1.75 (crystal), $2.00 (opal), or $2.50 (blue) each. All colors are scarce. Crystal: $125.00 – 150.00. Opal: $200.00 – 250.00. Blue: $250.00 – 280.00.

DM-2. ROMAN II CANDELABRUM, FROM 1877 CATALOG

Roman II candelabrum. 14½" high, 5½" diameter base. This candleholder consists of an arm attached to a Roman I candlestick that converts it into a two-light candelabrum. Like the Roman I this was originated by Ripley & Co., most likely in the 1860s. The base is marked with "RIPLEY & Co" and "PAT PENDING." The arm is also marked "PAT PENDING." The patent for the candleholder was issued in February of 1870 so the mold was logically produced before this. This candlestick was shown in an 1877 Geo. Duncan & Sons catalog where it was listed in crystal, blue, and opal. The insert consists of two Britannia metal candle cups attached to a glass arm with a 10" spread. Between the arms is a glass sphere, the upper half of which is removable and has a small cross. The lower hemisphere bears the letters "IHS." In 1877 the prices ranged from $5.00 to $8.00 each, quite expensive at that time. Scarce to rare in any color. Complete examples in good condition are quite rare. Crystal: $275.00 – 325.00. Opal: $375.00 – 450.00. Blue: $500.00 – 600.00.

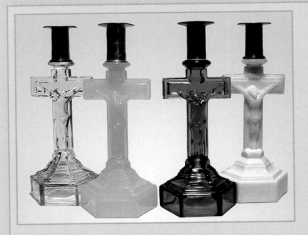

DM-3. CRUCIFIXES IN CRYSTAL, OPALINE, BLUE, AND OPAL

Crucifix candleholder. 10" high with a 3⅝" hexagonal base. Circa 1870s – 1891. Scarce in opal and crystal, rare in blue and opaline (a Ripley color). The crystal was advertised in plain or etched (frosted). Because these use the same metal socket as found on the Roman candleholders we assume they also originated with Ripley. In 1877 these were listed as being available in "all glass" or with a "Britannia [metal] top." Unfortunately, only the metal top version was shown. We have never seen an identical Crucifix candlestick with a glass socket. Perhaps the all glass version was from a completely different mold and is one of the many unattributed Crucifix candleholders in existence. Prices in 1877 ranged from $1.00 to $2.50 for the all glass version and $2.25 to $3.00 for the Britannia top version. By the next year the all glass versions were the same price as the Britannia top versions. This candleholder appeared in the first U.S. Glass 1891 Factory D catalog but was gone the next year. This mold may have been lost when Factory D burned in March of 1892. Crystal: $150.00 – 200.00. Opal: $225.00 – 275.00. Clambroth: $250.00 – 300.00. Blue: $300.00 – 350.00.

Pope Leo XIII candlestick. 9¾" high. Circa 1878 – 1886. Available in opal, crystal, and crystal etched (frosted). These originally sold for $3.00 each in opal, $3.50 for crystal etched, and $2.50 for plain crystal. Scarce. Crystal (plain or frosted): $225.00 – 300.00. Opal: $275.00 – 325.00.

DM-4. POPE LEO XIII CANDLESTICK, FROM EARLY CATALOG

Grecian candlestick. 10¾" high. Produced from 1878 to 1891 in crystal and crystal etched (frosted). Appeared in the U.S. Glass 1891 Factory D catalog but was gone the next year. This is another mold that may have been lost when Factory D burned in 1892. We have never seen one of these candlesticks and assume them to be scarce to rare. $350.00 – market.

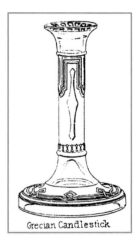

DM-5. GRECIAN CANDLESTICK, FROM CATALOG, CA. 1890

No. 358 candlestick. 10½" high. Introduced in 1891 as part of Geo. Duncan's No. 360 Pattern and continued in production through 1904 as U.S. Glass No. 16. Known only in crystal. Hard to find. $150.00 – 175.00.

DM-6. No. 358 CANDLESTICK, FROM CATALOG, CA. 1890

DM-7. No. 1 Early American Sandwich candelabrum

No. 1 Early American Sandwich candelabrum. 10" high with a 5¼" base. The predecessor to this Duncan & Miller staple was a large candelabrum introduced in the mid 1890s (DM-7a and DM-7b), and reissued from 1935 to around 1940. The smaller versions shown in DM-7 and DM-7c share many parts with their more elaborate cousin, but were not introduced until 1935. Production continued at least into the 1960s, well after Duncan had become a division of U.S. Glass. Screw-in sockets and metal connectors allowed this versatile candleholder to be sold as a single to five-light candelabra. It was also sold with a globe as a hurricane lamp. An epergne can also be found in place of the center candle cup. The hurricane globes can be found etched with various patterns, including First Love and Indian Tree. One-light: $70.00 – 85.00; with hurricane globe (plain): $100.00 – 125.00; with hurricane globe (etched): $150.00 – 200.00. Three-light: $250.00 – 300.00; with arm extension: $350.00 – 400.00.

DM-7a. No. 2 Early American Sandwich five-light candelabrum

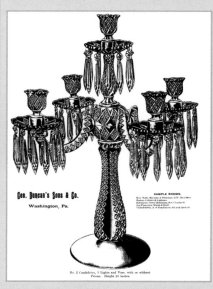

DM-7b. Geo. Duncan's Sons & Co. advertisement, *China, Glass & Lamps*, November 4, 1896. (Note difference in base compared to DM-7a.)

DM-7c. Duncan & Miller catalog, ca. 1940s

No. 65 or No. 120 candelabrum. 11" – 12" high. Consists of four main pieces: a 5" scalloped base, a screw in metal connector, a bobeche with 5, 8, 10, or 12 prisms, and a screw-on candle cup. Estimated to have been first produced in the early 1900s, they continued in production until at least the 1960s. Made primarily in crystal but for a short time during the 1950s these were also manufactured in milk glass as Duncan's No. 120 Monticello Candelabra. The milk glass versions came with crystal or ruby prisms and are eagerly sought after by collectors. Sometimes the base is flared more, as shown in DM-8a, making the height about an inch shorter. Although most of the Duncan items that continued to be manufactured by U.S. Glass were advertised as Duncan & Miller, it seems that Tiffin marketed these simply as Tiffin, with no mention of their Duncan heritage. One-light, crystal: $65.00 – 75.00; milk glass: $225.00 – 275.00. Two-light, crystal: $200.00 – 250.00; milk glass: market. Three-light, crystal: $250.00 – 300.00; milk glass: $500.00 – market.

DM-8. No. 65 (No. 120) CANDELABRUM

DM-8A. No. 65 (No. 120) TWO-LIGHT CAN-DELABRUM, FLARED BASE

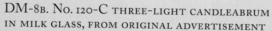

DM-8B. No. 120-C THREE-LIGHT CANDLEABRUM IN MILK GLASS, FROM ORIGINAL ADVERTISEMENT

No. 54 candlestick. 8½" high with a 5" diameter, nine-sided, scalloped base. Circa 1900 – 1923 in crystal. This was also offered with cuttings. $50.00 – 65.00.

DM-9. No. 54 CANDLESTICK

DM-10. No. 58
CANDLESTICK

No. 58 candlestick. 9" high, 5" diameter base. Circa 1900 – 1923 in crystal. An undated Lotus catalog shows this candlestick with their No. 17 cutting. $50.00 – 55.00.

DM-11. No. 61
CANDLESTICK,
FROM CATALOG,
CA. 1900

No. 61 candlestick. Sometimes called Sweet Sixty-one by collectors. 10" high. Skirted base. Circa 1900 – 1923. Known only in crystal. $55.00 – 60.00.

DM-12. No. 64 CHAMBER
CANDLESTICK

No. 64 chamber candlestick. 4" high, handled, with a 4½" diameter base. Circa 1900 – 1923 in crystal. Sold as part of the No. 61, five-piece bedroom set. The other pieces consisted of a pitcher, two glasses, and a tray. A similar handled chamberstick was made by Heisey as part of their No. 150 pattern from 1907 to 1930; the primary differences are in the shape of the candle cup and the distinctive pointed thumb guard on the handle of the Duncan candlestick. $20.00 – 25.00.

DM-12A. COMPARISON OF
DUNCAN NO. 64 CANDLE-
STICK AND HEISEY NO. 150
CANDLESTICK

No. 66 candlestick. Available in 4", 6", and 7½" heights. The 4" size is generally considered a toy candlestick and has a base 2½" in diameter. The base on the 7½" size is 4⅜" in diameter. Produced ca. 1900 to as late as 1937 in some sizes. Made in amber, black, and crystal. Cambridge, New Martinsville, and Paden City made very similar candlesticks. Cambridge's No. 2862 candlestick (in 6½" and 7½" heights) has the bulge closer to the center of its column. (See CB-22 on p. 55.) New Martinsville's No. 19 candlestick (7½" high) and Paden City's No. 114 candlesticks (6½" and 7½" high) are the closest in design to Duncan's, with the bulge higher up on the stem, and came in similar colors, but the Duncan & Miller has three mold seams and the others have two. Crystal: $25.00 – 30.00. Colors: $30.00 – 35.00.

DM-13. No. 66 CANDLESTICKS, 7½" SIZE WITH CUTTING AND 4" TOY

No. 67 candlestick. Unknown size. Produced ca. 1900 – 1937 in crystal. An undated catalog shows this candlestick with their No. 16 cutting. $55.00 – 65.00.

DM-14. No. 67 CANDLESTICK, FROM CATALOG, CA. 1900

No. 68 candlestick. 3⅝" high, 4¾" saucer base. Produced ca. 1900 – 1923 in crystal. This candlestick reappeared around 1940 with the base turned down and the pattern changed to No. 120. (See DM-77 on p. 164.) $30.00 – 35.00.

DM-15. No. 68 CANDLESTICK

No. 72 toy chamber candlestick. 2" high, 2½" hexagonal base. Circa 1900 – 1923 in crystal. This is a miniature stick that holds a slim taper candle. Other toy candlesticks by Heisey and Westmoreland have round loop handles; the shape of the Duncan handle is distinctive. $30.00 – 35.00.

DM-16. No. 72 TOY CHAMBER CANDLESTICK

No. 91 candlestick. Available in 9" (flared skirt) or 10" (straight skirt). Produced 1917 – 1927 in crystal. Edmondson Warrin & Co., a decorating company, advertised this candlestick with various sterling silver and enamel designs. Duncan advertised this pattern as "Almost as light as blownware," and stated emphatically that "We have been granted letters patent on this design — the greatest achievement in pressed glass making in the history of the industry — and will prosecute all infringers." Despite the warning, Diamond Glass Co. (DI-4 on p. 132) and Fostoria Glass Co. both made candlesticks similar to the straight skirt version. Josef Inwald, A.G., of Czechoslovakia, also made a very similar candlestick in the 1920s – 1930s. $45.00 – 50.00.

DM-17. No. 91 CANDLESTICK, STRAIGHT SKIRT, FROM CATALOG

DM-17A. 1917 ADVERTISEMENT FROM *POTTERY, GLASS & BRASS SALESMAN.* NOTE FLARED SKIRT.

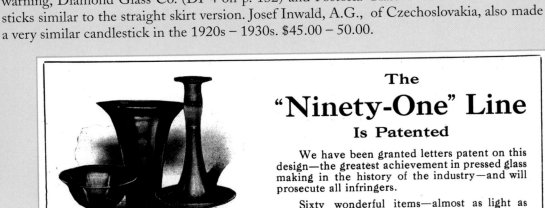

The
"Ninety-One" Line
Is Patented

We have been granted letters patent on this design—the greatest achievement in pressed glass making in the history of the industry—and will prosecute all infringers.

Sixty wonderful items—almost as light as blownware. A full line of Stemware and scores of Novelties and Specialties.

Write for Catalog and Price List today

The Duncan & Miller Glass Company
WASHINGTON, PA.

W. B. ANDREWS, 30 E. Randolph St., Chicago, Illinois
PAUL JOSEPH, 92 West Broadway, New York
THE MAUS-STEWART CO., 146 Southwest Temple, Salt Lake City, Utah

JOSEPH TOMKINSON, 213 Commercial Bldg., Philadelphia   MARSH & KIDD CO., 617 Mission St., San Francisco
GREEN & THOMAS, 33 So. Charles St., Baltimore   H. B. HOLLIS, 157 Summer St., Boston

DM-18. No. 70 CANDLESTICK, FROM CATALOG 24

No. 70 square tapered candlestick. Unknown size. From Duncan & Miller catalog #24, circa 1923. Listed in crystal. Other companies made very similarly shaped candlesticks. $35.00 – 40.00.

DM-19. No. 99 CANDLESTICK

No. 99 candlestick. 9⅝" high, 3½" base. Mold blown. Ca. 1922 – 1927 in crystal, sometimes with wheel cut design. Advertisements stated that the pattern was "suggested by the superb 'flutings' of the Stourbridge and Waterford glass cutters of the early nineteenth century." The pattern was designed to be used by cutters or other decorators as blanks. $55.00 – 60.00.

No. 35 low candlestick. Produced ca. 1923 – 1927 in crystal. This is the lowest of the No. 35 candleholders. It also has a different socket from the others in this line. Almost every company made a similar spool candleholder. $10.00 – 20.00.

DM-20. No. 35 LOW CANDLE-STICK, FROM 1927 CATALOG

No. 35 candlestick. Available in 3", 4½", 6½", and 8" heights. Produced ca. 1923 – 1927 in crystal and in crystal with an amber stain. Westmoreland made a similarly shaped 9" candleholder (No. 1041). An 8¾" example in one of the authors' collections in sky blue satin is probably Westmoreland, but may be a Tiffin reissue using the Duncan mold. Crystal, crystal with amber stain: $30.00 – 40.00.

DM-21. No. 35 TALL CANDLESTICK, FROM 1927 CATALOG

DM-21A. No. 35 3" CANDLESTICK, FROM 1927 CATALOG

DM-21B. No. 35 CANDLESTICKS WITH UNKNOWN DECORATIONS IN 4½" AND 6½" SIZES

No. 36 candlestick. Available in two heights: 8½" and 12". Produced 1922 – 1937. Made in plain crystal or cut and with an amber stain. $30.00 – 35.00.

DM-22. No. 36 CANDLESTICK WITH AMBER STAIN AND CUTTING

No. 83 Tavern handled candlestick. Introduced in 1923 and probably only in production briefly. Known only in crystal. $50.00 – 75.00.

DM-23. No. 83 TAVERN HANDLED CANDLESTICK, FROM CATALOG, CA. 1923

DM-24. No. 83
TAVERN CANDLE-
STICKS, 7½" AND 9"

No. 83 Tavern candlesticks. Available in 6", 7½", and 9" heights. Made ca. 1923 – 1927. Known only in crystal. Can be found stained or with a hand-painted floral decoration. $45.00 – 65.00.

DM-25. No. 40½ EARLY COLONIAL SPIRAL candle-stick in amber

No. 40½ (3½" high) and No. 40 (7½", 9½", and 11½" high) Early Colonial Spiral candlesticks. Circa 1924 – 1927. Made in amber, green, crystal, and rose; the small size is also known in Cape Cod blue and cranberry pink opalescent. The pattern was advertised as a reproduction of Steigel glass and is also known as Spiral Flutes by collectors. A 10½" kerosene lamp was also made in this pattern. 3½": $15.00 – 20.00. 7½": $45.00 – 55.00. 9½": $50.00 – 65.00. 11½": $90.00 – 125.00.

Note: The 7½" size of this candle-stick has been reproduced in cobalt and possibly other colors. The reproduction might be from the original mold but the glass quality is quite poor. We don't know who made it, but it has the appearance of glass imported from Taiwan.

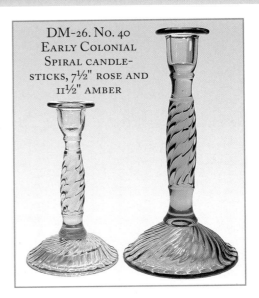

DM-26. No. 40 EARLY COLONIAL SPIRAL candle-sticks, 7½" ROSE AND 11½" AMBER

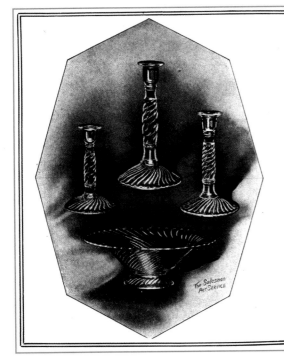

"40"

Early Colonial Spiral

IN the No. 40 Line we have reproduced a pattern in glassware that goes back to the earliest days of glass making in America. It is found among priceless specimens of Stiegel glass (Manheim, Pa., 1765) in museum and private collections and other early makes.

To carry out the revival completely we are making it in the delightful green and amber as well as crystal of Colonial days. All the staples and many novelties.

The
Duncan & Miller Glass Co.
Washington, Pa.

DM-26A. AD FROM FEBRUARY 4, 1926, EDITION OF *THE POTTERY, GLASS & BRASS SALESMAN*

No. 101 Ripple candle block. 1¼" high and 4¼" in diameter. Produced in 1927 in crystal and green. Other colors known in the pattern are likely, including amber and rose. Also called Rings. The pattern was advertised in 1928 as Corduroy, "after Stiegel, Manheim, Pa., 1765." $20.00 – 25.00.

DM-27. No. 101 RIPPLE CANDLE BLOCK IN GREEN

No. 101 Ripple low candlestick. 3" high with a 4⅜" diameter base. Produced 1927 and probably continued until the 1930s. Made in amber, cobalt, crystal, green, rose, and ruby. Also called Rings, offered as part of a console set, and advertised as a reproduction of Czechoslovakian glass. Other ads from 1928 called the pattern Corduroy, "after Stiegel, Manheim, Pa., 1765." Somewhat similar to Heisey's later No. 1485 Saturn candlestick (1947 – 1953), except that the latter has wider rings and does not have the knob above the base. Crystal, amber: $30.00 – 35.00. Rose, green: $35.00 – 45.00. Cobalt, ruby: $50.00 – 60.00.

DM-28. No. 101 RIPPLE LOW CANDLESTICK IN ROSE

No. 103 Georgian candlestick. 1¾" high, 5" across. Circa 1927 – 1937 in amber, crystal, green, and rose. Offered as part of a console set. Fenton also made a candlestick in the Georgian pattern, but the shape is totally different. $20.00 – 28.00.

DM-29. No. 103 GEORGIAN CANDLESTICKS IN ROSE

No. 44 candlestick. 3¾" high, 4¼" diameter base. Known as Swirled Diamond or Quilted Diamond. Introduced in 1927. Made in amber, cobalt, crystal, green, and rose. Advertised as part of a console set and sold with a No. 44 crimped flower bowl. $25.00 – 35.00.

DM-30. No. 44 CANDLESTICK IN GREEN

No. 28 short candlestick. 3¾" high, 4⅜" diameter base. Produced from 1927 to at least 1943. Made in ebony, amber, crystal, green, and rose. $15.00 – 20.00.

DM-31. No. 28 SHORT CANDLESTICK IN GREEN

DM-32. No. 28
TALL CANDLESTICK
IN AMBER

No. 28 tall candlestick. 5¾" high x 4⅜" base. 1927 to circa 1943. Made in amber, crystal, ebony, green, and rose. Lotus combined this with a Heisey Queen Ann bowl decorated with Trianon (non-tarnish silver overlay on black glass). Edmonson Warrin & Co. also decorated these candlesticks with non-tarnish silver on transparent colors and Lotus offered these candlesticks with their La Furiste etching and other decorations. $25.00 – 35.00.

DM-33.
PHARAOH
CANDLE-
STICK

Pharaoh candlestick. This is probably the No. 4 candlestick, described by *Pottery, Glass, and Brass Salesman* in 1929 as "rather futuristic with its stepped foot." 2¾" high, 3½" square base. Produced in 1929. Made in amber with a crystal top, crystal, green, and rose. Other colors of the period are likely. Advertised as part of a console set. Can be found with a wheel-cut design on the rim. McKee made a very similar candlestick as part of their Lenox design in similar colors; the steps on the base of the McKee candlestick curve outwards, whereas the Duncan candlestick is indented on the sides. Also, the McKee candlestick has a draped design on the candleholder. $45.00 – 60.00.

DM-34. No.
3 THREE-
LEAF CAN-
DLESTICKS
IN ROSE AND
GREEN

No. 3 Three-Leaf candlestick. 2¾" high with a 4¼" diameter base. Circa 1929. Made in crystal, amber, green, and rose. Shown as part of a console set with the bowl available in four different shapes. A photograph in the July 1929 issue of *Crockery and Glass Journal* shows this console set offered by Leon A. Anthony of New York with his No. 218 gold and enamel decoration. $25.00 – 30.00.

DM-35 UNKNOWN THREE-
LEAF PATTERN CANDLE-
HOLDER, POSSIBLY DUNCAN

Unknown candleholder in what appears to be Duncan's Three-Leaf pattern. Several things make us believe that this might have been a product of Duncan & Miller. The pattern, color, and glass quality are all consistent with Duncan's, plus there's something else (admittedly less tangible)… We purchased a pair of these from a flea market vender whose entire table was filled with rose (pink) Duncan & Miller glassware. They had what looked to be a complete table setting of Canterbury along with two pairs of candleholders. One was a pair of Duncan's #28 (DM-31) and the other was the pair in question. The dealer (who was not aware that any of this was Duncan & Miller) said that it had all come from one estate. Make of it what you will. If more evidence comes to light (for or against) we'll publish it in a future volume.

Puritan candlestick. 2" high, 2⅞" footed base with a 4⅜" diameter mushroom top. Introduced in 1929. Made in green, rose, crystal, and crystal with various cuttings and/or stains. Advertised as "reflecting all the charm and rare simplicity in Early American Design yet within the reach of the modest purse." This may be the No. 6 candlestick. *Pottery, Glass, and Brass Salesman* described the console set in 1929, stating that "it shows a ring foot of fancy nature [on the bowl] and shows lines pressed into the bowl and also ornamenting the candlesticks." Crystal: $25.00 – 30.00. Colors or decorations: $50 .00 – 65.00.

DM-36. PURITAN CANDLESTICK

DM-37A. 1930 AD SHOWING DUNCAN'S BLACK GLASS LINE

Deco candlestick. 6" high, 4¾" base. Introduced in 1930 in cobalt, ebony, rose, green, and crystal. These were often decorated. Shown here in ebony with gold encrusted etched base and gold trim. Crystal: $35.00 – 40.00. Rose, green: $40.00 – 45.00. Ebony: $45.00 – 50.00. Cobalt: $50.00 – 60.00.

DM-37. DECO CANDLESTICK IN EBONY, UNKNOWN PATTERN NUMBER

No. 16 candlestick. 6¼" high, 4⅝" base. Circa 1930 – 1939. Made in amber, cobalt, crystal, crystal with gold trim, ebony, green, ruby, and rose. Available as part of a console set with a 12" flared bowl. This blank was also decorated by Lotus with their Trianon silver overlay on black. It was also known to have been decorated by Rockwell with silver overlay. Crystal (plain or with gold), amber: $30.00 – 35.00. Rose, green, black: $35.00 – 50.00. Cobalt, ruby: $75.00 – market.

DM-38A. NO. 16 CANDLESTICK IN AMBER WITH SILVER DECORATION

DM-38. NO. 16 CANDLESTICK IN EBONY

DM-39. No. 21 PLAZA CANDLE-STICK IN EBONY

No. 21 Plaza candlestick. Two-light. 5⅜" high x 6⅝" wide, with a 4½" base. Introduced around 1930 and discontinued by the middle of 1942. Made in amber, crystal, ebony, green, rose, and ruby. Amber, crystal: $40.00 – 45.00. Rose, green, black: $45.00 – 55.00. Ruby: $75.00 – 90.00.

No. 118 low Hobnail candlestick. 1½" high and 3½" in diameter. Produced in 1930. Known in crystal and rose. We believe these to be Duncan & Miller. They were advertised as part of a Hobnail dresser set by a company called Spicer Studio in Akron, Ohio, and are shown with Duncan & Miller 8 oz. colognes and a 4" puff box. They were advertised in amber, amethyst, blue, and rainbow green; these were probably iridescent finishes, since this appears to have been a specialty of Spicer's. $25.00 – 35.00.

DM-40. No. 118 HOBNAIL LOW CANDLESTICK (BELIEVED TO BE DUNCAN)

DM-41. No. 118 HOBNAIL CANDLESTICKS IN CAPE COD BLUE OPALESCENT AND CRAN-BERRY PINK OPALESCENT

No. 118 Hobnail candlestick. 4¼" high, 4" base. Produced from the early 1930s through the 1940s. Reissued by Tiffin in the 1960s. Reported in amber, green, rose, sapphire blue, ruby, Cape Cod blue opalescent, cranberry pink opalescent, crystal, and crystal opalescent. Green opalescent and jasmine yellow opalescent are other possible colors. Was also sold as a candelabrum with a peg bobeche and six prisms. Shown by Tiffin as No. 718-25 as part of a console set in milk glass with a No. 718-27 crimped 11½" bowl. Tiffin colors (reissued as No. 518-25) included milk glass, plum, cobalt blue, golden banana, Tiffin rose, and empire green. Crystal: $15.00 – 20.00. Plum, rose: $25.00 – 35.00. Crystal (with prisms) or opalescent colors: $35.00 – 45.00. Cobalt: $45.00 – 55.00.

DM-42. No. 14 GRANDEE THREE-LIGHT CANDELABRUM

No. 14 Grandee candelabrum. Three-light. Later listed as part of the Duncan Diamond group. 7¾" high x 9¼" wide with a 5¼" base. Produced 1934 until sometime in the 1940s. Made in amber, cobalt, ruby, green, and crystal, plain or with frosted finish. The crystal was available with a lattice cutting (No. 35). Also available as a candelabra with bobeches and prisms added. Advertised as part of a console set with a No. 14 footed bowl or a No. 11 Eden 14" bowl. Crystal: $45.00 – 50.00. Amber, green: $175.00 – 225.00. Cobalt, ruby: $225.00 – 300.00.

No. 14 Grandee candelabrum. Later listed as No. 75 (14) as part of the Diamond pattern. 8" high with a 4¾" diameter base. One-light with attached bobeche and eight prisms. Probably originally made in the 1930s and then reissued circa 1940 – 1943 in crystal and sienna (pale amber on the pink side) as Diamond. (See DM-75 on p. 163 for the remaining candlestick in the Diamond group.) L. E. Smith made a similar candelabrum but the base on the Smith version is raised and patterned. $35.00 – 40.00.

DM-43. No. 14 GRANDEE/NO. 75 DIAMOND CAN-DELABRUM

DM-44. No. 128 TROPICAL FISH CANDLE-STICK, FROM 1943 CATALOG

No. 128 Tropical fish candlestick. 5" high. According to Hazel Marie Weatherman, this pattern was introduced in 1934 and was still in the 1943 catalog. Made in Cape Cod blue opalescent, cranberry pink opalescent, crystal, and crystal satin. Designed by Charles "Eddie" Westlake as part of the Sculptured Glass line. These are very difficult to find. Crystal, crystal satin: $200.00 – 400.00. Opalescent colors: $800.00 – market.

No. 128 Chrysanthemum candlestick. 5" diameter. These have a hobnail pattern on the base and a socket in the shape of a chrysanthemum. According to Hazel Marie Weatherman, this pattern was introduced in 1934, and was still listed in the 1943 catalog. Known in Cape Cod blue opalescent and crystal. Other opalescent colors are probable. All colors may be found with a frosted finish. These were part of Duncan's Sculptured Glass line. Crystal satin: $75.00 – 100.00. Opalescent colors: $100.00 – 125.00.

DM-45. No. 128 CHRYSAN-THEMUM CANDLE-STICK, FROM 1943 CATALOG

No. 111 Terrace low candlestick. 4" high. Produced 1935 to the 1940s. Made in amber, blue, crystal, crystal with First Love etching, and ruby. Offered as part of a console set. Crystal (plain): $25.00 – 30.00. Amber, crystal (etched): $35.00 – 45.00. Cobalt, ruby: $60.00 – 80.00.

DM-46. No. 111 TERRACE LOW CANDLESTICK

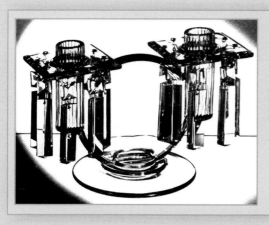

DM-47. No. 111
TERRACE
TWO-LIGHT
CANDELABRUM

No. 111 Terrace candlestick. Two-light. Unknown size. Produced 1935 – ca. 1940 in crystal. Available with or without bobeches and prisms. The accompanying illustration is from the *Crockery and Glass Journal,* September 1935. $125.00 – 150.00; with bobeches and prisms: $175.00 – 200.00.

DM-48. No. 111
TERRACE ONE-
LIGHT CANDE-
LABRUM, FROM
CATALOG

No. 111 Terrace candelabrum. 9" high with C prisms, square base. 1935 – ca. 1940 in crystal. $100.00 – 125.00.

DM-49. No. 112
CARIBBEAN CAN-
DELABRUM

No. 112 Caribbean candlestick. 7¾" high with a 4½" base. Introduced in 1936 as part of Duncan's new Wave line and discontinued before 1940. Made in sapphire blue, crystal, and crystal with ruby trim. Crystal: $65.00 – 75.00. Blue: $110.00 – 125.00.

DM-50. No. 112
CARIBBEAN
TWO-LIGHT
CANDLESTICK

No. 112 Caribbean candlestick. Two-light. 4¾" high x 5½" base. Introduced in 1936 and discontinued before 1940. Made in sapphire blue and crystal. Crystal: $70.00 – 80.00. Blue: $125.00 – 150.00.

Here are two candleholders often ascribed to Duncan & Miller's Caribbean line, however we can find no hard evidence of this and must therefore list them as unknown. While they may turn out to be Duncan, our opinion is that several things point away from it…

•The Caribbean line is fairly well documented, but we could not find these in any Duncan catalog or advertisement.

•They always seem to show up in amber, while (by far) the prevailing colors for Caribbean are crystal and sapphire blue.

•Other companies are known to have made very similar patterns; Jefferson for one.

•They often show up on eBay from European sellers, suggesting that they may have been made in England or elsewhere in Europe.

If additional information comes to light it will be published in a future volume.

DM-51. UNKNOWN CANDLESTICK OFTEN SEEN LISTED AS DUNCAN'S CARIBBEAN *(Artist's rendition)*

DM-52. UNKNOWN CANDLESTICK OFTEN SEEN LISTED AS DUNCAN'S CARIBBEAN

No. 5 candlestick. 6" high. Production was probably around the early to mid-1930s. Known in cobalt. Other colors are possible. Sometimes associated with the Venetian pattern, although this is actually a separate line. $70.00 – 80.00. *(Artist's rendition.)*

DM-53. No. 5 CANDLESTICK

No. 50 Venetian candlestick. 3" high. The base forms a triangle with rounded sides, approximately 4" in diameter. Produced ca. 1937 through at least the early 1940s. Made in cranberry pink opalescent, crystal opalescent, ruby, and plain crystal. Other opalescent colors are possible. A 7/24/42 Duncan document entitled "Items Discontinued from Price Lists" includes a No. 126 Venetian candlestick, 3" high, that was available with the Bridal Rose etching. We don't know if this is the same candlestick with a different pattern number or an otherwise unknown one. Crystal: $35.00 – 45.00. Opalescent colors: $40.00 – 50.00. Cobalt, ruby: $50.00 – 60.00.

DM-54A. No. 50 VENETIAN CANDLESTICK IN CRANBERRY PINK OPALESCENT

DM-54. No. 50 VENETIAN CANDLESTICK IN RUBY

DM-55. VIKING CONSOLE SET

Viking pattern candlestick. Unknown line number. Taken from a March 1937 ad in *Crockery & Glass Journal.* It is blown with an air twist stem in crystal and the bowl and feet in blue. Other colors are possible. We know nothing more about this candleholder, but suspect that it is the work of Aaron Bloom, who produced off-hand ware for Duncan from 1937 to 1940. $45.00 – 60.00.

DM-56. No. 301 TEAR DROP CANDLESTICK

No. 301 Tear Drop candlestick. 4" high with a 4½" diameter base. Circa 1937 – 1955 in crystal. Offered as part of console set with a 12" oval or round flower bowl. $15.00 – 20.00.

DM-57. No. 301 TEAR DROP TWO-LIGHT CANDLESTICK

No. 301 Tear Drop candlestick, two-light. 4½" high with a 5¼" diameter base. Circa 1937 – 1940 in crystal. Offered as a candelabrum with two peg bobeches and six stubby prisms. Available as part of a console set with a 12" oval bowl. $35.00 – 40.00.

Two additional candlesticks were added later to the Tear Drop pattern. See DM-88 and DM-89 on p. 167.

DM-58. No. 113 RADIANCE CANDLEHOLDER IN COBALT

No. 113 Radiance candleholder. 3⅞" high, 4¼" diameter base. Produced 1937 – circa 1940. Known colors are cobalt, sapphire blue, green, and crystal. Other pieces of this pattern were made in amber and ruby so it's possible that the candlestick was also. Crystal: $20.00 – 25.00. Light blue, green: $25.00 – 30.00. Cobalt: $30.00 – 35.00.

No. 115 Canterbury candlestick. Three-light. 5⅛"
high with a 4⅞" base, 8½" across the arms. Circa
1937 – 1939 in crystal. Also available as a No. 115
three-light candelabra with cut prisms and two
bobeches and as a two-light epergne candlestick.
$35.00 – 45.00; with bobeches and prisms: $65.00
– 105.00.

DM-59. No. 115
Canterbury
three-light
candlestick

No. 115 Canterbury candlestick. 6" high. Produced 1937 – 1950 in
crystal. Also advertised as a 7" high, one-light candelabrum with a
peg bobeche and U prisms. Crystal: $25.00 – 30.00; with bobeche
and prisms: $40.00 – 50.00.

DM-60. No.
115 Canter-
bury candle-
stick

No. 115 Canterbury candlestick. Three-light. 6" high,
10" wide, 4⅞" diameter base. Introduced in 1937 in
crystal and made until the 1950s. Also advertised as a
three-light candelabrum with either two or three peg
bobeches and U prisms (listed as 7" high x 11" wide).
$35.00 – 40.00; with bobeches and prisms: $80.00 –
100.00.

DM-61. No. 115 Canterbury
three-light candlestick

DM-61A. 1940 catalog

DM-62. No. 115-121 CANTERBURY LOW CANDLESTICK IN CHARTREUSE

No. 115-121 Canterbury low candlestick. Also listed as No. 115½. 3¼" high, 4½" base. Circa 1938 – 1980. Made in crystal, Cape Cod blue opalescent, chartreuse, cranberry pink opalescent, and jasmine yellow opalescent. Tiffin colors (after 1955) were copen blue, citron green, and desert red. Can be found etched with Bridal Rose, Charmaine Rose, First Love, Indian Tree, Language of Flowers, and Remembrance. Was also available with the Stratford cutting. Crystal (plain), chartreuse: $20.00 – 25.00. Opalescent colors, crystal (cut or etched): $40.00 – 50.00.

DM-63. No. 115-122 CANTERBURY TWO-LIGHT CANDLESTICK IN CHARTREUSE

No. 115-122 or No. 3 Canterbury candlestick. Two-light. 6½" high, 4¾" base, 7" wide. This was a late addition to the pattern, produced ca. 1949 to the 1950s. Made in chartreuse and crystal. The crystal can be found etched with Charmaine Rose, First Love, Indian Tree, and Remembrance. Tiffin colors (after 1955) were copen blue, citron green, desert red, and dawn. Like many other Duncan candleholders, this was also sold as a candelabra by adding a pair of peg bobeches. The top portion of the candlestick was available with the foot removed and replaced with a threaded insert to be used as part of a series of "candle-light garden" flower arrangers. Farber Brothers also marketed this insert as their No. 6133 candelabra with a metal foot. Crystal (plain): $25.00 – 30.00. Crystal (etched), chartreuse: $35.00 – 45.00. Copen blue, desert red, dawn (Tiffin): $75.00 – 100.00.

DM-64. No. 2 CANTERBURY TWO-LIGHT CANDLESTICK IN MILK GLASS

No. 2 two-light candlestick. 9½" high x 7½" wide with a 5" diameter base. Another late addition to the Canterbury line, made in crystal in the 1950s. Also known in milk glass, though it is unknown whether this version was made by Duncan or by Tiffin. Also offered as a candelabra with peg bobeches and cut prisms. Crystal: $50.00 – 65.00; with bobeches and prisms: $65.00 – 75.00. Milk glass: $75.00 – 100.00.

Do not confuse with Duncan's No. 115-122 (DM-63 above).

No. 117 Three Feathers cornucopia candlestick. Also listed as a vase. 4¼" high, 3¼" base. Produced ca. 1938 – 1943. Made in Cape Cod blue opalescent, jasmine yellow opalescent, cranberry pink opalescent, and crystal. The crystal can be found with Duncan's First Love and Adoration etchings or with the Tristan cutting. Crystal (plain): $40.00 – 45.00. Opalescent colors, crystal (etched): $50.00 – 65.00.

DM-65. No. 117 THREE FEATHERS CORNUCOPIA CANDLESTICK IN CAPE COD BLUE OPALESCENT

No. 30 two-light candlestick. 5¾" high with a 5" diameter base. Produced circa 1938 to the 1940s. Made in crystal, Cape Cod blue opalescent, cranberry pink opalescent, and jasmine yellow opalescent. Etchings on crystal include Adoration, First Love, Indian Tree, Language of Flowers, and Magnolia. Available cuttings were Stratford and Clematis. This was also sold as a candelabrum with peg bobeches and prisms. Lotus used this candlestick for their No. 17, No. 91 Hardy, and No. 793 cuttings. Crystal (plain): $30.00 – 35.00. Crystal (etched): $40.00 – 55.00. Opalescent colors: $175.00 – market.

DM-66. No. 30 TWO-LIGHT CANDLESTICK

No. 5323 Alden candlestick. 4¼" high with 2¾" square base. Appears to be made from the cocktail in this stemware line. The pattern was introduced in 1939. Known in green with a crystal stem. It isn't known if this was a production item, an experimental piece, or a whimsey. In addition to items in the Alden line, there were also a group of crystal vases with a similar foot. Unable to price. *(From the collection of Helen and Bob Jones.)*

DM-67. No. 5323 ALDEN CANDLESTICK IN GREEN WITH A CRYSTAL STEM

EARLY AMERICAN SANDWICH (LINE NO. 41) — DUNCAN'S MOST ENDURING PATTERN

This pattern, a copy of a nineteenth century Boston & Sandwich design, has outlived two companies and survives even today. Indiana Glass Company obtained the molds from U.S. Glass in the 1960s and it was still being marketed in recent years as part of the Lancaster Colony family of products (which includes molds from Indiana's own Sandwich pattern). Duncan's Sandwich pattern is reported as having first been introduced in 1925, but the earliest advertisements we have found for it were in 1928, when it was called Early American Lace Glass. Shortly after that Duncan's earlier five-light candelabrum was pressed (sic) into service as a part of this pattern and a series of smaller candelabra were designed to go along with it (see DM-7 on page 144). Sometime later additional candleholders were added to the line when it was expanded following a big advertising campaign that began in 1937. The production dates listed for the Sandwich items below are based on the first mention of them we can find in Duncan ads or catalogs. It's possible that any or all of them may actually have been introduced earlier.

No. 41 Early American Sandwich candlestick (later listed as No. 41-121). 4" high, 4¼" base. Circa 1939 – 1955. Made in amber, chartreuse, crystal, green, and rose. Reissued in milk glass as No. 741 by Tiffin from 1957 to 1963 as part of the White Lace pattern. Was sold with a 12" oblong bowl as part of a console set. Indiana Glass obtained the molds for this pattern in the 1960s and pieces in the pattern, including the candlestick, were reissued in 1967 as a Colony exclusive. (See CL-12 on p. 112.) The candlestick was also one of the items manufactured by Colony for one year only in crystal, green, blue, and a color called "sunset" (amberina) exclusively for Montgomery Ward's 100th anniversary in 1972. Crystal: $15.00 – 20.00. Rose, green, amber: $20.00 – 25.00. Milk glass, chartreuse: $25.00 – 30.00. Indiana colors: $20.00 – 25.00.

DM-68. No. 41 EARLY AMERICAN SANDWICH CANDLESTICK IN MILK GLASS (TIFFIN REISSUE)

DM-69. No. 41
EARLY AMERICAN
SANDWICH
TWO-LIGHT
CANDLESTICK

No. 41 Early American Sandwich candlestick. Two-light. 5" high by 9" wide with a 5" diameter base. Produced circa 1939 until sometime in the 1940s in plain crystal or with First Love etching. By 1950, this mold had been redesigned to become the No. 41-125 candlestick (see DM-71 below). Available cuttings included Eternally Yours. Crystal, plain: $35.00 – 45.00; etched: $45.00 – 55.00.

DM-70. No. 41
EARLY AMERI-
CAN SANDWICH
THREE-LIGHT
CANDELABRUM

No. 41 Early American Sandwich candlestick. Three-light. 7" high by 9" wide. Produced circa 1939 until sometime in the 1940s in crystal. Also available as a three-light candelabrum with stubby prisms. Crystal, plain: $40.00 – 50.00; etched: $50.00 – 75.00; with prisms and bobeches: $100.00 – 125.00.

DM-71. No. 41-125
EARLY AMERICAN
SANDWICH
TWO-LIGHT
CANDLESTICK

No. 41-125 Early American Sandwich candlestick. Two-light. 6" high, 5" base, and 7½" wide. Circa 1940s – 1955 in crystal with at least one etching, First Love, and the following cuttings: No. 773 Chantilly, Chinese Garden, Lily of the Valley, Wild Rose, and Willow. Also was offered as the No. 41-123 candelabrum, two-light. This was a redesigned version of the earlier No. 41 two-light candlestick (see DM-69 above). Crystal, plain: $35.00 – 45.00; etched or cut: $50.00 – 75.00.

DM-72. No. 122
SYLVAN CAN-
DLEHOLDER

No. 122 Sylvan candleholder. 3¼" high with a 2⅝" footed base. Produced circa 1939 – 1943. Made in Cape Cod blue opalescent, jasmine yellow opalescent, cranberry pink opalescent, and crystal. Designed by Robert A. May. Crystal: $35.00 – 40.00. Opalescent colors: $70.00 – 80.00.

No. 122 Sylvan two-light candle vase. Circa 1940 – 1943. Made in Cape Cod blue opalescent, cranberry pink opalescent, crystal, and jasmine yellow opalescent. Designed by Robert A. May. This was patented as D120,647, filed March 1, 1940, and approved May 21, 1940. Crystal: $40.00 – 50.00. Opalescent colors: $80.00 – 100.00.

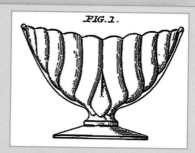
DM-73. No. 122 SYLVAN TWO-LIGHT CANDLE VASE, PATENT DRAWING

No. 122 Sylvan swan candleholder. 5½" long. Ca. 1940 – 1943. Made in crystal, Cape Cod blue opalescent, jasmine yellow opalescent, and cranberry pink opalescent. Crystal: $60.00 – 65.00. Opalescent colors: $120.00 – 130.00.

DM-74. No. 122 SYLVAN SWAN CANDLEHOLDER IN CRANBERRY PINK OPALESCENT

No. 75 Diamond candlestick. Listed as Provincial by Tiffin. 4⅛" high with a 4" round base. Introduced 1940 and made until 1949, when it was offered as part of a console set in the Montgomery Ward catalog. Made in crystal and sienna (pale amber). It is also used as a base for a one-light candelabrum and a hurricane lamp with prisms. Reissued by Tiffin 1956 – 1960. Original advertisements stated that the pattern was "inspired by the richness and elegance of life in the South before the Civil War." Crystal: $15.00 – 20.00. Sienna: $25.00 – 35.00.

DM-75. No. 75 DIAMOND CANDLESTICK

No. 120 candlestick. 3" high with a hexagonal base. Introduced about 1940 and discontinued by the middle of 1942. Made in crystal. $15.00 – 20.00.

DM-76. No. 120 CANDLESTICK, FROM 1940 CATALOG

DM-77. No.
120 CANDLE-
STICK, FROM
1940 CATALOG

No. 120 candlestick. 4" high with a turned down scalloped base. Introduced around 1940 and discontinued by the middle of 1942. Made only in crystal. This mold was originally used for Duncan's No. 68 candlestick. (See DM-15 on p. 147.) $20.00 – 25.00.

DM-78. No.
30 PALL MALL
SQUARE CAN-
DLEBLOCK,
FROM 1943
CATALOG

No. 30 Pall Mall candleblock. Square, 2" high. Introduced 1940 and made until sometime in the mid-to-late 1940s in crystal and crystal etched with Passion Flower. This very plain candleblock would be difficult to differentiate from other similar candleholders, such as Viking's No. 106 candleblock (which is 1¾" square). $15.00 – 20.00.

DM-79. No. 30
PALL MALL
TRIANGLE
CANDLEBLOCK,
FROM 1943
CATALOG

No. 30 Pall Mall candleblock. Triangle, 2" high. Circa 1943 in crystal. $25.00 – 30.00.

DM-80. No. 31
PALL MALL
CANDLESTICK,
FROM 1943 CAT-
ALOG

No. 31 Pall Mall candlestick. 3" high. Square. Circa 1943 in crystal. $20.00 – 25.00.

No. 30½ Pall Mall Swan. Made in two sizes: 7" and 10½" long. Sold as a candelite garden, circa 1943 – 1951. Made in avocado, Biscayne green, black, chartreuse, crystal, Cape Cod opalescent blue, cranberry opalescent pink, ruby, and teakwood. Rarely found in milk glass or milk glass with a ruby neck or green neck. Both size swans have elongated bodies and ground bottoms. Do not confuse with the far more common New Martinsville swan candleholders that have a rounder body and no ground bottom. Small, crystal: $35.00 – 45.00; ruby, chartreuse: $70.00 – 80.00; black, opalescent colors: unable to price; milk glass with colored neck: $325.00 – 375.00. Large, milk glass with colored neck: $400.00 – 450.00.

DM-81. No. 30½ PALL MALL SWANS IN MILK GLASS WITH GREEN NECK, RUBY WITH CRYSTAL NECK, AND CHARTREUSE

Duncan also made a swan candleholder in the No. 122 Sylvan pattern, with the "body" of the swan being leaf-shaped; the latter was made in opalescent colors. (See DM-74 on p. 163.)

No. 30½ Aladdin lamp. 7" long with an applied handle. Shown in the 1950 catalog. Made in crystal, chartreuse, and ruby. This is the same shape as the No. 30½ Pall Mall swan above, but seems to have been added to the pattern late; depending on its introduction date, some of the other colors mentioned for the swan are a possibility. Crystal: $20.00 – 25.00. Chartreuse: $25.00 – 30.00. Ruby: $35.00 – 40.00.

DM-82. No. 30½ ALADDIN LAMP IN CHARTREUSE

No. 130 Sanibel candle bowl. 1¾" high, 13¼" across. Based on the Sanibel oblong floating garden, but with raised candle cups added. Circa 1940s. We have only seen three of these, two in cranberry pink opalescent and one in Cape Cod blue opalescent. May have also been made in Jasmine yellow opalescent. Difficult to find. $175.00 – 200.00.

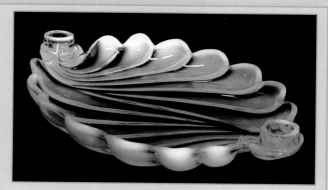

DM-83. No. 130 SANIBEL CANDLE BOWL IN CRANBERRY PINK OPALESCENT

DM-84. No. 125 Murano candle-stick flower arranger in cranberry pink opalescent

No. 125 and 127-121 Murano candlestick flower arranger. 2½" high. 6-footed. Produced circa 1943 – 1950. Made in Cape Cod blue opalescent, cranberry pink opalescent, jasmine yellow opalescent, crystal, Biscayne green, avocado, and teakwood brown. Another version can be found (probably made by Tiffin) in amber, plum, and possibly other colors. The variant is more poorly made than the example shown in DM-85. On the inferior versions the loop pattern (visible from the top) is missing and the feet are shorter. (See DM-84a.) Also known with the top turned-up basket style, in Tiffin's golden banana, plum, and rose colors. (See DM-84b.) Crystal, amber: $20.00 – 25.00. Opalescent colors, plum: $25.00 – 30.00.

DM-84B. No. 125 Murano candle-stick flower arranger in golden banana (Tiffin color), basket style

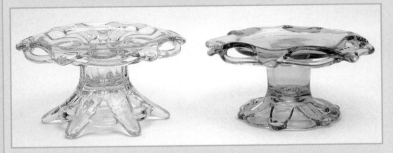

DM-84A. No. 125 Murano candlestick flower arranger. Duncan & Miller in crystal (left) vs. Tiffin ? in amber (right)

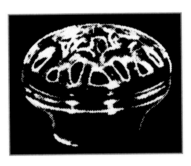

DM-85. No. 125 Murano "crown" candlestick, from 1943 catalog

No. 125 Murano "crown" candlestick. 5" high. Produced circa 1943 – 1950. Made in Cape Cod blue opalescent, cranberry pink opalescent, crystal, jasmine yellow opalescent, and crystal. Crystal: $25.00 – 35.00. Opalescent colors: $75.00 – 100.00.

DM-86. No. 4 four-light candlestick

No. 4 candlestick. Four-light. 10" high x 13" wide. Identified as new in a 1942 price list. Appears in the 1943 catalog in crystal. Probably only produced for a brief period. $120.00 – 145.00.

No. 71-D or 71-121 American Way 2" high "Leaf candlestick." Introduced about 1942 and continued until sometime in the 1950s. Made in ruby, milk glass, sapphire blue, green, crystal, crystal with satin (called Satintone Finish), chartreuse, Cape Cod blue opalescent, and cranberry pink opalescent. According to the 1943 catalog, this pattern was created by the decorating consultant of House and Garden. Offered in 1944 by Lotus Glass Company with philodendron vine "in relief in lovely shade of ruby and amber stain, all edges trimmed in 22-karat gold band." Crystal, light blue, chartreuse, green: $20.00 – 35.00. Opalescent colors, ruby: $35.00 – 45.00. Milk glass: $50.00 – 65.00.

DM-87. No. 71-D (No. 71-121) American Way leaf candleblocks in ruby, Cape Cod blue opalescent, and chartreuse

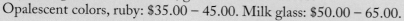

DM-87a. Comparison of Tiffin No. 71-D American Way leaf candleblock in citron (original version) with reworked versions in Tiffin Rosé

Also made by Tiffin in citron and possibly other colors. In 1962, Tiffin reissued this candlestick in rosé ("delicate shimmering gem color ... like Rosé wine ... with just a subtle suggestion of flame blue in its crystal depths"), amethyst, and golden banana. These reissues are reworked, with the petal feet stretched out, both pointing up (as on the original candleholders) and down. Whereas the originals measure approximately 4½" from point to point, the Tiffin versions range from 5½" to 6½", giving them a markedly different appearance. (See DM-87a.)

No. 301-121 Tear Drop candlestick. 4" high, 4¾" diameter base. Circa mid-1940s to the 1950s. Crystal only. Tear Drop was a very popular pattern that had been originally brought out around 1937 and that continued to be expanded following the war years. (See DM-56 and DM-57 on p. 158 for earlier candlesticks in the line.) Reissued by Tiffin from 1957 – 1963. $20.00 – 25.00.

DM-88. No. 301-121 Tear Drop candlestick

No. 301-122 Tear Drop candlestick. Two-light. 6¼" high, 5" diameter base. Circa mid-1940s to the 1950s in crystal. Reissued by Tiffin from 1957 – 1963. This was also offered as No. 301-123, a two-light candelabra with peg bobeches and prisms. $35.00 – 40.00.

DM-89. No. 301-122 Tear Drop two-light candlestick

DM-90. SYMPHONY CANDLESTICK

Symphony candlestick. 4¾" high with a 4½" base. Circa 1948 – 1949. Crystal only. This was advertised as being manufactured by Chartiers Glass (a division of Duncan & Miller) and was sold as part of a console set. The Symphony pattern was introduced with an unprecedented four-page advertising spread in *House and Garden* in December 1948, as "a brilliant new accomplishment in fine American crystal at less than pre-war prices." The three-piece console set, for instance, sold for $2.25. The glass quality is noticeably inferior to Duncan's usual quality, since the Chartiers Division was a short-lived experiment in the production of machine-made glass that began in 1947 and seems to have continued for only a very few years. The console set and some other pieces in the pattern were offered in the fall/winter 1949 Sears catalog with a sand carved morning glory decoration. $15.00 – 20.00.

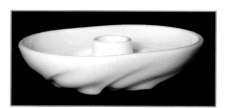

DM-91. No. 150 FLAIR CANDLELITE GARDEN IN MILK GLASS

No. 150 Flair candlelite garden. 1½" high and 6" oblong. Produced about 1950 – 1951 in crystal and milk glass. In the 1951 price list, the pattern name was given as Avalon. Available with or without hurricane shades. Crystal: $25.00 – 30.00. Milk glass: $30.00 – 35.00.

DM-92. No. 320-124 CANDELABRUM

No. 320-124 one-light candelabrum. 8¾" high, 5" hexagonal base. We believe this line was introduced around 1950, with this candelabrum and various other configurations appearing in a catalog from around that year. We don't have much information concerning it under Duncan's reign, but we do know that Tiffin advertised numerous configurations of this item with one to five lights and an endless assortment of vases, epergnes, and other decorative attachments. $65.00 – 80.00.

DM-93. No. 220-2 ONE-LIGHT CANDELABRA VASE

No. 220-2 one-light candelabra vase. 8¾" high, 5" hexagonal base. Like the 320-124 we believe this line was introduced in the 1950s. We know that Duncan used this unique base, with its built-in vases, to make one-to-three light candelabra and offered several attachments like a candy dish for where the center candle would normally be. Epergnes were another option. However, this specific base does not appear in either the 1950 catalog or Tiffin's 1956 catalog, suggesting limited production between those years. $80.00 – 100.00.

No. 153-121 Contour candle (tulip). 2" high candle block with a 1½" base. Made 1952 – 1960s. Often sold with a No. 153-98 6½" ashtray as a "candlelight garden set." Made in light blue, chartreuse, crystal, dawn (also known as twilight), and ruby. Can also be found as a crystal candleholder nested with a blue opalescent ashtray. To the best of our knowledge the candleholders themselves were never made in any opalescent color. Production continued under Tiffin with the following colors being offered: greenbriar, copen blue, citron green, desert red, dark green (possibly pine), smoke, and black (satin finish). Crystal: $8.00 – 10.00 (candleblock), $25.00 – 35.00 (with ashtray). Chartreuse, emerald, smoke: $10.00 – 12.00 (candleblock), $40.00 – 45.00 (with ashtray). Ruby, dawn, blue opalescent: $30.00 – 40.00 (candleblock), $100.00 – 125.00 (with ashtray).

DM-94. No. 153-121 CONTOUR CANDLEHOLDER

DM-94A. No. 153-121 CONTOUR CANDLEHOLDER AND ASHTRAY, PROBABLY IN PINE (TIFFIN COLOR)

DM-94B. CANDLEBLOCK NESTED INSIDE THE ASHTRAY

No. 152 Patio candlestick. 1⅝" high, 3⅜" square, four-footed. Introduced in 1952 and discontinued by 1955. Listed colors were crystal and chartreuse. Biscayne green and Key Largo blue are also possible. Crystal, plain: $20.00 – 25.00; with cutting: $25.00 – 35.00. Chartreuse: $35.00 – 40.00.

DM-95. No. 152 PATIO CANDLESTICK

No. 154/50 Laguna candlestick. 4" high. Introduced circa 1953 and probably in production until 1955. Made in Biscayne green, smoky avocado, and teakwood brown. They were also sold with a hurricane shade. The Laguna pattern was designed by James Rosati and was selected by the Museum of Modern Art in 1953 for its Good Design award. $40.00 – 50.00.

DM-96. No. 154/50 LAGUNA CANDLESTICKS, FROM 1954 CATALOG

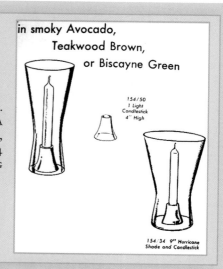

in smoky Avocado, Teakwood Brown, or Biscayne Green

154/50 1 Light Candlestick 4" High

154/34 9" Hurricane Shade and Candlestick

DM-97. No. 155/60 FESTIVE CANDLE-STICK, FROM 1950S CATALOG

No. 155/60 Festive candlestick. 5½" high. Made 1954 – 1955 in aqua, crystal, and golden honey with a removable mahogany disc separating the candle cup from the base. Michael Lax was the designer. (For other designs by Lax for Dunbar, see DB-8 on p. 140, and for Fenton, FN-59 on p. 195.) Crystal: $35.00 – 40.00. Honey: $40.00 – 45.00. Aqua: $45.00 – 50.00.

DM-98. No. 709-14 BETSY ROSS CANDLE-STICK IN MILK GLASS (DUNCAN DIVISION OF U.S. GLASS)

No. 709-14 Betsy Ross candlestick. 7⅞" high with a 5⅞" diameter base. Sawtooth pattern on the lower part of the column. This is one of the few candleholders to come from the Duncan & Miller division of U.S. Glass that the original Duncan & Miller Co. never made. Produced in 1957 in milk glass. Sold as part of a console set with a 9½" bowl (No.709-6). This was a reissue of U.S. Glass's earlier No. 19367 Pinafore pattern, originally offered in the early 1940s in crystal and crystal satin (sometimes with pink or green stain). Pinafore included reworked molds from the even earlier No. 309 Queen Anne pattern. Crystal, crystal satin (original U.S. Glass issue): $25.00 – 30.00. Milk glass: $35.00 – 40.00.

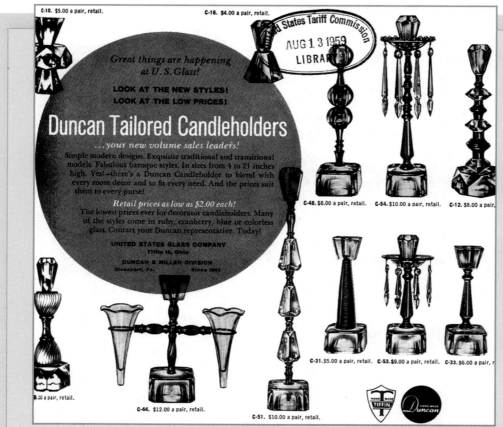

DM-99. AN INTERESTING AD FROM THE *CROCKERY AND GLASS JOURNAL* DATED AUGUST 13, 1959. IT SHOWS A NEW LINE OF CANDLEHOLDERS FROM THE DUNCAN & MILLER DIVISION OF U.S. GLASS. THESE TOO WERE NEVER PRODUCED BY THE ORIGINAL DUNCAN & MILLER GLASS COMPANY.

ECONOMY TUMBLER COMPANY, see Morgantown Glass Works (in volume 3 of this series).

ERICKSON GLASS WORKS, Bremen, Ohio (1943 – 1961). Founded by Carl Erickson and his brother Stephen. Their father had emigrated from Sweden and went to work for the Pairpoint Manufacturing Company. As a teenager, Carl joined his father as an apprentice and spent the next 20 years developing a high level of craftsmanship. Among many other skills, he learned to make pieces with controlled bubbles — a technique often associated with Pairpoint, but also widely used by Erickson in later years in his own glass designs.

In the early 1930s he was employed by Libbey Glass and then, later in the decade, by the Blenko Glass Company, where he was production manager and supervised production of the reproductions made for the Colonial Williamsburg Foundation. Not surprisingly when he started his own factory in Bremen, Ohio, in 1943, he capitalized on his years of experience by specializing in fine free-hand blown glass, all from his own designs and under his direct supervision. Most pieces have acid etched signatures.

In addition to the controlled bubble paperweight bases often featured on Erickson pieces, the company also introduced cased bubble glass in 1945 and flame in 1946 ("the startling effect of colored flame, encased between two layers of fine crystal" — *Giftwares and Housewares Magazine,* December 1950). Other pieces featured cased colors in unusual combinations, craquelle (a lightly crackled finish) and nailsea (a looped effect).

With Carl Erickson's strong emphasis on quality and no more than two dozen workers at any given time, the output of this firm was relatively small — perhaps 100,000 pieces in their 18-year existence. Erickson was chosen to blow the first pieces of glass at the restored Jamestown glass factory and also made reproductions for a number of museums, including the Smithsonian Institution, the Old Sturbridge Museum, the Metropolitan Museum of Art, and the Corning Museum of Glass (including at least one style of blown candlestick made for the latter). The candlesticks shown below are only a sample of those made by this firm.

A less expensive line, known as Holiday, was introduced in 1959, but by that time the company was already finding it difficult to compete with glass imported from Europe and Asia. When Carl Erickson retired in 1961, the decision was made to close the factory.

COLORS

Amber, amethyst (later replaced by heliotrope), aquamarine (introduced 1957), champagne, charcoal, cobalt, emerald, fire (orange), grape, honey (introduced 1957), lavender, opal (briefly in 1952), pink cranberry (gold-ruby, introduced in 1959), selenium red, shadow, smoke, sunlight (yellow), and turquoise (later replaced by azure).

No. 725CH candleholder. 3¼" high with a diameter of 4¼". Also made in a smaller size: 2¾" high with a diameter of 3½". Made ca. 1950 in emerald, champagne, smoke, and grape, encased in crystal. Also available with a hurricane shade that encircles the entire candleholder, resting on the table top. $35.00 – 45.00.

ER-1. No. 725CH CANDLE-HOLDER IN EMERALD CASED IN CRYSTAL

Candlestick. 5¾" high. Advertised in July 1957 as part of a console set consisting of "off hand bowl and candlesticks in hand-wrought glass with bubbles in the base." Known in crystal with a smoke top; probably also made in other colors. $50.00 – 60.00.

ER-2. CANDLESTICK, UNKNOWN PATTERN NUMBER, FROM 1957 TRADE JOURNAL

FAYETTE, see Smith (L.E.) Glass Company (in volume 3 of this series)

FEDERAL GLASS COMPANY, Columbus, Ohio (1900 – 1979). Federal began in 1900

as another maker of handmade glassware but before long they were developing methods of automating the glassmaking process. By the 1920s they were a leading supplier of low cost, machine-made tumblers. By the thirties entire table settings were being pressed by machine. They continued to prosper and expand through the 1940s. In 1958 Federal Glass became a division of the Federal Paperboard Company. They continued to supply glassware to the retail and commercial markets until their closing in 1979. Federal was responsible for several patterns popular with Depression glass collectors today, but they weren't a large manufacturer of candleholders.

COLORS

Known Federal colors include:

amethyst glow	1920s	rose glow (pink)	1931 – 1942
orange pekoe	1920s	Madonna blue (medium blue)	1933 – 1934
burgundy	1920s	iridescent (marigold)	1926 – 1935
orchid	1920s	limelight (avocado green)	1970s
springtime green	1926 – 1936	sun gold	1970s
golden glow (amber)	1931 – 1942	Aegean blue	1973

Madrid candleholder. 2¼" high, 3½" base. Circa 1932 – 1939 in golden glow, iridescent, and rose glow. Federal reproduced this pattern in amber from new molds in 1976 for the Bicentennial under the name Recollection Glassware and a '76' was added to each mold. However, when Federal went out of business the molds were bought by the Indiana Glass Company who removed the '76' and began making the glass again in crystal, pink, and blue, from 1982 to 1990. The Indiana reproductions are not marked, but have vertical ridges inside the candle socket to hold the candle more firmly. The originals do not have these and are smooth inside. The Archers list the pattern number as No. 2604. $10.00 – $12.00.

FD-1. MADRID CANDLEHOLDERS IN GOLDEN GLOW AND IRIDESCENT MARIGOLD

FD-2. No. 2826 DOUBLE CAN-DLESTICK IN ROSE GLOW

No. 2826 double candlestick. 4⅜" high with a 4¼" diameter base. Production dates circa 1938 to the 1940s. Made in crystal and rose glow. Sometimes called Wigwam or Windmill by collectors. Crystal: $10.00 – 12.00. Rose glow: $30.00 – 35.00.

No. 2806½ Plymouth candlestick bowl. Flared and ruffled saucer shape. Production dates circa 1938 – 1941 and probably beyond. Made in crystal and crystal with satin finish or red stain. Also known with a silvered backing, giving it a mirrored finish, with only the center design in red stain. Sold as part of the No. B-35 console set with an 11" scalloped edge bowl. Federal reissued this bowl in 1972 with a carnival finish, so it is possible that the candleholders were also brought out again at that time. $10.00 – 12.00.

FD-3. No. 2806½ Plymouth flower bowl and console set, from 1940 catalog

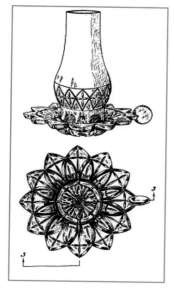

No. 2809 Petal hurricane lamp. 5¼" high with a base diameter of 4⅝". Introduced in 1940. This is a mini-hurricane, or child's size. Petal was a popular line for many years, so production probably continued until the 1950s. Known in crystal, sometimes with amethyst or yellow stain. A design patent was received for this piece as D122,877, filed August 14, 1940, and approved October 1, 1940. The designer was given as Albert H. Nicholson. The bases are often found without the easily broken shade. Complete hurricane lamp: $15.00 – 20.00.

FD-4A. Patent drawing

FD-4. No. 2809 Petal hurricane lamp

Park Avenue candleholder. This pattern was also marketed as Brighton. 1¾" high, 4¾" across the top. Production dates 1941 – early 1970s. Known only in crystal. The nappy that was used to make this candleholder was patented as D124,870, filed November 25, 1940, approved January 28, 1941. The designer was given as Albert H. Nicholson. $6.00 – 8.00.

FD-5. Park Avenue candleholder

No. 2727 candlestick. 2" high x 4½" across. Production dates unknown, but appears in the 1954 catalog. Known in crystal and marigold carnival. Vertical ribbed in pattern similar to Heisey's Crystolite. Sold as "The Candle Lite Twins." Crystal: $6.00 – 8.00. Marigold carnival: $8.00 – 10.00.

FD-6. No. 2727 candlesticks in crystal and marigold carnival

FD-7. No. 2758 PETAL CANDLE-HOLDER, FROM 1967 CATALOG

No. 2758 petal candleholder. 3" square by 2" high. Made in the late 1960s, early 1970s. Offered in crystal and sundown (a smoke color). This candleholder was apparently redesigned to become the No. 2658 Glacier Ice candleholder (see FD-9 below). $5.00 – 10.00.

FD-8. No. S-500 CELESTIAL CANDLEHOLDER IN GEM-TONE

No. S-500 Celestial candleholder. 1¼" high and 5¼" in diameter. Produced ca. 1972 – 1979. Made in Gem-Tone (crystal with purple and marigold iridescent edges), limelight (avocado green), and other colors and treatments. Reissued by Fostoria under the same pattern name as their No. 318 candle in 1985 in crystal, blue, or sun gold with iridescent finish. Also since reissued by Indiana Glass Company with a hurricane globe. $5.00 – 10.00.

No. 2658 Glacier Ice candleholder. Described in the catalog as being 4". Made from 1977 to 1979 and reissued by the Indiana Glass Company in 1980 (see book 2 of this series). This appears to be a redesigned version of the No. 2758 petal candleholder (FD-7 above). Offered in crystal. $5.00 – 10.00.

FD-9. ADVERTISEMENT FOR THE GLACIER LINE, *CHINA, GLASS & LAMPS*, DECEMBER 1977

FENTON ART GLASS COMPANY, 700 Elizabeth Street, Williamstown, West Virginia 26187 (1907 to the present). Brothers Frank L. and John W. Fenton founded the Fenton Art Glass Company in 1905. Initially, they were strictly a decorating company, applying hand-painted designs to glass blanks made by various other companies. However, as they grew more successful they began to have trouble obtaining blanks from their suppliers, so within two years of their inception they decided to move from their old factory in Martins Ferry, Ohio, to a brand new one in Williamstown, West Virginia. From there they started to produce their own glass in January of 1907.

The firm has been family owned and in continuous operation since its beginning and it's still going strong today. Fenton glass is sold through gift shops, specialty dealers, glass shows, and on cable home-shopping shows. Their website (www.fentonartglass.com) claims them to be "The largest manufacturer of handmade colored glass in the United States."

Known for their innovative colors, finishes, and hand-painted designs, Fenton was a pioneer in the development of the process that brought the iridescent glassware known today as carnival glass to the masses. This popular glassware of the early twentieth century mimicked the iridescent glass being produced at the time by Tiffany and Steuben, but at much lower prices.

In the late 1940s Frank M. Fenton and Wilmer C. (Bill) Fenton took over as president and vice president and in 1986 the torch passed to the third generation when Frank's son, George W. Fenton, became the company's president. Frank M. & Bill Fenton both remain active as company spokesmen and Frank M. also serves as the company's historian.

In the early 1970s Fenton began marking their glass with the word "Fenton" in an oval. By 1973 all pieces bore this mark (small items may have Fenton's stylized "F" within the oval). The mark is usually located on the bottom and you sometimes must look closely to see it. In the 1980s they added a small "8" under the logo and in the 1990s it was changed to a "9." The exceptions to this are private mold work (where someone contracts with Fenton to produce glass from their own molds). Fenton did private mold work for L.G. Wright, the Sandwich Glass Museum, and other companies. Some items made especially for QVC and Tiara Exclusives were also not marked. Prior to 1970, pieces were only marked with various styles of paper label.

LOGO, EARLY 1950S

LOGO, 1956 – 1970S

CURRENT LOGO

COLORS

During its lengthy history Fenton has made about every color imaginable. When two names are listed for a color it indicates that the same color formula was marketed under both names. The dates listed here indicate the approximate years the color was in production. Use the production dates listed with the candleholders along with the color listings to determine when an item may have been made in a particular color.

Note: Because Fenton Art Glass is an on-going concern, colors are constantly being discontinued and revived. Therefore some production cut-off dates may no longer be accurate and the dates given should not be assumed to always be continuous. Also, this list does not include colors made for special customers, occasional pieces, or limited edition colors. Many of these colors may also be found with satin or carnival finishes, crackled, etc.

amber	dark brownish yellow	1926 – 1939 & 1959 – 1960
antique amber & colonial amber	slightly lighter than the earlier amber	1959 – 1982, 1987 – 1988
apple blossom	milk glass with an opaque pink edge	1960 – 1961
apple green	cased green over milk glass	1961
aqua crest	milk glass with a blue edge	1941 – 1942 & 1948 – 1953
aqua opalescent	light blue with white highlights	1927 – 1928
aquamarine* & azure blue	light blue [stretch]	1927 & 1932
aquamarine	light transparent bluish-green	2000
autumn gold	bright amber	1994
autumn gold opalescent	amber with white highlights	1994
black or ebony	opaque black	1911 – present (not continuous)
black crest	milk glass with a black edge	Late 1960s (special order)
black rose	cased peachblow with a black crest	1953 – 1955

blue crest	milk glass with a deep blue edge	1963 only
blue marble	turquoise with swirls of white	1970 – 1973
blue opalescent	blue with white highlights	1939 – 1954, 1959 – 1964 & 1978 – 1981
blue opaline	semi-opaque blue	1960
blue overlay & opaque blue	cased blue over milk glass	1943 – 1953 & 1962 – 1965
blue pastel	opaque pale blue	1954 only
blue ridge	blue opalescent with an applied blue border	1939
blue royale	rich transparent blue	1990 – 1991
blue satin	opaque blue with frosted finish	1971 – 1984
Burmese	custard with pink edges	1970 – 1995
cameo opalescent	light brown with white highlights	1926 – 1927 & 1979 – 1982
candleglow	yellow	1982 – 1983
carnival (original formula)	carnival iridescent finish on amethyst	1970 – 1983
cased jade opaline	semi-opaque baby blue	1990
cased lilac	turquoise cased over gold ruby	1955 – 1956
Celeste blue*	medium blue [stretch]	1921 – 1928
champagne satin	pink with white highlights & carnival finish	1997 – 2000
Chinese yellow & jade yellow	semi-opaque yellow	1922 – 1933
chocolate	light brown slag	1907 & 1975 – 1976
colonial blue	deep sapphire blue	1962 – 1979
colonial green	olive green	1963 – 1976
colonial pink	bright transparent pink	1962 – 1968
coral	peach cased over milk glass	1961
cranberry	deep transparent pink	1990 – present
cranberry opalescent	red with white highlights	1940 – present (not continuous)
cranberry opaline	semi-opaque milk glass cased over bright pink	1990
crystal crest	milk glass with a crystal and white edge	1942 only
crystal velvet	crystal with satin highlights	1977 – 1989
custard	opaque light yellow	1975 – 1976
custard satin	opaque light yellow with frosted finish	1972 – 1989
dusty rose & empress rose	transparent lavender-pink	1984 – present
emerald crest	milk glass with a green edge	1949 – 1955
federal blue	medium blue	1984
flame	opaque marbleized orange	1924 – 1926
flame crest	milk glass with a red/orange edge	1963 only
Florentine green	iridescent light green stretch	1917 – 1928
forget-me-not blue	pale transparent blue	1982
French opalescent	crystal with white highlights	1956 – 1968
fuchsia	deep cranberry	1994
gold amberina	yellow shading to ruby	1999
gold crest	milk glass with a amber edge	1943 – 1945 & 1963 – 1964
gold overlay & goldenrod	cased amber/yellow over milk glass	1949 & 1956 only
gold pearl	iridescent yellow stretch	1992 – 1993
Grecian gold	iridescent marigold stretch	1921 – late 1920s
green opalescent	green with white highlights	1939 – 1940 & 1959 – 1961
green overlay	cased green over milk glass	1949 – 1953
green pastel	opaque pale green	1954 – 1955
green transparent	came in many distinct shades	1921 – 1939
honey amber	yellow cased over milk glass	1961 – 1967
ice blue pearl	iridescent finish on medium blue	2000 – present
independence blue	carnival finish on cobalt blue	1974 – 1976
iridized opal	carnival finish on milk glass	1993
ivory crest	opaque ivory with a crystal edge	1940 – 1941

jade green	semi-opaque green	1921 – 1939 & 1980
Jamestown blue	dark aquamarine cased over turquoise	1957 – 1958
Jamestown blue transparent	dark aquamarine	1957 – 1958
jonquil yellow	semi-opaque bright yellow	1968 – 1969
lavender lady	violet cased over milk glass	2000
lavender satin	opaque lavender with frosted finish	1977 – 1978
light amethyst carnival	iridescent finish on amethyst	1991
lilac	opaque lavender	1932 – 1933 & 1955
lilac	transparent pastel lavender	1990 – 1991
lime green	light transparent green	1974 – 1976
lime opalescent	cased French opalescent over green	1952 – 1954
lime satin & lime sherbet	opaque green with frosted finish	1952 – 1954 & 1973 – 1980
lotus mist Burmese	light green shading to pink with satin finish	2000
Mandarin red & Venetian red	opaque marbleized red	1932 – 1935
mermaid blue	light steel blue	1934 only
milk glass	semi-opaque white	1924 & 1933 – 1957
milk glass & Valley Forge white	opaque white (formula change)	1958 – present
misty blue satin	blue with white highlights & carnival finish	1997 – 1998
Mongolian green	opaque marbleized green	1934 – 1935
moonstone	translucent white opal	1932 – 1934
mulberry	cased cranberry over light blue	1942 only
mulberry opalescent	transparent blue shading to deep lavender	1990 – 1996
ocean blue	carnival finish on teal	1993
opaline	teal with white highlights	1996
orange satin	transparent orange with a frosted finish	1968 only
orchid	lavender	1927 – 1928
orange	transparent yellowish-red	1963 – 1977
orange carnival	iridescent finish on orange	1972 – 1973
patriot red	dark opaque marbleized red	1976 only
peach crest	cased milk glass over pink w/crystal crest	1940 – 1969
peaches 'n cream	bright pink with white highlights	1987 – 1988
Pekin blue & Peking blue	semi-opaque robin's egg blue	1932 – 1933, 1968 – 1969 & 1980
Periwinkle blue	opaque marbleized blue	1934 – 1943
Periwinkle blue	transparent grayish-blue	1986 – 1988
Persian pearl	iridescent crystal stretch	1911 – 1927 & 1933
Persian pearl	iridescent teal	1992 – 1993
petal pink	light pink	1990 – 1994
pink chiffon opalescent	light semi-opaque pink	2000 – present
pink opalescent	transparent pink with white highlights	1988
pink opaline (Jacqueline)	semi-opaque light purplish-pink	1960
pink pearl	transparent pink with iridescent finish	1992
plated amberina	ruby cased over milk glass	1962 – 1963
plum	deep amethyst	1993 – 1997
plum carnival	iridescent finish on purple	1997 – 1998
plum opalescent	deep purple with white highlights	1959 – 1962
plum overlay	deep purple cased over milk glass	1997 – 1998
plum slag	marbleized amethyst	1994
powder blue	light blue cased over milk glass	1961 – 1962
provincial blue opalescent	medium blue with white highlights	1987 – 1988
rosalene	milk glass with bright pink highlights	1976 – 1978
rose	pink	1927 – 1939
rose crest	milk glass with a semi-opaque rose edge	1944 – 1947
rose magnolia	bright pink with white highlights	1993 – 1994

rose overlay & wild rose	cased pink over milk glass	1943 – 1948 & 1961 – 1962
rose pastel	opaque pink (pink milk glass)	1954 – 1957
rose pearl	carnival finish on pink	1993
rose satin	opaque pink with frosted finish	1954 – 1954 & 1974 – 1977
royal blue	cobalt blue	1907 – 1939 & 1966 – present (not continuous)
royal purple	dark amethyst	1998
rubina verde	green shading to deep amethyst	1997
ruby*	ruby red [stretch]	1907 – 1939
ruby	transparent red	1966 – 1998
ruby iridescent & red carnival	carnival finish on ruby	1976 – 1977 & 1990 – present
ruby overlay	cranberry cased over milk glass	1956 – 1974
ruby silver crest	crystal edge on ruby glass	unknown, but very limited
sage mist	opaque green	1990 – 1991
Salem blue	light medium blue	1990 – 1992
sapphire blue opalescent	cobalt with light blue highlights	1990
sea green satin	light opaque green with iridized finish	1998
sea mist green	light transparent green	1991 – 1997
sea mist opalescent	light green with white highlights	1992 – 1993
sea mist slag	marbleized light green	1994
shell pink	iridescent finish on opaque pink	1990 – 1991
silver crest	milk glass with a crystal edge	1940 – 1986, 1992
silver Jamestown	milk glass cased over turquoise with crystal edge	1957 – 1959
silver rose	opaque pink with a crystal edge	1956 – 1957
silver turquoise	opaque turquoise with a crystal edge	1956 – 1958
snow crest	colored glass with a milk glass edge	1950 – 1954
spruce green carnival	iridescent greenish-purple finish	1999 – 2000
Stiegel blue opalescent	deep turquoise with white highlights	1991
Stiegel green stretch	iridescent green stretch	1994
tangerine*	transparent orange [stretch]	1927 – 1929
teal marigold	bluish-green carnival finish	1989
teal royale	medium-dark green	1987 – 1989
topaz	iridescent yellow-green stretch	1921 – 1930s
topaz opalescent	yellow-green with white highlights	1941 – present (not continuous)
turquoise	opaque pale blue-green	1955 – 1958
twilight blue	medium transparent blue	1992 – 1994
Velva rose	iridescent pink stretch	1926 – 1928 & 1980 – 1982
violet	medium amethyst	2000 – present
violet satin	purple carnival finish	1999
white satin (ivory)	milk glass with frosted finish	1972 – present
willow green opalescent	reissue of Florentine green stretch	2000 – present
wisteria*	amethyst [stretch]	1933 – 1939
wisteria	transparent amethyst	1977 – 1978
wisteria opalescent	amethyst w/white highlights	1933 – 1935
yellow opaline	semi-opaque light yellow	1960

*Indicates that the color was available in regular transparent or iridescent stretch.

No. 349 colonial candleholder. 10¼" high, 4⅛" base. No. 449 colonial candleholder. 8½" high, 3⅞" base.

A classic design taken from silver candleholders of the era. Both sizes were introduced in 1921 or before. The 10¼" was discontinued about 1933. The 8½" is Fenton's most enduring candlestick. It's still being made today as No. 9071 and we believe that it's been in near continuous production since its introduction. Two smaller sizes, 6¼" and 3¾", were added around 1989, in teal royale, green, and probably other colors. (See FN-94 on p. 204.)

Early colors include ebony, Celeste blue, Chinese yellow, Florentine green, Grecian gold, jade green, Pekin blue, Persian pearl, Rosaline (only one pair known), royal blue, ruby, ruby stretch, tangerine (rare), topaz, turquoise, Velva rose, Venetian red, and wisteria stretch. In recent years, made in many transparent and opaque colors, including blue royale, candleglow (yellow), cobalt, dusty rose, empress rose, federal blue, petal pink, plum, ruby slag, sea green satin, sea mist green, spruce green, twilight blue, violet, and white satin. Almost any color, including those with a stretch, carnival, or opalescent finish is possible. Some pieces have gold trim or hand-painted decorations and some have oval wheel-cuttings on the corners. Shown in the 2001 catalog with a hurricane globe as No. 9471.

No. 349, Grecian gold, crystal: $60.00 – 70.00; Celeste blue, Persian pearl, Florentine green, Velva rose: $70.00 – 80.00; royal blue, ruby, black, jade: $85.00 – 95.00; Peking blue, Chinese yellow, Venetian red, wisteria: $110.00 – 130.00; ruby stretch, topaz: $225.00 – 275.00. Cuttings: add 50 – 100%.

No. 449, Celeste blue, Persian pearl, Florentine green: $65.00 – 75.00; Grecian gold, jade, ruby, black: $80.00 – 90.00; Peking blue, Mandarin red, wisteria: $100.00 – 110.00; ruby stretch, topaz: $175.00 – 225.00. Cuttings: add 50 – 100%.

FN-1. No. 349 AND No. 449 COLONIAL CANDLEHOLDERS IN FLORENTINE GREEN AND CELESTE BLUE

Several other companies made candleholders similar to Fenton's #449 but only Northwood and Vineland also made a 10" size. Westmoreland lists a 9" (actually 9½") and an 11" size, but Fenton never made those sizes. Both sizes of the Northwood have a knob finial just above the base where all of the others have a smaller flared detail. The Vineland sticks were made in a three-piece mold (causing three seams). All the others are from two-piece molds and therefore have two seams.

FN-1A. WE'VE PLACED THE EASIEST DIFFERENCES TO SPOT IN SQUARE BRACKETS []. 1. NORTHWOOD No. 695 [KNOB FINIAL]. 2. WESTMORELAND No. 1034, SOLID BASE [FLAT BOTTOM]. 3. FENTON No. 9071 (CIRCA 1990S). 4. INDIANA [⅝" STEP-UP BASE]. 5. LANCASTER [15⁄16" STEP-UP BASE]. NOT SHOWN: WESTMORELAND No. 1043, HOLLOW BASE [?]

FN-2. No. 314 CANDLEHOLDER
IN WISTERIA

No. 314 candleholder. 1½" high, came with either a 3⅞" round or hexagonal base. Production dates from the mid-1920s through the early 1930s. Made in cameo opalescent, Celeste blue, Chinese yellow, Velva rose, Florentine green, Grecian gold, green transparent, jade green, rose, ruby, and wisteria stretch. Many companies made a candleholder similar to the round base No. 314 and Tiffin's No. 94 is almost identical to the octagonal base version, but the Fenton candlesticks can sometimes be identified when they appear in one of Fenton's distinctive colors. Green transparent: $12.00 – 15.00. Celeste blue, cameo opalescent, Florentine green, jade, rose, Velva rose: $15.00 – 20.00. Ruby, Chinese yellow, wisteria: $25.00 – 30.00.

FN-3. No. 315 PRINCESS CAN-DLEHOLDER IN VENETIAN RED

No. 315 Princess candleholder. Heights vary from 3" to 3½", saucer base is 4¾" in diameter. Production dates 1924 – 1925. Made in amber, Celeste blue, Chinese yellow, Florentine green, Grecian gold, jade green, opal, topaz, Venetian red, and wisteria. Later reissued with a crimped base in 1941 as No. 680. (See FN-34 on p. 190.) Celeste blue, Florentine green, Grecian gold: $35.00 – 45.00. Topaz stretch, wisteria, Chinese yellow, Venetian red: $50.00 – 65.00.

FN-4. No. 316 CANDLEHOLDERS IN TOPAZ, PER-SIAN PEARL, AND TANGERINE

No. 316 candleholder. 3½" high with a 4¼" diameter base. Production 1926 – 1933. Made in ebony, jade green, ruby, green transparent, Celeste blue, Florentine green, Cameo opalescent, Grecian gold, Persian pearl, rose, Velva rose, tangerine, and topaz. Many other companies made similar candleholders but the No. 316s are different enough to avoid much confusion. According to Madeley and Shettlar's *American Iridescent Stretch Glass*, an early version was made with two rings on the stem. Green transparent, rose, black: $20.00 – 25.00. Celeste blue, Velva rose, cameo opalescent, jade, Persian pearl, Florentine green: $25.00 – 35.00. Topaz stretch, tangerine stretch: $40.00 – 55.00.

FN-5. No. 317 CANDLEHOLDER IN FLORENTINE GREEN

No. 317 candleholder. Was also listed as No. 1623. 3⅝" high with a 5" round base. Produced only in 1927 – 1928. Made in Florentine green, Grecian gold, green, orchid, rose, royal blue, ruby, tangerine, topaz, Celeste blue, and Velva rose. Jade, green transparent, rose: $22.00 – 25.00. Celeste blue, Florentine green, Velva rose, Grecian gold: $25.00 – 30.00. Topaz stretch, tangerine stretch, ruby, orchid, royal blue: $40.00 – 60.00.

No. 318 candleholder. Also listed as No. 7572. Was also made as No. 1502 with diamond optic and as No. 1503 with spiral optic patterns on the base. 2¾" high with a 4⅜" diameter base. Production dates: 1927 – 1935. Reintroduced in 1980 in jade green, Peking blue (for about four months), and Velva rose. Originally made in aquamarine, black, cameo opalescent, Chinese yellow, Florentine green, transparent green, Mandarin red, orchid, Pekin blue, Persian pearl, rose, royal blue, ruby, tangerine, and tangerine stretch. Jade, green transparent, black: $15.00 – 20.00. Rose, Persian pearl, cameo opalescent, Florentine green, ruby: $20.00 – 25.00. Velva rose, Chinese yellow, aquamarine: $30.00 – 35.00. Peking blue, Mandarin red, tangerine stretch: $40.00 – 55.00. Cuttings: add 50 – 100%.

FN-6. No. 318 CANDLESTICKS IN VELVA ROSE STRETCH, ROYAL BLUE, AND VELVA ROSE WITH SPIRAL OPTIC BASE

No. 249 candleholder. 6¼" high, hexagonal base measures 3½" across. Produced from 1921 to 1937 in ruby, Celeste blue, Persian pearl, Grecian gold, jade green, Florentine green, Venetian red, ruby stretch, and wisteria stretch. In 1936 it was produced in crystal with Fenton's satin San Toy etching. In 1937 it was offered with a different etching (named Snow Fern by William Heacock). All colors are difficult to find. Reissued in 1984 as No. 5527VC in white satin with Golden Pine Cone, a hand-painted decoration by Martha Reynolds. Several other companies made candlesticks with a similar shape, including Heisey, Imperial, and Paden City, but they were all larger. The size and Fenton's distinctive colors are enough to make identification no problem. Grecian gold, Persian pearl, Celeste blue, ruby: $35.00 – 45.00. Topaz stretch: $50.00 – 65.00. Ruby stretch, wisteria: $110.00 to market.

FN-7. No. 249 CANDLESTICKS IN PERSIAN PEARL, CELESTE BLUE, RUBY, AND JADE GREEN

No. 549 candleholder, 8⅜" high, 3¾" diameter base; No. 649 candleholder, 10" high; and No. 749 candleholder, 12" high.

Production dates 1924 – 1928. Made in ebony, Celeste blue, Pekin blue, marigold, flame, ruby, Persian pearl, royal blue, Chinese yellow, orange, moonstone, milk glass, Grecian gold, jade, Florentine green, topaz, wisteria, and Venetian red. Can be found in many two-tone combinations of the above colors with the base a contrasting color to the rest of the stick. The 10" size is scarce and the 12" is very scarce. Two-tone versions should be considered scarce to rare, depending on the size and color combination.

No. 549, Grecian gold, moonstone, Celeste blue, Persian pearl: $65.00 – 75.00. Royal blue, wisteria, topaz, jade, Peking blue, Florentine green: $80.00 – 90.00. Flame, Chinese yellow, ruby, Venetian red: $110.00 – 130.00. Two-tone combinations: double the value of the color of the upper half. No. 649: Add 15 – 20% to prices of No. 549. No. 749: Add 30 – 40% to prices of No. 549.

FN-8. No. 549 & No. 649 CANDLESTICKS IN JADE GREEN, MOONSTONE WITH BLACK BASE, FLAME, WISTERIA, AND CELESTE BLUE

FN-9. No. 232
CANDLESTICK
IN CAMEO
OPALESCENT

No. 232 candleholder. 8⅜" high, 4" diameter base. Production dates 1926 – 1927. Vertical ribbed stem and candle cup. Made in Cameo opalescent, wisteria (both believed to be rare), Celeste blue, Florentine green, Grecian gold, jade green, topaz, and Velva rose. Most often seen in Florentine green and Celeste blue, but this is a difficult candlestick to find in any color. This candlestick was reissued in teal royale during the late 1980s. The reissue is mold marked with the Fenton logo. Teal royale (reissue): $20.00 – 25.00. Celeste blue, Florentine green, Grecian gold: $50.00 – 70.00. Jade green, Velva rose: $70.00 – 90.00. Cameo opalescent, wisteria, topaz: $120.00 to market.

FN-10. No. 1700
LINCOLN INN
CANDLESTICK

No. 1700 Lincoln Inn candleholder. 3⅞" high with a round base. Production date is probably late 1920s or early 1930s. There is only one of these known in black, reported in *Glass Candlesticks of the Depression Era* by Gene Florence. $110.00 to market. *(Artist's rendition.)*

FN-11. No. 1621 CANDLESTICK, FROM
CATALOG

No. 1621 Dolphin handled candle dish. Production dates 1928 – 1936. Available crimped, round, folded, flat and oval. Advertised colors were aquamarine, crystal, jade, rose, and royal blue. It was also available with a satin acid-etched finish. Crystal (acid etched): $25.00 – 30.00. Aquamarine: $28.00 – 32.00. Royal blue: $35.00 – 40.00.

FN-11A. No. 1621, CRIMPED
VERSION

FN-12. No. 1623 CANDLESTICKS IN RUBY AND IRIDIZED
DUSTY ROSE (QVC REISSUE)

No. 1623 Dolphin handled candleholder. 3½" high with a 4" round base. Production dates 1927 – 1937. Reissued in 1994 for QVC in iridized dusty rose, which is not marked with the Fenton logo. The socket rim is slightly smaller on the reissue and dusty rose (iridescent pink) was not an original color so identification should not be difficult. Original colors include ebony, crystal, ruby, gold, green, jade, rose, royal blue, topaz, lilac (rare), orchid, Florentine green, and Velva rose. All have either a floral or ribbed pattern under the base. Crystal, iridized dusty rose: $15.00 – 20.00. Ruby, green transparent, rose: $22.00 – 25.00. Royal blue, ebony: $50.00 – 65.00. Florentine green, Velva rose, topaz stretch: $80.00 – 100.00. Lilac: $110.00 – 130.00.

No. 2318 candelabra. 6" high. Two-light. Production dates 1927 – 1935. Made in black, crystal with Ming decoration, French opalescent, jade, ruby, moonstone, Mandarin red, and lilac (both of the latter are rare). Crystal (Ming etch), moonstone: $40.00 – 50.00. Black, French opalescent: $50.00 – 65.00. Jade, ruby: $80.00 – 100.00. Mandarin red, lilac: $110.00 to market.

FN-13. No. 2318 TWO-LIGHT CANDELABRA IN FRENCH OPALESCENT

No. 1611 Georgian candlestick. 4⅛" high with a 4½" diameter base. Introduced in 1930 under the name Agua Caliente. Original colors were ruby, royal blue, jade green, ebony, crystal, rose, green, and amber. It was reissued in milk glass about 1952. The milk glass version has a somewhat smaller base (4¼") due to the absence of the broad rim seen on the original. The newer milk glass and highly promoted ruby are the easiest colors to find. All other colors are scarce to rare. Ruby, milk glass, green, rose, crystal, amber: $25.00 – 35.00. Royal blue, jade, ebony: $55.00 – 75.00.

FN-14. No. 1611 GEORGIAN CANDLESTICK IN RUBY

No. 1092 candleholder. 2¼" high, 5" diameter. Basket Weave pattern. Three footed with open edge. Production dates 1930 – 1937. Made in ebony, jade green, crystal, ruby, royal blue, green opalescent, and possibly in milk glass from 1933 to 1936. Some pieces of the Basket Weave pattern were reissued in 1970. We aren't sure if the candleholder was included, but reissued pieces carry the Fenton logo. Also made with the top edge flat, not ruffled. Crystal: $10.00 – 15.00. Ebony, green transparent: $15.00 – 25.00. Ruby, jade, green opalescent: $25.00 – 35.00.

FN-15. No. 1092 BASKET WEAVE candleholders in RUBY (CRIMPED TOP) AND GREEN OPALESCENT (FLAT TOP)

No. 848 candleholder. 1⅝" high with 4½" diameter bowl. Also marketed as No. 1234. It was usually shown with nine petals but can be found with six. It is dish shaped with three feet. Production dates 1932 – 1936. The nine petaled version is known in royal blue, light blue, jade green, ebony, ruby, and Pekin blue and the six petaled version in green, ebony, crystal, and Chinese yellow. Other colors are probable for both styles. These were often sold with a matching petaled bowl. Crystal: $6.00 – 8.00. Ruby, jade, ebony, green transparent: $10.00 – 15.00. Royal blue: $15.00 – 20.00. Chinese yellow, Peking blue: $25.00 – 30.00.

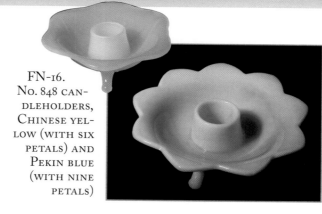

FN-16. No. 848 CANDLEHOLDERS, CHINESE YELLOW (WITH SIX PETALS) AND PEKIN BLUE (WITH NINE PETALS)

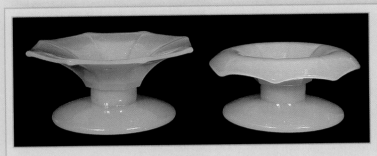

FN-17. No. 1672 OCTAGON EDGE CANDLEHOLDERS IN JADE, FLARED AND ROLLED EDGES

No. 1672 Octagon Edge candleholder. 2⅜" high with a 3¾" round base, 4¾" across top. Production dates 1931 – 1933. Available with a flared or rolled rim. This candleholder was sometimes marketed as No. 1676. The stock number seemed to depend on the style bowl that it was being sold with. Made in jade, ruby, black, wisteria, and lilac (very scarce). Jade, black, ruby: $35.00 – 50.00. Lilac: $80.00 – 100.00.

FN-18. No. 1673 OCTAGON EDGE CANDLE VASE

No. 1673 candle vase. 8" high. Produced in 1933 in jade, ruby, and ebony. Very scarce in all colors. Jade, ebony: $80.00 to market. Ruby and jade: $100.00 to market.

Lest you think that these "to market" prices are due to laziness or lack of research let us relate a turn of events as we were about to go to print… In the spring of 2002 a ruby No. 1673 in excellent condition sold on eBay for $510.00. Less than one month later another, identical in all respects, brought only $99.00. Both were similarly and correctly advertised as "Rare Fenton #1623 ruby candle vase." Both photos were clear and both sellers had good feedback. Luck of the draw and auction fever were all that could account for the difference. In this case the $100 price is probably closer to the value we would place on this item. The seller in the $510.00 auction had a $75.00 reserve on the piece, meaning that he was willing to sell for that price, and the third highest bidder in that auction stopped at $49.00. *(Artist's rendition.)*

FN-19. No. 950 CORNUCOPIA CANDLEHOLDERS IN RUBY (WITH FLAT TOP) AND OPALESCENT AMETHYST (WITH FLARED TOP)

No. 950 cornucopia candleholder. 5½" high, 4¼" oval base. Produced from 1932 to 1939 in amber, azure blue, ruby, green, crystal, ebony (scarce), royal blue, milk glass, jade green, moonstone, rose, Persian pearl, Mongolian green (very scarce), Mandarin red (scarce), and opalescent amethyst (only four known). Four satin etchings were also available. These were Ming, Poinsettia, San Toy, and Silvertone. This mold was resurrected in 1941 to make Fenton's No. 951, which is identical to the No. 950 except for the addition of a crimped, crested edge. (See FN-29 on page 188.)

Note the flat top on the ruby No. 950 shown on the left in figure FN-19. This is a variation to the more commonly seen style shown on the right. We couldn't find the flat rim pictured in any Fenton catalog but believe this to be the earliest version of this candlestick. Probably during its first year of production, someone discovered that a few slight tweaks to rim of the still warm glass would give the design some extra "flare." This later style continued in production throughout the life of the No. 950 and was also used on the later crested and hobnail versions of this cornucopia candleholder. The flat-top style is known in milk glass, Mandarin red, ruby, and jade green.

Moonstone, amber, green transparent, rose, Persian pearl, crystal etched: $22.00 – 30.00. Azure blue, royal blue, ruby, rose etched, green etched, jade: $35.00 – 55.00. Mongolian green, Mandarin red: $55.00 – 80.00. Amethyst opalescent: $125.00 to market.

No. 1790 Leaf Tiers candleholder. 2" high, 5¾" across the top. This scarce, three-footed candleholder has a pressed leaf design on the underside of the bowl. Production dates 1934 – 1941. Made in crystal, crystal satin, milk glass, and topaz opalescent. Other possible colors include royal blue, jade, Mandarin red and blue opalescent. Crystal, milk glass: $40.00 – 50.00. Topaz opalescent: $90.00 to market.

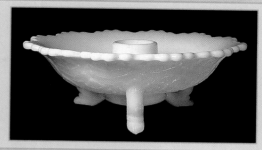

FN-20. No. 1790 LEAF TIERS CANDLE-HOLDER IN MILK GLASS

No. 1800 Sheffield candleholder. 4¼" with a 4½" diameter base. Produced 1937 – 1938, reissued during the 1980s as No. 6672, sometimes called New Sheffield. (Note the difference in the base of the reissue, as shown in FN-21a.) Made in amber, aquamarine, blue, blue opalescent, French opalescent, minted cream, peaches and cream opalescent, gold, ruby, and the more commonly found crystal. Can also be found with the acid etched Silvertone decoration. A version of this candlestick is also known that has no ribs on the center column and only three ribs, separated by panels, on the candle cup. It has been seen with the Poinsettia etching. The Sheffield pattern is very similar to Heisey's Ridgeleigh, but the candlestick is completely unlike any of the candleholders included in that pattern. Crystal: $15.00 – 20.00. Peaches and cream opalescent, minted cream, blue opalescent, crystal Silvertone, amber: $25.00 – 30.00. Ruby, aquamarine: $35.00 – 40.00.

FN-21. No. 1800 SHEFFIELD CANDLESTICK

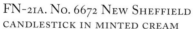

FN-21A. No. 6672 NEW SHEFFIELD CANDLESTICK IN MINTED CREAM

No. 1010 candleholder, flared (shown), 1¾" high, 4¼" diameter; and No. 1011 candleholder, tri-cornered or club shaped (not shown).

"Three-toed." This pressed pattern was called Silvertone, but don't confuse it with Fenton's Silvertone acid-etched decoration. Production dates: 1936 – 1937. Made only in amber, crystal, and wisteria. The No. 1011 is the same except the bowl is formed into a triangular shape. Crystal: $10.00 – 12.00. Amber: $15.00 – 18.00. Wisteria: $25.00 – 30.00.

FN-22. No. 1010 SILVERTONE CANDLEHOLDER IN AMBER

No. 349 candleholder. The straight-sided version is 3½" with a 3¾" round base and octagon rim. The flared version is 3⅛" high, 4½" across, with a 3⅝" base. There are three beads on either side of the bowl surrounding the socket. Produced circa 1937 in crystal and crystal satin with the Wisteria, San Toy, and Ming acid etches. Made with "straight" sides or with the sides flared, as seen here. This was most likely made from the No. 1672 Octagon Edge mold (see FN-17 on p. 184). Note that this stock number was previously used for a completely different candleholder (see FN-1). Difficult to find. Crystal, plain: $30.00 – 40.00; etched: $65.00 – 95.00.

FN-23. No. 349 CANDLESTICK, WITH MING ETCH

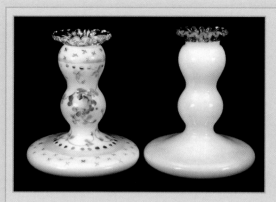

FN-24. No 1523 CANDLESTICKS IN DECORATED SILVER CREST AND AQUA CREST

FN-24A. No. 1523 CANDLESTICKS WITH SPIRAL OPTIC IN CRANBERRY AND BLUE OPALESCENT (NOTE VARIANCE IN TOPS)

No. 1523 candlestick. 4¼" to 4¾" high with a 3¾" base. Unlike most of Fenton's candleholders, these are blown rather than pressed. They were made in Spiral Optic, plain milk glass, and cased (peach crest). The Spiral Optic sticks can be found with plain or ruffled tops. The milk glass versions were made with various "crests" including aqua, gold, crystal, silver, peach, rose, ivory, and emerald. Of the optic patterns: Cranberry opalescent was produced from 1938 to 1940. French opalescent, green opalescent, blue opalescent, and blue ridge were produced in 1939 only. A limited amount of topaz opalescent may have been produced in early 1940. In 1939 another candleholder with the same stock number was advertised in Ring Optic (see FN-24b). These could have been made in any of Fenton's Spiral Optic colors and are believed to be rare. Sometime between 1948 and 1953 the stock number was changed to 7270. Due to a change in Fenton's milk glass formula, pieces made after 1957 are opaque white and have none of the pearl-like opalescence of the earlier pieces. Silver crest: $20.00 – 25.00. Gold crest, ivory crest, rose crest, peach crest, aqua crest: $30.00 – 40.00. Emerald crest, blue spiral optic: $55.00 – 75.00. Pink spiral optic: $65.00 – 85.00. Blue ridge: $110.00 to market.

FN-24B. 1939 CATALOG PHOTO-GRAPH OF A VARIANT No. 1523 IN THE RING OPTIC PATTERN

FN-25. No. 2000 PINEAPPLE TWO-LIGHT CANDELABRA IN MERMAID BLUE

No. 2000 Pineapple two-light candelabra. 5¾" high with a 5⅜" round base. (Listed as 5".) Production dates: 1936 – 1939 and again in 1992 for QVC in petal pink iridized. Other known colors include crystal and rose in plain or satin finishes, jade, mermaid blue, and ruby (made for a third party). Ming is the only listed decoration. Crystal, petal pink iridized: $35.00 – 50.00. Rose, jade, ruby: $50.00 – 65.00. Mermaid blue: $70.00 – 80.00.

FN-25A. No. 2000 PINEAPPLE TWO-LIGHT CANDELABRA IN PETAL PINK IRIDIZED (QVC REISSUE)

No. 6 Swan candlestick. 6⅜" high (cupped base version). There is a great deal of discussion among collectors as to whether Fenton ever made the candleholder shown in figure FN-26. The Diamond Glass-ware Company originally manufactured these as part of an entire line of swan items. When they went out of business in the early 1930s, Fenton acquired the molds for Diamond's swan line. There is a 1938 Fenton catalog that shows the swan candlestick with a flared base being offered in crystal, crystal satin, and milk glass (see FN-26a) but nothing to document that Fenton ever produced the cupped base version. We have tried to compare colors to determine the maker of our cupped based swans and have to report the results as inconclusive. Both cupped and flared versions were probably made from the same mold, with the final appearance being determined by the way the base was "worked" after being removed from the mold. The only other color that we're aware of for the flared base version is opalescent blue (rare). Known colors for the cupped base version are amber, ebony, green, pink, and amethyst.

FN-26. No. 6 Swan candlesticks with cupped bases in pink and amethyst — Fenton? (Diamond mold)

No matter who made them, a pair of these with a matching console bowl makes a beautiful table centerpiece. In fact, Fenton must have agreed since they resurrected the swan candleholder in 1971 for inclusion into their Original Formula Carnival Glass line. The item number at that time was listed as No. 5172 and the mold had been reworked to include more patterning on the candle cup and stem (see FN-77 on page 199). The initial color was amethyst carnival. In the 1990s they made complete console sets in colonial pink, turquoise opalescent, and possibly other colors. All of the No. 5172s that we've seen have cupped bases. Amber, crystal, ebony, green, pink: $40.00 – 60.00. Milk glass, amethyst: $50.00 – 75.00. Blue opalescent: $150.00 – market.

FN-26A. No. 6 Swan candlestick with flared base, from 1938 catalog

No. 1974 Daisy and Button two-light candleholder. 4¼" high with a 5" round base. Sometimes found with a domed base, making the height 5". Production dates 1937 – 1963. Introduced circa 1937 – 1939 as part of the No. 1900 Cape Cod line. Originally made in crystal and transparent colors, then in 1953 it was reissued with a slightly reworked socket in milk glass and other opaque colors. Known in amber, Cape Cod green, colonial blue, crystal, French opalescent satin, mermaid blue, milk glass, plum opalescent (experimental color, only one pair known), royal blue, vaseline, and wisteria. Milk glass, crystal: $20.00 – 25.00. Amber, Cape Cod green, colonial blue: $25.00 – 30.00. Royal blue, vaseline, wisteria: $60.00 – 75.00. Plum opalescent: $135.00 – market.

FN-27. No. 1974 Daisy & Button two-light candleholder in milk glass

FN-28. No. 7676 VIKING TWO-LIGHT CANDLEHOLDER (REISSUE IN PLUM CARNIVAL)

No. 7676 Viking two-light candleholder. 4¼" – 4½" high, 5⅜" on-center, across the arms. Originally produced in 1938 with a satin finish called Velvatone. Advertised as having a "figure-head motif," it was sold with a bowl that resembled a Viking ship. It was reissued in plum carnival in 1998. The reissues have the Fenton logo and a "9" mold marked on the bottom. The base of the reissue is also worked into a dome shape (figure FN-28) whereas the original's is almost flat. This makes the reissue stand 5½" high. The original version is rare. Velvatone: $110.00 – 150.00. Plum carnival: $45.00 – 65.00.

FN-29. No. 951 CORNUCOPIA CANDLEHOLDERS IN RUBY SILVER CREST (RIBBED VERSION) AND ROSE CREST (SMOOTH VERSION)

No. 951 Cornucopia candleholder. 5¾" to 6¼" high with a 4¼" oval base. Produced 1940 – 1966. First introduced in ivory crest and quickly followed by aqua crest, crystal crest (1942 only), gold crest, silver crest, ivory crest, jade snow crest (1942 only), peach crest, rose crest, and ruby silver crest (scarce). The early production units had a vertical ribbing on the sides like the No. 950 cornucopia candleholder from which they were derived. (See FN-19 on p. 184.) The ribbed detail had given way to a smooth surface by the time of the 1950 catalog. In the early 1950s the stock number was changed to No. 7274. By this time they were only being made in silver crest and rose crest. Silver crest: $25.00 – 30.00. Gold

crest, ivory crest, rose crest, peach crest, aqua crest, crystal crest: $35.00 – 45.00. Ruby silver crest, jade snow crest, opal with jade crest: $110.00 – 150.00.

Note the edge detail in FN-29a. This is crystal crest, which was Fenton's only crest to have two layers of applied glass. This gives a nice effect but was found too difficult to produce so it was quickly discontinued and replaced with the popular silver crest.

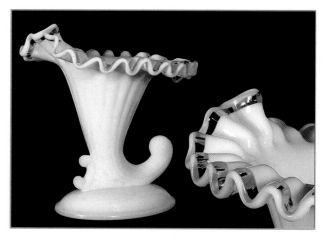

FN-29A. No. 951 CORNUCOPIA CANDLEHOLDER IN CRYSTAL CREST

NO. 389 HOBNAIL LINE

When first introduced in quantity around 1940 all of the items in Fenton's Hobnail line had the same pattern number (389). It was not until 1952 that individual items got their own stock numbers. We'll use the individual numbers whenever possible.

Due to the popularity of what turned out to be Fenton's largest and longest-lived line, new items were continually added over a period of many years. Our attempt at a chronological presentation means that Hobnail candlesticks will be interspersed throughout most of the remaining pages in this chapter.

No. 3971 miniature Hobnail cornucopia. 3¾" high, 2¾" oval base. Production dates 1940 – 1957. Holds a thin candle. Produced in French opalescent, blue opalescent, topaz opalescent, and milk glass. All but the milk glass were discontinued in 1954. Milk glass, French opalescent: $15.00 – 20.00. Blue opalescent: $20.00 – 25.00. Topaz opalescent: $30.00 – 40.00.

FN-30. No. 3971 MINIATURE HOBNAIL CORNUCOPIA IN BLUE OPALESCENT

No. 3874 Hobnail cornucopia. 5¾" high with a 4¼" oval base. Production dates 1942 – 1965. Like the No. 3971, this was offered in French opalescent, blue opalescent, green opalescent, topaz opalescent, and milk glass. All but the milk glass were discontinued in 1954. Milk glass, French opalescent: $25.00 – 30.00. Blue opalescent: $35.00 – 40.00. Green opalescent: $40.00 – 45.00. Topaz opalescent: $50.00 – 65.00.

FN-31. No. 3874 HOBNAIL CORNUCOPIAS IN GREEN AND BLUE OPALESCENT

No. 3974 Hobnail candleholder. There are two distinct shapes to this candleholder and much variation with each size. The first version introduced in 1941 had a rather flat base giving a typical size of 2¾" high with a 4⅝" diameter base. This style was in limited production until at least 1962. Meanwhile, sometime in the early 1950s a taller version with a slightly domed base appeared using the same number. The typical size for this version is 3⅝" high with 4⅛" diameter base. Version 2 was still in production in the 1980s and was reissued in 1994 – 1995 in milk glass. Version 1 known colors include milk glass, green pastel, blue opalescent, French opalescent, green opalescent, plum opalescent, and topaz opalescent (reissued in 1980 for Levay). Version 2 is known in Pekin blue II (scarce), amber (1959 only), blue jade, blue marble, blue pastel, jonquil yellow (sample color only), milk glass (plain or with a hand-painted holly decoration) rose pastel, ruby and turquoise. Ruby, French opalescent, blue marble, amber, milk glass: $10.00 – 15.00. Turquoise, rose, green: $15.00 – 20.00. Blue opalescent, blue pastel: $20.00 – 25.00. Topaz opalescent, green opalescent, jonquil yellow: $30.00 – 35.00. Cranberry opalescent: $45.00 – 55.00. Plum opalescent: $65.00 – 85.00.

FN-32. No. 3974 HOBNAIL CANDLEHOLDERS IN TOPAZ OPALESCENT (FLAT BASE) AND RUBY (CUPPED BASE)

No. 36 candle vase. 4" high with a 2¼" round base, and "double crimped" top. Production dates 1941 – 1942. Known in ivory crest and aqua crest (both scarce). This was made from Fenton's much more common No. 36 vase. To be the candleholder it must have a distinct candle socket in the bottom of the "vase." $40.00 – 60.00.

FN-33. No. 36 CANDLE VASE IN IVORY CREST

FN-34. No. 680 CANDLE-HOLDER IN EMERALD CREST

No. 680 candleholder. 3¼" high, 5" saucer base. Produced 1941 – 1952. Made in silver crest, aqua crest, and emerald crest. Additionally, silver crest and ruby silver crest, both with the acid etched Silvertone pattern were made in 1941 as a special order. All are considered hard to find. Made from the same mold as Fenton's earlier No. 315 (see FN-3 on p. 180). Silver crest: $45.00 – 55.00. Aqua crest: $55.00 – 70.00. Emerald crest: $70.00 – 90.00. Ruby silver crest: $100.00 – market.

FN-35. No. 192 MELON RIBBED CANDLEHOLDERS IN PEACH CREST AND BLUE OVERLAY — LOW

No. 192 candleholder. Melon ribbed. 3¼" high, 1⅞" base. This was another one of Fenton's mold-blown candlesticks. Production dates 1942 – 1949. Made from the same mold as the cologne in the No. 1405 vanity set. The inside of the neck will be slightly larger and not ground, as the cologne is for the stopper to fit. Made in aqua, crystal, gold, peach, and silver crests, French opalescent with dot optic, melon with a silver crest, mulberry, ruby overlay with diamond optic, and blue and rose overlay. Hard to find. Silver crest, rose overlay, blue overlay: $25.00 – 35.00. Aqua crest, crystal crest, peach crest, gold crest: $30.00 – 40.00.

FN-36. No. 192 MELON RIBBED CANDLEHOLDER IN BLUE OVERLAY — TALL

No. 192 candleholder. Melon ribbed. 4⅞" high with a 3¾" diameter base. Mold blown. Production dates 1942 – 1943. Made in aqua and gold crest, and in blue overlay. All colors are scarce to rare. Blue overlay: $35.00 – 40.00. Other colors: $50.00 – 70.00.

FN-37. No. 1524 COIN DOT CAN-DLEHOLDER IN FRENCH OPALESCENT

No. 1524 candleholder, Coin Dot. 5½" high x 3¾" round base. Mold blown. Production dates 1947 – 1954. Made in blue opalescent, cranberry opalescent, and French opalescent. The catalog designation was later changed to No. 1470. French opalescent: $60.00 – 75.00. Blue opalescent: $70.00 – 90.00. Cranberry opalescent: $100.00 – 150.00.

No. 1948 Diamond Lace candleholder. 1½" high, 4⅜" diameter. Production dates 1949 – 1954. In 1952 the number was changed to No. 4874 and these were sold with a 9½" (No. 4824) bowl as part of the No. 4804 console set. Made in blue opalescent and French opalescent. Also known in ruby with a ruffled edge and pink opalescent with a white edge. French opalescent: $15.00 – 20.00. Blue opalescent and other colors: $20.00 – 25.00.

FN-38. No. 1948 DIAMOND LACE CANDLEHOLDER IN FRENCH OPALESCENT

No. 1948A Diamond Lace cornucopia candleholder. 5" high with a 3¼" base. Production dates 1948 – 1950. Made in blue opalescent, blue opalescent with a silver crest, French opalescent, and French opalescent with an aqua or emerald crest. French opalescent: $45.00 – 50.00. Blue opalescent: $50.00 – 60.00. French or blue opalescent with crest: $60.00 – 75.00.

FN-39. No. 1948A DIAMOND LACE CORNUCOPIA CANDLEHOLDER IN FRENCH OPALESCENT WITH EMERALD CREST

No. 752 candleholder. 1½" high, 4"x 5" diameter with a "tiered leaf" design around the perimeter. Limited production dates, 1951 – 1952. Made in milk glass and emerald green. Sold as part of a console set that included two or four candlesticks and a matching bowl. Milk glass: $20.00 – 25.00. Emerald green, crystal with satin border: $25.00 – 30.00.

FN-40. No. 752 CANDLE-HOLDERS IN EMERALD GREEN

No. 68 candleholder. Unknown size. Produced during 1952 in amber, green, and milk glass. This bowl-shaped candleholder was sold as part of a console set with an 11½" oval bowl. $15.00 – 20.00.

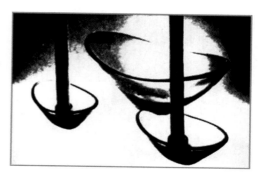

FN-41. No. 68 CONSOLE SET, FROM *GIFTWARES*, FEBRUARY 1952

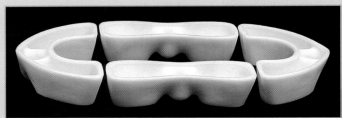

FN-42. No. 9002 (or No. 1952) Clusterettes four-piece flower set in milk glass

No. 9002 Clusterettes four-piece flower set. Also listed as No. 1952. 1⅝" high. Production dates 1952 – 1958. Clusterettes consist of two rectangular pieces that are 6¼" long and two curved pieces that

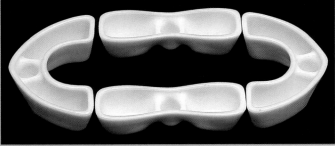

FN-42A. No. 9002 (or No. 1952) Clusterettes four-piece flower set in milk glass, top view

are 6¼" x 3¾". They could be arranged in various combinations. Made in amber, dark green (both discontinued in 1956), and milk glass (discontinued in 1954, but still offered to florist accounts until 1958). Milk glass, amber: $60.00 – 70.00. Emerald green: $70.00 – 80.00. (Prices are for complete sets.)

FN-43. No. 3998 Hobnail candle lamp in ebony with pink pastel shade

No. 3998 Hobnail hurricane candle lamp, two piece. 8¼" high overall, consists of a 1¼" high x 5⅛" handled base with a hobnail shade, 7⅝" high x 2⅛". Production dates were 1952 – 1970. Made in blue pastel, pink pastel, milk glass, and ebony. The base will sometimes be found without a shade. Despite being part of the No. 389 Hobnail pattern, note that the base is plain, without hobnails. Also known in ruby with a plain ruby shade. Milk glass: $40.00 – 50.00. Colors: $70.00 – 100.00.

FN-44. No. 3870 Hobnail handled candleholder in cranberry opalescent

No. 3870 Hobnail handled candleholder. 3¼" high. Production dates 1953 – 1978. Made in cranberry opalescent, blue opalescent, French opalescent, lime opalescent (scarce), and milk glass. Milk glass: $20.00 – 25.00. Cranberry opalescent: $55.00 – 65.00.

FN-45. No. 7272 candleholder peach crest

No. 7272 candleholder. 4¾" high x 2¾" footed base. Produced 1953 – 1963. Made in black rose, peach crest, silver crest, silver turquoise. Rare in goldenrod , which was produced for only six months. Silver crest: $35.00 – 45.00. Peach crest: $50.00 – 60.00. Silver turquoise: $95.00 – 125.00. Black rose: $120.00 – 150.00. Goldenrod: $135.00 – market.

No. 7073 candleholder. 3" high (3¼" to top of handle), 2¼" oval base. Mold blown. Produced 1954 – 1956. Made in the opaque colors of blue pastel, green pastel, pink pastel, and milk glass. One each of a milk glass with a black handle and a black with a milk glass handle are known. Milk glass: $15.00 – 20.00. Pastels: $30.00 – 40.00.

FN-46. No. 7073 CANDLEHOLDER IN BLUE PASTEL

No. 5670 Block and Star handled candleholder.
No. 5671 Block and Star square candleholder.
No. 5672 Block and Star flared candleholder. (FN-49, not pictured.)
No. 5673 Block and Star cupped candleholder.

1¾" to 2" high, 4" diameter. All were introduced in 1955. Nos. 5671 and 5672 were gone by July 1956. The others survived until 1959. They all appear to be made from the same mold and worked into the desired shape. The No. 5670 is just the No. 5673 with an applied handle. Made in milk glass and turquoise. Sample turns of moonstone and rose pastel may also have been produced. Milk glass: $15.00 – 20.00. Turquoise: $25.00 – 30.00.

FN-47. No. 5670 BLOCK & STAR HANDLED CANDLEHOLDER IN MILK GLASS

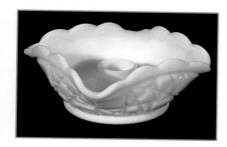

FN-48. No. 5671 BLOCK & STAR SQUARE CANDLEHOLDER IN MILK GLASS

FN-50. No. 5673 BLOCK & STAR CUPPED CANDLEHOLDER IN TURQUOISE

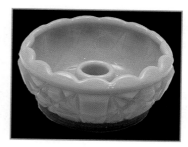

No. 7271 candleholder. 3½" high with a 4½" ruffled, crested base. Produced 1955 – 1980s. Made in silver turquoise, silver crest, black crest (scarce) or apple blossom crest. The silver crest can be found with Fenton's hand-painted decorations of Apple Blossoms, Yellow Roses, or Violets in the Snow (as shown). Silver crest: $12.00 – 16.00; hand-painted: $20.00 – 25.00. Silver turquoise: $25.00 – 30.00. Apple blossom crest: $30.00 – 35.00. Black crest: $70.00 to market.

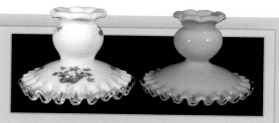

FN-51. No. 7271 CANDLEHOLDER IN SILVER CREST (WITH HAND-PAINTED VIOLETS IN THE SNOW DECORATION) AND SILVER TURQUOISE

No. 6974 Teardrop candleholder. 5½" high, vertical ribbed, with a 4½" diameter base. Produced 1957 – 1959 in milk glass. $15.00 – 20.00.

FN-52. No. 6974 TEARDROP CANDLEHOLDER IN MILK GLASS

FN-53. No. 4498
THUMB-PRINT
HURRICANE LAMP
IN MILK GLASS

No. 4498 Thumb-print [Fenton spelling] hurricane lamp. 10" high with a 6" diameter base. Two piece, handled. The thumbprint pattern is on the base and the shade. Production dates 1956 – 1958 in milk glass. The base can be found with a plain round or a tab handle. In 1960 Fenton marketed a line of thumbprint pattern glass as part of their "Olde Virginia Glass" line. However, this item was already discontinued by then and was not part of that offering. $70.00 – 85.00.

FN-54. No. 6674
PETITE
EPERGNES

No. 6674 petite epergne. 5¾" wide and 3" tall, including the peg. Designed to be inserted in any candlestick and to hold flowers. Made circa 1958 in crystal. The pattern is very similar to Fenton's earlier Sheffield and to Heisey's Ridgeleigh. $12.00 – 15.00.

FN-55. No. 3770
HOBNAIL CANDLE-
HOLDER IN MILK
GLASS

No. 3770 Hobnail candleholder. 3½" high, 6" diameter footed. Cupped bowl. Production dates 1959 – 1965 in milk glass and 1959 – 1960 in topaz opalescent. Milk glass: $30.00 – 35.00. Topaz opalescent: $85.00 – 100.00.

No. 3771 Hobnail candle bowl. 3¾" high, 8" in diameter. Flared, ruffled bowl. Production dates 1959 – 1969. Made in milk glass, green opalescent, plum opalescent, topaz opalescent, and blue opalescent. All colors except the milk glass were discontinued between 1960 – 1961 and are hard to find. This is made from the same mold as the No. 3770 candle bowl. Milk glass: $30.00 – 35.00. Plum opalescent, topaz opalescent: $90.00 – 110.00. Other colors: $65.00 – 80.00.

FN-56. No. 3771 HOBNAIL CANDLE BOWL
IN MILK GLASS

No. 3774 Hobnail candlestick. 9" high, 4⅝" base. Production dates 1958 – 1971. Made in milk glass and antique amber. Antique amber was only made during the first half of 1959 and is therefore difficult to find. $35.00 – 40.00.

FN-57. No. 3774 HOBNAIL CANDLESTICK IN MILK GLASS

No. 3474 Cactus candleholder. 3½" high. Production dates 1959 – 1960 in milk glass and topaz opalescent. Cactus was reintroduced as Desert Tree in 1967 – 1968 as part of the Olde Virginia Line. Colors at that time were milk glass and colonial amber. Milk glass, amber: $35.00 – 45.00. Topaz opalescent: $80.00 – 100.00.

FN-58. No. 3474 CACTUS CANDLEHOLDER IN MILK GLASS

No. 8175 Horizon candleholder, 5" high; No. 8176 Horizon candleholder, 6½" high; No. 8177 Horizon candleholder, 8" high. Production dates: 1959 – 1960. Horizon was an attempt by Fenton to market a contemporary line of glassware. The line, designed by Michael Lax, included three candleholders, all basically the same except for size. Horizon did not sell well and only lasted one year. Colors were amber, French opalescent (see below), and Jamestown blue. All candleholders have a porcelain candle cup insert. Michael Lax also worked as a designer earlier for the Dunbar Glass Corporation and Duncan & Miller. (See DB-8 on p. 140 and DM-97 on p. 170.) Amber: $12.00 – 18.00. Other colors: $20.00 – 28.00.

FN-59. HORIZON ADVERTISING BROCHURE

FN-59A. HORIZON BOWL AND CANDLEHOLDERS IN FRENCH OPALESCENT, FROM *CHINA, GLASS & LAMPS*, FEBRUARY 1959

No. 7474 candleholder. 5¾" high with a 4½" ruffled, crested base. Produced 1960 – 1978. Made in apple blossom crest, blue crest, ebony crest, flame crest, gold crest, and silver crest. From 1968 to 1972 the silver crest No. 7474s were offered with Fenton's hand-painted Violets in the Snow decoration (as shown). This candlestick was later reissued in 1984 with a dome base (and without the ruffled crest) as No. 7475. (See FN-89 on p. 203.) Silver crest: $20.00 – 25.00. Silver crest (hand painted), gold crest: $40.00 – 55.00. Apple blossom crest, flame crest, ebony crest: $60.00 – 80.00.

FN-60. No. 7474 CANDLEHOLDER, SILVER CREST WITH HAND-PAINTED VIOLETS IN THE SNOW DECORATION

FN-61. No. 3673
HOBNAIL FOOTED
CANDLEHOLDER

No. 3673 Hobnail footed candleholder. 2⅞" high, 4⅛" in diameter. Sherbet style. Production dates 1962 – 1976. Milk glass only. Almost identical to the No. 3670, but not as wide and with a 3" round foot added. $15.00 – 20.00.

FN-62. No. 3670
HOBNAIL CAN-
DLEHOLDER IN
MILK GLASS

No. 3670 Hobnail candleholder. 2" high, 4⅞" in diameter. Round or square versions offered. The round version was also available with a peg bottom, to enable it to be inserted in another candleholder as an epergnette. Production dates 1961 – 1969. Milk glass only. $15.00 – 20.00.

FN-63. No. 3672
HOBNAIL TWO-
LIGHT CANDLE-
STICK IN MILK
GLASS

No. 3672 Hobnail two-light candleholder. Round dome base. Production dates 1961 – 1971. Milk glass only. $35.00 – 45.00.

FN-64. No. 3674
HOBNAIL CAN-
DLEHOLDER IN
MILK GLASS

No. 3674 Hobnail candleholder. 5⅞" high with a 4¼" base. Production dates 1961 – 1985. Made in milk glass, crystal, blue opalescent, and Almost Heaven (a blue slag color). Milk glass pieces can be found with Fenton's hand-painted Holly decoration. The No. 3674 was reissued in green Persian pearl (an iridescent finish) in 1992 as a limited edition item for Fenton's Persian Pearl Historical Collection promotion. Milk glass (plain), crystal: $12.00 – 15.00. Milk glass (hand painted), blue opalescent: $30.00 – 35.00.

FN-65. No. 4473
THUMBPRINT CAN-
DLESTICK IN MILK
GLASS

No. 4473 Thumbprint candleholder. 8⅝" high, 4¾" diameter base. Production dates 1961 – 1970. Made in colonial amber, colonial blue, colonial green, colonial pink, crystal, and milk glass. Pattern also known as Olde Virginia Glass. Crystal, amber, green: $12.00 – 15.00. Milk glass, blue, pink: $22.00 – 25.00.

No. 4474 Thumbprint low candleholder. 2" high, 4⅛" diameter. Produced in 1961 in milk glass. Pattern also known as Olde Virginia Glass. $12.00 – 18.00.

FN-66. No. 4474 THUMBPRINT LOW CANDLE-HOLDER IN MILK GLASS

No. 3678 Hobnail crescent candleholder. 3" high, 8" across. Produced in 1962 using the No. 3798 bowl with a candle receptacle added. Made in milk glass. $100.00 to market (One sold on eBay in the spring of 2002 with original label for $370.52).

FN-67. No. 3678 HOBNAIL CANDLEHOLDER IN MILK GLASS

No. 4470 Thumbprint candleholder. 3¾" high x 4" base. Production dates 1964 – 1970. Made in colonial amber, colonial blue, colonial green, colonial pink, and orange. $8.00 – 12.00.

FN-68. No. 4470 THUMBPRINT CANDLEHOLDER IN COLONIAL AMBER

No. A-018 Hobnail candleholder. 5¾" high, 3¼" diameter base. We don't have a production date for this piece but believe it was manufactured sometime during the 1960s. Known only in milk glass. Made by adding a candle receptacle to the No. 3728 footed comport (which was made circa 1956 – 1980s). $15.00 – 20.00.

FN-69. No. A-018 HOBNAIL CANDLEHOLDER IN MILK GLASS

No. 9270 Rose candleholder. 3¼" high with 4½" diameter base. Produced 1967 – 1981. Made in blue marble, colonial amber, colonial blue, colonial green, colonial pink, milk glass, Mongolian green, and lavender opalescent, which was an experimental color in 1981. Amber, milk glass, green: $12.00 – 15.00. Blue, pink, blue marble: $16.00 – 20.00.

FN-70. No. 9270 ROSE CANDLE-HOLDER IN BLUE MARBLE

FN-71. No. 3570
SPANISH LACE
CANDLEHOLDER
WITH SILVER CREST
EDGE

No. 3570 Spanish Lace candleholder. 3⅞" high, 4½" base. Production dates: 1968 – 1984. Spanish Lace is a textured, or embossed, pattern with a Silver Crest edge. Available plain or hand painted with Fenton's popular Violets in the Snow decoration. Reissued in 1988 for QVC in teal with a milk glass crest. Milk glass (plain): $15.00 – 20.00; hand painted: $20.00 – 25.00. Teal with milk glass crest: $22.00 – 28.00.

FN-72. No. 3872 HOBNAIL CRE-
ATIVE CANDLE BOWL IN EBONY

No. 3872 Hobnail Creative candle bowl. 3½" high x 6½" diameter. Production dates 1968 – 1980+. Made in colonial blue, colonial green, colonial amber, blue marble, shiny custard, lime sherbet, milk glass, ebony, and ruby, and the following experimental colors of crystal iridescent, jonquil, and Pekin blue. Other colors are possible. The outside held five slim taper candles while the center would accept a regular taper or a pillar candle. In 1970 these were boxed and offered with various floral arrangements and a 9" scented pillar candle and proved to be very good sellers. Covered by patent 3,547,569, filed December 11, 1968, and approved December 15, 1970, with the inventors given as Wilmer C. Fenton and Anthony J. Rosena. This patent was not for the design of this particular piece, but for the concept of a candle bowl ("a single decorative structure for containing candles, flowers, and other articles"). The same patent also applied to the No. 9172 Fine Cut & Block candle bowl. (See FN-79 on p. 200.) Amber, green: $10.00 – 14.00. Blue, pink, milk glass: $12.00 – 16.00. Blue marble, ebony, custard, lime green: $18.00 – 22.00.

FN-73. No. 3873
HOBNAIL MINIA-
TURE CANDLE
BOWL IN MILK
GLASS

No. 3873 Hobnail miniature candle bowl. 3¼" high. Scalloped foot. Production dates 1969 – 1977. Made in colonial blue, colonial green, colonial amber, colonial orange, and milk glass. Amber, green, orange: $12.00 – 16.00. Milk glass, blue: $18.00 – 22.00.

FN-74. No. 8374 VALENCIA FOOTED CANDLEHOLDERS IN ORANGE,
PROVINCIAL BLUE, AND DUSTY ROSE

No. 8374 Valencia candleholder. 4¾" high with a 4" diameter scalloped footed base. Produced 1970 – 1972 and occasionally reissued since. Known in the following colors: colonial amber, colonial blue, colonial green, crystal, dusty rose, holly berry, orange, provincial blue opalescent (1987 – 1988), rose corsage, and teal royale. Was also sold with a hurricane globe as No. 8376. Amber, green, crystal: $10.00 – 14.00. Colonial blue, orange: $12.00 – 16.00. Provincial blue opalescent, dusty rose: $20.00 – 25.00.

No. 9193 mini-arranger. 3¾" in diameter. Produced 1971 – 1973. Made in crystal only. Designed to hold five taper candles and a 1" or 2" candle. Could be used in the No. 3778 MI 8" ashtray, any bowl, or by itself. $15.00 – 20.00.

FN-75. No. 9193 MINI-ARRANGER

No. 3895 toothpick/candleholder. Unknown size. Production dates 1971 – 1976 in milk glass only. A very similar candleholder has been seen, marked "Made in Taiwan." $20.00 – 25.00.

FN-76. No. 3895 TOOTH-PICK/CANDLE-HOLDER, FROM CATALOG

No. 5172 Swan candleholder. 6½" high with a 3¼" diameter base. This candleholder was first manufactured by Fenton in the 1930s (see FN-26 on p. 187) and before that by the Diamond Glass-ware Company. This reissue, first produced as part of Fenton's Original Formula Carnival line in 1971, used a modified mold with additional detailing on the upper stem and candle cup. It was produced again during the 1990s, this time in colonial pink, green opalescent, and possibly other colors. Colonial pink: $25.00 – 30.00. Amethyst carnival: $40.00 – 55.00. Other colors: $30.00 – 45.00.

FN-77A. COMPARISON OF FENTON'S No. 6 (LEFT, IN PINK) AND No. 5172 (RIGHT, IN COLONIAL PINK)

FN-77. No. 5172 SWAN CAN-DLEHOLDER IN GREEN OPALESCENT (DIAMOND MOLD)

No. 3775 Hobnail candleholder. 4" high with an eight-sectioned, round base. Production dates 1972 – 1977 in milk glass. $20.00 – 25.00.

FN-78. No. 3775 HOBNAIL CANDLEHOLDER IN MILK GLASS

No. 9172 Fine Cut and Block candle bowl. 3⅞" high and 6½" across. Produced around 1972. Made in cameo opalescent, colonial amber, colonial green, crystal, custard, and milk glass. Offered as part of the Olde Virginia Glass line. Marked on the bottom, "Patent No. 3547569." This patent, filed December 11, 1968, and approved December 15, 1970, was not for the design of this particular piece, but for the concept of a candle bowl ("a single decorative structure for containing candles, flowers, and other articles"). The inventors were Wilmer C. Fenton and Anthony J. Rosena. The same patent also applied to the No. 3872 Hobnail candle bowl. (See No. FN-72 on p. 198.) Milk glass, amber, green: $25.00 – 35.00. Custard, cameo opalescent: $35.00 – 45.00.

FN-79. No. 9172 FINE CUT & BLOCK CANDLE BOWL IN CUSTARD

No. 1970 Daisy and Button, one-light candleholder. 4⅝" high x 4½" round base. Production dates 1973 – 1976 when colors were discontinued. Crystal continued to be produced through 1984 and should be marked with the Fenton logo/8. Made in cameo opalescent, colonial amber, colonial blue, colonial green, crystal, custard, milk glass, opaque blue, violet, orange, and French opalescent (in 2002). Daisy and Button was offered as part of the Olde Virginia Glass line. Amber, green, crystal: $12.00 – 15.00. Colonial blue, orange, milk glass: $15.00 – 20.00. Custard, opaque blue: $20.00 – 25.00. Cameo opalescent: $25.00 – 30.00.

FN-80. No. 1970 DAISY & BUTTON CANDLESTICKS IN CUSTARD AND MILK GLASS

FN-80A. No. 1970 DAISY & BUTTON CANDLESTICK IN OPAQUE BLUE

FN-81. No. 3745 HOBNAIL CANDLESTICK IN MILK GLASS

No. 3745 Hobnail candleholder. 7¼" high with 5" round, eight-sectioned base. Production dates 1973 – 1976 in milk glass. This candleholder was used with various combinations of candle bowls and epergnes to form centerpieces. $25.00 – 30.00.

No. 8472 Orange Tree candlestick. 5" high with a 4¼" base. Produced 1974 – 1975. Made in blue satin, lime sherbet, and white satin. Reissued in cobalt marigold carnival, 1983 – 1984. A sample in Favrene (a carnival finish) was made in 1985. Offered as part of a console set with an Orange Tree and Cherry patterned bowl (No. 8233). Lime sherbet, blue satin, white satin: $15.00 – 20.00. Blue iridescent, Favrene: $25.00 – 30.00.

Note: A No. 9173 candle bowl, listed as 8", was earlier made in the Orange Tree pattern in amethyst carnival sometime in the 1970s.

FN-82. No. 8472 ORANGE TREE CANDLESTICK IN COBALT MARIGOLD CARNIVAL

Art glass candleholder. 8" high with a 2¼" diameter base. Circa mid-1970s. Acid etched Fenton logo on bottom. According to James Measell and Dave Fetty of the Fenton Art Glass Company, this stick was probably made by Delmer Stowasser who, along with Fetty, worked with Robert Barber during his short career at Fenton making "offhand" ware. Many limited-production and experimental items were made by Stowasser and Fetty during this time period and were sold through Fenton's gift shop. Amethyst, cobalt, and ivory iridescent: $130.00 – market.

FN-83A. ACID ETCHED FENTON LOGO ON ART GLASS CANDLEHOLDER

FN-83. OFFHAND ART GLASS CANDLESTICK IN COBALT AND IVORY IRIDESCENT.

No. 8473 Water Lily candleholder. 3" high with a 5⅛" base. Produced 1976 – 1990s. Made in blue satin, colonial blue, crystal velvet, lime satin, rosalene (translucent opal shading to pink), and turquoise. Listed as a No. 611 in an old catalog reprint. Made for Tiara Exclusives in ruby (as No. 146, July – December 1990 only), teal mist (as No. 401, Nov. 1991 only), green (as No. 592, July – December 1990), white lace crystal (crystal opalescent, as No. 611, 1987 – 1989), and provincial blue (blue opalescent, as No. 694, 1990 – 1991). Other colors are possible. Usually marked with the Fenton logo, but the Tiara pieces will not be marked. Crystal velvet, blue satin, lime satin, white satin, green, red: $20.00 – 25.00. Blue opalescent, rosalene: $30.00 – 35.00. Topaz opalescent: $40.00 – 45.00.

FN-84. No. 8473 WATER LILY CANDLEHOLDER IN WHITE SATIN

FN-84A. No. 8473 WATER LILY CANDLEHOLDERS IN WHITE LACE CRYSTAL AND GREEN (MADE FOR TIARA EXCLUSIVES)

FN-85. No. 3971 HOBNAIL CANDLE BOWL IN AMETHYST CARNIVAL

No. 3971 Hobnail candle bowl. 5" high. Footed with a paneled base. The top measures 7½" across. Production dates 1978 – 1980. Made in milk glass, blue opalescent, and amethyst carnival (ca. 2002). This was a later addition to Fenton's popular Hobnail line. The earlier No. 3971 miniature cornucopia (FN-30 on p. 189) shares the same number. Milk glass: $40.00 – 50.00. Blue opalescent, amethyst carnival: $50.00 – 60.00.

FN-86. No. 8475 LILY OF THE VALLEY CANDLEHOLDERS IN BLUE OPALESCENT AND CAMEO OPALESCENT

No. 8475 Lily of the Valley candleholder. 3⅝" high x 5⅝" base. Produced 1970 – 1982 and reissued in 1997. Made in cameo opalescent, topaz opalescent, blue opalescent, and champagne satin in 1997 – 1998. Champagne satin: $15.00 – 20.00. Cameo opalescent: $30.00 – 35.00. Blue opalescent: $35.00 – 40.00. Topaz opalescent: $45.00 – 55.00.

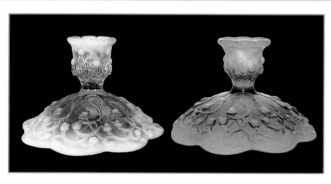

No. 6370 Flower Band candlestick. 6" high with a 4⅛" round base. Produced 1982 – 1984. Made in country peach, crystal, and forget-me-not blue. Reissued as No. 6371 in 2002 in emerald green and ruby. Crystal: $10.00 – 12.00. Colors: $25.00 – 30.00.

FN-87. No. 6370 FLOWER BAND CANDLESTICK

FN-87A. No. 6371 FLOWER BAND CANDLESTICK IN RUBY

FN-88. No. 9574 BASKET WEAVE CANDLEHOLDERS IN CUSTARD SATIN AND MILK GLASS, WITH HAND-PAINTED DECORATIONS

No. 9574 Basket Weave candleholder. 4½" high x 5" handled, scalloped bell base. Produced 1983 – 1984. Made in blue satin, custard (plain and satin), iridescent topaz, and milk glass with the hand-painted floral decorations: Violets in the Snow, Love Bouquet, Daisies, and at least one other floral decoration. Also sold with a decorated glass shade as No. 9504. Without shade: $40.00 – 45.00. With shade: $100.00 – market.

No. 7475 candlestick. 6" high with a 4⅛" diameter dome base. Produced 1984 – 1985. Made in pink or opal satin and decorated with hand-painted designs, Berries and Blossoms, Winter, and probably others. This candlestick was originally issued as No. 7474 with a ruffled base with various colored crests. (See FN-60 on p. 195). $20.00 – 30.00.

FN-89. No. 7475 CANDLESTICK IN OPAL SATIN, WITH HAND-PAINTED WINTER DECORATION

No. 7573 candleholder. 2½" high, 4⅞" across, with a base diameter of 3½". Produced 1984. Made in custard and opaline with Petite Fleur decoration. Produced exclusively for the Stretch Glass Society in emerald green stretch in 2002 (marked SGS 2002 on the bottom). This candleholder is footed and has a flared and ruffled top. Plain: $20.00 – 25.00. Hand painted: $35.00 – 45.00.

FN-90. No. 7573 CANDLEHOLDER IN OPALINE, WITH HAND-PAINTED PETITE FLEUR DECORATION

No. 9578 two-way candleholder. 4¼" high, 3½" in diameter at its widest point. Produced 1988 – present. Made in antique rose, aquamarine, blue opalescent, champagne, cobalt, dusty rose, empress rose, French opalescent, ice blue pearl, petal pink, plum, sea-mist green, teal royal, twilight blue, yellow, and red. Also available with hand-painted decorations. This has also been listed as No. 9596. It can be used two ways. As shown it holds a taper candle, turned over it will hold a votive candle. Current catalog prices, plain: $17.50 – 18.50. Decorated: $25.00 – 30.00.

FN-91. No. 9578 TWO-WAY CANDLEHOLDER IN RED, WITH HAND-PAINTED DECORATION

No. 9372 candlestick. 4½" high with a 4⅝" diameter base and Ram's Head column. Produced 1989 – 1991. Made in black with Copper Rose hand-painted decoration, teal royale (a bluish green), ruby, opal satin with the Holly Berry hand-painted decoration, iridized opal, and probably other colors and decorations. This is a reissue of a Cambridge candleholder made from the original mold (No. 3500/74), which originally was produced in the 1930s. (See CB-96 on p. 77.) Imperial then owned the mold for a number of years before it was obtained by Fenton. Fenton's reissues will be mold marked with their logo. All colors, plain: $15.00 – 20.00. Hand painted: $35.00 – 45.00.

FN-92. No. 9372 RAM'S HEAD CANDLESTICK IN TEAL ROYALE (CAMBRIDGE MOLD)

FN-93. BUTTERFLY CANDLEHOLDER IN
AMETHYST CARNIVAL

Three-light Butterfly candleholder. 7½" long with a 5" body. Unknown line number. Originally only a few test pieces were made around 1974, reportedly less than 20 in a dark amethyst carnival, as well as a few more in non-iridized amber and blue. In 1989, somewhat more than 150 were made in ruby carnival to be sold as the annual convention souvenir for the Fenton Art Glass Collectors of America (see front cover). Prior to this a number of test pieces were made in a variety of colors, including dusty rose iridized, ruby and white marble, milk glass with marigold carnival finish, teal, teal iridized, and milk glass iridized. In 1992 it was reportedly made again in frosted ruby carnival. Milk glass: $50.00 – 60.00. Ruby carnival: $75.00 – 90.00. Amethyst carnival: $80.00 – 100.00.

FN-94. No. 5528
CANDLEHOLD-
ER, 6¼" SIZE, IN
TEAL ROYALE,
WITH APPLIED
DECORATION

No. 5528 candleholder. Made in two sizes, 6¼" and 3¾" (the No. 5528 refers to the 6¼" size). These are shorter versions of Fenton's very popular and long-lived No. 349 and 449 colonial candleholders. (See FN-1 on p. 179.) They were introduced around 1989, in teal royale, green, and probably other colors. $12.00 – 15.00.

FN-95. No. 556 DESERT BLOSSOMS TWO-LIGHT CAN-
DLEHOLDER IN SAGE MIST

No. 556 Desert Blossoms two-light candleholder. 1¾" high and 8½" long. Produced in 1991 in sage green for Tiara Exclusives. Made from an original Indiana Glass Company mold originally introduced in the 1930s or 1940s as No. 1009 Leaf in crystal and later reissued in milk glass in 1957. (See book 2 of this series.) Sage green: $15.00 – 20.00.

FN-96. No. 559
DESERT BLOS-
SOMS FOOTED
CANDLEHOLDER
IN SAGE MIST

No. 559 Desert Blossoms candleholder. 3¾" high with a 3¼" diameter round footed base and a top diameter of 4⅛". Produced from 1990 to 1991 in sage green for Tiara Exclusives. Made from an original Indiana Glass Company mold from a pattern originally introduced in the 1930s or 1940s as No. 1009 Leaf, though it isn't known if the footed candleholder was made then or if it was a later addition to the line, modified from the sherbet, exclusively for Tiara. Earlier colors made by Indiana for Tiara include sunset (amberina), burnt honey, and black. (See book 2 of this series.) Sage green: $10.00 – 12.00.

No. 9674 Beauty candleholder. 3¾" high with a 4½" base. Produced 1990 – 1991 and later. Made in aquamarine carnival and dusty rose. Dusty rose opalescent was offered for Fenton's 95th anniversary in 2000. Aquamarine carnival, dusty rose: $20.00 – 25.00. Dusty rose carnival opalescent: $25.00 – 30.00.

FN-97. No. 9674 BEAUTY CANDLEHOLDER IN IRIDIZED DUSTY ROSE

No. 754 Baroness candleholder. Made in two sizes: 7⅛" high with a 3¾" diameter base (1990 – 1993) and 5" high (1991 – 1993). Both sizes were made in dusty rose for Tiara Exclusives. The taller size was also offered as the base for a No. 727 candle lamp. This candlestick was originally made by Imperial in the 1920s and then again from 1969 to 1982 as No. 532 (or No. 41790) as part of the Collector's Crystal pattern. The smaller size (not pictured) was originally made from 1982 to 1983 as No. 41793. After Imperial closed, the molds were obtained by the Indiana Glass Company and put back into production in the late 1980s. (See book 2 of this series.) Tall candlestick: $16.00 – 20.00. Small size: $8.00 – 10.00.

FN-98. No. 754 7⅛" BARONESS CANDLEHOLDER IN DUSTY ROSE (FROM TIARA EXCLUSIVES 1992 CATALOG)

No. 8372 Barred Oval candlestick. 5¾" high with a 4½" base. Made circa 1985 – 1987. Known in ruby, but other colors are possible. $20.00 – 30.00.

FN-99. No. 8372 BARRED OVAL CANDLESTICK IN RUBY

No. 2911 candleholder. 3" high. Produced during 1995 as part of Fenton's 90th anniversary collection. Originally made only in Celeste blue, with experimental runs in forest green and French opalescent made ca. 2002 and sold through Fenton's gift shop in Williamstown, West Virginia. $25.00 – 35.00.

FN-100. No. 2911 CANDLEHOLDER IN CELESTE BLUE

Grape and Cable candleholder. 1½" high with a top diameter of approximately 4" and a bottom diameter of 1½". Made in 1982 in cobalt marigold carnival. This was a special order for Dorothy Taylor, of Kansas City, publisher of *Carnival Glass Encore*, a bimonthly newsletter. Marked on the bottom "Encore, Fenton, 1982, KC MO." $18.00 – 22.00.

FN-101. GRAPE AND CABLE CANDLEHOLDER IN COBALT MARIGOLD CARNIVAL

FN-102. SPIRAL CANDLEHOLDER IN SEA GREEN SATIN (WESTMORELAND MOLD)

Spiral candleholder. 7" high. This appears to be from an old Westmoreland mold, made in the 1930s as No. 1710 with a domed base. Most Fenton examples have a flattened foot, though some were also made with domed bases similar to the Westmoreland originals. Known colors are ruby (made for Christmas 1999), cobalt, seafoam green opalescent, and satin sea green (for QVC). Other colors are likely. Introduced during the 1990s and was still being made in 2001. $30.00 – 40.00.

FN-103. No. 4672 RING & PETAL CANDLESTICK IN STIEGEL BLUE OPALESCENT (WESTMORELAND MOLD)

No. 4672 Ring and Petal candlestick. 3½" high with a 5½" base. Made in 1991 in Stiegel blue opalescent. This is a reissue of Westmoreland's very popular No. 1875 candlestick. $25.00 – 30.00.

FN-104. No. 5526 LOTUS CANDLE-HOLDER IN STIEGEL GREEN STRETCH (WEST-MORELAND MOLD)

No. 5526 candleholder. 3½" high with a 5" petal base. Originally manufactured by Westmoreland as No. 1921 Lotus. Made by Fenton in 1992 in Stiegel green stretch, transparent green, and gold pearl. Other colors are likely. Some are hand decorated and like most of Fenton's newer hand-painted items are signed by the artist. All of them are marked with the Fenton logo in the mold. $25.00 – 30.00.

FN-105. No. S5474 DOLPHIN CANDLESTICK IN DEEP BLUE. (REPRODUCTION OF SANDWICH CANDLESTICK MADE FOR THE SANDWICH GLASS MUSEUM)

No. S5474 Dolphin candlestick. 7" high with a hexagonal base. Made in cobalt blue, amberina, topaz opalescent, and possibly other colors. This is a reproduction of a Boston & Sandwich Dolphin candlestick (see BS-18 on p. 40) made by Fenton for the Sandwich Glass Museum from 1995 to 1998. Marked SGM or SM under the base, at least some of these were sold with a Fenton paper label. Note: This mold is owned by the Sandwich Glass Museum and these candle-holders have been alternately manufactured by both Fenton and Pairpoint. Opalescent colors: $45.00 – 65.00. Other colors: $35.00 – 45.00.

FN-106. No. 5473 PANELED GRAPE CANDLESTICK IN EMPRESS ROSE (WESTMORELAND MOLD)

No. 5473 Paneled Grape candlestick. 4" high, 4" skirted base. Originally manufactured by Westmoreland as part of their very successful No. 1881 Paneled Grape line. Produced by Fenton during 1998 in Empress rose and more recently in spruce green and cobalt. Other colors are possible. $20.00 – 25.00.

APPENDIX

IDENTIFYING DOLPHIN & FISH CANDLEHOLDERS

The stylized dolphin motif has been a staple of the American pressed glass industry since the mid-1800s when the Boston & Sandwich Glass Company began manufacturing candleholders and oil lamps with dolphin stems. Soon, other New England and Pittsburgh glasshouses followed suit, with some adding matching comports and bowls so that a complete table centerpiece could be assembled. The dolphin shape remained popular for several decades but by the end of the nineteenth century most of the New England glass companies were gone and the flood of dolphin candleholders was reduced to a trickle. This lull lasted until the 1920s when the Westmoreland Glass Company introduced a new line of dolphin items, including two new candleholders. Once again, several manufacturers from the U.S. and abroad quickly joined the fray. These items were often advertised as being "authentic reproductions" of earlier designs from the by-then defunct New England glass companies. Although many of the Westmoreland pieces were later discontinued, the candleholders remained in production until the company's demise in 1984. Viking, and then Dalzell Viking continued to make dolphin candleholders using the Westmoreland molds until they too closed in 1998. Currently, candleholders from the Westmoreland molds are being made by the Mosser Glass Company in a light alexandrite color similar to Dalzell Viking's cranberry mist. Other U.S. manufacturers producing dolphin candleholders are the Summit Art Glass Company (from Cambridge molds) and the Pairpoint Glass Company (for the Sandwich Glass Museum).

Since so many collectors are attracted to this design, and because it's been so widely produced (and reproduced) over the years, we thought it would be beneficial to include this section to assist the reader in identifying these items of beauty and interest. Proper identification is especially important with these candleholders because pieces that are virtually identical in appearance can be vastly different in age and value.

You may have noticed that the majority of these candleholders bear little resemblance to a dolphin. Most have scales and look more like fish, but there is good evidence that The Boston and Sandwich Glass Company referred to them as dolphins and that's been the name that has stuck with collectors. Some companies have made items with fish motifs that were clearly not meant to be dolphins. Duncan & Miller's Tropical Fish line is one example. For completeness, we've included these and other similar items in this grouping.

The following chart should enable you to determine the manufacturer of almost any pressed glass dolphin candleholder. Please note that this appendix is only meant to be an aid for identification. All other information about the item will be found in the chapter concerning the manufacturer of the item (located in the appropriate volume of this series). If you are unfamiliar with any of the terms used in the chart please refer to the glossary section.

To use the chart: Measure the height of your candleholder and select the chart entries whose ranges straddle your measurement. Then read the description for the first selected entry from left to right. Discard the entry and move to the next as soon as you find something in the description that disagrees with the item in question. Once you get a complete match, see if any of the other listings also match 100%. In the event of two or more items meeting all listed criteria, you can usually compare the color of your item with those listed in the manufacturers' chapters to make the final determination.

A RARE BOSTON AND SAND-
WICH GLASS COMPANY 9" HEX-
BASED DOLPHIN CANDLEHOLDER
IN CANARY

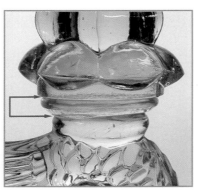

TWO VIEWS OF A BOSTON & SANDWICH HEX-BASED
CANDLEHOLDER. THE LEFT-HAND IMAGE SHOWS
THE THREE CONCENTRIC RINGS THAT MUST BE
PRESENT FOR A 9" – 9½" HEX BASED DOLPHIN TO
BE FROM BOSTON & SANDWICH. THE RIGHT-HAND
IMAGE SHOWS A WAFER OR GLASS BUTTON THAT IS
USED TO JOIN THE SOCKET TO THE BASE ON ALL
DOLPHIN CANDLEHOLDERS FROM BOSTON & SAND-
WICH AND SOME OTHER MAKERS. NOTE THE WAFER
IS NOT ALWAYS THIS WELL FORMED. SOME ARE
DEFORMED AND/OR IRREGULARLY SHAPED.

Height	Base Shape	Base Description	Socket Description	Head	Marked	Remarks	Manufacturer Date
1¼" – 3½"	Round	Dish shaped	Round	Solid	No	#1621. Two small dolphin handles are attached to the rim	Fenton Art Glass Co. 1920s & 1930s
2¾" – 2⅞"	Square	1⅛" stepped	6 petal	Solid	No	Toy or miniature	The Glass Workshop, Kirk Nelson 1990s
3¼" – 3½"	Round	4" with various patterns pressed from beneath	Hex with round rim	Solid	No	#1623. Two small dolphins are attached to socket, 180 degrees apart	Fenton Art Glass Co. 1920s & 1995
3⅞" – 4⅛"	Hex	3¼"	10 petal	Solid	Later items will have a WG	#1049. The detail is better on the older. Depression era examples, early and late colors are different	Westmoreland Glass C 1924 – 1984
3⅞" – 4⅛"	Hex	3¼ "	10 petal	Solid	No	#1937. From Westmoreland's mold, colors are different and detail is not as good as Westmoreland's	Viking 1985-1986 Dalzell Viking 1988 – 1998
4" – 4¼"	Round	3⅜"	Round with seashell wax catcher	Solid	No	#SS66. Part of Krystolshell line	Cambridge Glass Co. 1940s – 1950s
4" – 4¼"	Round	3⅜"	Round with seashell wax catcher	Solid	No	Made from Cambridge's #SS66 mold	Summit Art Glass Co. 1990s – present
4" – 4¼"	Round	3⅜"	Round	Solid	No	Has ocean wave pattern on base	Tiffin Glass Co. 1940s
4½" – 5"	Round	A variant has a skirted base 4¼"	Round	Solid	No	Has swimming tropical fish as stem	Unknown foreign manufacturer
4½" – 5"	Square	Rounded ends and notched sides	Round with attached bobeche and 6 prisms	Solid	No	Has rim to hold hurricane globe, height is without globe attached	Czechoslovakian Impo (unknown factory)
4¾" – 5¼"	Irregular		Candle sits in fish's mouth	Solid	No	#128. Tropical Fish. Fish has a "mane"	Duncan & Miller Co.
4¾" – 5¼"	Round	4⅛"	Two light, Round	Solid	No	#67	Cambridge Glass Co. 1936 – 1954
4¾" – 5¼"	Round	4⅛"	Two light, Round	Solid	No	Made from Cambridge's #67 mold, colors differ from Cambridge's.	Summit Art Glass Co. 1990s
4⅞" – 5⅛"	Square	3" (early) 3¼" (late)	8 petal	Solid	Late production marked IG	#779 Empire pattern. A rim added to the late production bases caused the size to increase.	Imperial Glass Co.
5" – 5¼"	Irregular		Candle sits in dolphin's mouth	Solid	No	#1550	A.H. Heisey & Co. 1942 – 1948
5" – 5¼"	Irregular		Candle sits in dolphin's mouth	Solid	Yes, IG	Limited production from Heisey's #1550 mold for the Heisey Collectors of America	Imperial Glass Co. 1982
5" – 5¼"	Irregular		Candle sits in dolphin's mouth	Solid	Yes, HCA 95 D	Limited production from Heisey's #1550 mold for the Heisey Collectors of America	Dalzell Viking 1995
5½" – 5¾"	Round	Petticoat flared, 4¾"	Round	Solid	No	#109. A copy of Northwood's petticoat dolphin	A.H. Heisey & Co. 1925 – 1935

Height	Base Shape	Base Description	Socket Description	Head	Marked	Remarks	Manufacturer Date
5⅞" – 6⅛"	Three-toed	Dolphin feet attached to a bulbous base	Round	Solid	Usually. H in a diamond	#1401 Part of Empress line	A.H. Heisey & Co. 1929 – 1935
5⅞" – 6⅛"	Three-toed	Dolphin feet attached to a bulbous base	Round	Solid	Yes. CG in a circle	Made from Heisey's #1401 mold for the Collector's Guild	Imperial Glass Co. 1981
6¼" – 6½"	Round	Petticoat cupped, 3⅞"	Round	Solid	No	#109. A copy of Northwood's petticoat dolphin	A. H. Heisey & Co. 1925 – 1935
6¼" – 6¾	Round	Has a short step on top, 16 scallops around edge, and two groups of concentric rings underneath	Round with 12 petals on rim, connected to base via a wafer	Partially hollow	No	Rare in crystal and opal, very rare in other colors	Cape Cod Glass Co. or Boston & Sandwich 1855 – 1870
6½" – 6¾"	Round	Petticoat cupped, 3¾"	Round Opalescent	Solid	No	Socket will usually have an opalescent edge. Colors differ from the Heisey copies	Northwood Glass Co. 1890s
6¾" – 7"	Hex	Two groups of concentric rings 3⅝"	Hex. Wafer attached. Hole depth >= 1¼"	Solid	No		Boston & Sandwich 1855 – 1870
6¾" – 7"	Hex	Two groups of concentric rings 3⅝"	Hex. Stuck. Has pseudo wafer with no seam	Solid	Yes. SM or SGM	Made for the Sandwich Glass Museum. "Wafer" is actually part of the socket.	Pairpoint Late 1980s
6¾" – 7"	Hex	Two groups of concentric rings 3⅝"	Hex	Solid	Yes. SM or SGM	Made for the Sandwich Glass Museum from the Museum's mold	Pairpoint 1980s – 1994 & 1998 to present. Fenton 1995 – 1997
6⅞" – 7¼"	Oval	Stepped with square sides and very rounded corners	Round with attached bobeche and 8 prisms	Solid	No	Has rim to hold hurricane globe. Height is without globe attached.	Czechoslovakian Import (unknown factory)
7½" – 7¾"	Round	3¾". Base height is approx. 1⅛"	Round	Solid	No	The transparent colors have a wave pattern on the base.	Tiffin Glass Co. 1930s
7½" – 8"	Square	Notched corners. 4⅜"	8 petal	Solid	No		Cambridge Glass Co. 1940s – 1950s
7⅞" – 8"	Twelve-sided	4¾"	Octagonal Bonded	Hollow	No	Looks like a sea serpent or Chinese dragon	PV (France) 1920s – 1930s

THIS MARK SHOWN HERE (SGM) IS ONE TYPE THAT HAS BEEN USED BY THE SANDWICH GLASS MUSEUM ON THEIR 7", HEX BASED, DOLPHIN CANDLEHOLDERS. THE STICKS USING THIS MARK WERE VERY AUTHENTIC LOOKING COPIES MADE BY PAIRPOINT DURING THE 1980S AND SOLD THROUGH THE MUSEUM GIFT SHOP. BEWARE AS THIS MARK IS OFTEN VERY DIFFICULT TO SEE! THE WAFER ON A GENUINE BOSTON & SANDWICH CANDLESTICK WILL NOT HAVE A SEAM, NEITHER HORIZONTALLY OR VERTICALLY. SIMILAR STICKS ARE STILL BEING SOLD BY THE MUSEUM BUT THEY'RE NOT AS DIFFICULT TO DISTINGUISH FROM THE ORIGINALS AND THEY ARE ALSO MORE CLEARLY MARKED.

THIS IS ANOTHER MARK USED ON THE SANDWICH GLASS MUSEUM'S 7" REPRODUCTION DOLPHINS DURING THE 1980S. IT CONSISTS OF THE LETTERS "SM" PRESSED INTO THE BASE OF THE CANDLESTICK. WHILE EASIER TO SEE THEN THE MARK SHOWN IN THE PRECEDING PHOTO IT IS STILL SOMETIMES HARD TO MAKE OUT WHAT IT SAYS. THE ORIGINALS HAD NO MARKINGS.

Height	Base Shape	Base Description	Socket Description	Head	Marked	Remarks	Manufacturer Date
7⅞" – 8"	Twelve-sided	4¾"	Octagonal Bonded (early), later one piece	Hollow	No	From PV (France) mold, imported, probably from Taiwan	A.A. Imports 1950s – present
7⅞" – 8"	Round	4" diameter Rayed	Round	Solid	No	Looks like a sea serpent or Chinese dragon	Gus Crystal, Russia current production
8" – 8½"	Round	Has a short step on top, 16 scallops around edge, and two groups of concentric rings underneath	Octagonal, long and connected to base via a wafer	Partially hollow	No	Rare in crystal and opal, very rare in other colors	Cape Cod Glass Co. or Boston & Sandwich 1855 – 1870
8" – 8½"	Round	3¾". Base height is approximately 1⁵⁄₁₆"	Round with rim for attaching a lamp socket	Solid	No	Same basic design as the 7½" – 7¾" version but made for use as a lamp base	Tiffin Glass Co. 1930s
8½" – 8¾"	Round	Flat and plain 4¾" diameter	8 petal	Solid	No	Same as Cambridge's Mount Vernon petticoat dolphin except for base	Cambridge Glass Co. 1928
8¾" – 9¼"	Square	3⅞" stepped	16 petal	Solid	No	#2562	Consolidated Glass Co. 1920s – 1930s

THIS IS THE WAFER ON A 7" DOLPHIN CANDLEHOLDER BY BOSTON & SANDWICH. TO BE AUTHENTIC THE WAFER CANNOT HAVE MOLD SEAMS, EITHER VERTICALLY OR HORIZONTALLY.

HEISEY #109, 5¾" PETTICOAT DOLPHIN WITH FLARED BASE, CIRCA 1925 – 1935. FLAMINGO

HEISEY #109, 6½" PETTICOAT DOLPHIN WITH CUPPED BASE, CIRCA 1925 – 1935. MOONGLEAM

NORTHWOOD 6¾" PETTICOAT DOLPHIN, CIRCA 1890s – 1900s. CANARY OPALESCENT

6½" PETTICOAT DOLPHIN IN CRYSTAL. NO OPALESCENCE, POSSIBLY NORTHWOOD*

A RARE MCKEE DOLPHIN, CIRCA 1850s – 1870s

*THIS CANDLESTICK IS UNUSUAL IN THAT IT IS FROM THE SAME MOLD AS THE NORTHWOOD PETTICOAT DOLPHINS BUT IT HAS A SLIGHTLY SHORTER SOCKET AND DOES NOT HAVE ANY OPALESCENCE. OVER THE YEARS THIS CANDLEHOLDER HAS BEEN ATTRIBUTED TO MANY MANUFACTURERS FROM BOTH THE NEW ENGLAND AND PITTSBURGH AREAS. RESEARCH BY OTHERS NOW EXISTS SHOWING THAT NORTHWOOD ALMOST CERTAINLY MANUFACTURED THE OPALESCENT VERSIONS AT ABOUT THE TURN OF THE LAST CENTURY. HOWEVER, THIS EXAMPLE APPEARS TO BE EARLIER, POSSIBLY FROM NORTHWOOD, BUT IT MIGHT SHOW THAT ANOTHER COMPANY WAS THE ORIGINAL MANUFACTURER OF THIS CANDLESTICK. THINGS LIKE THIS ARE WHAT MAKE THIS HOBBY BOTH FUN AND FRUSTRATING AT THE SAME TIME. AT THIS POINT WE'LL HAVE TO CALL IT "UNKNOWN, POSSIBLY NORTHWOOD."

Height	Base Shape	Base Description	Socket Description	Head	Marked	Remarks	Manufacturer Date
8¾" – 9¼"	Square	3⅞" stepped	16 petal	Solid	No	#188. Possibly made from Consolidated's #2562 mold or copied from it	Haley Glass Co. 1948
8¾" – 9¼"	Square	3⅞" stepped	16 petal	Solid	Yes. IG	#90. Possibly made from Consolidated's #2562 mold or copied from it	Imperial Glass Co. 1957 – 1980
9" – 9⅜"	Hex	4"	6 petal. Hole depth <= 1½"	Hollow	No	#1049. Will have bead detail on back, above head, 9⅜" with ring for lamp socket	Westmoreland Glass Co. Type I 1924 – 1940
9" – 9¼"	Hex	4"	6 petal. Hole depth <= 1½"	Hollow	Usually. WG	#1049. No bead detail (see photo on p. 213)	Westmoreland Glass Co. Type II 1940 – 1970s
9" – 9¼"	Hex	4"	6 petal. Hole depth <= 1½"	Solid	Yes. WG	#1049. No bead detail (see photo on p. 213)	Westmoreland Glass Co. Type III 1970s – 1984
9" – 9¾"	Hex	4"	6 petal. Wafer attached. Hole depth >= 1¾"	Hollow	No	Appears identical to the Boston & Sandwich listing directly following this one except for the lack of the three rings beneath the base	Unknown but believed to be circa 1800s
9" – 9¾"	Hex	4", three raised concentric rings beneath	6 petal. Wafer attached. Hole depth >= 1¾"	Hollow	No	Rare! Canary and crystal are the only known colors but others are possible. Must have all listed characteristics!	Boston & Sandwich 1845 – 1870
9⅛" – 9¼"	Hex	4"	6 petal. Hole depth <= 1½"	Solid	No	Made from Westmoreland type III mold. No bead detail (see photo on p. 213)	Viking 1985-1986 Dalzell Viking 1988 – 1998

This is the Portieux-Vallerysthal (PV) version of the dolphin footed candleholder which is now imported from Taiwan by A.A. Imports. Notice the sharper detail and larger socket when compared to the A.A. Import version.

These candleholders have been imported from Taiwan since the 1970s by A.A. Imports. Various colors have been manufactured over the years. They are both from molds originally owned by the French glass manufacturer, Portieux-Vallerysthal (PV).

This is the Portieux-Vallerysthal (PV) version of the dolphin which is now imported from Taiwan by A.A. Imports. Note that the spine that the arrow points to is noticeably larger and sharper on the original.

Height	Base Shape	Base Description	Socket Description	Head	Marked	Remarks	Manufacturer Date
9¼" – 9½"	Round	Dolphin-footed	Round. Broad, wax-catcher rim	Solid	No	Slim round stem. #1844 "Gossips" candlestick	PV(France) 1920s – 1930s
9¼" – 9½"	Round	Dolphin-footed	Round	Solid	No	PG16045. Slim round stem. Crudely made from PV mold. Socket is cut down from original. Imported from Taiwan	A.A. Imports 1980s – present
9¼" – 9½"	Round	4⅞"	Hex. Stuck	Hollow	No	Rare in crystal. Would be very rare if found in color.	McKee & Brothers 1850s-1870s
9¼" – 9¾"	Hex	4"	6 petal. Stuck. Hole depth is >= 1¾"	Hollow	No	Czechoslovakian import	Unknown (Czech) 1920s
9⅜" – 10"	Square	4" "short step"	Hex, w/small dolphins and shells. Wafer attached	Hollow	No	Rare!	Boston & Sandwich 1845 – 1870
9½" – 9¾"	Round	5" petticoat w/ diamond pattern	8 petal	Solid	No	Part of Mount Vernon pattern	Cambridge Glass Co. 1920s
10" – 10¾"	Square	3⅝" with a ¾" step	6 petal. Wafer attached. Hole depth is >= 1¾"	Hollow. 2¾" long	No	Center of eye is ¹¹⁄₁₆" above base	Boston & Sandwich 1845 – 1870
10¼" – 10½"	Square	4⅜"	6 petal	Hollow	No	#110. Converted to a lamp base by the Ideal Cut Glass Company	A.H. Heisey & Co. 1925 – 1930s
10¼" – 10¾"	Square	3¾" flat top	6 petal. Wafer attached	Hollow	No		Boston and Sandwich 1845 – 1870

ANOTHER IMPORT. THIS TIME BY GUS CRYSTAL IN RUSSIA. THIS IS OF HIGHER QUALITY THAN THE TAIWANESE IMPORTS AND SO FAR AS WE KNOW IS AN ORIGINAL MOLD. IT IS IN CURRENT PRODUCTION.

RARE BOSTON & SANDWICH DOLPHIN ON HALF-STEP BASE WITH DOLPHIN AND SHELL SOCKET. 9⅝" HIGH. THE INSERT SHOWS THE SOCKET DETAIL.

9½" HIGH, HEX BASED, WAFER JOINED DOLPHIN CANDLEHOLDER OF UNKNOWN ORIGIN. THIS IS VERY SIMILAR TO THE RARE, MID-1800S BOSTON AND SANDWICH CANDLEHOLDER OF THE SAME DESIGN, BUT WITHOUT THE CONCENTRIC RINGS BENEATH THE BASE. IT IS NOT THE 1920S CZECH VERSION AND IS THOUGHT TO BE FROM A COMPETING NEW ENGLAND OR PITTSBURGH COMPANY OF THE SAME ERA. SCARCE TO RARE.

Height	Base Shape	Base Description	Socket Description	Head	Marked	Remarks	Manufacturer Date
10¼" – 10¾"	Square	3¾" flat top	6 Petal	Hollow	Usually. GHC	Imported from Taiwan	General Housewares Corporation
10¼" – 10½"	Square	3¾" flat top	6 petal. Bonded to pseudo wafer	Solid	Yes. MMA	Made for the Metropolitan Museum of Art	Imperial Glass Co. 1972 – 1980s
10½" – 11"	Square	3⅝" with a ¾" step	6 petal. Wafer attached. Hole depth is >= 1¾"	Hollow 3" long	No	Center of eye is ⅞" above base. Czechoslovakian import	Unknown (Czech) 1920s
10½" – 11"	Square	4" "short step"	6 petal. Wafer attached. Hole depth is >= 1¾"	Hollow	No		Boston & Sandwich 1845 – 1870
10½" – 11"	Square	4" "short step"	Hex, w/small dolphins and shells. Wafer attached.	Hollow	No	Rare!	Boston & Sandwich 1845 – 1870
10¾" – 11"	Square	4" "short step"	Hex. Bonded. Decorated with dolphins and shells	Solid	Yes. MMA	Made for the Metropolitan Museum of Art	Imperial Glass Co. 1972 – 1980s. Dalzell Viking in 1993

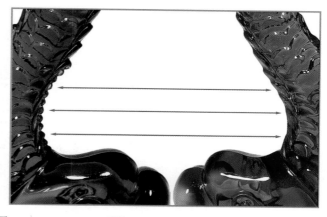

TWO VERSIONS OF WESTMORELAND'S #1049, 9" DOLPHIN CANDLEHOLDERS. THE LEFT SIDE OF THE PHOTO SHOWS THE ORIGINAL MOLD, INTRODUCED IN THE 1920S. IT HAS A DISTINCTIVE BEAD DETAIL ON THE BACK THAT IS NOT THERE ON LATER VERSIONS. WE REFER TO THIS EARLY MOLD AS TYPE I. BY THE 1950S THE TYPE II MOLD WAS IN USE AND THIS DETAIL WAS GONE. TYPE I AND TYPE II MOLDS BOTH HAVE HOLLOW HEADS. THE LATEST WESTMORELAND MOLD REVISION (TYPE III) CAME ABOUT IN THE 70S AND HAS A SOLID HEAD. THE TYPE III MOLD WAS LATER USED BY VIKING AND DALZELL VIKING. STICKS FROM TYPE I MOLDS ARE NEVER MARKED. STICKS FROM TYPE II MOLDS ARE SOMETIMES MARKED WITH THE W OVER G. STICKS FROM TYPE III MOLDS ARE ALWAYS MARKED IF THEY ARE FROM WESTMORELAND. UNMARKED TYPE III MOLDS ARE VIKING, DALZELL VIKING, OR MOSSER GLASS CO. IT IS POSSIBLE THAT SOME EARLY STICKS FROM VIKING WILL STILL HAVE THE W OVER G MARK.

THIS IS A GROUPING OF VENETIAN CANDLEHOLDERS UTILIZING THE DOLPHIN MOTIF. BEING NEITHER U.S. MADE NOR PRESSED GLASS PUTS THEM OUTSIDE THE SCOPE OF THIS BOOK BUT THE STYLE IS QUITE DISTINCTIVE SO WE WANTED TO POINT THEM OUT.

SHELF 1:
CAMBRIDGE #109, 9½" MOUNT VERNON PETTICOAT DOLPHIN, CIRCA 1920S, AMBER
CAMBRIDGE #109, 9½" MOUNT VERNON PETTICOAT DOLPHIN, CIRCA 1920S, BLUEBELL
CAMBRIDGE #109, 9½" MOUNT VERNON PETTICOAT DOLPHIN, CIRCA 1920S, EMERALD GREEN
CAMBRIDGE 8½" DOLPHIN WITH FLAT ROUND BASE, CIRCA 1928, ROSE

SHELF 2:
TIFFIN 7½" DOLPHIN, JADE
TIFFIN 4¼" DOLPHIN, REFLEX GREEN
TIFFIN 7¾" DOLPHIN LAMP BASE (NOTE RIM ON TOP OF SOCKET), CRYSTAL
TIFFIN 7½" DOLPHIN, SKY BLUE
TIFFIN 4¼" DOLPHIN, ROSE
TIFFIN 7½" DOLPHIN, REFLEX GREEN
TIFFIN 4¼" DOLPHIN, AMBER
TIFFIN 7¾" DOLPHIN LAMP BASE, JADE

SHELF 3:
CAMBRIDGE #50, 7¾" SQUARE BASE DOLPHIN, CROWN TUSCAN
CAMBRIDGE #67, 5" KRYSTOLSHELL DOLPHIN TWO-LIGHT, CROWN TUSCAN
CAMBRIDGE #50, 7¾" SQUARE BASE DOLPHIN, MILK GLASS
CAMBRIDGE #66, 4" KRYSTOLSHELL DOLPHIN, CROWN TUSCAN
CAMBRIDGE #50, 8" SQUARE BASE DOLPHIN CANDELABRA, CRYSTAL

SHELF 4:
BOSTON & SANDWICH 10¼" DOUBLE-STEP BASE DOLPHIN, CRYSTAL
BOSTON & SANDWICH 10½" SQUARE BASE DOLPHIN, CLAMBROTH
BOSTON & SANDWICH SHORT-STEP BASE DOLPHIN (SOCKET BROKEN OFF), CANARY
BOSTON & SANDWICH 10¼" DOUBLE-STEP BASE DOLPHIN, CLAMBROTH
BOSTON & SANDWICH 10½" SQUARE BASE DOLPHIN, CRYSTAL

SHELF 1:
MMA 10¾" SHORT-STEP DOLPHIN BY IMPERIAL, CIRCA 1970S –
 1980S, DEEP BLUE
MMA 10¾" SHORT-STEP DOLPHIN BY IMPERIAL, CIRCA 1970S –
 1980S AND DALZELL VIKING IN THE EARLY 1990S, CRYSTAL
MMA 10¾" SHORT-STEP DOLPHIN BY IMPERIAL, CIRCA 1970S –
 1980S, EMERALD
CZECH 10⅞" DOUBLE-STEP DOLPHIN, CIRCA 1920S, CRYSTAL
MMA 10¾" SHORT-STEP DOLPHIN BY IMPERIAL, CIRCA 1970S –
 1980S AND DALZELL VIKING IN THE EARLY 1990S, AZURE BLUE

SHELF 2:
IMPERIAL #779, 5" EMPIRE DOLPHIN, CIRCA 1930S, AMBER
IMPERIAL #90, 9" DOLPHIN, CIRCA 1970S FROM CONSOLIDATED
 MOLD, FERN GREEN
IMPERIAL #779, 5" EMPIRE DOLPHIN, CIRCA 1950S, MILK GLASS

IMPERIAL #90, 9" DOLPHIN, CIRCA 1970S FROM CONSOLIDATED
 MOLD, AMBER
IMPERIAL #779, 5" EMPIRE DOLPHIN, CIRCA 1930S, LIGHT BLUE
IMPERIAL #779, 5" EMPIRE DOLPHIN, CIRCA 1960S, CARAMEL SLAG

SHELF 3:
MMA 10⅝" FLAT SQUARE BASE DOLPHIN BY IMPERIAL, CIRCA
 1970S – 1980S, OPAQUE BLUE
MMA 10⅝" FLAT SQUARE BASE DOLPHIN BY IMPERIAL, CIRCA
 1970S – 1980S, CANARY
GHC 10½" FLAT SQUARE BASE DOLPHIN, IMPORTED FROM TAI-
 WAN, CIRCA 1980S, MEDIUM BLUE
MMA 10⅝" FLAT SQUARE BASE DOLPHIN BY IMPERIAL, CIRCA
 1980S, CLAMBROTH WITH OPAQUE BLUE SOCKET, HAND PAINT-
 ED
HEISEY #110, 10" SQUARE BASE DOLPHIN, CIRCA 1925 – 1930S,
 MOONGLEAM

GLOSSARY

Amberina. Coloring that shades from a light yellow to red or fuchsia. Created by adding gold powders to a batch of amber glass and then reheating portions of the finished product.

Art deco. A style popularized in the 1920s and 1930s. The name is a shortened from the Exposition Internationales des Arts Decoratifs et Industriels Modernes, the exhibition in Paris that first introduced the style in 1925, though it has roots dating back earlier. Sometimes called Art Moderne. Design elements tend to be geometric, almost architectural at times, with simple lines and restrained decoration.

Blank. A completed piece of glassware with no decoration (other than that produced in the mold).

Bobeche. A disk or saucer affixed beneath the candle socket of a candlestick or candelabrum to catch wax drippings. Often has prisms suspended from it. May be either permanently attached or removable. A peg bobeche has a fitting on the bottom that inserts into a candle cup.

Carnival glass. See Iridescent.

Cased glass. Two or more layers of different colored glass, sometimes with the outer layer cut back to reveal the color underneath. Crystal or another transparent color may also be cased over an opaque color or used to "sandwich" another decorating technique between the layers.

Clambroth. A semi-opaque glass with a slightly smoky look. See also Opaline.

Console set. A combination of candlesticks and a floral bowl, usually in the same pattern, used as a centerpiece for a table setting. This practice became popular in the latter half of the 1920s, with most companies producing these combinations well into the 1950s or 1960s. Many decorating companies bought bowls and candlesticks from various sources, putting them together with their own decorations added, so that it is possible to find "matching" sets with pieces originally made by different glass factories.

Controlled bubbles. A decorative technique where bubbles in the glass are created intentionally by rolling the molten glass over a spiked form, then applying a second layer of glass to trap the resulting air cavities.

Copper wheel engraving. See Engraving.

Crackle glass. Decorative treatment that resembles cracked ice. Created by plunging the article while still in a molten state into cold water. The resulting thermal shock creates fine cracks on the surface. The glass is then reheated and final shaping takes places.

Crest. A rim applied to an existing piece, usually in crystal or a contrasting color. This technique was used by many companies, most notably by Fenton who often combines crests with milk glass bodies. The technique is also referred to as "rimming."

Crystal. Clear, colorless glass. In general usage, "crystal" denotes any colorless glass, though technically it must contain a minimum of 24% lead to be officially labeled as such. Crystal is also made with potash-lime. Our use in this book simply reflects a lack of color.

Cutting. A method of decorating glass by use of rapidly turning iron, stone, and wooden wheels (for roughing, smoothing, and polishing, respectively). Usually a three-stage process in which an abrasive agent such as sand, pumice powder, or putty powder is used along with the grinding and polishing wheel to effect the cutting. Cutting often involves deep lines and curved miter designs. See also Engraving.

Depression glass. Refers to machine-made glass produced in the late 1920s and 1930s. Collectors today often refer to "Depression-era" glass, which also includes the handmade glassware from the same period.

End of day glass. See Slag glass.

Engraving. A method of decorating glass by use of rapidly turning copper wheels of many sizes, some as small as an eighth of an inch. An abrasive agent of emery or pumice mixed with water and oil is used. In engraving, the glass blank is held under the wheel so that the view of it is cut off by the wheel itself, unlike cutting, where the blank is held over or on top of the wheel. Engraving involves much shallower cuts and results in much more detailed, intricate designs. Engravings may be left "gray" or may be polished with acid to return them to a state of clearness. The term "rock crystal" is often used to refer to acid polished engravings. See also Cutting.

Etching. A method of decorating glass by applying designs created by hydrofluoric acid eating into the surface of the glass, leaving a frosted finish. There are several techniques for applying etchings, with plate etching being one of the more common forms. This involves the transfer of a design from a metal plate covered with acid resistant beeswax to a piece of special tissue paper. The tissue coated with beeswax is then applied to the blank to be decorated so that the wax transfers onto the glass. The portions of the glass that remain uncovered with the acid resist or beeswax are the portions that make up the design. The item is immersed in hydrofluoric acid for fifteen to twenty minutes. When the wax is removed, the etched design appears on those surfaces that were not protected by the acid resist. See also Satin finish.

Fired-on color. A solid color, usually applied to all surfaces of a blank. Often found both in crystal and milk glass. The coated piece is then fired in a kiln. Sometimes referred to as "baked-on."

Flint glass. Originally referred to nineteenth century glass made with fine silica produced from quartz (or flint) that had been pulverized. Some early companies also began using oxide of lead in their glass batch, which resulted in flint glass being used synonymously for lead glass. In the later nineteenth century and early twentieth century, after it had been discovered that crystal could be produced using lime, flint glass remained in common usage to describe this less expensive glass, as well.

Free hand. Glassware created entirely by hand, without the use of molds to impart the final shape of the piece.

Frosted. See Satin finish.

Gravic cutting. A form of cutting where multiple cuts could be made simultaneously. Characterized by simple floral designs made up of several parallel cuts, close together, generally left gray without polishing, this was a less expensive form of decoration than full cutting or engraving. Also known as "gang cutting."

Hobnail. A popular pressed pattern made by many companies, featuring evenly distributed small knobs, so named because they resemble the heads of the hobnails used for studding shoe soles. Sometimes called Dewdrop.

Hurricane lamp. A candleholder fitted with a globe to protect the flame from being snuffed out by the wind. Most hurricane lamps have removable globes, but some are formed as a single unit.

Iridescent. A rainbow-like colored finish with a metallic appearance, often referred to as carnival glass. Some lustres (a form of staining) also have an iridescent finish. Iridescence is created by spraying metallic salts on the glass while it is still hot. See also Stretch glass.

Jadite. A light green opaque glass, made in large quantities by McKee, Jeannette, and Anchor Hocking. Opaque green shades produced by other companies are often referred to as jadite, as well.

Knop. A solid knob or rounded shape, usually applied to the stem of a piece. See also Prunt.

Lustre. See Iridescent.

Marbleized glass. See Slag glass.

Matte finish. See Satin finish.

Milk glass. Popular name for opaque white glass. Most early companies referred to this color as opal and some milk glass will have opalescent highlights. Today's collectors use milk glass to refer to all opaque glass, including blue opaque, green opaque (jadite), and even black. See also Slag glass.

Mosaic glass. See Slag glass.

Novelties. A term used by glass companies to refer to individual items that were not part of larger patterns, including some utilitarian pieces. Most novelties were occasional pieces, often in unusual or imaginative shapes or with brightly colored hand-painted decorations. Opal novelties included smoking items, toothpick holders, candlesticks, and other small items.

Offhand glassware. Blown pieces created without the use of molds. Most blown glassware is made by blowing the glass into a mold that gives it its basic shape. Offhand glassware, also known as freehand glassware, was made using only a blowpipe and could be decorated with a variety of techniques while still in a malleable state.

Opal. See Milk glass.

Opalescent. Transparent glass with milky white edges, with a fiery appearance resembling opals. Created by adding calcium phosphate (or bone ash) to the glass batch. When the pieces are reheated, the edges (and often raised portions of the pattern) turn opalescent.

Opaline. Partly translucent glass, less dense then milk glass, but with a generally even distribution of color, unlike opal or opalescent glass. Sometimes has a slightly smoky look, referred to as clambroth.

Optic. A decorative technique used mostly in blown items consisting of faint lines in the glass that catch the light. Popular optics include diamond, panel, festoon (or drape). Created by inserting the partially blown item into a mold to pick up the optic pattern and then blowing it to its full shape and size, which causes the optic pattern to become less distinct.

Peg nappy. A small bowl with a fitting on the bottom that allows it to be inserted into the socket of a candlestick, converting it into a comport or container for a floral arrangement.

Plate etching. See Etching.

Pontil. Also called a pontil rod or punty rod. The iron tool used to hold a piece of pressed glass while it is still hot enough to be shaped into its final form. When the item is removed from the rod, it leaves a rough scar, referred to as a pontil mark or punty mark. Some manufacturers ground and polished this mark away, sometimes leaving a smooth, circular, concave impression, also referred to as a puntied bottom.

Prescut. A molded design that could be augmented by simple cutting to give the impression of being a full-cut piece. The cut portions were often left gray, or might be polished. Cambridge's Nearcut patterns are examples of Prescut designs.

Prunt. A rough blob of glass added to the surface of a piece as decoration. See also Knop.

Puntied. See Pontil.

Reissue. A piece made in the original mold years after the initial production dates, by either the same company or a subsequent owner of the mold.

Reproduction. A piece made in a newly created mold in imitation of an earlier issued item or pattern. This includes items added to a reproduced line that were not initially made by the original company.

Rock crystal cutting. See Engraving.

Ruby stain. See Stain.

Satin finish. A form of etching where the entire piece is dipped in acid to give it a frosted or matte finish. Some companies added the satin finish to portions of an item, leaving the remainder clear. The finish can range from dull gray to lustrous.

Silver deposit/overlay. A decorative technique where a thin layer of silver is deposited permanently on the glass in various designs. There are several different techniques used in applying the silver, resulting in a technical distinction between overlay and deposit, though the final product in both cases presents a similar appearance. An inexpensive means of decorating with silver involved brushing the liquid silver on, but this did not have the permanence of either silver deposit or overlay.

Slag glass. Two or more colors combined to give the appearance of natural, variegated marble. Also known as marble glass or mosaic glass. Frequently referred to as "end of day" glass, implying that pieces were made using leftover batches of glass mixed together. In fact, slag glass is produced using carefully controlled formulas heated to very precise temperatures. Most slag glass is a mixture of milk glass with one or more transparent colors.

Stain. A form of decoration achieved by spraying or painting a part or whole of an item and then reheating it so that a transparent color becomes a permanent part of the glass. When metallic oxides were used, the result was a lustre stain, with iridescent qualities. Ruby and amber are the most common colors used for staining, though other colors have been popular at various times. Often referred to as "flashing," which is an erroneous term. Some companies, such as Consolidated, used similar techniques to apply semi-opaque colors, which they referred to as "washes."

Stretch. A form of iridescent glass that is reheated in the furnace after it has been sprayed with the metallic salts, then reworked by hand until it has been formed into the desired shape. This causes the iridescent finish to develop a web-like network of overall "stretch marks."

Wafer. Many early pressed glass pieces (or combination pressed and blown items) were formed in two or more parts. In the case of candlesticks, this often meant that the candle cup, the stem, and sometimes the foot were all pressed separately. The individual pieces were joined together, while still hot, by using a small glob of molten glass pressed flat between them, so that it takes on a rough wafer shape. (Some pieces may have multiple wafers.) A true wafer can be identified by tracing the mold marks on the rest of the finished item. A mold mark will not appear on the wafer and often the marks on the top and bottom pieces will not even line up with one another. As companies got away from this manufacturing technique and began making entire candlesticks in one molded piece, they often continued to produce popular styles with a "pseudo-wafer" — a molded wafer that mimicked the real thing. Pseudo-wafers will also be found on many twentieth century reproductions.

Wash, colored. See Stain.

Whimsey. A one-of-a-kind item, created by changing the shape of a production piece (or making an entirely new piece freehand), usually during a workman's off time. It is sometimes difficult to know whether a previously unreported shape in a pattern is a whimsey or a short-lived production piece (or feasibility item) that never made it into a catalog.

In compiling the terms related to decorated glass above, the authors are particularly indebted to the series of articles by Helen and Robert Jones on "Glass, the many ways it's decorated," in *Glass Collector's Digest.*

BIBLIOGRAPHY AND RESOURCES

FACTORIES, COLLECTORS' CLUBS, AND MUSEUMS

Akro Agate Collector's Club, Inc, 10 Bailey Street, Clarksburg, WV 26301-2524. Website: www.mkl.com/ akro/club/index.htm. Newsletter: *The Clarksburg Crow*.

Anchor Hocking Corporation. Website: www.anchorhocking.com

Blenko Glass Company, P.O. Box 67, Fairgrounds Road, Milton, WV 25541. Website: www.blenkoglass.com

Boyd's Crystal Art Glass, Inc. 1203 Morton Ave., Cambridge, OH 43725. Website: www.boydglass.com

Corning Museum of Glass, One Museum Way, Corning, NY 14830-2253. Website: www.cmog.org/

Fenton Art Glass Collectors of America, Inc., P. O. Box 384, Williamstown, WV 26187.

Fenton Art Glass Company, 700 Elizabeth Street, Williamstown, WV. Website: www.fentonartglass.com. Newsletter *Glass Messenger*.

National Cambridge Collectors, Inc., P.O. Box 416, Cambridge, OH 43725-0416. Website: www.cambridgeglass.org Newsletter: *Cambridge Crystal Ball*.

National Duncan Glass Society, 525 Jefferson Avenue, Washington, PA 15301. Website: www.duncan-glass.com

National Fenton Glass Society, P.O. Box 4008, Marietta, OH 45750-7008. Website: axces.com/nfgs/. Newsletter: *The Fenton Flyer*.

National Milk Glass Collectors Society. Website: www.nmgcs.org/. Newsletter: *Opaque News*.

Pacific Northwest Fenton Association, 8225 Kilchis River Road, Tillamook, OR 97141.

Sandwich Glass Museum, P.O. Box 103, 129 Main St., Sandwich, MA 02563. Website: www.sandwichmuseum.org

West Virginia Museum of American Glass, P.O. Box 574, Weston, WV 26452. Website: members.aol.com/wvmuseumof glass/. Newsletter: *The Glory Hole*.

BOOKS AND PERIODICALS

Archer, Douglas. "Whoseits." *Glass Review*, October 1983, p. 4 – 5.

Archer, Margaret & Douglas. *The Collector's Encyclopedia of Glass Candlesticks*. Paducah, KY: Collector Books, 1983.

_____. *Glass Candlesticks*. Paducah, KY: Collector Books, 1975.

_____. *Glass Candlesticks, Book II*. Paducah, KY: Collector Books, 1977.

Ash, Cynthia. "Ferlux, Beaumont's Mystery Glass." *Glass Collector's Digest*, April/May 1997, p. 50 – 55.

Ash, Roy D. "Co-operative Flint Glass Company's 'Sunset' glass." *Glass Collector's Digest*, August/September 1994, p. 31 – 38.

_____. "Santa Maria: Flagship of Consolidated Glass." *Glass Collector's Digest*, August/September 1995, p. 90 – 95.

Barlow, Raymond E. & Joan E. Kaiser. *The Glass Industry in Sandwich, Vol. 3*. West Chester, PA: Schiffer Pub., 1987.

_____. *The Glass Industry in Sandwich, Vol. 4*. Windham, NH: Barlow-Kaiser Pub. Co., 1983.

_____. *The Glass Industry in Sandwich, Vol. 5*. Atglen, PA: Schiffer Pub., 1999.

_____. *A Guide to Sandwich Glass: Pressed Tableware*. Atglen, PA: Schiffer Pub., 1993.

Belknap, E. M. *Milk Glass*. New York: Crown Publishers, 1959.

Bennett, Harold & Judy. *The Cambridge Glass Book*. Des Moines, IA: Wallace-Homestead Book Co., 1970.

_____. *1903 Catalog of Pressed and Blown Glass Ware*: reprint. Cambridge, OH: Bennett, 1976.

Blenko glass, 1962 – 1961 catalogs. Atglen, PA: Schiffer Pub., 2000.

Bones, Frances. *The Book of Duncan Glass*. Des Moines, IA: Wallace-Homestead Book Co., 1973.

_____. *Genuine Duncan*: catalog reprints (1939 – 1951). Fresno, TX: Bones, n.d.

Boyd, Bernard. *Boyd's Crystal Art Glass*. Cambridge, OH: Boyd's Crystal Art Glass, 1980

Bredehoft, Neila, George A. Fogg & Francis C. Maloney. *Early Duncan Glassware*. Boston: Fogg, 1987.

Bredehoft, Tom & Neila. *Fifty Years of Collectible Glass, 1920 – 1970, Vol. 1*. Dubuque, IA: Antique Trader Books, 1997.

Brenner, Robert. *Depression Glass for Collectors*. Atglen, PA: Schiffer Pub., 1998.

Burkholder, John R. & D. Thomas O'Connor. *Kemple Glass, 1945 – 1970*. Marietta, OH: Antique Publications, 1997.

Burns, Carl O. *Imperial Carnival Glass*. Paducah, KY: Collector Books, 1996.

Chiarenza, Frank & James Slater. *The Milk Glass Book*. Atglen, PA: Schiffer Pub., 1998.

Coe, Debbie & Randy. *Elegant Glass: Early, Depression & Beyond*. Atglen, PA: Schiffer Pub., 2001.

Doty, David. *A Field Guide to Carnival Glass*. Marietta, OH: Glass Press, 1998.

Edwards, Bill & Mike Carwile. *Standard Encyclopedia of Carnival Glass, 6th Ed.* Paducah, KY: Collector Books, 1998.

Cige, Eason & Rick Wilson. *Blenko Glass, 1930 – 1953*. Marietta, OH: Antique Publications, 1987.

Cige, Eason. *A Century of Glassmaking in West Virginia*: exhibition, June 8 – September 1, 1980. Huntington, WV: Huntington Galleries, 1980.

Everett, Larry. "The Everglade Line." *Cambridge Crystal Ball*, Nov. 2001, p. 1, etc.

Felt, Tom & Bob O'Grady. *Heisey Candlesticks, Candelabra and Lamps*. Newark, OH: Heisey Collectors of America, 1984.

Florence, Gene. *Anchor Hocking's Fire-King & More*. Paducah, KY: Collector Books, 1998.

_____. *Collectible Glassware from the 40s, 50s, 60s, 4th Ed*. Paducah, KY: Collector Books, 1998.

_____. *The Collector's Encyclopedia of Akro Agate Glassware*. Paducah, KY: Collector Books, 1975.

_____. *Collectors Encyclopedia of Depression Glass, 14th Ed*. Paducah, KY: Collector Books, 2000.

_____. *Glass Candlesticks of the Depression Era*. Paducah, KY: Collector Books, 2000.

Fogg, George A. *Reprint of Geo. Duncan and Sons Catalog of Fine Flint Glassware*, circa 1890. Boston: Fogg, 1984.

Frost, Marion & Sandra. *The Essence of Pairpoint*. Atglen, PA: Schiffer Pub., 2001.

Garmon, Lee & Dick Spencer. *Glass Animals of the Depression Era*. Paducah, KY: Collector Books, 1993.

Grizel, Ruth Ann. *The Collector's Guide to Lesser Known Modern Milk Glass*. Iowa City, IA: FSJ Pub. Co., 1996.

Glass factory year book directory, 1944 ed. Pittsburgh: American Glass Review, 1944.

Hardy, Roger and Claudia. *The Complete Line of Akro Agate: Marbles, General Line, and Children's Dishes, with Prices*. Clarksburg, WV: Hardy, 1992.

Heacock, William, James Measell & Berry Wiggins. *Dugan/Diamond: The Story of Indiana, Pennsylvania Glass*. Marietta, OH: Antique Publications, 1993.

Heacock, William. *Fenton Glass: The First Twenty-five Years*. Marietta, OH: O-Val Advertising Corp., 1978.

_____. *Fenton Glass: The Second Twenty-five Years*. Marietta, OH: O-Val Advertising Corp., 1980.

_____. *Fenton Glass: The Third Twenty-five Years*. Marietta, OH: O-Val Advertising Corp., 1989.

_____. "Religious Figures in Glass." *Glass Collector's Digest*, June/July 1987, p. 80 – 91.

Hemminger, Ruth, Ed Goshe & Leslie Pina. *Tiffin Glass 1940 – 1980: Figurals, Paperweights, Pressed Ware*. Atglen, PA: Schiffer Pub., 2001.

Humphrey, Audrey L. "Handmade by Erickson." *Glass Collector's Digest*, Dec. – Jan. 1988, p. 70 – 76.

Innes, Lowell. *Pittsburgh Glass, 1797 – 1891: A History and Guide for Collectors*. Boston, MA: Houghton Mifflin Co., 1976.

Owen, Meg. "Canton: the Glass Company that Refused to Die!, pt. II." *Glass Collector's Digest*, Feb. – Mar. 1999, p. 73 – 82.

Jones, Helen & Bob. "Glass: The Many Ways it's Decorated." *Glass Collector's Digest*, Dec. – Jan. 2000, p. 38 – 47; Feb. – Mar. 2000, p. 63 – 70; Apr. – May 2000, p. 42 – 47; June – July 2000, p. 34 – 42.

Kamm, Minnie Watson. *A Second Two Hundred Pattern Glass Book, 3rd Ed*. Grosse Point, MI: Kamm Publications, 1950.

King, W. L. *Duncan & Miller Glass: ca. 1950 catalog reprint, 2nd Ed*. Venetia, PA: Victoria House Museum, n.d.

Kovel, Ralph & Terry. *The Kovels' Illustrated Price Guide to Depression Glass and American Dinnerware*. New York: Crown Publishers, 1980.

Krause, Gail. *The Encyclopedia of Duncan Glass*. Hicksville, NY: Exposition Press, 1976.

_____. *Hand-made Duncan: Catalog No. 93*: reprint. Heyworth, IL: Heyworth Star, 1982.

_____. *The Years of Duncan: 1865 – 1955*. Heyworth, IL: Heyworth Star, 1980.

Lechler, Doris Anderson. *Children's Glass Dishes, China, and Furniture*. Paducah, KY: Collector Books, 1983.

Lehner, Lois. *Ohio Pottery and Glass Marks and Manufacturers*. Des Moines, IA: Wallace-Homestead Books, 1978.

Lucas, Robert Irwin. *Tarentum Pattern Glass*. Tarentum, PA: Lucas, 1981.

Mauzy, Barbara & Jim. *Mauzy's Depression Glass, 2nd Ed*. Atglen, PA: Schiffer Pub., 2001.

McKearin, George S. & Helen. *American Glass*. New York: Crown Publishers, 1948.

Measell, James, editor. *Fenton Glass: The 1980s Decade*. Marietta, OH: Glass Press, 1996.

_____. *Fenton Glass: The 1990s Decade*. Marietta, OH: Glass Press, 2000.

_____. *Imperial Glass Encyclopedia, Vol. I*. Marietta, OH: Glass Press, 1995.

Measell, James & Berry Wiggins. *Great American Glass of the Roaring 20s & Depression Era*. Marietta, OH: Glass Press, 1998.

_____. *Great American Glass of the Roaring 20s & Depression Era, Book 2*. Marietta, OH: Glass Press, 2000.

Miller, C. L. *Depression Era Dime Store Glass*. Atglen, PA: Schiffer Pub., 1999.

National Cambridge Collectors, Inc. *The Cambridge Glass Company: Catalog Reprints, 1930 – 1934*. Paducah, KY: Collector Books, 1976.

_____. *Colors in Cambridge Glass*. Paducah, KY: Collector Books, 1984.

_____. *Fine Handmade Table Glassware by Cambridge: 1940 Catalog Reprint*. Cambridge, OH: National Cambridge Collectors, 1995.

_____. *Fine Handmade Table Glassware by Cambridge, 1949 – 1953: Catalog Reprints*. Paducah, KY: Collector Books 1978.

_____. *Fine Handmade Table Glassware by Cambridge: 1956 Catalog Reprint*. Cambridge, OH: National Cambridge Collectors, n.d.

_____. The Cambridge Buffs, Study Group #7. *Nearcut: 1910 Catalog Reprint*. Cambridge, OH: Cambridge Buffs 1985.

National Duncan Glass Society. *Duncan, Highest Quality Glass Catalogue: Reprint of 1940 Catalog*. [S.l.: s.n., n.d.]

_____. *Genuine Duncan: 1943 Catalog Reprint*. [S.l.: s.n., n.d.]

Newbound, Betty & Bill. *Collector's Encyclopedia of Milk Glass*. Paducah, KY: Collector Books, 1995.

Newman, Harold. *An Illustrated Dictionary of Glass*. London: Thames and Hudson, 1977.

Nye, Mark A. "Candlesticks, Candelabra, and Epergnes, pt. I." *Cambridge Crystal Ball*, Jan. 1991, p. 4 – 7.

_____. *Caprice*. Cambridge, OH: National Cambridge Collectors, 1994.

_____. "Lyre Candlestick." *Cambridge Crystal Ball*, Aug. 2002, p. 12 – 15.

Page, Bob & Dale Frederiksen. *Seneca Glass Company, 1891 – 1983: A Stemware Identification Guide*. Greensboro, NC Replacements, 1995.

Pendergrass, Paula & Sherry Riggs. *Glass Candleholders: Art Nouveau, Art Deco, Depression Era, Modern*. Atglen, PA: Schiffer Pub., 2000.

Peterson, Arthur G. *400 Trademarks on Glass*. DeBary, FL: Peterson, 1971.

Pina, Leslie. *Crackle Glass in Color: Depression to '70s*. Atglen, PA: Schiffer Pub., 2000.

_____. *Depression Era Glass by Duncan*. Atglen, PA: Schiffer Pub., 1999.

_____. *Popular '50s and '60s Glass: Color Along the River*. Atglen, PA: Schiffer Pub., 1995.

Reilly, Gerald I., editor. *Wheeling Glass, 1829 – 1939*. Wheeling, WV: Oglebay Institute, 1994.

Revi, Albert Christian. *American Pressed Glass and Figure Bottles*. Nashville: T. Nelson, 1964.

Rice, Ferill J., editor. *Caught in the Butterfly Net*. Williamstown, WV: Fenton Art Glass Collectors of America, 1991.

Riggs, Sherry & Paula Pendergrass. *Glass Candle Holders of the Depression Era and Beyond*. Atglen, PA: Schiffer Pub., 2001.

_____. *20th Century Glass Candle Holders: Roaring 20s, Depression Era & Modern Collectible Candle Holders*. Atglen, PA Schiffer Pub., 1999.

Roller, Dick, compiler. *Indiana Glass Factories Notes*. Paris, IL: Acorn Press, 1994.

Schroy, Ellen T. *Warman's Depression Glass: A Value & Identification Guide*. Iola, WI: Krause Publications, 1997.

Six, Dean. *Central Glass Works: 1896 – 1939, Successor to Central Glass Company, Wheeling, West Virginia*. Weston, WV West Virginia Museum of American Glass, 1999.

_____. *Dunbar Glass: 1950s Modern to the End*. Weston, WV: West Virginia Museum of American Glass, 2002.

_____. *Weston, West Virginia, Glass: Selected Catalog Page Reprints & a Brief History*. Weston, WV: West Virginia Museum of American Glass, 1999.

Smith, Bill & Phyllis. *Cambridge Glass, 1972 – 1929: Catalog Reprint*. Springfield, OH: Smith, 1986.

Spillman, Jane Shadel. *Glass Tableware, Bowls & Vases*. New York: A. A. Knopf, 1982.

_____. *Glass 2*. New York: A. A. Knopf, c. 1983.

Stout, Sandra McPhee. *Depression Glass III*. Des Moines, IA: Wallace-Homestead Book Co., 1976.

Taylor, Dorothy. *Encore by Dorothy, Book I*. Kansas City, MO: Taylor, 1979.

Teal, Ron, Sr. *Tiara Exclusives: Company Catalog Reprints*. Marietta, OH: Glass Press, 2000.

Walk, John. *The Big Book of Fenton Glass, 1940 – 1970*. Atglen, PA: Schiffer Pub., 1998.

Weatherman, Hazel Marie. *Colored Glassware of the Depression Era 2*. Springfield, MO: Weatherman Glassbooks, 1974.

Welker, John & Elizabeth. *Pressed Glass in America: Encyclopedia of the First Hundred Years, 1825 – 1925*. Ivyland, PA Antique Acres Press, 1985.

Welker, Mary, Lyle & Lynn. *Cambridge Ohio Glass in Color*. New Concord, OH: Welker, 1969.

_____. *Cambridge Ohio Glass in Color, Book II*. New Concord, OH: Welker, 1973.

Whitmyer, Margaret & Kenn. *Fenton Art Glass, 1907 – 1939*. Paducah, KY: Collector Books, 1996.

_____. *Fenton Art Glass, 1939 – 1980*. Paducah, KY: Collector Books, 1999.

Wilson, Jack. D. *Phoenix & Consolidated Art Glass, 1926 – 1980*. Marietta, OH: Antique Publications, 1989.

Wilson, Kenneth M. *New England Glass and Glassmaking*. New York: T. Y. Crowell, 1972.

Ziegler, Roserita. "Erickson Glass Works." *Glass Review*, Aug. 1980, p. 42 – 43.

INDEX

AKRO AGATE

AK-1&2

AK-3

AK-4

AK-5

AK-6

AK-7

AK-8

AK-9

AK-10

ANCHOR HOCKING

AH-1

AH-2

AH-3

AH-4

AH-4A

AH-5

AH-5A

AH-5B

AH-6

AH-7

AH-8

AH-9

AH-10

AH-11

AH-12

AH-13

AH-14

AH-15

AH-16

AH-17

AH-17B

AH-18

AH-19

AH-20

AH-21

AH-22

AH-23

ATTER-BURY

AT-1

AT-1A

BAKE-WELL

BP-1

BARTLETT

BC-1

BEACON

BE-1

BEAU-MONT

BU-1

BU-1A

BU-2

BU-2A

BU-3

BU-4

BU-5

BU-6

BISCHOFF

BI-1

BI-2

BLENKO

BL-1

BL-2

BL-3

BL-4

BL-5

BL-6

BL-7

BL-8

BL-9

BL-10

BL-11

BL-12

BL-13

BL-14

BL-15

BL-16

BL-17

BL-18

BL-19

BL-20

BL-21

BL-22

BL-23

BL-24

BL-25

BL-26

BL-27

BL-28

BL-29&30

BL-31

BL-32

BL-33

BL-34

BL-35

BL-36

BL-37

BL-38

BL-39

BL-40

BL-41

BL-42

BL-43

BL-44

BL-44A

BL-45

BL-46

BL-47

BL-48

BL-49

BL-50

BL-51

BOSTON SANDWICH

BS-1

BS-2

BS-3

BS-4

BS-5

BS-6 & 6A

BS-7

BS-8

BS-9

BS-10

BS-11

BS-12

BS-13

BS-14

BS-15

BS-16

BS-17

BS-18

BS-19

BS-20

BOYD'S

BO-1

BO-2

BO-3

BO-4

BO-5

BO-6

BO-6A

BRILLIANT

BR-1

BROOKE

BK-1

BRYCE BROS.

BB-1

CAM-BRIDGE

CB-1

CB-2

CB-3

CB-4

CB-5

CB-6

CB-7

CB-8

CB-9

CB-10

CB-11A

CB-12

CB-13

CB-14

CB-15

CB-16

CB-17

CB-18

CB-19

CB-20

CB-21

CB-22

CB-23

CB-24

CB-25

CB-26

CB-27

CB-28

CB-29

CB-30

CB-31

CB-32

CB-33

CB-34

CB-35

CB-36

CB-37

CB-38

CB-39

CB-40

CB-41

CB-42

CB-43

CB-44

CB-44A

CB-45

CB-46

CB-47

CB-48

CB-49

CB-50

CB-51

CB-52

CB-53

CB-54

CB-55

CB-56

CB-57A

CB-58

CB-59

CB-60

CB-61

CB-62

CB-63

CB-64

CB-65

CB-66

CB-66A

CB-67

CB-68

CB-69

CB-70

CB-71

CB-72

CB-72A

CB-73A

CB-73B

CB-74

CB-75

CB-76

CB-77

CB-78

CB-78A

CB-78B

CB-79

CB-80

CB-81

CB-82

CB-83

CB-84

CB-85

CB-86

CB-87

CB-88

CB-89

CB-90

CB-90A

CB-91

CB-92

CB-93

CB-94

CB-95

CB-96

CB-97　　CB-98　　CB-99　　CB-100　　CB-101　　CB-102

CB-102A　　CB-103　　CB-104　　CB-105　　CB-106　　CB-107

CB-108　　CB-109　　CB-110　　CB-111　　CB-112　　CB-113

CB-113B　　CB-114　　CB-115　　CB-116　　CB-117　　CB-118

CB-119　　CB-120　　CB-121　　CB-122　　CB-123　　CB-124

CB-125　　CB-126　　CB-127,128,129　　CB-130　　CB-131　　CB-132

CB-133　　CB-134　　CB-135　　CB-136　　CB-136A　　CB-136B

CB-137

CB-138

CB-139

CB-140

CB-141

CB-142

CB-143

CB-144

CB-145

CB-146

CB-147

CB-148

CB-149

CB-150

CB-151

CB-152

CB-153

CB-154

CB-155

CB-156

CB-157

CB-158

CB-159

CB-160

CB-161

CB-162

CB-163

CB-164

CB-165

CB-166

CB-167

CB-168

CB-169

CANTON

CN-1

CN-2

CN-3

CN-4

CN-5

CN-6

CN-7

CN-8

CN-9

CN-10

CN-11

CN-12

CN-13

CN-14

CN-15

CAPE COD

CC-1

CC-2

CENTRAL

CE-1

CE-2

CE-3

CE-4

CE-5

CE-6

CE-7

CE-8

CE-9

CE-10

CE-11

CE-12

CE-13

CE-14

CE-15A

CE-16

CE-17

CE-18

CE-19

CE-20

CE-21

CE-22

CE-23

CE-24

CHALLI-NOR

CH-1

CO-OPER-ATIVE

CO-1

CO-2

CO-3

CO-4

CO-5

CO-6

CO-7

CO-8

CO-9

CO-10

CO-11

CO-12

CO-13

CO-14

CO-15

COLONY

CL-1

CL-2

CL-3

CL-4A

CL-5

CL-6

CL-7

CL-8

CL-9

CL-10

CL-11

CL-12

CONSOLI-DATED

CS-1

CS-2

CS-3

CS-4

CS-5

CS-6

CS-7

CS-8

CS-8B

CS-9

CS-10

CS-11

CS-12

CS-13

CS-14

CS-15

CRESCENT

CR-1

DALZELL VIKING

DV-1

DV-2

DV-3

DV-4

DV-5

DV-6

DV-7

DV-8

DV-9

DV-10

DV-11

DV-12

DV-13

DV-14

DV-15

DV-16

DV-17

DV-18

DV-19

DV-20

DELL

DL-1

DL-2

DIAMOND

DI-1

DI-2

DI-3

DI-4

DI-5

DI-6

DI-7

DI-7B

DI-8

DI-9

DI-10

DI-11

DI-12

DITH-RIDGE

DT-1

DT-2 & 3

DT-4 & 5

DRITZ

DR-1

DR-2

DR-3

DUNBAR

DB-1

DB-2

DB-3

DB-4

DB-5

DB-6

DB-7

DB-8

DUNCAN MILLER

DM-1

DM-2

DM-3

DM-4

DM-5

DM-6

DM-7

DM-7A

DM-8

DM-8A

DM-8B

DM-9

DM-10

DM-11

DM-12

DM-13

DM-14

DM-15

DM-16

DM-17

DM-18

DM-19

DM-20

DM-21

DM-21A

DM-22

DM-23   DM-24   DM-25   DM-26   DM-27   DM-28

DM-29   DM-30   DM-31   DM-32   DM-33   DM-34

DM-35   DM-36   DM-37   DM-38   DM-39   DM-40

DM-41   DM-42   DM-43   DM-44   DM-45   DM-46

DM-47   DM-48   DM-49   DM-50   DM-51   DM-52

DM-53   DM-54   DM-55   DM-56   DM-57   DM-58

DM-59   DM-60   DM-61   DM-62   DM-63   DM-64

DM-65

DM-66

DM-67

DM-68

DM-69

DM-70

DM-71

DM-72

DM-73

DM-74

DM-75

DM-76

DM-77

DM-78

DM-79

DM-80

DM-81

DM-82

DM-83

DM-84

DM-84B

DM-85

DM-86

DM-87

DM-88

DM-89

DM-90

DM-91

DM-92

DM-93

DM-94

DM-95

DM-96

DM-97

DM-98

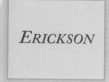

ERICKSON

ER-1

ER-2

FEDERAL

FD-1

FD-2

FD-3

FD-4

FD-5

FD-6

FD-7

FD-8

FD-9

FENTON

FN-1

FN-2

FN-3

FN-4

FN-5

FN-6

FN-7

FN-8

FN-9

FN-10

FN-11

FN-11A

FN-12

FN-13

FN-14

FN-15

FN-16

FN-17

FN-18

FN-19

FN-20

FN-21

FN-21A

FN-22

FN-23

FN-24

FN-24A

FN-24B

FN-25

FN-25A

FN-26

FN-26A

FN-27

FN-28

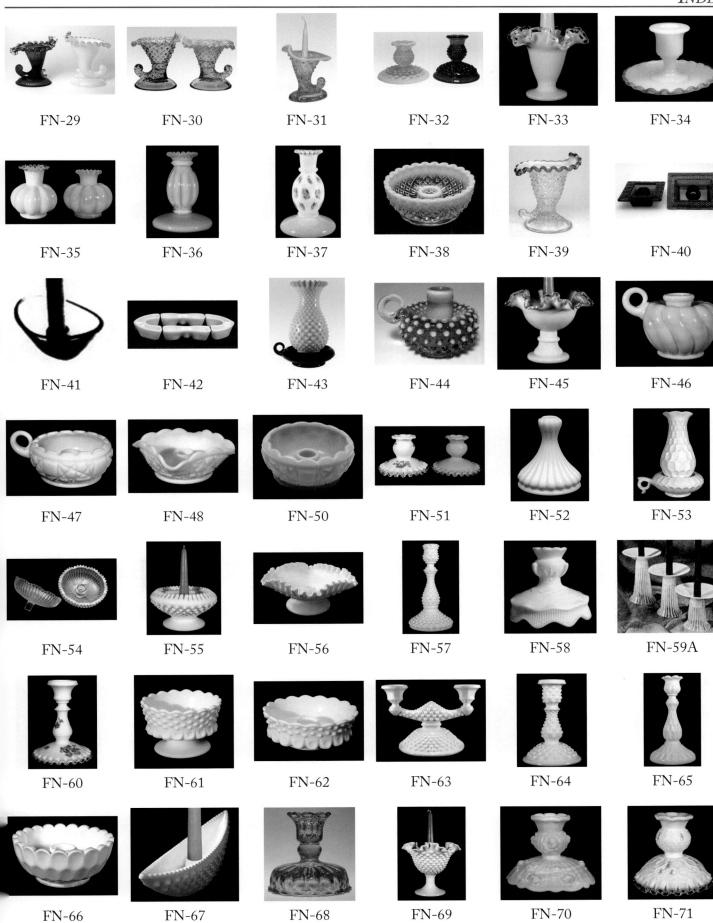

FN-29

FN-30

FN-31

FN-32

FN-33

FN-34

FN-35

FN-36

FN-37

FN-38

FN-39

FN-40

FN-41

FN-42

FN-43

FN-44

FN-45

FN-46

FN-47

FN-48

FN-50

FN-51

FN-52

FN-53

FN-54

FN-55

FN-56

FN-57

FN-58

FN-59A

FN-60

FN-61

FN-62

FN-63

FN-64

FN-65

FN-66

FN-67

FN-68

FN-69

FN-70

FN-71

FN-72　　　FN-73　　　FN-74　　　FN-75　　　FN-76　　　FN-77

FN-78　　　FN-79　　　FN-80　　　FN-81　　　FN-82　　　FN-83

FN-84　　　FN-85　　　FN-86　　　FN-87　　　FN-88　　　FN-89

FN-90　　　FN-91　　　FN-92　　　FN-93　　　FN-94　　　FN-95

FN-96　　　FN-97　　　FN-98　　　FN-99　　　FN-100　　　FN-101

FN-102　　　FN-103　　　FN-104　　　FN-105　　　FN-106

HOW TO USE THE SHAPE INDEX

The following index is intended to help you if you are trying to identify a candlestick, but do not know its manufacturer. You will find all of the candlesticks in this book grouped by shared characteristics to make your search a little easier.

Here are a few helpful hints:

If your candlestick holds multiple candles, you will find all two-, three-, four-, and five- light candlesticks grouped at the end of the index, regardless of whether they might also fall into one of the other named categories.

If it is a single light, you may find it first in one of the following sections:

Toy or miniature candlesticks

Candleblocks (usually a solid "block" of glass without a separate foot)

Crucifix or other figural candlesticks

Dolphins, objects, plants/flowers, etc.

Hurricane lamps (with a globe or shade)

If it doesn't fall into any of the above categories, the remainder of the index is divided according to the shape of the base.

Toy or miniature
AK-10, CB-15, CB-19, CN-4, CN-5, CE-3, CE-5, CE-6, DM-16

1-light, candleblock
AK-1 & 2, AK-3, AK-4, AK-5, AK-6, AK-7, AH-12, BE-1, BL-9, BL-11, BL-12, BL-13, BL-14, BL-18, BL-20, BL-27, BL-31, BL-34, BL-35, BL-37, BL-40, BL-41, BL-42, BL- 43, BL-45, BL-47, BL-49, BL-50, BL-51, BR-1, CB-124, CB-125, CB-126, CB-127, CB- 128, CB-129, CB-140, CB-150, CB-153, CL-6, CL-3, DM-27, DM-40, DM-78, DM-79, DM-87, ER-1, FD-1, FD-6, FN-75

1-light, round base
AK-9, AH-1, AH-2, AH-4A, AH-22, AH-23, BC-1, BI-1, BI-2, BL-1, BL-2, BL-3, BL-4, BL-5, BL-6, BL-8, BL-19, BL-24, CL-29 & BL-30, BL-38, BS-6, BS-6A, BK-1, BB-1, CB-13, CB-44, CB-44A, CB-47, CB-53, CB-54, CB-55, CB-56, CB-57, CB-58, CB-59, CB-61, CB-63, CB-64, CB-65, CB-66, CB-66A, CB-72A, CB-73, CB-82, CB-93, CB-94, CB-96, CB-97, CB-123, CB-130, CB-134, CB-135, CB-137, CB-146, CB-151, CB-161, CN-3, CN-8, CN-9, CN-10, CN-11, CN-13, CN-15, CE-14, CE-16, CE-17, CE-18, CE- 21, CE-22, CE-23, CS-1, CS-2, CS-8, CS-8B, CO-8, CO-10, CO-14, DV-9, DV-11, DV- 13, DV-18, DI-2, DI-6, DI-9, DB-1, DB-4, DB-7, DM-5, DM-20, DM-21, DM-21A, DM- 28, DM-31. DM-32, DM-34, DM-37, DM-38, DM-41, DM-43, DM-46, DM-55, DM-60, DM-62, DM-75, DM-88, DM-90, DM-98, ER-2, FN-2, FN-3, FN-4, FN-5, FN-6, FN-8, FN-9, FN-10, FN-12, FN-21, FN-24, FN-24A, FN-32, FN-57, FN-68, FN-92, FN-99

1-light, round base, domed or skirted
BL-7, BS-8, CB-5, CB-18, CB-37, CB-38, CB-39, CB-40, CB-42, CB-45, CB-46, CB-47, CB-49, CB-50, CB-84, CE-15, CS-11, CO-9, CO-11, CO-12, DV-7, DI-4, DI-5, DI-7, DI-7B, DR-2, DM-8, DM-11, DM-17, DM-22, DM-24, DM-25, DM-26, DM-30, DM-49, DM-52, DM-53, DM-54, DM-56, DM-97, FN-14, FN-52, FN-59, FN-64, FN-65, FN-70, FN-71, FN-78, FN-80, FN-81, FN-82, FN-86, FN-87, FN-89, FN-97

1-light, round base, scalloped or paneled
AH-9, AH-13, BU-1, BU-2, CB-22, CB-33, CB-86, CB-88, CB-91, CB-106, CB-158, CB-159, CB-167, CE-19, CE-24, CL-12, CO-5, DV-6, DV-16, DL-2, DI-6B, DI-10, DB- 2, DM-6, DM-7, DM-10, DM-13, DM-14. DM-15, DM-68, DM-77, FN-34, FN-51, FN- 58, FN-60, FN-98, FN-99, FN-102 (old FN-101), FN-103 (old FN-102), FN-104 (old FN- 103), FN-106 (old FN-105)

1-light, round base, beaded
AH-11, BO-5, CS-15

1-light, round base, ridged
BL-17, CB-95, CB-118, CB-119, CB-120, CL-1, FN-21A

1-light, round with feet
AH-4, AH-7, AH-12, DM-35

1-light, oval base
CS-3, CS-4

1-light, square/rectangular base
BS-1, BS-2, BS-4, BS-5, CB-14, CB-16, CB-23, CB-24, CB-27, CB-31, CB-32, CB-34, CB-41, CB-42, CB-51, CB-52, CB-68, CB-92, CB-131, CN-2, CN-6, CE-1, CE-9, CD- 10, DV-5, DV-12, DV-14, DI-12, DT-4, DR-1, DB-3, DM-18, DM-48, DM-67, DM-80, FN-40

1-light, hexagonal base
AH-15, AH-18, BP-1, BS-7, BS-9, BS-10, CB-7, CB-8, CB-10, CB-11, CB-12, CB-20, CB-25, CB-26, CB-28, CB-30, CB-35, CB-36, CB-157, CE-4, CE-6, CE-7, CE-11, CE- 12, CE-13, CO-3, CO-4, CO-6,

Watch for future volumes of
THE
GLASS
CANDLESTICK
BOOK

from
COLLECTOR
BOOKS

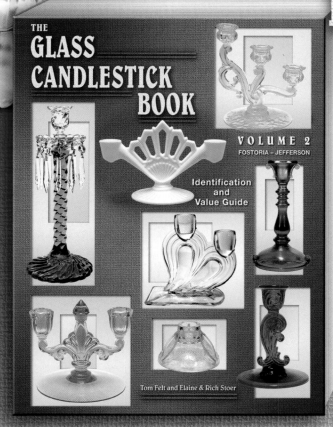

THE GLASS CANDLESTICK BOOK

VOLUME 2
FOSTORIA – JEFFERSON

Identification
and
Value Guide

Tom Felt and Elaine & Rich Stoer

The second volume picks up where the first left off in the identification and illustration of hundreds of glass candlesticks. Covering pieces made by 15 different American companies, alphabetically from Fostoria to Jefferson Glass, the book features hundreds of candlesticks. More than 800 color photographs and catalog reprints from old trade journals and advertisements light up the book. This volume will be of particular interest to collectors of Fostoria, Heisey, Hobbs Brockunier, Imperial, Jeannette, and Indiana Glass.

Volume 3 begins with the Kanawha Glass Company and ends with Wright Glass. Over 50 companies are represented in this final volume, including Morgantown, New Martinsville, Northwood, Paden City, U.S. Glass, and Westmoreland. Once again a plethora of photographs appears, this time exceeding 900, as well as more catalog reprints and trade advertisments that collectors are sure to enjoy.

Each chapter of both volumes includes a history of the factory and information about production colors and trademarks used. Every candlestick is described with dimensions, production dates, known colors, information on reissues and reproductions, the current location of the mold, as well as current values. A glossary and an extensive bibliography round out both books. Each features an illustrated index which includes thumbnail photographs of all the candlesticks in the book.

With this three-volume set, collectors will own the most complete reference work ever done on the subject. Other books on the subject don't hold a candle to this series!

COLLECTOR BOOKS
P.O. Box 3009
Paducah, KY 42002–3009
www.collectorbooks.com

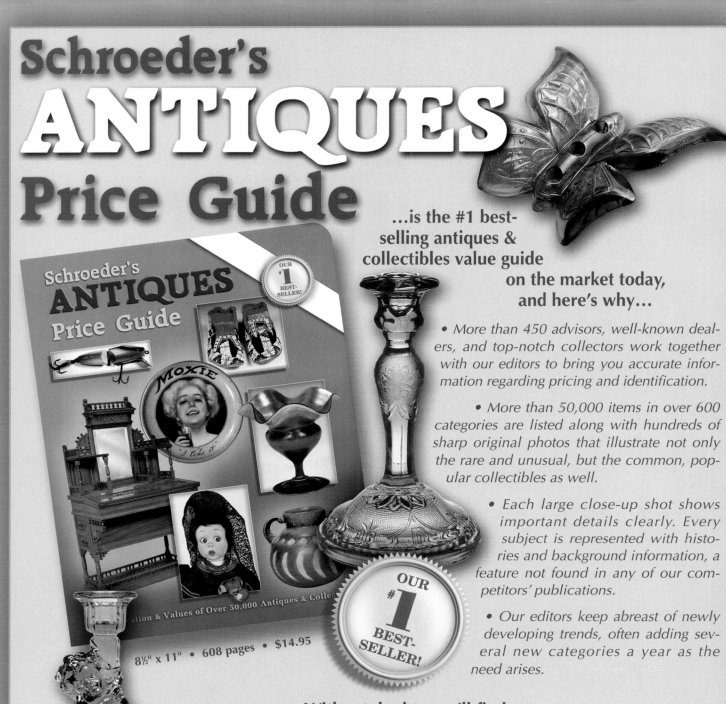